Tug of War

Tug of War

The battle for Italy, 1943–1945

Dominick Graham

and

Shelford Bidwell

PEN & SWORD MILITARY CLASSICS

The extract from "Rural Raid" by Denton Welch which appears on page 191 is reproduced with
the kind permission of David Higham Associates and is taken from *The Terrible Rain: The War
Poets 1939-1945* published by Methuen.

First published in 1986 by Hodder & Stoughton.
Published in 2004, in this format, by
PEN & SWORD MILITARY CLASSICS
an imprint of
Pen & Sword Books Limited
47 Church Street
Barnsley
S. Yorkshire
S70 2AS

ISBN 1 84415 098 4

A CIP record for this book
is available from the British Library.

Printed and bound in Great Britain by
CPI UK

For a complete list of Pen & Sword titles please contact:
PEN & SWORD BOOKS LIMITED
47 Church Street, Barnsley, South Yorkshire, S70 2AS, England.
E-mail: enquiries@pen-and-sword.co.uk
Website: www.pen-and-sword.co.uk

ACKNOWLEDGMENTS

We are greatly indebted to our fellow historians and other distinguished persons for help we received when working on this study of the Italian campaign. As they are variously located in Canada, England, France, New Zealand and the United States and we consulted them separately, we consider it appropriate to express our gratitude separately.

Bidwell thanks Lieutenant-General Sir Ian Jacob for an authoritative view of the problems of command and commanders at the highest level; General Sir Frank Simpson and Major-General Eric Sixsmith for answering questions on organisational matters; Major-General Adam Block, Colonel John Mennell, Lieutenant-Colonel P. S. Turner and Michael Glover for their impressions of events at the operational level, together with their perceptions of some commanders and national contingents. He received valuable advice and information from the military historians Correlli Barnett, Carlo D'Este, Nigel Hamilton, the late Ronald Lewin and, in particular, from John Terraine, with whom he has long enjoyed a profitable dialogue. Roy Smith provided useful information concerning air support, and Michael Wasilewsky indicated sources to consult on the Polish Forces. He also consulted W. McAndrew (see under Graham).

To these names must be added those of J. Harding, Historical Branch (Army), Ministry of Defence; Patricia Methven, The Liddell Hart Centre for Military Archives, King's College, London; Air Commodore H. A. Probert and Group Captain T. Flanagan, Royal Air Force Historical Section; Roderick Suddaby, the Imperial War Museum, and Richard Tubb, Librarian, the Royal United Services Institute for Defence Studies, together with the staffs of those establishments.

We are both especially indebted to Lieutenant-Colonel H. R. D. Emery, The French Embassy, London, for his help, and to Monsieur le Général Delmas, *Chef de Service Historique* for the gift of three volumes on the French participation in the Italian campaign.

Graham thanks Dr Alec Douglas and his staff at the Directorate of History, National Defence Force HQ, Ottawa and in particular

5

Acknowledgments

Brereton Greenhous and William McAndrew for showing him material concerning their tour of the Gothic Line; Justice Sir John White for recalling events at General Freyberg's HQ during the Battles of Cassino; the staff of the National Archives in Wellington, New Zealand; Martin Blumenson for conversations concerning Mark Clark and the Italian campaign, and his kindness in allowing him to see his biography of Mark Clark in manuscript; Richard Kohn and the staff at the Office of Air Force History for their kindness; and Richard Sommers at the Archives of the Military History Institute, Carlisle Barracks, Pennsylvania for the trouble he took to find relevant documents. He is immensely grateful to Nick Straker, whose research in the British Cabinet Offices in 1970 laid the foundation for our study of the battles of Salerno, Cassino, Anzio and the Gothic Line. To these names he adds those of the late John Sherman, Robert Tooley, Valerie Graham, Pat Harahan and David Zimmerman for their comments on draft chapters; and of James Parton for providing information about Ira C. Eaker's part in the operations at Cassino, and also *The History of the Mediterranean Air Forces*, which he wrote in the spring of 1945.

We wish to emphasise that though we researched separately we are both equally and jointly grateful to all the above.

Ion Trewin, now Editorial Director of our publishers, Hodder & Stoughton, provided encouragement, advice and criticism which has resulted, we hope, in a greatly improved and enlarged text. This was polished by the meticulous editing of Christine Medcalf, who also coordinated the sometimes mutually conflicting views of the co-authors with skill and tact. We thank them both.

Alec Spark drew the maps, adroitly compressing the essential information into a limited space without loss of clarity.

Jean Walter, whose flair as a sub-editor and reader is equal to her accomplishments as a copy-typist of the books of many authors, decrypted an often chaotic typescript to provide a text fit for the publisher.

Our last and warmest expression of thanks is to our wives, who provided the moral and logistic support on which we depended as draft chapters and mutual criticisms winged their way back and forth across the Atlantic.

In conclusion, we state formally that the responsibility for all expressions of opinion advanced by us and for errors of fact is ours alone.

CONTENTS

VI – AT LAST A PLAN

VII – FRANCE WINS THE DIADEM

VIII – THE GOTHIC LINE

ILLUSTRATIONS

Acknowledgements
1. The Imperial War Museum
2. Bundesarchiv
3. Public Archive, Canada
4. United States Historical Archiv

MAPS

I

A Soft Target

1

TWO ARMIES IN SEARCH OF A
BATTLEFIELD

No-one starts a war – or, rather, no-one in his senses should do so – without
being clear in his mind what he intends to achieve by that war and how he
intends to conduct it.

Karl von Clausewitz

At 4.30 a.m. on September 3, 1943 the citizens of Reggio Calabria, at
the tip of Italy's toe, were awakened by a thunderous bombardment.
Cascades of aerial bombs, hundreds of shells from warships and 400
tons of ammunition fired by field artillery on the western shore of the
Straits of Messina fell on the beaches north of the town. Then, as the
barrage lifted, three brigades of Canadian and British infantry disembarked from landing craft and waded ashore, to claim the honour of
being the first Allied troops to set foot on the soil of Nazi-dominated
Europe with the firm intention of staying there. Their passage had
neither been molested by the legendary monster Scylla, whose habit it
was to snatch seamen from the decks of passing ships and devour them,
nor troubled by the whirlpools of Charybdis. Nor was there any
interference from a more real danger, the 26th Panzer and the 29th
Panzer Grenadier Divisions defending the eastern shore of the nar-
rows. Their commanders, alerted by the preliminary bombardment of
their gun positions, and following their orders, prudently had faded
away into the mountainous interior of Calabria two days before, leaving
their Italian comrades to offer what resistance they could, which was
little. A few long-range guns opened fire from far inland, to be rapidly
silenced by Allied air attack. The Italians in the coastal defences
surrendered with alacrity, even lending willing hands to help unload
the landing craft.

15

The historic return of a British army to continental Europe, three years after the ignominy of Dunkirk, was therefore something of an anti-climax. Not that the soldiers in the ranks cared much about that. They had already sampled the fighting qualities of the German infantry in Sicily, and were only too happy to be ashore safely without having to fire a shot. Nor was the commander of the renowned Eighth Army put out at being so thoroughly hoaxed. He was always careful of his soldiers' lives, and for him it would have been inconceivable to land his troops on a coast defended by artillery without the elementary precaution of first silencing it. It was only a week since the Royal Navy had tested the defences by sailing through the Straits of Messina, every gun blazing, and part of Montgomery's mission was to open them for the passage of convoys carrying the troops for another assault on the mainland at Salerno.

He had, in fact, an inkling that Italian morale was crumbling and that the Germans might be thinning out, for on August 27 a special forces patrol returned from the farther shore and reported that the civil population was taking to the hills and the Italian soldiers deserting in droves, bringing a willing informant, an Italian railway worker, with them to confirm the story. Five more patrols were sent across the Straits that night with orders to find out how widespread this movement was and report by radio. There followed two days of silence, and it was assumed that all five had been captured before they could even open radio communications. Montgomery decided that he had no other course open but to hold to arrangements for an assault crossing preceded by a bombardment.[1]

Once ashore the operations proved equally undramatic. There was a little skirmishing, and a sharp fight after a brigade had been sent a short distance up the west coast in landing craft in the hope that it could cut in behind the enemy line of retreat, but the real battle was between the opposing engineers over the problem of marching two mechanised divisions through the gorges and over the crags of the Calabrian mountains. The German engineers had created a web of demolitions along every road from south to north and from coast to coast. Every corniche had been blown down, every junction cratered and every bridge cut. Five days' toil saw the leading elements of the 13th Corps 100 miles north of Reggio and approaching the narrow neck of land where the "toe" of Italy joins the foot, and the engineers running out of stores and bridging material. On the 8th Montgomery decreed a halt to improve his line of communications and build up stores before resuming his advance.

On the same day a great Allied invasion fleet was approaching the

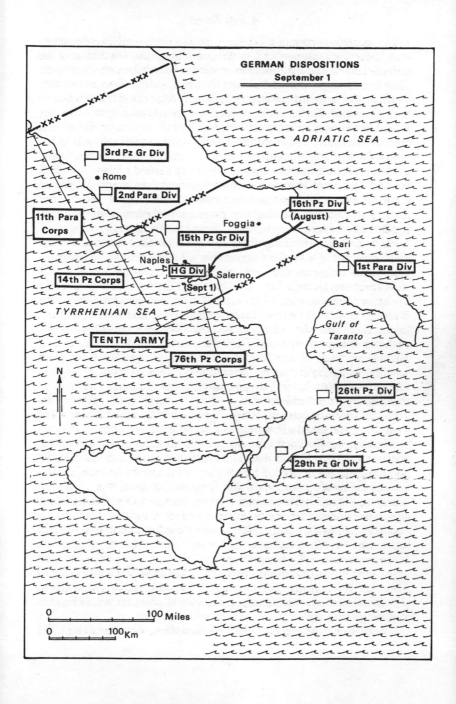

GERMAN DISPOSITIONS
September 1

ADRIATIC SEA

3rd Pz Gr Div

• Rome

2nd Para Div

11th Para Corps

16th Pz Div (August)

Foggia •

15th Pz Gr Div

• Bari

Naples

HG Div (Sept 1)

Salerno

1st Para Div

14th Pz Corps

TYRRHENIAN SEA

Gulf of Taranto

TENTH ARMY

76th Pz Corps

N

26th Pz Div

29th Pz Gr Div

0   100 Miles

0   100 Km

Bay of Salerno, carrying the United States Fifth Army headquarters and Lieutenant-General Mark Wayne Clark, the US 6th and the British 10th Corps for the main assault on the Italian mainland, the objective being the port of Naples. That evening the ships picked up a broadcast from the Allied Forces station in Algiers with the glad news that the Italian Government wished for an armistice and no longer intended to continue the war. This was loudly cheered by the troops. Shortly afterwards they received a rude shock when Luftwaffe bombers launched a fierce attack on the fleet, and a yet ruder one in the early hours of the morning, when they were shelled while still in their landing craft, shot up as they came ashore and then attacked, as some terrified units believed, by hundreds of tanks before they pulled themselves together and began to carve out and consolidate a bridgehead. Their leaders were, perhaps, more alarmed than the troops.

On September 10, General Sir Harold Alexander, commander-in-chief over both Clark and Montgomery, having received Montgomery's signal announcing his halt, urged him to accept all administrative risks and hurry to the aid of the Fifth Army. On the 12th he followed it up by sending his own chief of staff to repeat and emphasise the message. In fact the German high command had long been expecting a major descent on the Italian coast, probably in the region of Naples, and the commander-in-chief of the south, Field-Marshal Albert Kesselring, had already deduced that Salerno was the most likely landing place. On the 9th he ordered that all the German divisions in Calabria should withdraw, leaving only the thinnest of screens to watch the Eighth Army, and he prepared for a battle royal between the invaders and the German Tenth Army, with the object of throwing them back into the placid waters of Salerno Bay.

Marshal Ferdinand Foch once said something to the effect that warfare was not a well-ordered or intellectual affair, but "a dreadful and impassioned drama". The opening moves of the invasion of Italy were certainly of the stuff of drama: General Montgomery, the victor of Alamein, piqued at being given a minor part and displeased that his advice not to make two landings 200 miles apart separated by difficult country had been ignored, sulked in his caravan. At one stage during the battle for the Salerno bridgehead General Clark prepared to re-embark the US 6th Corps, but the US artillery saved the situation when the German battle-groups were within a couple of miles of HQ Fifth Army. Meanwhile a decisive battle was fought for the control of the air over Salerno Bay between the Luftwaffe and the Allied fighters and the guns of the invasion fleet moored off-shore.

There were to be other dramatic moments later in the campaign; the

German counter-offensive at Anzio and in the Auruncan mountains, the scene of the only truly brilliant stroke of the war when the French Expeditionary Force led by General Alphonse Juin broke through a German defence line that had so far baffled the soldiers of four armies, and the tragic and heroic moment when the 12th Podolski Lancers hoisted the flag of Poland and the Union Jack over the ruins of the Abbey of Montecassino. The rest of the war was, however, in the strict literal meaning of the word, dreadful. Many officers who had served on the Western Front in 1916–18 declared that Italy was as cruel. The weather was vile, the ground largely Napleon's "fifth element", mud, where it was not granite or limestone, and the line of advance perpetually barred by a succession of fast-flowing rivers and mountain crests. It was a bloody affair, a war of attrition designed to wear down the German strategic reserves by lasting a year and a half, claiming some 312,000 Allied killed, wounded and prisoners and some 435,000 German. The wretched Italian people, paying for the sin of supporting a gimcrack dictator, suffered terribly, as much from the bombs and shells of their liberators as from the brutality of their erstwhile German ally. The destruction of the Abbey on Montecassino was a tragic event, but nothing compared to the misery of civilians, their beautiful towns and villages destroyed by the retreating Germans or smashed above their heads by the Allied artillery and air force.

Wherein, therefore, does the interest of that stark conflict lie? First and foremost, in the human predicament of men at war. Counting the Germans and non-German auxiliaries as one, altogether the armies of eight nations played a part, each with its own style of fighting, and with different reasons for fighting at all. Their successes and failures were dramatic, and on an epic scale, as was the clash of will, not only between the opposing generals but among the Allies. Generals as a rule are strong-minded, self-opinionated men of high mettle, and in Italy inevitable differences of opinion were exacerbated by rival national aims. They made many mistakes, but war is not a game of chess, and commanders in war cannot be judged against some impossibly perfect model. If history is to be written faithfully the historian is forced to be critical, but as our story unfolds the reader will perceive that the leading actors in the drama were all men fitted to endure the acute stresses and strains of war and breathe the rarefied air at the summits of command.

The campaign in Italy is an example of how an operation of war begun to achieve rational and limited goals develops a momentum of its own. As each is reached another even more desirable appears. Like the black holes believed to exist in space, inexorably sucking matter into their gravitational fields, a local war once started develops an increasing appetite for men and materials. The invasion of Sicily (the first major amphibious landing on a coast line held by an enemy and embarked on with some trepidation) was a logical conclusion to the campaign in North Africa. Until it was in Allied hands the sea route through the Mediterranean was still hazardous. Its success, and signs of the imminent collapse of the Fascist regime in Italy, led to the next step.

In 1942 Britain and the United States joined together to study the problems of how to assemble a very large American force in England, and how their united armed forces could best cross the English Channel and open operations in northern France. After much discussion the British point of view prevailed: that there were insufficient resources available, particularly of specialised shipping and landing craft, to attempt the crossing that year. Instead, after some American misgivings, it was decided that rather than stand idle the limited resources available could in the meantime be used to carry the war to French North Africa with the aim of clearing the whole Mediterranean coast by a coordinated offensive eastwards from Algeria and westwards by the British Eighth Army from the sands of the Western Desert. This was a wise decision for a reason which was not expressed overtly in the councils of the two nations. Neither army as yet was fully trained or tough enough to meet head on the best soldiers in the world in that most difficult of all operations in war, an opposed landing. In the summer of 1942 an Axis force inferior in numbers led by General Erwin Rommel had routed the Eighth Army in the Western Desert, and early in 1943 the Americans received a salutory bloody nose in Tunisia. Both learnt valuable lessons, and the Allies found in General Montgomery and General Patton commanders who were able to reanimate their battered and somewhat discouraged troops. On those occasions there had been space to withdraw and time to rally, but in a seaborne invasion to withdraw is to drown.

The weather, stiff resistance and mismanagement of the western arm of the pincers delayed the completion of the African campaign until the spring, and the question was where to go from there. Once again it was agreed, after much debate, to postpone the great invasion of France until spring the following year, and to take the obvious step of capturing and occupying Sicily, thus ensuring control of the Mediterranean from end to end and hemming in the Axis on its southern perimeter. Sicily was successfully occupied and proved a tonic for the Allies. The successful landings exorcised the ghosts of Suvla Bay and Gallipoli which appeared whenever they contemplated landing on an enemy-held coast.* The Americans, who had struck a bad patch in Tunisia, showed that they could outfight the best of German troops, and recovered their habitual confidence. As a campaign, however, it was badly bungled by the Allied high command, and in Sicily there appeared the jealousies and lack of grip which were to bedevil the war in the mainland almost to its victorious end. The initial plan for invasion, made by Major-General Charles Gairdner, chief-of-staff to Alexander, and a specially assembled planning staff, was for separate landings by General Patton at one corner of the island and by General Montgomery, who was in Cairo while the planning staff worked in Algiers, at another. It drew strong objections from Montgomery, and was eventually changed, although not without friction.[2]

Montgomery, having succeeded in altering the plan so that the Eighth and Seventh armies landed side by side, tactlessly gave Patton the impression that his role was subordinate to that of the Eighth Army. The airborne component of the invasion was wrecked by a fearful error, caused by poor air force navigation and rough weather, which led to the incoming aircraft being engaged by the anti-aircraft artillery of the fleet. Patton, sensing the lack of grip from the top, departed from the operational plan and went off at a tangent with Palermo as his objective, covering a good deal of ground but engaging few German units. He thus effectively ruined the plan for a concentrated thrust by the whole of the 15th Army Group.

Patton then made for Messina, revealing the obsession of US Army commanders for geographical goals which could be easily exploited for the purpose of publicity. The Eighth Army, not to put too fine a point on it, dawdled. Patton's attempts to speed up his advance by employing landing craft in short "hooks" behind the withdrawing Axis troops proved fiascos. The Axis command wasted no time in exploiting these mistakes. Establishing a powerful defensive ring round the area of Messina and covering the crossing of the straits with a concentration of anti-aircraft guns and such few fighters as remained, it succeeded in extricating the bulk of the Axis forces and much valuable equipment without any interference from the Allied air forces or fleet.[3] Patton made his vaunted entry into Messina only when the German defenders chose to withdraw, and not a moment sooner. None of this augured well for the invasion of the mainland. It was the business of the army group commander to ensure a good plan agreed by both army commanders; that his two fractious subordinates acted in a spirit of

---

* To say nothing of the débâcle at the port of Tanga in German East Africa, November 1914.

cooperation and obeyed their orders; and that every step was taken to destroy or capture the defeated Axis forces. In all these Alexander conspicuously failed.

For the general conduct of the war world-wide the Americans and British had set up a loose but effective staff and system for consultations. At the top stood the President of the United States, Franklin D. Roosevelt, and Prime Minister and Minister of Defence, Winston Churchill, for Britain. The two heads of state attended by the Combined Chiefs of Staff (CCS) met at frequent intervals, and their decisions were conveyed to the commanders-in-chief in the theatres of war, who were officers serving the Alliance and not national commanders. General Dwight D. Eisenhower held the first appointment of this kind, in North Africa. In spite of separation by the breadth of the Atlantic, inevitable differences of opinion over strategy and rival national aspirations, its members worked together, if not in harmony, at least with a remarkable capacity to agree.

Four main questions tugged the decisions of this great council of war in different directions. The first concerned the strategic priorities of the Alliance. There was a strong feeling in the American camp, arising from a combination of anti-British and anti-European sentiments never very far from the surface of American thinking, a natural desire for revenge for the Japanese attack on the US Navy at Pearl Harbor and the loss of the Philippines, that the war in the Pacific should have priority over the war against Germany. The second was the fate of Soviet Russia, and the consequences of its possible defeat, which had at all costs to be avoided, for were Hitler given time to defeat Russia and consolidate his German hegemony in Europe the war might well be lost in the Western hemisphere, or in the worst case last for years. The third and fourth concerned method. General George C. Marshall, the dominating figure of the United States Chiefs of Staff, argued successfully that the war against Hitler should be the first task of the Allies, and that their strategy should be the destruction of Nazi Germany, beginning with the invasion of north-west Europe and the liberation of France. The British chiefs of staff could only support such a decision, but did not adopt so rigid and fundamentalist an attitude as General Marshall's. They were prepared to exploit any weaknesses on other parts of the perimeter of German-dominated Europe. The fourth concerned the priority given to the strategic bombing campaign against German war industry, her sources of oil and the morale of the working population by the destruction of German cities. This was the only area of the Alliance where there was total unanimity because the leaders of the United States Army Air Force and of the Royal Air Force shared a fanatical belief that Germany could be defeated by the bomber offensive alone.

All these factors came into play the moment the Allied leaders perceived that the battle in Sicily was going so well that they had to make a rapid decision on how far it should be exploited. General Marshall feared that all secondary fronts were "operations [that] invariably create a vacuum into which it is essential to pour more and more means". He also feared that the ease with which Churchill was seduced by the political prospects of far-flung, harassing operations on the perimeter of Europe was evidence of his secret intention to distort the whole Allied strategy by making the major effort in the Mediterranean. Churchill countered this by saying one more push might force a dejected and demoralised Italy out of the war altogether with many resultant benefits, to which he added the irrefutable argument that as all were agreed that the cross-Channel invasion could not possibly be launched until the spring of 1944, the Allies could not suspend operations until then while the embattled Russians were grappling with no fewer than 156 German divisions. The voice of the airmen gave Churchill support. The occupation of mainland Italy up to a line north of Naples–Foggia would give them two valuable constellations of military airfields from which they could launch fresh offensives at a favourable range against southern and eastern Germany and also her main supplier of oil, Romania.

While these deliberations were taking place exciting news arrived from General Eisenhower's headquarters in Algiers. On July 25, 1943 a group of conspirators led by the senior Italian soldier – Marshal of Italy Pietro Badoglio – and the King of Italy nerved themselves to depose and imprison the dictator Mussolini, who had so far brought only defeat and ruin to Italy, and established a new government free from the taint of Fascism. On the 31st it decided in secret to approach the Allies and ask for an armistice.

The transactions that followed resembled the plot of a political thriller and, if they had not involved matters of life and death, could be seen as a comedy. Four different emissaries were sent to sound out the Allies; their brief being to obtain the best terms for Italy in return for her active participation on the Allied side. On July 31 two distinguished civilians were sent to the British Ambassador in Madrid and the British Consul in Tangier. This producing no result, a general officer, Castellano, the chief of the department of plans and operations in the Italian high command, was also sent to Madrid in disguise as a civilian but without any credentials, in case he was caught by the Germans who were already deeply suspicious of the loyalty of the new Italian

Government to the Axis. He arrived on August 15 and was sent on to Lisbon, where he was interviewed by General Eisenhower's Chief of Staff, General W. Bedell Smith, US Army and his chief intelligence officer, Brigadier Kenneth Strong, British Army. Castellano achieved little as he wanted to take back some assurance that the Allies would intervene in great strength in Italy to protect the new Government, while the two Allied representatives refused to reveal Allied plans and told him that the only condition on which an armistice would be granted was the unconditional surrender of the Italian Government. All this took some time, so the Italian Government sent their fourth emissary, a General Zanussi, taking with him as a proof of sincerity the British General Sir Adrian Carton de Wiart, VC, who was a prisoner of war in Italian hands.

Providentially these missions coincided with the important QUAD-RANT conference in Quebec, where the two Allied heads of government, the Combined Chiefs of Staff and their other advisers were conveniently assembled. The Italian proposals were not, however, received with sympathy. As Churchill put it when he first heard the news: "Badoglio admits that he is going to double-cross someone but ... [it is] ... more likely Hitler will be the one to be tricked ... meanwhile the war should be carried on *in every way the Americans will allow*" (authors' italics).

All the same, this put a completely different complexion on the place of Italy in future operations. There were those, like General Montgomery, who believed that the new Government of Italy was composed of men of straw, but that if the Italian armed forces possessed sufficient spirit to resist any German attempt to interfere with Italian sovereignty, Italy might be gained with little trouble. Sheer military necessity might persuade the Germans, who already had large forces committed to holding down the populations of the Balkan countries, to cut their losses in Italy and retire to a defensive line in the north, perhaps along the foothills of the Alps. All, then, that would be required of the Allies would be to commit sufficient forces to the Italian operation as would serve to reassure the Italian Government and stiffen the resistance of the armed forces. All the glittering rewards of an Italian surrender, the blow to German morale, the raised hopes of other peoples under the Nazi heel, the liberation of Rome, possession of the airfields, the winding down of the expensive war in the Mediterranean, could be obtained on the cheap. The buck was promptly passed to General Eisenhower. His directive was a compromise between the views of Marshall and Churchill. He was to prepare to part with seven British and American divisions together with a large proportion of his assault shipping and landing craft required in England for the invasion of Europe by November 2. At the same time he was to undertake such operations as were best calculated to eliminate Italy from the war, and contain as many German divisions in that country as possible.[4]

Eisenhower therefore faced a difficult problem, full of incalculable factors. In this he was not alone. The view from Hitler's headquarters was deeply depressing. In February 1943 there had been a great disaster on the Russian front, ending in the surrender of the German Sixth Army at Stalingrad. In July a counter-offensive launched at Kursk in the hope of stopping the remorseless Russian advance had been completely defeated by the 17th. In comparison the surrender of the Axis forces in Tunisia and the loss of Sicily on August 17 were only dents in the curtain wall of Fortress Europe, but all the signs taken together pointed to a Germany under siege and facing ultimate defeat. To be sure, the German commanders in Sicily had with great courage and professional skill not only halted Generals Patton and Montgomery, but removed 60,000–80,000 men and much equipment across the Straits of Messina to the mainland in spite of the attacks of the Allied air forces. Wars, however, are not won by glorious retreats. The German divisions in central and southern Italy were mere wrecks, requiring to be re-manned, re-equipped and re-trained. The German commanders on the spot could only wonder why the Allies did not embark at once, or had not forestalled the evacuation of Sicily by landing in Calabria ahead of them, and they thanked God for the respite their unenterprising opponents had given them.

In August Hitler was the target of contradictory advice. His favourite, Rommel, assured him that the British and Americans, supported by their overwhelming air-power, could not possibly be contained in the south of Italy. He recommended that the Reich could best be defended in the north, and that the centre and south should be abandoned. Field-Marshal Albert Kesselring, who held the appointment of Commander-in-Chief (South) over all German and Italian forces, was more optimistic. He believed that if he were allowed time to rebuild his German forces the terrain of Italy was eminently suitable for a slow, deliberate withdrawal. Hitler, who was temperamentally incapable of giving up territory once conquered, however cogent the strategic reasons, could not respond completely to the logic of either course, so he backed both Rommel and Kesselring. Rommel was ordered to assemble an army group in northern Italy, and Kesselring to create the Tenth Army in the south, whose role would be to repel the Allied invasion (expected to land anywhere between the Straits of Messina and Naples), and, with a strong contingent located in the area of Rome, to take care of any hostile move by the Italian forces. These arrangements gradually took shape during the month of August until each of the rival commanders had eight divisions.

It must be borne in mind that Hitler at his headquarters strictly controlled any alterations in these dispositions, and also that Kesselring's were divisions in name only, except for the 16th Panzer Division, refitting after being decimated in Russia, and being fleshed out to full establishment before returning to that theatre. As for the Italians, the Germans realised after the coup of July 25 that they could no longer be relied on to resist an Allied invasion. Accordingly they made arrangements for all Italian forces to be disarmed at the first sign of treachery. The members of the provisional Government were well aware of their own personal danger should their Axis partners get wind of the peace negotiations, or if there were a premature announcement of an armistice, but were too timid to make their own plans or reveal their fears directly to the Allies. Eisenhower was only to discover the full extent of Italian irresolution on the very eve of AVALANCHE, launched in the hope that the landing at Salerno would be unopposed. On September 9 the British and American servicemen of the Fifth Army were to be suddenly and brutally disillusioned.

2

GENERAL EISENHOWER'S PROBLEMS

Plan followed plan in swift succession
Commanders went, commanders came
While telegrams in quick succession
Arrived to fan or quench the flame.

Rhyme composed in the British
Fourteenth Army during a planning frenzy

Italy is a boot. You have to enter it from the top.
Napoleon

One of the most fortunate events in the early history of the Anglo-American alliance was the discovery of Colonel Dwight D. Eisenhower, US Army, and his rapid ascent to the post of commander-in-chief of the Allied forces in North Africa. He was not a "great captain" in the classical sense, although it can be said that he had the same flair for coalition war as the Duke of Marlborough and the same earthy American horse sense as his fellow countryman Ulysses S. Grant and like him became a president of the United States. He was never a battle-fighting general, able to "ride the whirlwind and direct the storm", nor would he have regarded such metaphor as anything but highfalutin, for he was at heart a simple boy from the Middle West of the United States, with a taste for open-air pursuits like golf and fishing, who seldom read anything other than thrillers for relaxation. Though he was no intellectual he had plenty of brains, and had he not been trained as a soldier he might well have proved the successful head of a large international business corporation. Eisenhower was however well-educated in military affairs and a commander with a will of his

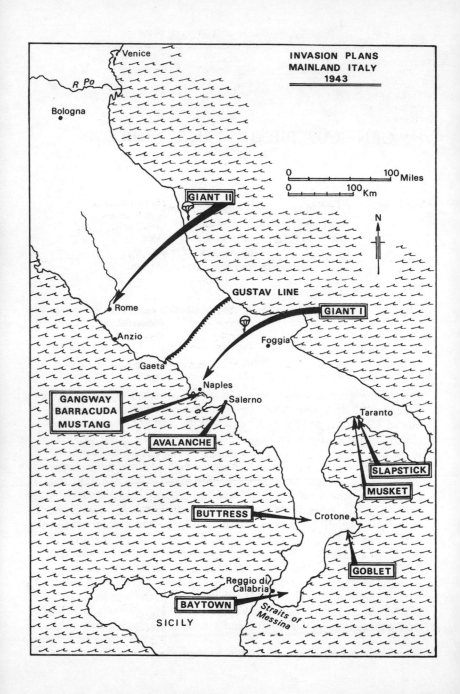

CODE-NAME	OBJECTIVE	FORCES ALLOTTED	OUTCOME
BARRACUDA GANGWAY MUSTANG	Naples	None	All discarded
MUSKET	Taranto	US Fifth Army: 6th Corps, 2 infantry, 1 armoured, 1 airborne divs	Discarded
SLAPSTICK	Taranto	Br. 1st airborne div.	Hastily mounted, Sept. 9, troops carried in RN ships
GOBLET	Crotone	Br. Eighth Army: 3 Br. infantry, 1 US airborne divs	Discarded
BUTTRESS	Gulf of Gioia	Br. 10th Corps: Eighth Army: 2 infantry, 1 armoured divs	Discarded. Force transferred to AVALANCHE
BAYTOWN	Reggio in Calabria	Br. 13th Corps 1 Br., 1 Cdn infantry divs	Launched, Sept. 3
AVALANCHE	Naples, landing in Bay of Salerno	US Fifth Army: assault echelon, 2 infantry, 1 armoured Br. divs, 1⅔ US infantry divs	Launched, Sept. 9
GIANT I	Approaches to AVALANCHE bridgehead from north	1 US airborne div.	Cancelled
GIANT II	Coup-de-main, Rome	1 US airborne div.	From AVALANCHE
GIANT III (?) (afterthought)	Avellino and Paestum	Part of US airborne div.	To reinforce Fifth Army at Salerno. Launched hastily Sept. 13

own. That glamorous species, the "great captain" of old, deciding on his strategy, making his own plans and personally directing his troops in battle, was not only extinct but obsolete. The complexity of twentieth-century warfare demands an altogether new sort of commander at the top level; below the purely political direction of a war, yet fully aware of the political dimension and able to respond sensibly to its pressure; an organiser and director of operations by air, land and sea, remote from the hurly-burly of the battlefield, yet watchful and involved in its events. Like the head of a great corporation he is concerned with goals, the allocation of resources and the appointment of "top managers", but the analogy may not be pressed too far, because the modern comman-der must continue to be "a general" in the full sense of the term and not pretend to be the chairman of a board. He is still a commander, not a manager, able to withstand the emotional stresses of warfare and take cruel decisions without agonising over the possible consequences.

Eisenhower had many of the attributes of such a paragon, though he had no experience on the staff or in command of the conduct of active operations. He had in full the American genius for managing very large enterprises. He was a very likeable man, able to win not only the respect but the affection of his subordinates. His career in the Philippines, when he was staff officer to General Douglas MacArthur during the transition of that country to independence, and later in London, when the great American force build-up for the invasion of France and the liberation of Europe was being planned, had made him familiar with politics, politicians and command problems at the highest level. All this was to stand him in good stead, for when he arrived in North Africa every strategic problem had a political dimension. Like all successful politicians Eisenhower had a strong sense of the possible, and under-stood that the essential prerequisite for success is to survive.

His first requirement, therefore, was to keep in the good books of his powerful superior, George Marshall, while dealing even-handedly as an international commander, trying to please all his masters. Next, he had to assert his authority over the young bulls of the herd, men like the British Air Marshal Sir Arthur Tedder and the American Lieutenant-General Carl Spaatz, respectively the British and American air force chiefs. They formed a powerful combination, for the RAF and the USAAF were bound together by common interest as well as the freemasonry of the air. Tedder was a firm believer in the doctrine that the air force was an independent service and not in any way the handmaiden of the army. He had agreed to an ingenious system of command and control by which the army could obtain direct support on the battlefield, but he insisted that his first priority was to win the battle for air control against the opposing air force, in his own way and using his own judgment. Only then would he consider providing fighter cover for the army over the battlefield, or invasion beaches, or act as its flying artillery. The USAAF, though still nominally part of the army, held the same views and was anxious to acquire the autonomy enjoyed by the RAF, and so the two air forces presented a united front to the supreme commander and the other services. Eisenhower therefore had to combine tact with authority to obtain the full and cheerful cooperation of the airmen in operations that were essentially tri-service and combined.

He had no problems with the admirals. The sea service is a thing apart, seamen have a strong sense of superiority over land soldiers, and whether it was due to the common bond that unites seamen being stronger than the past history of conflict between the two navies, or a fortunate rapport between Vice-Admiral H. Kent Hewitt, USN, and the Fleet Admiral Sir Andrew Cunningham, RN, and their subordinates, the naval aspects of the war caused Eisenhower little anxiety as far as command relationships were concerned. (What friction there was occurred between the sailors and the airmen. During the Battle of Salerno Admiral Hewitt was incensed when the British Air Marshal Sir Arthur Coningham, far away in Algiers, took upon himself to decide the level of fighter cover the fleet required. Montgomery and Admiral of the Fleet Sir Andrew Cunningham were incompatible and quarrelsome, and Eisenhower had to intervene between them over the provision of landing craft.)

On land the situation was not so simple. The US Army commanders in North Africa were not predisposed to like or admire their British colleagues, by reason of history (many regarding Britain as their ancient enemy), their isolation and their upbringing. As yet inexperienced, they were extremely sensitive to criticism spoken or implied. Many British officers, understandably at that stage in the war, felt that they had given the Germans one good beating and they knew the answers, but were foolish and tactless enough not to conceal their opinions.* Eisenhower's first and important success was to organise a model, international, integrated HQ, the first of its kind, using all his authority, political skill and undoubted charm to ensure harmony.

As regards his own role he found as soon as he had arrived in Africa

---

* One British general at a press conference was asked his opinion of the US Army's performance to date in Tunisia. In all innocence, or ignorance, he gave an all too candid reply, which exacerbated the already frosty Anglo-American relationship and damaged his career.

that he was involved in the most complicated negotiations with the French, while at the same time discussing strategic options of every variety with the Combined Chiefs of Staff, London and Washington. He needed a land forces commander on a level with the two other services, who shared his views, and the British provided him in General Sir Harold Alexander, who, as commander of the 18th Army Group had the role of coordinating the converging operations of the British-Indian-New Zealand Eighth Army and the British First Army, with British, US Army and French units under command.* Alexander was a man with whom Eisenhower found he could deal comfortably.

Eisenhower's first operational mission in Africa was simple and straightforward. The Axis forces had been caught in a vice between the converging Allied armies and all that was required was to coordinate their efforts. London and Washington had hoped for a quick kill, but the problem although simple to pose was difficult to solve, because of the realities of war, and the Axis forces in Africa were not liquidated until April 1943. Nevertheless it was a victory for Eisenhower and his unique command apparatus, and he had consolidated his position both militarily and politically.

The second, in Sicily, was straightforward as far as the purely military factors went. The object was clear, the resources ample and both the army commanders, Montgomery and Lieutenant-General George Patton, the commander of US Seventh Army, were experienced warriors. To be sure, a more experienced supreme commander and one with full disciplinary powers over his subordinates might possibly have anticipated and corrected the mismanagement and jealousies which marred the battle for Sicily, but Eisenhower should not have had to bother with current operational issues; that was the very reason for which he had asked for a land commander. His concern was with future strategy, and there he had problems difficult enough to daunt any general.[1]

Primarily these stemmed from the need to steer a cautious path between the opposed intentions of his real master, George Marshall, who was against any Italian involvement, and Churchill, who was still at heart the same unregenerate advocate of an "eastern" strategy he had been in 1915. On the one hand Eisenhower, as said, had by November to part with a substantial part of his forces and landing craft, and

---

* The titles of army groups were arrived at by juggling the numbers of armies. In Sicily the same HQ became the 15th (the Seventh and the Eighth) which it remained until it became HQ Allied Armies in Italy, reverting to the numerical title in December 1944.

Marshall also refused to allow the US strategic air forces to be diverted from the Combined Bomber Offensive for the preliminary air battle to wear down the Luftwaffe before the projected invasion of the mainland. On the other, in accordance with the directive given to Eisenhower by the Combined Chiefs of Staff, he had to develop operations calculated to knock Italy out of the war, which would only be done by invading the mainland. In short, he was expected to obtain grand political-military results with slender means. His reactions were, as usual, politically astute. He was not a Montgomery, given to writing forthright appreciations ridiculing sloppy strategical thinking. He set his planning staffs to work churning out every possible combination of plans for landings from north of Naples round the coast to Taranto, leaving the adverse balance between the force levels required as deduced by the planners and those he could actually convey to the objectives to speak for itself. (See sketch map and connected table on pp. 28–9.)

These fell into two distinct groups. The first was made up of plans aimed at the capture of Rome or Naples, either by direct attack or envelopment by air and sea; all strategically rewarding if they came off but operationally very risky. Eventually Eisenhower took the advice of his naval and air commanders and settled for the Bay of Salerno, as the point furthest north where cover by land-based fighter aircraft from airfields in Italy could be provided. The second was of landings in the south of Italy, safe and certain to succeed but strategically unrewarding. They were too far from Rome to make a sharp political impact, and the terrain and communications offered infinite possibilities for delaying tactics. Eisenhower kept all his options open and waited on events, as we have said, which proved startling.

When Mussolini fell and the secret emissaries of the Badoglio Government arrived the situation was, as it were, stood on its head. Eisenhower's problem was no longer how to inflict another swingeing defeat on the Axis on the scale of Tunis and Sicily, but to exploit an Italian surrender. It became imperative, therefore, to take operational risks which so far had been unacceptable. This new factor dominated Eisenhower's strategic concept. If he could act boldly and quickly he might secure great gains: Italy as a co-belligerent and a German withdrawal to the northern Apennines, or even the line of the Alps. It is only with hindsight that he can be condemned for entertaining an illusion based on a common intelligence fallacy, that of assuming that your opponent's mind works like your own. Eisenhower's real difficulty was that he had no reliable intelligence coming out of Italy on German intentions. It is no wonder that he became irritated with the far more canny Montgomery who was raising every difficulty about hopping over the Messina strait, which Eisenhower believed could be crossed in "row-boats". He was not alone in his optimism. The invasion of the mainland would be conducted as if it were a pursuit until the Allied land commanders came hard up against reality at the end of the year in the shape of the Italian winter, the Italian mountains and the fortifications of the Gustav Line.

While negotiating with the Italians and juggling with future plans Eisenhower had to consider commanders. Alexander fell naturally into place as commander overall with his army group HQ. Montgomery was in position to undertake the invasion of Calabria and in fact, bored with the closing stage of the battle for Sicily, had already delegated control of operations there to the commander of the 13th Corps, Lieutenant-General Sir Oliver Leese, and on his own initiative directed the unemployed commander of his 10th Corps, General Sir Brian Horrocks, to begin to plan. What emerged was BAYTOWN, the direct crossing of the Straits of Messina, and BUTTRESS, a landing on the west face of the toe of Italy in the Gulf of Gioia. Of the American commanders General George Patton, Seventh Army, was fully occupied in Sicily and in any case his future employment was in doubt because of an indiscretion. (A highly strung and impulsive man, he had struck a psychiatric casualty he found in a field hospital, believing that he was a malingerer, and even repeated the same offence on another victim later.) Omar Bradley, who might have altered the history of the Italian campaign, had been appointed an army commander designate to OVERLORD. There remained the commander of the US Fifth Army stationed in North Africa, the obvious choice. In this way the fateful conjunction of Alexander and Mark Wayne Clark came about.

Harold Alexander was the third son of the Earl of Caledon in the peerage of Ireland. Educated at Harrow and Sandhurst he seems to have drifted into the army without any great sense of purpose – he had toyed with the idea of becoming an artist. Commissioned in 1911, he was accepted by the Irish Guards, to spend the whole war in the firing line with the infantry with only two interruptions, to recover from wounds. He was twice decorated, commanded a battalion and briefly a brigade, and ended the war as a lieutenant-colonel. He then chose to dedicate himself to the profession of arms. In the 1920s the only sure road to advancement was through the Army Staff College (which was also in effect a war college) and he insisted on being allowed to attend it, even though this meant that he had to accept a reduction in rank. The regime was extremely competitive and testing, and Alexander did not impress two of the directing staff who observed him closely – the future

Chief of the Imperial General Staff, Alan Brooke, and Bernard Montgomery. This did not impede his promotion. He was, most unusually as a British service and Guards officer, appointed commander of an infantry brigade in the Indian Army and distinguished himself in active operations on the North-West Frontier of India. (He astonished its officers by learning to speak Urdu.) By 1939 he was commanding a division, part of the British Expeditionary Force. In 1940 he was given command of a corps.

Fate then decreed that he would be given in succession three missions in the hope that he could retrieve an impending disaster. The first was to extricate the British forces trapped at Dunkirk. There his courage and sangfroid proved a tonic and he succeeded. He was the last man to leave the beaches, after searching them from end to end for stragglers. In March 1942 he was given the impossible task of winning a battle already lost in Burma. In August of the same year Churchill selected him to succeed General Auchinleck as Commander-in-Chief in the Middle East. There again, he was able to achieve little, but for happier reasons. The only force engaging the enemy, the Eighth Army, had just been gripped by his former instructor, Montgomery, now his subordinate, and he could do little but lend him support and encouragement. Nevertheless, the lustre of the Eighth Army's victories was naturally shared by the commander-in-chief, and Alexander seemed the best choice for commander of the ground forces (and later 15th Army Group commander) under Eisenhower during the last phase of the war in North Africa.

There were mixed feelings about the wisdom of this choice. Alexander had never had any experience of planning and directing a major, successful offensive operation. His first big battle, to crush the Axis forces holding the western front in Tunisia, was a failure, and the *coup de grâce* had to be organised by Lieutenant-General Brian Horrocks, a corps commander lent by Montgomery. Brooke felt strongly that Alexander required the assistance of a first-class chief of staff, to think for him. The intolerant Montgomery regarded his chief as incompetent. In sharp contrast, Harold Macmillan, a politician but also a Guardsman and a veteran of the Western Front, was impressed by Alexander's qualities.* What Alexander had was something Macmillan admired, *style*. His unshakable calm, courtesy, readiness to listen to the views of his subordinates and sensitivity to the undercurrents of

---

* Harold Macmillan, created Earl of Stockton in 1984, and future Prime Minister, was appointed British Minister Resident in North Africa, remaining in the Mediterranean theatre until the end of the war.

national prejudice and jealousy were all essential to the successful command of a coalitionary army group.

The mess of an ordinary field headquarters was a place where hard-pressed staff officers snatched a hasty meal and continued to transact business. Alexander's own mess, as Macmillan recorded in his diary, resembled rather the high table of a college in Oxford or Cambridge. The war was "politely ignored". The conversation dwelt on such topics as "the campaigns of Belisarius, the advantages of classical over Gothic architecture or the best ways to drive pheasants in flat country . . ." The arrival of an urgent operational signal was not allowed to interrupt this flow of civilised chat. Alexander would ask permission to read it, continue the conversation for a minute or two and if necessary "unobtrusively retire" from the table. "There was no fuss, no worry, no anxiety – and a great battle in progress!"[2]

This was all very well, but behind the urbanity Alexander's own views were concealed by an impenetrable reserve. (A distinguished officer who served under him for many months said that he knew him no better at the end of that period than the day when he first took up his appointment.) His admirers, like Macmillan, believed that his style of command, by throwing out suggestions, inviting opinions and compromising, was the only way to manage a team of fractious Allied generals. His detractors maintained that his reserve concealed a mind empty of strategic ideas, incapable of deciding the best course in any set of circumstances. Whatever the reason, Alexander either would not or could not impose his will as a commander should. Mark Clark, of whom Macmillan said that he was the cleverest general in the theatre, was quick to observe this weakness, with unhappy results. Clark was a staff officer of immense ability who had first made his name as the right-hand man of the commander of the US Ground Forces, General Lesley McNair, at the time of the great expansion of the US Army in 1941–2, when Clark made a notable contribution both in organisation and the training of the new divisions by mass production methods. He was far from popular, as it fell to him to weed out incompetent officers; a task he carried out with ruthlessness. In England Clark had given Eisenhower invaluable assistance in taking care of all the organisational details of the Allied landings in North Africa, after which he revealed an unsuspected flair for diplomacy when he made a hazardous mission in a submarine to meet the French commanders to persuade them not to oppose the Allied landings. Clark's real ambition, however, was to command in war. His operational experience had been cut short on the Western Front in 1918 when he had been seriously wounded soon after the battalion he commanded entered the front line. In 1943 in Africa, when Clark saw that Eisenhower had found an ideal chief of staff (in W. Bedell Smith), he pressed for his release and requested the command of the newly raised Fifth Army. Since then he had been occupied in planning notional operations and training US Army units in North Africa in amphibious warfare. Salerno was to be his first test in battle.

That Clark was an officer of enormous ability, intelligence and drive was the opinion of McNair, Eisenhower, Brooke, that harsh critic of US Army officers, and Churchill, who called him "the American Eagle". He was also intensely ambitious, which is no bad thing, longing to be and be seen as a great field commander. He was to drive his troops hard and to accept heavy casualties as the price of success. He had great physical courage and he was no stranger in the front line. He had, however, two serious shortcomings. He lacked something granted to many lesser soldiers, that almost instinctive faculty for discerning what was operationally sound and what was not. His "schemes of man-oeuvre" were designed mechanically from a set of rules imbibed at the Staff College, drawn on a map and invariably faulty. (For instance, the reason he gave for his ill-judged warning order to Admiral Hewitt to re-embark the 6th Corps at Salerno was that it is what he was taught at staff school.)[3] Moreover, he seemed secretly conscious of his inadequacy; where Alexander would discuss endlessly and never give orders, Clark gave orders and refused to discuss them. The other side of his (honourable) ambition was bitter jealousy of his rivals and an avid desire for publicity. He had suspicions amounting to paranoia that the British were stealing his limelight and trying to take the credit for the achievements of his army. This was unfortunate, for it was a conviction that nothing could modify, let alone eradicate. It was to colour his attitude towards Alexander and distort all his operational planning. On the contrary, his antipathy, though carefully dissembled and revealed only to his diary, became more intense as one battle succeeded another.

The opponent of the ill-matched team of Clark and Alexander was Generalfeldmarshall Albert Kesselring, a Franconian, originally commissioned in the garrison or heavy branch of the Bavarian Artillery, who during 1914–18 had served largely on the artillery staff. After the Armistice he was engaged in building up the post-war German Army, until 1933 when he was transferred to the Luftwaffe. The better to assert his authority in the new service he learnt to fly, a remarkable accomplishment for a man of forty-eight. As Commander-in-Chief South (*Oberbefehlshaber Sued*) in Italy and later theatre commander he had to steer a careful course between the wishes of his master, Hitler, and the realities of the situation. This he did with great skill, concealing any misgivings he had behind a mask of optimism – he was nicknamed

37

"Smiling Albert" – that infuriated his army commanders; but from them he stood no nonsense. He was a master of defensive operations and withdrawal, keeping his troops in position until the eleventh hour and then disengaging them intact. He was very shrewd. As an airman he did not have to be told by his intelligence staff that the most likely landing place was Salerno. He was aware that his Italian ally might rat on him, and had a plan ready to be put into action at the first sign of treachery. When we trace the course of the war in Italy and describe the setbacks and disappointments of the Allies, the reader should bear in mind that they were facing as good a general as emerged from the German Army in the Second World War and certainly the best on either side in the Italian theatre.

We can now return to Eisenhower, who was cutting his suit to fit his cloth. He soon realised that he could only carry out two landings, both on a scale much reduced in the weight of the initial assault and the rate of build-up. MUSKET was cancelled. The Fifth Army was to land at Salerno (AVALANCHE) with three divisions and a floating reserve amounting to about two-thirds of a fourth one. The US 82nd Airborne Division complete was also allotted to Fifth Army, which Clark intended to use in its airborne role in the Naples plain to engage German units that might otherwise join the fight at Salerno.* The Eighth Army operation was cut down. GOBLET was cancelled, and the 10th Corps of two divisions after having been told to be prepared to carry out either BUTTRESS or AVALANCHE was finally ordered to come under command of the Fifth Army, and Montgomery's role for the moment reduced to BAYTOWN with only the two divisions of the 13th Corps. Loading was started on August 19 and the assault landing craft and ships stowed by September 1. Clark produced his outline plan on August 26. D-day for BAYTOWN was September 3, for AVALANCHE the 9th.

On September 3 the Badoglio Government concluded a secret agreement with the Allies for an armistice. Eisenhower had had to push them very hard, for the Italians were under no illusions about what their fate might be if the Germans discovered their treachery. They were anxious to discover what the Allied plans were, and had tried to stipulate that a minimum of fifteen divisions should be landed in the Rome area, but Eisenhower was adamant that he would not in any circumstances disclose his plans in advance. He felt, however, that at least a gesture demonstrating Allied support was necessary. If an

* This was GIANT I, the first of several abortive plans to use the division in other than a straight infantry role in the Salerno bridgehead.

airborne force could be dropped in the Rome area it might serve to encourage the Italian Army and act as a focus for a general rising. On the 3rd he informed a dismayed Mark Clark that he was removing the 82nd Airborne Division from his command and using it for this purpose.

Eisenhower understandably felt that though he considered that this extremely risky operation was worth while he had no firm intelligence of what in fact the Italian plans or intentions were. Accordingly the last act of the drama of the Italian surrender was played, fortunately, as a comedy-thriller. Two courageous officers from the airborne division were sent on a clandestine mission to Rome where they were able to have a private interview with Marshal Badoglio, who was horrified by the whole project. It was clear that the Italians had neither plans nor the intention for a rising against the Germans. It became clear also that the agreement to declare an armistice entered into by the Italian emissary was seen in Rome as conditional on the major Allied landing being made in the Rome area, whereas the Italian staff had correctly deduced that it was to be at Salerno. On the 8th the mission was able to transmit by radio the code-words "situation Innocuous" to Algiers, signifying that the operation should not take place, and orders to call it off arrived at the airfields just in time, after the first flights had actually taken off. Clark was not informed, or at least was not aware that the 82nd Division was once more at his disposal, for four days. The Taranto operation was then revived, as Eisenhower felt able at least to rely on Italian assurances that it was not occupied by the German forces and that the Italians would not resist. In a hastily improvised operation, SLAPSTICK, the British 1st Airborne Division was rushed to Taranto on the decks of ships of the Royal Navy and disembarked over the dockside on the 9th, where it saw units of the Italian fleet depart to surrender in Malta.

Eisenhower now made one of the few political miscalculations of his military career. From optimism about Italian intentions he had veered to distrust, even of Badoglio's promise to surrender as agreed and not oppose the landings, and he determined to force his hand. On the 8th he broadcast personally from Radio Algiers announcing the Italian surrender. Picked up by the Germans it led to the code-words "bring in the harvest" being sent to the German troops, who at once proceeded to disarm all the Italian units. All meekly obeyed except one general, who was shot down at once in front of his staff. The broadcast therefore had the very consequence Eisenhower wished to avoid, as his bold moves were based on the hopes of the active collaboration of the Italians. The news was also picked up by the ships in the Salerno convoys, now only hours away from their beaches, where it was greeted with some astonishment by the senior officers, including Admiral Hewitt and General Clark, who had not been forewarned. Admiral Hewitt, somewhat perplexed, issued a conditional order on opening fire with naval guns as the flotillas approached the beach; that fire should be held unless the batteries on shore opened fire first. In the event the US Corps had decided to land without a preliminary bombardment as it might sacrifice surprise, which proved a costly mistake. The British, already aware that German reconnaissance aircraft had spotted the huge invasion fleet, did the opposite, and profited by it.

The Allied commanders had yet to discover that the Italians had been disarmed. The Germans were in full operational control, Kesselring had correctly judged that the invaders would land at Salerno and the 16th Panzer Division was deployed in readiness to defend the beaches. Instead of being alerted to that possibility, the news of the Italian surrender spread quickly among the troops, with the adverse effect of relaxing their pre-battle tension. Expecting a walk-over, they were greeted not with cheers from the general public and flowers and kisses from beautiful *signorini* but a storm of well-directed fire, which led to a degree of demoralisation in some units during the first hours of the assault.

Seen from a distance of forty years the disjointed and haphazard approach to so dangerous an enterprise seems fumbling and inept to a degree. That the staff were able to cope with all the chopping and changing was a miracle, for even after the AVALANCHE fleet had sailed mail-bags full of amendments to operations orders were being delivered to ships – and left unopened. Montgomery's harsh criticisms of the dissipation of effort, the lack of a coordinated operational plan and of a plan for strategical development were, in strict military terms, justified. Before passing judgment, however, we must enter into Eisenhower's predicament. To say a man has done the best he could is the most damning of criticisms, but Eisenhower really did very well, beset as he was by every difficulty.

Generals can only do so much to win or lose a battle. In Brussels in 1815 a friend asked Wellington how he thought the impending clash with the Grand Army would turn out. He pointed at a private soldier strolling past them looking at the strange sights of a foreign city. "It all depends on that article," said the duke. This, as we shall see in the ensuing chapters, was to prove the case on the beaches of Salerno.

II

Salerno

3

THE BOARD AND THE PIECES

If hopes were dupes, fears may be liars;
It may be, in yon smoke concealed,
Your comrades chase e'en now the fliers,
And, but for you, possess the field.
Arthur Hugh Clough 1819–61

The field which the German Tenth Army proposed to defend and the
Allies to secure can be visualised as a walled garden, triangular in
shape, open to the sea on one side. The wall itself was a lofty and
imposing structure, tumbled down in parts, and pierced by four
gateways, one in the south, in the angle between the wall and the sea,
one in the apex leading inland towards the east, and two in the north.
The "garden" was represented by the low coastal plain, richly culti-
vated, intersected by rivers and irrigation ditches and covered with
vineyards, orchards of olives, tobacco plants and corn; all affording
cover for a deadly game of hide-and-seek between invaders and
defenders. Tactically, the key points included the Montecorvino
airfield and the numerous villages, each on a hillock or low ridge
commanding the plain. The vital objectives were gateways in the
mountain wall.

As a full-size field of battle it was inconvenient. The seaward edge of
the triangle was thirty miles in length, the other two eighteen, too big
for the base line of an attack, too small for the manoeuvre of an army,
and hemmed in by mountains whose summits rose to 3,500 feet. An
invader was in effect thrusting his head into a bag. The approach by sea
was plain sailing, unobstructed by sandbanks or shallows, the beaches
good with easy access inland through sand-dunes, but while it seemed
easy enough to land, how to get out was another question. On closer

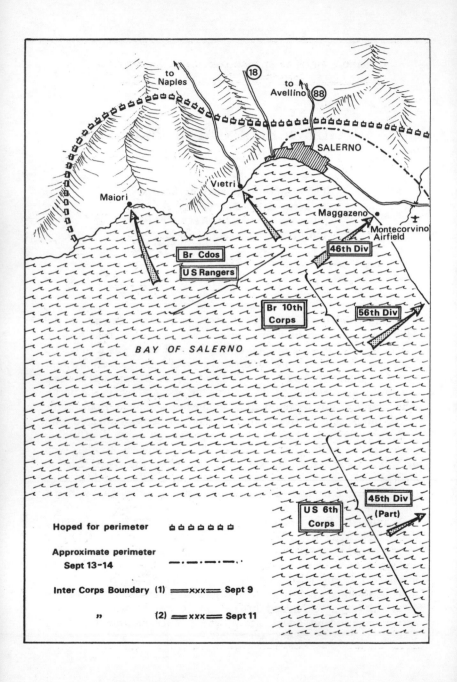

to Naples

18

to Avellino 88

SALERNO

Vietri

Maiori

Maggazeno

Montecorvino
Airfield

Br Cdos

U S Rangers

46th Div

Br 10th
Corps

56th Div

BAY OF SALERNO

US 6th
Corps

45th Div
(Part)

Hoped for perimeter ᶿᶿᶿᶿᶿᶿ

Approximate perimeter
Sept 13-14

Inter Corps Boundary (1) ══xxx══ Sept 9

„ (2) ══xxx══ Sept 11

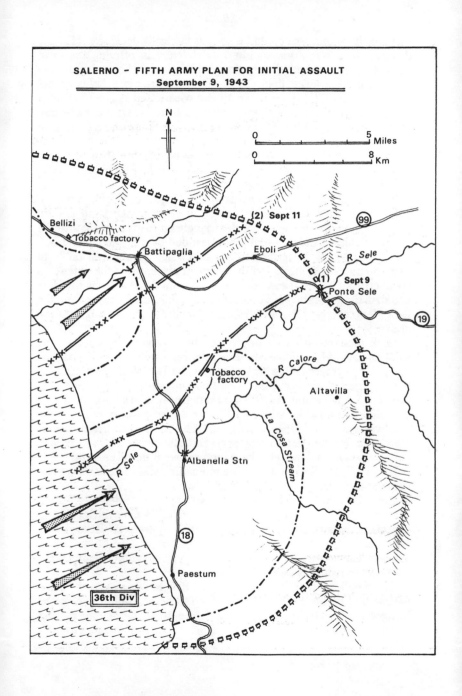

SALERNO – FIFTH ARMY PLAN FOR INITIAL ASSAULT
September 9, 1943

N

0 _____ 5 Miles
0 _____ 8 Km

Bellizi
Tobacco factory
Battipaglia
(2) Sept 11
Eboli
99
R Sele
(1) Sept 9
Ponte Sele
19
Tobacco factory
R Calore
Altavilla
La Cosa Stream
Albanella Stn
R Sele
18
Paestum
36th Div

analysis the whole area could be seen as tactically deceptive. Had the designer of a war-game sought a model terrain offering the most difficult options to both the attackers and defenders he could not have made a better choice than the smiling orchards and fields of the Salerno plain. To begin with, small and constricted as it appears on a map, it was large enough to absorb troops as desert sand absorbs rain from a cloudburst. The regiments on both sides knew about fighting in the open spaces of Africa or the steppes of Russia, but amid the vines or tobacco plants fields of fire and view were no more than fifty or a hundred yards, sometimes zero. It was indeed a place for hide and seek, but of a nerve-racking and deadly kind.

As a point of entry Salerno held out advantages or difficulties to both sides. To be sure, the invaders could not develop their strategy until they had forced their way out of the triangle up roads running through narrow defiles many miles long commanded by crags looming 1,000 feet above them. Nevertheless the first stage of an invasion is to consolidate a bridgehead as a jumping-off place, while the defenders try to crush it before it can be reinforced from the sea. If the invaders can slam the gates and keep them shut, the tables can be turned and the defenders can, possibly, be defeated before their reserves can enter the arena.

High mountains have a deceptive effect, largely on morale. The soldiers in the plain below cower, imagining that the frowning heights are full of eyes watching their every move (we shall see later how Montecassino hypnotised the Allied commanders) but tactically it is the foothills that count. Anything from twenty-five to a hundred feet of elevation and a field of fire of 1,000 yards are good enough for the machine-gunner or artillery observer. The plain itself was not completely flat, but rumpled with ridge and hillock, increasing in altitude as the invaders moved inland, where picturesque little villages and towns perched on the lower slopes of the mountain mass. These were to be the scenes of many a small but bloody contest.

From Ogliastro to the mountain passes north of Salerno and so to Naples, there ran one good road, Highway No. 18. Control of this, and especially the stretch from the village of Battipaglia to Bellizzi, was essential for a successful defence, so that reserves could be moved laterally. Conversely, possession of the high ground immediately to the north of the road was essential for the invaders.

To complicate matters further, the battlefield was awkwardly compartmented by the River Sele, too deep to be crossed except by the bridges, and also by its tributary, the Calore, smaller, but none the less an obstacle, flowing from the east and joining the Sele six miles from its mouth. The pocket between the Sele and Calore could be either a pistol pointing at the beach-head, or a trap for a counter-attacker. Any aggressive manoeuvre involving cooperation between the right and left wings of the invading army depended on the possession of the bridges over the Sele. Such was the board of what was to prove a deadly war-game.

The number of pieces available, the "ratio of troops to space", was tiny. Nominally von Vietinghoff's Tenth Army could dispose of six or seven divisions according to what could be spared from the task of coping with a possibly hostile Italian Army, but they were divisions in name only. Two of them, the Hermann Goering Panzer and 15th Panzer Grenadier Divisions, were in the process of being rebuilt and re-trained after evacuation from Sicily. Generalleutnant Hermann Balck, commanding the 14th Panzer Corps (in the absence of Hans Valentine Hube who was on leave), had only one unit approaching full strength, the 16th Panzer Division, covering the beaches of the Bay of Salerno. The Hermann Goering Division (originally a Luftwaffe division, hence its title) could only bring to the battle a regiment of two motorised infantry battalions, twenty tanks in its tank battalion, a company of assault guns, a battalion of field howitzers (three batteries of four guns), a reconnaissance battalion and a battalion of engineers.

The lessons of the war in Russia had led to a reorganisation and re-equipment of the panzer divisions and the creation of motorised infantry divisions as distinct from the standard marching infantry divisions of First World War pattern with their horse-drawn artillery. Panzer divisions were strengthened by the adoption of the Mark IV PKW with its long 75-mm gun as main battle tank, and the addition of the heavy Mark V PKW "Panther". Mark Vs were used later in Italy, although none was available at Salerno, and by 1944 the super-heavy Mark VI "Tiger" tanks mounting the much-feared 88-mm guns organised in separate units were encountered by the Allies. In addition to tanks a large number of armoured self-propelled guns with their armament, usually a long 75-mm mounted in a fixed casemate instead of a revolving turret, were manufactured to make good the enormous tank losses in Russia. They were a supplement and not a substitute for tanks proper, but frequently reported as tanks by the Allied infantry. They were known as *Sturmgeschutzen*, "assault guns", or *Panzerschutzen*, "armoured guns". The infantry in armoured units were renamed *"Panzer Grenadieren"*, a "grenadier" being anciently an elite infantry-man. Panzer grenadier divisions comprised two regiments of three battalions in armoured carriers, and a battalion of tanks, together with artillery and engineers. In Italy they were regarded as more useful than full panzer divisions. At Salerno the German strength therefore was greatly overestimated.

Hermann Goering was supposed to be an elite division, but it had a large number of young and green recruits in its ranks and its training was not complete. The 15th Panzer Grenadier Division was at roughly the same strength, but as it had to leave detachments behind to watch other sectors of the coast in case the Allies chose to land at more than one point, it was able to bring only two infantry battalions, its reconnaissance unit and its engineer battalion to Salerno. The 3rd Panzer Division was also much under strength and, moreover, was composed of ethnic but non-national Germans and believed to be of doubtful morale. It was located near Rome.

(It is important to note that there was a divergence of opinion in Fifth and in Eighth Army about real enemy strengths, owing, in part, to their not knowing how many casualties the Germans had suffered in Sicily. Fifth Army Intelligence spoke of "weak divisions" but the operations staff assumed that they approached full strength. Montgomery wrote and spoke as though he believed German divisions south of Rome were still powerful. In preparing the "enemy narrative" for Martin Blumenson's *Salerno to Cassino* [in "The US Army in World War II Series"] Mavrogordato wrote that, by the end of August, the 76th Corps comprised 27,000–30,000 men in the 26th Panzer and 29th Panzer Grenadier Divisions and as many as 17,000 in the 1st Parachute Division. The 14th Corps had 45,000 in the area between Salerno and Gaeta, including 17,000 in the 16th Panzer. In this he follows the Fifth Army's operational staff and, incidentally, supports the traditional view of the battle as a near-run thing, contradicting not only German documents but also contemporary Allied Intelligence estimates made before the battle. Afterwards they changed their tune.)

The 76th Corps, General of Panzer Troops Traugott Herr, in Apulia and Calabria, was equally badly off. The 1st Parachute Division was well below strength and some of its units had been detached to strengthen the security force in the area of Rome. Of the two divisions facing the British 13th Corps in Calabria the 26th Panzer Division was reduced to two companies of tanks, only one of which reached the battle. The 29th Panzer Grenadier Division had only a few tanks, as it was felt that there was no scope for large armoured units in such rugged country. Both were stronger in infantry, although the 26th lacked one of its battalions and was very short of artillery. One of the great difficulties all the German panzer commanders faced was the shortage of petrol for training, and for moving their units for long distances in operations. On the mountain roads armoured vehicles, especially, used twice the standard staff allotments of fuel.

It is commonplace in warfare that the view from both sides is often equally alarming and equally dismal, but the predicament facing "Smiling Albert" Kesselring was enough to depress even that ever-optimistic commander. The real strength of the "mass of manoeuvre" he could hope to bring against the invader consisted of only one and a half divisions, without heavy tanks or medium artillery and seriously below strength in light field artillery; how soon they could be concentrated in the face of attack by the Allied air forces was uncertain. To complete the catalogue of his woes he had a creaking and makeshift command machine. His own headquarters, "OB(Sued)", was designed to deal with the strategic problems of the Axis and with all three services. An all-German headquarters, *Armee Oberkommando 10*, or Tenth Army, to control the operations of the 14th and 76th Corps had been created only on August 22, under General of Panzer Troops Heinrich von Vietinghoff *gennant* Scheel. He had no logistics branch, and was seriously deficient of signals operators, equipment and cypher staff. His divisions had to deal with Kesselring's HQ for all supplies. Because of these weaknesses he was never to have a clear or up-to-date picture of the situation at Salerno after the Allies had landed.

Kesselring had decided on his strategy before the Allied landings. A strong, almost impregnable natural defence line ran across southern Italy from the mouth of the Garigliano river on the Tyrrhenian coast through Cassino and along the Sangro to the Adriatic. There he intended to stand, and he set his engineers to work fortifying it. To give them enough time he would conduct a fighting withdrawal, avoiding the obvious trap of becoming too involved in the south when the Allies landed, as he accurately forecast, at Salerno. He had already reacted to Montgomery's crossing of the Messina strait by thinning out in Calabria and Apulia behind a belt of demolitions. His only problem was how to deal with Salerno. His two corps – the 14th Panzer (General-leutnant Hermann Balck) and 76th Panzer (General der Panzertruppen Traugott Herr) were disposed to cover all likely invasion points, but ready to move to Salerno. The most favourable outcome would be if von Vietinghoff could complete his concentration there quickly enough to mount a full-scale counter-attack against the invaders before they could be reinforced and drive them back into the sea. If this failed there was to be no question of investing the bridgehead and being taken in the rear by the advancing Eighth Army. In that case von Vietinghoff's orders were to break off the battle, pivot on his right, form a line of battle across Italy and continue the withdrawal to what was to become famous as the Gustav Line.

Whether the invading Fifth Army could be defeated on the beaches depended on the ability of Generalmajor Rudolf Sieckenius* to hold a thirty-mile-wide front at Salerno until his division was reinforced, and the speed at which Balck and Herr could come to his assistance. There was a good chance of this as it was the strongest German unit in Italy. The 16th Panzer Division had been badly mauled at Stalingrad and withdrawn first to France and then to what was hoped to be the comfortable backwater of southern Italy to receive replacements, re-equip and re-train. By the beginning of September its strength was 15,000 all ranks (not 17,000 as estimated by Allied Intelligence), the majority raw recruits. Collective training had been hampered by the shortage of motor-fuel, but the division's cadre of battle-hardened officers and NCOs had in full the remarkable German flair for turning recruits into aggressive fighters in a short time, as the Fifth Army soldiers were to find.

Compared with the other German divisions the 16th Panzer Division was well equipped, but it still lacked its heavy battalion of the new Mark V tanks and the medium artillery battalion of 150-mm howitzers. Otherwise it was very strong. Sieckenius had one hundred tanks, of which eighty-seven were the excellent Mark IVs with the long 75-mm gun, and fifty-five assault guns, supported by a regiment of field artillery with thirty-six 105-mm howitzers. Light anti-tank guns were distributed throughout the infantry and in addition two batteries (eight guns) of the dual-purpose 88-mm guns were attached. Ideally, the four panzer grenadier infantry battalions were carried in armoured half-tracks, but the division had yet to receive its full complement. However, apart from his tanks and assault guns Sieckenius had another 176 armoured fighting vehicles, including those in the armoured reconnaissance regiment, which the German Army often used as infantry. Sieckenius had therefore what was virtually a fully mobile division, with a high ratio of fire-power to men. A German division, unlike its British or American counterpart, did not normally fight in regiments separately arm by arm, but in mixed groups of all arms formed *ad hoc* appropriate to the mission, known as *Kampfgruppen*, and identified by the name of the commanding officer, who might be from any

---

* General officers' ranks in the German Army are not quite the equivalent of British or American. A *Generalmajor* was the equivalent of the US brigadier-general, a *Generalleutnant* of a British or US major-general, and rank was not fixed rigidly to the level of command.

arm.* Long practice and training that ensured that all officers had a full understanding of the tactics of arms other than their own enabled them to form and re-form these "battle-groups" with extraordinary speed and flexibility, composed not only of divisional troops accustomed to working with each other, but also in an emergency of any hastily collected groups of soldiers.[1]

The German "doctrine" (or policy) for protracted defence, developed on the Western Front in 1914–18 and later adapted to armoured, mobile warfare was a weak front, depth, and instant counter-attack to regain lost ground. Ideally, the front was covered by a first line of outposts with few men but strong in machine guns and anti-tank guns. Behind this, far enough back to be out of range of reconnaissance patrols and the surveillance of artillery observation posts was the second or main line of resistance. From it would be launched local counter-attacks to check penetration of the outpost line, while its own reserve units were poised to counter-attack in strength to restore dents in the main line. Behind this was a third or reserve line of units whose task it was to mount a coordinated counter-offensive in the event of a breakthrough of the main line. Like all formulae designed to cover a variety of military situations this was only valid if there were adequate forces available. Until he was reinforced Sieckenius was without any third-line reserve and had little to spare for immediate counter-attacks while at the same time covering his front. The one clear advantage he did have was that his division was fully mobile while the bulk of the invading force was marching infantry. Accordingly he modified the accepted doctrine by reducing the outpost line to eight strongpoints manned by a platoon of infantry backed by anti-tank guns and machine guns, covered by field artillery fire and protected by minefields along the long sweep of beach at the most likely landing places.[2] Behind them, two to five miles back, he placed four *Kampfgruppen*, well concealed and ready to deal with any incursion inland either by fire or counter-attack:

KG Dornemann, Major Dornemann, his 16th Reconnaissance Battalion less a detachment with von Doering and plus a company of assault guns from von Holtey, in the area Baronissi–Salerno.

KG Stempel, Colonel Stempel, his 64th Panzer Grenadier Regiment,

---

* The British had taken some time to absorb this idea, but did reinforce infantry brigades with armour or *vice versa* in "brigade groups" but kept their artillery under central control. The US Army formed similar "regimental combat teams" (RCTs) in the infantry divisions, and "combat commands" and "task forces" in its armoured divisions in exactly the same way as in the panzer divisions.

the 3rd Assault Gun Battalion from von Holtey, less the company with Dornemann, in the area Pontecagnano–Montecorvino airfield –Battipaglia.

KG von Doering, Colonel von Doering, his 79th Panzer Grenadier Regiment, two companies of tanks from von Holtey, detachment 16th Reconnaissance Battalion, in the area Albanella–Paestum.

KG von Holtey, Colonel von Holtey, his 2nd Panzer Regiment, less the detachments with the other battle-groups, in reserve in the area between Battipaglia and Eboli.[3]

All the battle-groups included a battery of field artillery and detachments from the divisional engineer battalion and 75-mm anti-tank guns. The panzer grenadier regiments had surrendered a platoon from each battalion to man the beach strongpoints. Any artillery not directly in their support or sited to engage landing craft remained under centralised control. This, it will be agreed, was not much to pit against a complete invading army. Although Sieckenius had knowledge of the ground, good observation and surprise to the extent that some at least of the invading units were not aware that they were likely to face tanks, he faced a grim struggle.

We must now turn to the details of the Allied invasion plan for AVALANCHE. Fifth Army had been reduced below the level which some planners believed essential because shortage of shipping limited the first lift for the assault to the equivalent of three and a half strongly reinforced divisions. One of Eisenhower's reasons for committing troops to BAYTOWN and SLAPSTICK (Calabria and Taranto) was because they made no large demands on shipping but got troops ashore somewhere on the mainland. The effect, however, was to spread the effort when it should have been concentrated. After the battles in Tunisia and Sicily some Allied divisions were either under strength or had to be cannibalised to provide equipment for those destined for Italy, or were preparing to depart for OVERLORD. The troops available to Eisenhower therefore, were fewer than might be thought, and certainly fewer than Kesselring feared. But if the offensive capability of the Allied air forces is reckoned on the credit side, the total strength of the force to be landed in the assault phase should have inspired confidence that it would survive until the 7th Armoured Division and the remaining American infantry began to disembark in the follow-up phase, beginning on D plus four (September 13).

Clark's force was indeed considerable. There were two special service brigades, one of US Rangers and one of British Commandos which, it was hoped, would seize by *coup de main* the exits from the north-western angle of the bridgehead leading to the plain of Naples;* twenty-seven battalions of infantry reinforced by some 150 tanks and numerous anti-tank guns, supported by 144 field guns of 88 mm (British 25-pounders), 24 105-mm-calibre self-propelled howitzers and 44 medium guns of 5.5 in. (140 mm) in the British 10th Corps, and 156 105-mm and 155-mm howitzers plus a number of the M10 self-propelled anti-tank guns in the US 6th Corps. All were to be put ashore by nightfall on D-day; enough to handle any possible enemy response, it was thought.

All the same, some misgivings were expressed that the tasks Clark had given his force exceeded its capacity. Indeed, the Fifth Army plan had serious flaws, the result of a combination of inexperience and the rush in which the planning process had been completed. It is conventional military wisdom when crossing a river or landing on a defended coast to spread the effort widely, so as to dissipate the enemy defensive effort, and then reinforce success and join up the landings into a single bridgehead. In AVALANCHE however there were not several landings but two completely separate ones ten miles apart, with the barrier of the Sele between them. The US 36th Infantry Division, commanded by Major-General Walker, strongly reinforced with tanks and tank-destroyers, was to secure the right of the bridgehead against any counter-thrust from the south up the coast and from the north-east. Its left flank rested on the Sele. It was to be joined on D-day plus one by part of Major-General Middleton's US 45th Division; two Regimental Combat Teams, one of three battalions and one with only two, a limitation imposed by lack of assault landing craft.

The role of Major-General Graham's British 56th Division was similarly defensive. It was to capture Montecorvino airfield and secure the ground commanding it to the north so that it could be used by the Allied air forces as soon as possible, obtain control of the vital stretch of road between Bellizzi and Battipaglia, push out north of it to deny the enemy observation over it and then, implausibly, to extend to its right across the gap and join hands with the 36th Division on the line of the Sele river. This gave it a total frontage of fifteen miles, with its units strung out in a thin cordon, and was to prove impossible.

The mission given to the 46th British Infantry Division, commanded by Major-General J. T. L. Hawkesworth, was equally ill-conceived. The US Rangers and British Commandos were to land on the

* US Ranger Force, three battalions Lieutenant-Colonel William O. Darby; Special Service Brigade, two Commandos (battalions), Brigadier R. Laycock.

Sorrento peninsula. Hawkesworth was to disembark five miles south of the port of Salerno, which he was to capture, and then advance north to link up with the special forces brigade and secure the long mountain passes through which ran highways Nos 18 and 88, the exits from the plain of Salerno leading to Naples. To do this he had to wheel left exposing his inland flank to the enemy, so he had to use one brigade to extend the 56th Division's defensive line to the north. The whole plan was an example of the Fifth Army staff's propensity to make plans on the map without any study of the ground or possible enemy reaction. The result was that of the nine brigades or RCTs available (counting the special force as one) only two were allotted to the task of breaking out of the bridgehead: both infantry, marching on foot.

Hindsight is always to be deplored but it would have been far better to land the 6th Corps complete north of the Sele, which would have given it a defensive obstacle on its open right flank. In fact dissentient voices had already been heard, notably that of General Patton. As a matter of routine he had been appointed the reserve commander of the Fifth Army, in case something unexpected befell General Clark. When he was briefed on the AVALANCHE plan by Major-General A. Gruenther, the Fifth Army Chief of Staff, he immediately put his finger on the wide gap between the two corps, observing that if the Germans knew their business they would soon find it, which in the event they did. Gruenther made no reply and nothing came of it. When the British commander of the 10th Corps, Lieutenant-General Richard McCreery, was briefed on the plan he too perceived that it was fundamentally unsound, but his appointment as commander was made too late for alterations to be considered. In any case the rigid US Army system of command did not normally allow for plans once made to be discussed by subordinates. The original mistake made in the Sicily planning had been repeated in the space of a few months, but there was no Montgomery to argue the toss.

So much for the plan of operations. How it was to turn out was decided by the actors. Of Clark we have already spoken. His touch in what was, after all, his maiden battle was to prove uncertain, but his admirable resolution only faltered once, and then only briefly. His principal lieutenants, like him, had considerable experience on the staff and in training troops, but little experience in the field. Major-General Ernest J. Dawley, commander US 6th Corps, had smelt powder only once, in the American punitive expedition to Mexico in 1916. In 1918 he had been staff officer to General George Marshall, and his subsequent work on the staff and as commander 40th Infantry Division in 1941 had led to his appointment to command the 6th Corps in March

1942. His headquarters remained unemployed, except for valuable work in training and planning. Dawley was one of those meritorious but unlucky officers who, had he made his debut in action in a normal operation under a sympathetic army commander, might have done well. As it was he was placed in a difficult command situation and lacked what the British call the necessary "bloody-mindedness" to assert himself. It was as much pressure from above as from the enemy in front that wore him down.

Poor Dawley flits briefly across the scene. Lieutenant-General Richard McCreery, 10th Corps, was to stay the course and become the last commander of the British Eighth Army. If Clark is the epitome of one type of West Point officer, highly professional, authoritarian and single-minded, McCreery represents perfectly a British type, the Anglo-Irish eccentric. He was, as British cavalry officers would aver, a typical cavalryman in that he did not conform to type. He was obsessed with horses and the best amateur steeple-chase jockey of his day, but he was also an utterly professional soldier. Like Clark he was tall, with great presence, and physically courageous, but there the resemblance ended. He was an intensely private man, detested publicity, relaxed only in the intimate circle of his personal staff in his field mess, drawing out their ideas and testing them against his; not always a very comfortable process, as he would pounce on any loose thinking like a tiger. He was greatly respected and liked by his divisional commanders, listening to their views and often taking their advice, but his seniors found him rebarbative, as he denounced unsound orders or ideas in the bluntest of terms. Those who knew him well found him simple and sweet-natured, although his staff warned newcomers that the wintry smile that occasionally illuminated his severe features was in fact a danger signal, presaging a violent and sometimes profane outburst of rage. He was an upright man of great integrity who was, privately, deeply religious. He read his Bible daily and often had his chaplain join him in prayers for guidance on the eve of battle. All in all, "Dick" McCreery could have served as the model for Macaulay's Cromwellian trooper, the Ironside "Obadiah-Bind-Their-Kings-in-Chains-and-Nobles-in-Links of Iron". Like many characterful or eccentric commanders the troops liked him, and nicknamed him "Hopalong Cassidy" because his wounds had left him with a limp.

Professionally McCreery stood out from the ruck of cavalry officers who had so foolishly obstructed the abolition of British horsed cavalry in the inter-war years. Perhaps as the result of observing the impotence of the mounted arm in France in 1916–18 (where he was severely wounded and decorated for bravery), he had made a close study of armoured warfare, and was enthusiastic in the conversion of his own regiment, the 12th Royal Lancers, which was to earn the reputation for efficiency second to none. In infantry tactics he was self-taught, but well taught, during his term as senior staff officer (GSO 1) to Harold Alexander in the 1st Infantry Division. He commanded an armoured force with credit if only briefly in 1940, earning a DSO and a useful lesson in the art of *Blitzkrieg* as seen from the side of the victim. In 1941 he raised and trained the British 8th Armoured Division, was posted to Headquarters, the British Middle East Forces as adviser on tanks and armoured tactics (Major-General, Armoured Fighting Vehicles), and in 1942 was packing his bags, having given General Sir Claude Auchinleck a piece of his mind on the subject of his misconceptions of armoured warfare. He was however saved by the change of command when Alexander, finding him in Cairo, immediately appointed him his chief of staff. McCreery succeeded to command of the 10th Corps when the incumbent General Brian Horrocks was severely wounded in an Axis air raid on Bizerta shortly before AVALANCHE was launched.

All the divisions, British and American had their origin in the volunteer formations of part-time soldiers which were maintained in peace as a reserve for the regular army.* After embodiment their ranks were filled by conscripts, and their higher command and staff stiffened by posting in regulars, but once they trained they proved excellent troops, because though "amateurs" or "weekend" soldiers their average standard of intelligence and alertness was superior to that of peacetime regular recruits. The weakness in the 36th Division was in the staff and the commanders of infantry regiments, as it was in the more experienced 45th Division. The US 36th Infantry Division, commanded by Major-General Fred L. Walker, was composed entirely of Texans, and retained much of its National Guard characteristics. There is no doubt that, like the two British divisions, the 36th had had insufficient training for so difficult and hazardous a task as an assault landing on defended coast line, doubly necessary in view of the fact that it had seen no active service, but it was to recover from the initial unpleasant shock of battle to acquit itself well. Five battalions of the US 45th Infantry Division grouped in two regimental combat teams under Major-General Troy H. Middleton formed the 6th Corps floating reserve. It was also a National Guard unit, recruited from Arizona, Colorado, New Mexico and Oklahoma. It had seen some fighting in Sicily, but its infantry regiments were poorly trained and lacked spirit, though its artillery was very good.

* The British Territorial Army, US National Guard.

The Board and the Pieces

The British units had had varied experience and were of uneven value. The 56th Infantry Division, Major-General D. A. H. Graham, consisted of the 201st Guards Brigade (Grenadier, Coldstream and Scots battalions) which had seen much fighting in the very different environment of the open desert in 1942, but the division as a whole had been engaged only briefly, at the end of the war in Tunisia. Its best brigade was probably the 169th, of three territorial battalions of the Queen's Regiment. The 46th Infantry Division had a newly appointed commander, Major-General J. T. L. Hawkesworth. Its Territorial Army battalions came from as far afield as Hampshire, which provided a complete brigade from the county regiment, the Midlands, Yorkshire and Durham. As a division it was dogged rather than dashing, good in defence, as it had proved in March 1943, when it had defeated one of the main thrusts of the Axis offensive in Tunisia, but it was very slow, at times tactically careless and unenterprising in the attack.

The artillery of the British and the United States armies was well equipped, well trained and with a strong *esprit de corps*. In many respects it was their most effective arm and both armies came to rely on it increasingly as the war dragged on. At Salerno the fire of the field artillery was powerfully reinforced by the guns of the combined fleet, either firing "direct" at shore targets visible from the ships, or controlled by artillery observers ashore in contact with the troops. The field artillery and the ships' guns were in the long run to break the German will to continue the fight at Salerno.

AVALANCHE AND HURRICANE

On September 7 the code-word *Fueurbrunst* – "the fire's hotting up" – was flashed to all the units of the 16th Panzer Division, alerting them that the expected Allied invasion fleet was at sea and shaping a course for Naples. At 4.30 p.m. on the 8th the code-word *Orkan* – "Hurricane" – reached the 16th Reconnaissance Battalion, the main unit of KG Dornemann. Sub-Lieutenant Rocholl, commander of a *Funkspaeh-truppe*, who was supervising the frying of some potatoes, a rare treat, ordered them to be put away carefully and reported to his headquarters for instructions and to draw a set of fresh cyphers. Then he ordered the men of his little command of two armoured cars and a radio vehicle to start up their engines and mount, and led it off to his pre-selected observation post on a hill just south-west of Salerno overlooking the sea-shore. He was to have an unrivalled view of the drama of D-day of AVALANCHE or, as he remembered it, the "Hurricane" bursting on the coast.

He set up his radio-transmitter, 80 kilowatts, as powerful as Radio Cologne, he noted with pride. He wondered whether to use its full power, for fear of interception, but decided to risk it, for he knew that his information might be vital and was determined that it should get through. In addition he had an immediate and difficult task for so junior an officer. The Italians, he was shocked to learn, had surrendered to the Allies, and he had to disarm the garrisons of two positions nearby. An infantry section proved tractable. The men threw down their arms and departed with alacrity. A battery of artillery nearby proved more difficult, but after Rocholl hinted that he might have to use force, its commander agreed to abandon his guns, and he and his men also disappeared into the twilight. "It was all over in forty-five minutes." The potatoes were brought out, replaced on the cooker, and pronounced delicious by all ranks.

Rocholl then made his arrangements for the morning, posted his sentries and settled down for what was to prove a noisy night. Shortly after dark he heard the sound of explosions in Salerno harbour as the demolitions went off. Later the sky above him resounded with the drone of aircraft flying out to sea, and the horizon was suddenly lit up from end to end as the invasion fleet opened on them with every gun. "After midnight" – it was actually 3 a.m. – "cruisers and *Nebelwerfers**" began to shell the beaches some five miles down the coast from Rocholl's position: the first blast of the hurricane. Dawn revealed a "magnificent spectacle". Rocholl might well have been awed. The modern battlefield is empty of all but a scurrying figure there or a tank here, incapable of being captured by brush or camera, but Salerno exceeded the wildest imagination of a film director planning a set: a vast array of ships, the anchored cruisers, like metal castles, banging away with their guns at the coast, the defending artillery replying, their shells throwing up pillars of water that seemed to stand for minutes, landing craft plying busily from ships to shore, destroyers dashing in to silence an obstinate defence post, tanks and infantry disembarking and moving inland.

Rocholl had sent his two cars down to watch the beaches below, and remained observing and reporting the more distant scene until about 6 p.m., when his preoccupation almost prevented him from noticing the cautious approach of two men in berets and khaki battledress stalking him with tommy guns. They were chased away, but Rocholl, whose duty it was to observe and not become involved in fighting, changed position. The reaction was probably mutual, as the intruders were from his battalion's opposite number, the Reconnaissance Regiment of the British 46th Division, whose commander in a most praiseworthy manner had wasted no time in pushing out to Salerno town. So far he had met no enemy. Dornemann, having posted his screen of observation posts, had had quite enough to do, establishing a road-block at Ponte Fratte, finding out what troops had landed at Vietri sul Mare and engaging them. He called in Rocholl's troop, and as it drove inland it suffered the irony of being pelted with flowers by the local populace, to cries of "Viva Inglesi".[1]

The naval side of operation AVALANCHE went perfectly, all the units of the Fifth Army being landed within a few minutes of the planned H-hour and, except for a muddle at the junction point between the 46th and 56th Divisions, all at the right place. This did not obviate the desperate air of confusion that attends any landing in the dark on a

* By *Nebelwerfers* Rocholl meant the multi-barrelled launchers mounted on landing craft operated by the Royal Navy.

coast held by the enemy: landing craft cannot guarantee to beach in parade-ground order, the various components of a combat team are momentarily lost or muddled up with other units, the ground does not seem to fit the map. One infantry company plodded on knee-deep in water, wondering why it seemed such a long way to dry ground, until it discovered that it was wading up the Tusciano river. Soldiers exposed for the first time in their lives to fire understandably feel that hostile shelling, fired blind, is aimed at them personally, and tend to take cover or dig in instead of moving inland.[2] Both British and American units were temporarily thrown into disorder or even paralysed by enemy defensive fire on the beaches in the first hours of the invasion.

By daylight appearances are, if anything, worse. There is the terrifying roar of fighter-bombers, the shocking sight of sinking vessels, burning vehicles and the newly dead. The first sight of battle for one young British private was a long row of corpses, neatly laid out: some of the Hampshire battalion that had landed in an earlier wave and been caught by a machine gun.[3] In both corps, it must be remembered, many of the assault troops were very young and unacclimatised either by experience or realistic training. It was remarkable how soon they recovered from their initial shock and how well they acquitted themselves later.

Nowhere was this process better seen than on the American beaches. The 36th Division had wisely landed on a broad front, two RCTs side by side, each with two battalions abreast in the assault wave. This ensured that a hitch or even the repulse of a whole regiment would not block the advance of the division. There were momentary crises on beaches near Paestum when von Doering's tanks fired at short range into the sandhills and there was a danger that troops would go to ground. In fact, 141 RCT on the right made little progress in the first twenty-four hours, but its role was the least important of all. Elsewhere, the Americans never lost the initiative, thanks to the bravery of individuals who got to their feet, sometimes to their own astonishment, threw grenades, fired sub-machine guns and gave the lead to others who followed them. It was scoring the first goal that settled the team, but a division consists of many teams and needs to experience many successes and at least one failure before they settle into winning combinations.

Learning by experience is an expensive process, but in the 36th Division it was fired by enthusiasm. Fifty minutes behind the rifle companies the regimental self-propelled 75-mm guns came ashore to support the rush inland. At a place where hostile fire had upset the orderly landing of the divisional artillery three guns from different units were put together in battery and fought as such. Those troops which were not pinned by fire were carried forward by their sense of purpose, but this elan carried a penalty. The main feature of D-day on the 6th Corps beaches was the degree of disorganisation just inland. There was a necessary pause lasting most of the next day while things were sorted out.

The profligate waste of modern war was never more evident than on the Salerno beaches. Half-sunken and stranded ships, vehicles burnt out or stuck in sand up to their axles together with a mass of stores littered the sands as far as the eye could see. Radio sets, batteries, weapon magazines and necessities like ground sheets and medical supplies, soon to be urgently required inland, lay jettisoned by the assault troops. Two days later and a quarter of a mile inland order had been created out of apparent chaos. All the scattered items had been sorted, marked and arranged in tidy dumps. Incoming vehicles that had "waded" ashore and been dried out, their water-proofing gear removed, were assembled in orderly parks until they were required, and a control post was established to run the operation.

In both armies a special task force based on a spare battalion providing the labour under a naval officer was landed on each RCT or brigade beach. In the 36th Division, by good fortune or good judgment, a senior officer was appointed to exercise command overall who proved to be a one-man task force. This was Brigadier-General John W. ("Iron Man") O'Daniel, who until the invasion had been commandant of the Fifth Army Amphibious Warfare School in North Africa. He owed his appointment to the army commander, who knew his mettle. O'Daniel and Clark had served in the same battalion on the Western Front in 1918, and when Clark was seriously wounded shortly after taking command O'Daniel succeeded him. His appointment as a sort of beach-master-in-chief was a happy one. He proved full of energy and gripped the administrative situation on the beaches as soon as he landed. He also found time to assess the operational situation ashore and to use his own communications to signal his reports direct to Clark who, on board USS *Ancon*, the command vessel, was completely in the dark about the situation ashore, as the official link between the 36th Division and the command ship had temporarily failed. Later O'Daniel was to take over command of a sector of the 36th Division's front.

(Someone of O'Daniel's rank and assertive character would not have been amiss on the 10th Corps beaches, where in places there occurred scenes of indiscipline amounting to farce. In spite of the protests of the officers of the Royal Navy, some army officers made no attempt to prevent their troops from discarding their extra loads of ammunition inside the landing craft even before they landed. One beach-master found the men of a famous regiment landing a piano for the sergeant's mess; another, a fat pig in a crate, intended for another regiment's officers' mess victory dinner in Naples!)

Despite the check to the 141st RCT, General Walker and his division had opened the ball with a marked success, greater than he knew. His push forward had cut off KG von Doering from its direct line of withdrawal while it was engaged in battering the 141st RCT. On the 10th Sieckenius, having reviewed the situation over the whole of his divisional front, wanted to bring him back into reserve in his centre, but to do so von Doering had to make a long march south, east and then north. He was therefore effectively *hors de combat* until the 11th.

The fortunes of the two divisions on the beaches chosen by the British 10th Corps were varied. The 46th Division, for no good reason, elected to land on a single brigade front; the 56th, on two with the 169th Infantry Brigade on the left and the 167th on the right. It so happened that two of the beach strongpoints manned by the 16th Panzer Division coincided with the choice of beaches; *Moltke*, as it was called, on the 46th Division's left-hand beach, and *Lilienthal* on the boundary line of the two divisions marked by the Asa stream. *Moltke* was blown up by one of the rocket-firing landing craft covering the British assault, but there was some doubt about the exact location of *Lilienthal*. The fire of the rocket craft detailed to bombard it fell, not north of the mouth of the Asa, but south of it. The craft carrying the right-hand battalion of the 128th Brigade had been ordered to land their passengers where the rockets fell, and as a result, they disembarked on the wrong side of the river, in 56th Division territory, and the craft carrying the 169th Brigade were shouldered off to their right and thus in turn landed in the wrong place.

This led to a good deal of shuffling about, in the course of which both the Hampshires of the 128th Brigade and the Queen's of the 169th took action against *Lilienthal* and eliminated it. Euphemistically, a faint radio message to KG Stempel reported that it had been "broken into".[4] The 128th eventually sorted itself out on its own side of the inter-divisional boundary, to run into trouble at the hands of KG Stempel. The commander of the 169th, a brigade made up of three territorial battalions all from the Queen's Regiment, discovered that he had landed too far south, and getting a grip of his force, ordered it to face left and march to its proper jump-off line for his task, the capture of Montecorvino airfield. Brigadier L. O. Lyne was an outstanding commander and trainer of troops, with the utmost confidence in his brigade, and he was determined to waste no time. As soon as it was light he sent off his 2nd/6th Queen's Battalion, with two troops of tanks of the Royal Scots Greys, a troop of the divisional anti-tank regiment equipped with the new and formidable 17-pounder guns and a troop of armoured self-propelled 105-mm howitzers of the 142nd Regiment Royal Artillery. Why the German aircraft were all still on the ground in spite of the warning implicit in the noise of battle, and why they were not engaging the anchored ships congesting the bay remains a mystery. In a mad quarter of an hour the Queen's battalion group destroyed no fewer than thirty-nine aircraft on the ground, and in addition a number of assault guns, tanks and half-tracks belonging to KG Stempel. In three successive shots one of the battalion 6-pounder anti-tank guns set a tank, an assault gun and an armoured half-track on fire. A rifleman, using a shoulder-controlled "PIAT" anti-tank projector, also hit a tank and an assault gun. The aircraft fell victim mostly to the tanks of the Scots Greys, but the field artillery dashingly pushed forward to fire "direct" at close range also scored a few hits. KG Stempel's riposte was prompt and savage, but it could not budge Lyne, and the Queen's and the panzer grenadiers remained facing each other across the runway for the next three days.

By the 11th (D-day plus two) Lyne's brigade was nine miles inland and holding firm. What worried him, and also his divisional commander, was a gap of 3,000 yards between two of his battalions, the inevitable result of the absurdly wide front the division had been allotted. He had to put his company of Royal Engineers into the line. (He recalled that they used their devilish skills to such purpose, surrounding their position with mines and booby-traps, that he counted it a greater risk to visit them than to visit forward localities under fire.) Lyne prevented the Germans from exploiting the gap by an ingenious and sustained piece of bluff. Such machine guns as he could spare sprayed the front occasionally with fire, his handful of tanks when not otherwise urgently needed paraded up and down, and from time to time his field artillery put down a smoke screen. Everything was done to suggest that he was about to make a thrust into the unguarded sector, and his bluff was convincing enough to unnerve his opponent; so much so that he more than once brought down his defensive artillery fire to repel an imaginary attack.[5]

By the morning of the 10th the 56th Division had built up a strong shoulder on its left. On its right the 167th Brigade had pushed out a battalion to S. Lucia, and the 9th Royal Fusiliers, by great efforts and the expedient of commandeering farm carts, hand barrows and bicycles to augment its meagre "assault" scales of vehicles, occupied the little town of Battipaglia commanding the key stretch of road linking the

16th Panzer Division's northern and southern wings. The 8th Fusiliers was for the moment unengaged, and the 201st Guards Brigade was ashore in good order preparing to send a battalion up to Highway No. 18 west of Battipaglia. All this was to change very rapidly within hours, as Sieckenius began to put the second phase of his defensive plan into action.

It developed right across the front of the 10th Corps in a series of small actions, never more than a battalion, as invader and defender probed the vineyards and olive groves and suddenly clashed with mutual surprise. In such fighting success goes to the side which reacts more quickly and aggressively. In one encounter the 10th Corps nearly lost its commander. General McCreery, visiting the forward troops in his Jeep escorted by two armoured cars, had halted to read his map and discover where he was. Fortunately he had dismounted, as suddenly some well-aimed shots from a concealed anti-tank battery had destroyed his Jeep and his escort. McCreery took to his heels, lame as he was, out-running his aide-de-camp. While on his way back, still running, McCreery ordered his ADC to shoot at a German fighter-bomber overhead, but the young officer confessed that during their flight the magazine had fallen off his tommy gun. "A – fine – pair – of – bloody – soldiers – we – are!" panted the general, continuing to run, but he slowed up and entered his command post as cool as if nothing untoward had happened. There he found General Sir Harold Alexander, to whom he immediately gave a lucid picture of the situation on his front.[6]

By the morning of the 10th Sieckenius might well have concluded that his worst case had occurred. The invaders had succeeded in getting ashore in strength complete with artillery and tanks and were still landing, Allied elements had been reported at Vietri and were approaching Salerno, his front was split, with KG Stempel in two parts, one on either side of the stretch of Highway No. 18 now in enemy hands, KG von Doering was out of the battle, and as yet there was no sign of the reinforcing divisions of the 14th and 76th Corps. In fact, his battle-groups had struck one severe blow at the 46th Division, wrecking the whole 10th Corps' plan, and two more at the 56th Division, throwing it back from the vital stretch of road by nightfall on the 10th.

The 46th Division's plan was for the 1st/4th Hampshire Battalion to land on the left on "Uncle Green" beach, and the 2nd Hampshire on the adjacent "Uncle Red" on the right, with the 5th Hampshire following the 2nd. Once ashore the 128th Brigade would push inland to take up positions to protect the move of the 138th Brigade, the "ball-carrier", whose role was to push on as fast as possible to Salerno and the mountain passes. The 139th Brigade was to follow in reserve. The landings were to be covered by an intense bombardment from destroyers, landing craft carrying 4.7-inch guns and the very effective multi-barrelled rocket launchers.

The landing by the 1st/4th Hampshires on Uncle Green went well. One company disregarding the defensive fire on the beaches marched inland in the dark with great determination and occupied the village of Pontecagnano, the battalion objective. The remainder found strong-point *Moltke* in its path and silenced it after a short fight and then followed the leading company to Pontecagnano. The 2nd Hampshires soon discovered that they were on the wrong beach where they came under fire from *Lilienthal*. Unexpectedly it lay just south of the shallow Asa river, but it was correctly engaged by the Royal Naval rocket craft. The battalion sent one company to silence it and then crossed the Asa into its own divisional sector where they dug in around a group of buildings called the *Maggazeno* (store-house) and waited for daylight.

The 5th Hampshires, which landed behind the 2nd Battalion, fell into confusion. The battalion radio net was not working properly (the portable sets of those days were crude and fragile) and the battalion commander was able to rally only two rifle companies and his support company and move to his proper beach, where his men became almost inextricably mixed with those of the 2nd Battalion. There followed a fatal pause, with a great deal of shouting by officers and NCOs trying to collect their companies and platoons, their voices barely audible above the noise of bursting shells and the racing of engines by drivers striving to extricate their vehicles from the boggy exits from the beach. Landing craft had been hit and were on fire, there was smoke everywhere, and slightly dazed groups of men were standing about or digging in where they were. There was great delay and no understanding that it was more important to move inland than wait until every man had answered the roll-call. Whatever the cause the 5th Hampshire did not move off the beach until 8 a.m.

Meanwhile the commander of the 1st Battalion, 64th Panzer Grenadiers (part of KG Stempel) was worried about the situation at *Lilienthal*. Except for the brief radio message at 4 a.m. saying that the invaders had "broken in" he had heard nothing. At about 6 a.m. he sent Oberleutnant Gustav Meierkord, a company of grenadiers and three tanks to its assistance. About three miles from the Maggazeno, and expecting to meet the enemy well inland, Meierkord ordered his grenadiers to dismount from their vehicles and deploy in battle formation. He had advanced cautiously for about two hours when, still some way short of the Maggazeno, he heard the sound of a large body

65

of men. The 5th Hampshires, at last, were on the move. Three tracks led in that direction, the middle one walled on both sides. He put a tank on each, ordered his men to be ready to attack and set off to meet them.

The encounter was a massacre. The Hampshires do not appear to have been told that they were likely to meet tanks, their 6-pounder anti-tank guns had become separated in the confusion of landing, the "PIAT" hand-held anti-tank weapons were not in working order (which hardly mattered as their operators had not had any training in their use) and no tank support had been arranged nor had artillery observers been attached, although both had been available since about 7 a.m. The battalion advanced without any precautions such as points, scouts or vanguard, in three columns of route up the tracks making, as Meierkord noted, a great deal of noise. Unwarned, it collided with the alert and expectant panzer grenadiers, no more than 100 strong, and was routed. The tank on the middle track drove into the column of marching men machine-gunning as it went and crushing any who were slow to leap over the walls. About 100 of the Hampshires were killed and wounded and 300 more surrendered in the ensuing panic. (A contributory factor may have been that this was the battalion's second unfortunate encounter with tanks. It had been overrun only five months before when placed in an isolated position at Sidi Nasir in Tunisia.) Only thirty escaped to run back to the Maggazeno and alert the defenders. Meierkord's charge had led him to within fifty yards of that place, but by then he was accompanied by only a single platoon, so he prudently withdrew for a mile and a half to collect his stragglers and take up a defensive position. He had done more than enough. He had ruined the 10th Corps plan.[7]

The fact that the landings were still proceeding smoothly merely added to the congestion on the divisional beaches. All movement stopped for a short but fatal pause. The local commanders, convinced that a large force of tanks lay in wait just inland, decided it would be better to stand firm at the Maggazeno until the division was strong enough to deal with it. At length, at 3 p.m., a battalion from Uncle Red beach with three tanks was sent to sweep the ground inland of Uncle Green. It met a small enemy force a mile inland, drove it away after a tank battle and reported the area clear by nightfall. It was not until the following day, D-day plus one, that the units on Uncle Green began to advance and leave the way free for the 138th Brigade to move on Salerno and the passes, but the golden opportunity had vanished. General Hawkesworth considered that he had to secure his base before attempting any daring manoeuvre, and as a result he failed to seize the passes when they were unguarded and his for the taking. "Ask me for anything except time," Napoleon once said, and Hawkesworth had asked for twenty-four hours. Before long Balck's panzer grenadiers would be rushing down to bottle up the invaders, but their work had already been done for them by three tanks and a hundred men of KG Stempel's battle-group.

The night of the 9th/10th saw a frenzy of activity in the 16th Panzer Division and there was little sleep for its staff. Arrows on the situation map in the operations van showed the 169th Brigade penetration past *Lilienthal* at 10 a.m. and the direction of Meierkord's counter-attack. More serious, at 2 p.m. the 2nd/64th Panzer Grenadiers, part of KG Stempel, was hemmed in by enemy in Pontecagnano on one side and Bellizzi on the other. An order went out to establish a base at Battipaglia for a divisional counter-attack but the town was found to be in enemy hands.

The actions of Sieckenius' superiors had been unhelpful, to say the least. The supply of petroleum was vital, of course, but OB(Sued) had miscalculated the demand and forgotten to inform Tenth Army of the location of the Italian depots. Down in Calabria a German naval officer had panicked, and emptied a shipload of petrol into the sea, fearing that it might fall into enemy hands. This effectively immobilised the 29th Panzer Grenadier Division, whose march north to Salerno was delayed for forty-eight hours. When von Vietinghoff tried to take charge of the battle he caused further confusion. He planned to transfer the 16th Panzer Division and the area for which it was responsible from Balck's 14th Panzer Corps to Herr's 76th Panzer Corps in mid-battle as soon as Herr's troops arrived. Consequently Sieckenius was bombarded with advice and orders from Balck, his present superior, Herr, his future commander and from von Vietinghoff himself, whose chief of staff rang up to say, obviously and somewhat unhelpfully: "Der Kerl muss raus!" (literally, "the guy must [get] out", more colloquially, "kick the bugger out".)

Balck, whose corps included the Hermann Goering, 15th and 3rd Panzer Grenadier Divisions marching to the sound of the guns from the north to help the 16th Panzers, soon found his way to HQ 16th Panzer Division. With him was his chief of staff, Colonel von Bonin who, giving the orders, although his general was present, as was the practice with the German General Staff, also insisted that the invader be thrown back into the sea within forty-eight hours, before his build-up had made him too strong to shift. Soon afterwards Herr, obeying his orders to take over as soon as his troops arrived on the scene, also turned up to see what was happening and started to breathe down Sieckenius' neck. In response to the urging of Balck, Sieckenius had already collected Colonel von Holtey, commanding his reserve battle-group, and set off rashly in the dark to inspect the ground, apparently disregarding KG Stempel's report that the enemy had closed up to Highway No. 18 and that his 1st Battalion/64th Panzer Grenadiers were now north of it.

Meanwhile all three brigades of the 56th Division had been actively engaged. On the left the 2nd Queen's of 169th Brigade had had a sharp but successful fight, losing some 172 casualties it could ill afford, but it was firm on its objective. The 201st Guards Brigade had closed up to Highway No. 18 and was preparing to attack the following morning. On the right the 8th Royal Fusiliers in 167th Brigade had, after some fighting, secured the flank of the division at S. Lucia, while the 9th Fusiliers had dug into a position north and east of the town of Battipaglia. Sieckenius and his party, motoring unwittingly into Battipaglia, were fired on by the Fusiliers' anti-tank guns. His tactical HQ vehicle and the radio section were destroyed and von Holtey badly wounded. (He was relieved, but we will continue to refer to KG von Holtey to avoid confusion, though the name of the group changed when his adjutant took command.) When Sieckenius got back to his main HQ the 14th Corps was still talking about a combined attack, although the 15th Panzer Grenadier Division had not yet arrived. What did arrive on the morning of the 10th was the 1st Battalion of the 3rd Parachute Regiment from Apulia, and the reconnaissance battalion of the 29th Panzer Grenadier Division. Sieckenius immediately ordered them to combine with KG von Holtey and clear the invaders away from Battipaglia. Shortly afterwards General Herr arrived to tell him that he would pass from Balck's command to his the next morning and meanwhile he was to be prepared to attack south to cover Ponte Sele, where Highway No. 19, the route by which Herr's units in Calabria would arrive to join the battle in the bridgehead, crossed the river.

By mid-afternoon, therefore, the situation resembled the artificial confusion of a staff college map exercise designed to pose a succession of difficult problems rather than the normal logic and simplicity of a real German operation. Sieckenius had been ordered to attack westward by HQ 14th Corps and southward by HQ 76th Corps. Part of the divisional engineer battalion reported that it was still fighting in the area of S. Lucia, "but," as the note in the war diary reads, "as they have no officer, who knows what the situation really is?" There was no information about the moves of the Americans, but the staff view was that their apparent inactivity could not last long, and if they thrust along the north bank of the Sele towards Eboli where there was nothing to stop them, the 16th Panzer Division might then be cut in two.

Sieckenius was right when he saw that the key to the situation was Battipaglia, where von Holtey's tanks knocked out all the Fusiliers' anti-tank guns and then drove their rifle companies back into the town where they were trapped. The tanks then drove up and down the streets blasting away with their guns, forcing the Fusiliers from house to house until their ammunition ran out. Major Delforce, who was awarded the DSO, succeeded in extricating 200 men and took up a defensive position south of the road, but 300, many of them wounded, including the commanding officer, were captured. Their defeat was partly due to the over-extension of the front and partly to the lack of support. As the Americans were soon to discover, it was unwise to post battalions out in the blue in the face of an aggressive armoured division, but that was no consolation for a serious reverse. Battipaglia was a key position and to Clark it looked as if the British had failed him. At 14th Corps, Balck, much elated by the success, ordered a grander operation to clear the British from the area bounded by Salerno town, S. Mango, Battipaglia and the River Tusciano to the sea.

Next morning, the 11th, Sieckenius received his staff's reports at the pre-breakfast briefing. The good news was that the reconnaissance battalion of the 15th Panzer Division had reinforced Dornemann in the area north of Salerno, and that KG von Doering had not only completed its circuitous march, but had picked up a battalion of the 15th Panzer Grenadier Regiment of the 29th Division marching up from Calabria on the way. (This was the 3rd Battalion. Later in the day the 2nd Battalion of the 71st Panzer Grenadier Regiment arrived.) He felt that he now had the resources to deal with the two remaining and imminent dangers. He sent the battalion of panzer grenadiers to hold Altavilla and the high ground at Point 424 commanding the village, to ensure against any American move towards the Ponte Sele from that direction. Von Doering was to move into the void north of the Sele, wheel northwards, drive in the British at S. Lucia and make for the bridge over the Tusciano at Fosso; his attack to be coordinated by one in the opposite direction with the same objective by the 2nd Battalion/ 64th Panzer Grenadier Regiment.

The main attack failed. General Graham had pulled his now contracted right wing together and coordinated his divisional artillery, and von Doering was stopped cold short of S. Lucia by its intense defensive fire; the 2nd/64th receiving the same treatment. The battalion ordered to Altavilla had occupied it without opposition and then been withdrawn by its parent division of which the headquarters was, by then, at Postiglione. This infuriated Sieckenius who, no longer able to endure the contradictory flow of orders, demanded to be told who was in charge of operations. The reply that it was Herr was followed by a warning order from the 76th Corps. A concerted full-scale attack would be mounted against the bridgehead as soon as the main body of the 29th Panzer Grenadier Division and the 9th Panzer Grenadier Regiment from the 26th Panzer Division arrived from the south, on September 13 or 14. It was now the afternoon of the 11th and assistance from the south was badly needed before the 13th. Heavy concentrations of artillery fire were falling on Battipaglia and it seemed that another attack was imminent, but there were no reserves to meet it. Montecorvino airfield had been finally lost to the British, helped by the support of heavy naval guns whose never-ending bombardment was beginning to wear down the morale of the hard-pressed German defence. At this stage, ironically, the commanders on both sides were apprehensive of the latent danger of the void between the two British corps and the two wings of the 16th Panzer Division. While Clark was only too conscious of the fact that he had two inner open flanks Sieckenius saw a clear run for the invaders up to Eboli and a lack of troops to plug the gap. He was alarmed by reports that the Americans were showing signs of activity in the area.[8]

After its unrealised success on D-day when it had shouldered KG von Doering off the battlefield, the 6th Corps on the 10th occupied the high ground in front of the 36th Division as far as Albanella village without opposition, while the administrative muddle behind was sorted out. Early in the morning part of the floating reserve, the 179th RCT of 45th Division, landed, followed in the afternoon by the two-battalion 157th RCT, without orders, on the initiative of the naval commander concerned who had become impatient with standing on and off while his craft presented moving targets in a shooting gallery for German guns and fighter-bombers. General Middleton and his headquarters landed, collected both RCTs under his command, attached tanks and M10 tank-destroyers to each, deployed his field artillery and prepared to function as a division. General Dawley now had two divisions and could function as a corps commander, had he been allowed to, and not had an anxious and eager army commander breathing down his neck.

When General Clark came ashore from USS *Ancon* to visit his commanders on the 10th, McCreery without any beating about the bush told him what was obvious: he was involved in heavy fighting all along his front, especially at Battipaglia, he had had to refuse his right flank at S. Lucia as it was wide open, and he had no troops to spare to send eight miles away to the east to capture Ponte Sele, one of the objectives allotted to the 10th Corps in the operational plan. Clark agreed. He saw that McCreery was being distracted from his primary mission, to open the roads to Naples and Avellino, so he decided to move the 6th Corps boundary northwards in 10th Corps' favour, and to send a battalion group from the 36th Division by sea to Maori to reinforce the US Ranger Force, at that moment holding on to the pass over M. di Chiunzi leading down to Nocera on the Naples road. He then repaired to HQ 6th Corps where he ordered Dawley to assume the offensive and made his plan for him. (The relationship between Dawley and Clark ended in open disagreement, with Dawley calling his army commander a "boy scout" and being finally dismissed. It seemed to have been fraught from the first hour of the invasion with lack of confidence and understanding, when Clark had impulsively ordered him ashore on D-day to command a single division and without his staff.) The 6th Corps attack would be made on three thrust lines. On the left the 157th RCT, which had been landed just south of the mouth of the Sele, was to cross over by the bridge near Albanella railway station, demolished by the Germans but repaired by the US Engineers. This would automatically take care of the northward shift of the inter-corps boundary. It was then to advance along the secondary road leading from the junction with Highway No. 18 to Eboli as its objective, an ambitious manoeuvre involving a march of eight miles. The 179th was to advance with two battalions between the Sele and the Calore, and its third battalion south of the Calore, to secure the Ponte Sele, while a battalion from the 142nd Infantry of 36th Division occupied Altavilla.

In the meantime, General Graham, though he had lost Battipaglia, was not prepared to relinquish his hold on the road; he was about to send the Scots Guards battalion of the 201st Guards Brigade to capture a strongly built and fenced group of warehouses known as the "British" tobacco factory commanding the road east of Bellizzi. (Two almost similar groups of buildings, stoutly built, fenced and arranged in a circle were the scene of hard fighting and were both confusingly known to the Allies as "the" tobacco factory. This one, unsuccessfully attacked by the Scots Guards, was on Highway No. 18. The other, the "American" tobacco factory was just north of Persano on the other side of the River Sele and was about to be the scene of a clash between the 157th RCT and elements of KG von Doering.) Thus an interesting situation was about to develop as both sides launched simultaneous offensives. Parts of KGs Stempel, von Holtey and von Doering were about to fail in their attempt to drive back the 56th Division, KG von Doering more or less crossing the thrust line of the 157th from right to left, while the Panzer Grenadier battalion that had been withdrawn

71

from Altavilla just before the 142nd Infantry occupied it, was ordered to retake it.

Partly due to the compartmented nature of the battlefield, and partly due to lack of contact and knowledge of where the enemy was, the Americans did not mount well-prepared attacks but simply marched off into the blue. Preoccupied with organising themselves after the confusion of unplanned landings, they neither sent out reconnaissance patrols nor showed any inquisitiveness about the strength or whereabouts of the enemy. They were also very slow. The 157th RCT did not move off until the afternoon of the 11th. It crossed the river and turned off Highway No. 18 on to a secondary road that led northwards towards Eboli. Some two miles on the vanguard stopped to examine a group of buildings used as a storage depot and drying sheds where the tobacco crop was cured, the "American" tobacco factory. The ground was open, and the company of Sherman tanks attached to the 157th RCT approached it cautiously, only to lose seven tanks to a sudden burst of fire. It was held by some carefully concealed tanks and anti-tank guns of KG von Doering, posted to act as flank protection for the attack against the 56th Division. Feeling out to his left, the commander of the 157th came into contact with other German positions, while still further over on that side he could hear heavy firing. In fact what he heard was the terrific defensive fire which the British artillery was laying down in front of the attack by von Holtey and von Doering on Graham's right flank. The Germans had been halted there, and had the commander of the 157th Infantry shown the slightest curiosity or, better, in the old phrase "marched to the sound of the guns" he might have caused the German attack to finish not merely in defeat but disaster. Instead, he decided to halt his advance and remained where he was doing nothing until the following day.

The 179th RCT proved equally unenterprising. While one battalion advanced as a flank guard south of the Calore, the others entered the Sele–Calore pocket and were fired on from Persano, by then held by a detachment from KG von Doering and some recently arrived parachutists. Leaving the supporting tanks and tank-destroyers behind to cover the village, they moved on tentatively towards Ponte Sele, their objective. One battalion halted after advancing 1,000 yards, the other found the objective defended, occupied it briefly after a brisk fight, but then withdrew. In fact, the bridge was held by a weak guard scratched up from some engineers and reconnaissance troops, KG Kleine Limburg, which could have been easily driven off by a determined attack, but the commander of the 179th RCT decided not to attempt it as night was falling. He fell back on his other battalion and also did nothing until the following day. His third battalion had been directed, somewhat ambitiously, on the village of Serre on Highway No. 19, eight miles from its jump-off line. It ran into stiff resistance at a bridge over the Calore from a battalion of the 71st Panzer Grenadier Regiment and, feeling exposed, fell back to the La Cosa stream early on the 12th and dug in behind it.

The 1st Battalion of 142nd RCT of 36th Division found Altavilla unoccupied and put it into a state of defence, but its position would have been tenable only if the rest of the corps operation had been successful and Eboli and Ponte Sele captured. During the night of the 11th, the battalion of the 15th Panzer Grenadier Regiment ordered to re-occupy Altavilla by Sieckenius, using the aggressive tactics that made the German infantryman so dangerous an opponent, infiltrated between the companies of the 1st/142nd Infantry, waited for daylight and defeated them one by one. In fact, the plan made by General Clark was bad; the effort dispersed in three different directions, the objectives chosen without any consideration of the enemy or, indeed, any knowledge of his locations or strength or consideration of how they were to be secured when captured. Sieckenius' entire resources – little more than the two powerful RCTs sent against him – were fully occupied against the other corps, and a well-coordinated attack by the Americans might have won a considerable success. As it turned out, the outcome of the operations of the 11th did not win any laurels for either side.

General Clark, in the meantime, had been shanghaied. As it had not yet been possible for him to establish even a small command post ashore, he had returned to USS *Ancon*, whose identity as a command ship, bristling with radio antennae, was obvious to the enemy. On the 11th the radio intercepts of Luftwaffe traffic revealed instructions for a mass attack on her after dark. Admiral Hewitt accordingly ordered her to put to sea and was later rewarded by intercepts of the Luftwaffe pilots' transmissions, enquiring of each other if they could see *Ancon*. This was satisfactory from Admiral Hewitt's point of view, but it kept Clark away from the battle until late on the 12th. That morning the 179th nerved itself to attack Persano, to find its defenders had vanished, and the 157th wrested possession of the tobacco factory from von Doering's 79th Panzer Grenadiers, successfully repelled a counter-attack and captured the bridge over the Sele leading to Persano. So ended the 6th Corps' first attempt at an offensive.

General Clark returned from his unwanted cruise in USS *Ancon* in a pardonable mood of rage and frustration. He had been cut off from the battlefield at the very moment when he should have been in hourly touch with events, and returned on the 12th to learn that his offensive had failed, although, by securing the "American" tobacco factory, Persano village and the bridge over the Sele between those two places, the 157th RCT had given him, had he but realised it, possession of a key area in the 6th Corps sector. Instead, his chagrin at the failure of his plan led him to upbraid Dawley. In reality the principal responsibility for the failure was his, for he had dissipated the strength of his powerful RCTs instead of concentrating them on one vital objective. The blame had to be shared with the two divisional commanders and, indeed, lack of training in Africa and Sicily was evident. The regimental commanders and battalion commanders clearly had not been drilled to the point when the process of locating the enemy, closely reconnoitring his position, making a coordinated plan for the use of infantry, tanks and artillery, briefing all ranks and then striking hard was second nature. Instead they marched and counter-marched to no effect and withdrew into a shell of defence, like snails, at the first sign of opposition. Dawley was not a man capable of inspiring or driving on his divisional commanders. In this connection one might speculate on how the battle would have gone had Eisenhower not turned down General Patton's plea to be given the 6th Corps after Seventh Army had been side-tracked following the end of the Battle of Sicily. Dawley had been on the wrong foot from the start of the battle. He was irritated by Clark's sudden and unexplained orders, and chagrined by Clark blaming him for not anticipating them. On his side, Clark's concept of the art of command did not embrace the idea that as well as driving his subordinates he should support and encourage them. The unhappy rift between the two men dated from the 12th.

On that day Clark analysed the situation as follows (to quote Martin Blumenson):

> To General Clark, who came ashore again on the 12th September and who found the 45th Division "badly bruised", the German strength near Persano seemed to be a spear pointing towards the center of the bridge-head. If the Germans pushed to the sea, they could turn the inner flank of either or both corps . . . Dawley, Clark believed, had either misinterpreted the failure of the 45th Division's thrusts towards Ponte Sele and Eboli or was oblivious to its meaning. To Clark, it was clearly evident that the enemy intended to launch a major attack in that area, and that adequate measures had to be taken to meet it.[9]

It is not at all clear how much of this estimate was the result of sitting down with his staff and how much instinctive and "off the top of his head", but he was both right and wrong. He had at last seen the potential danger of the gap between the two corps, and also the mistake of allotting the 10th Corps so absurdly long a front, and agreed to shift the boundary between the corps northward. His expectation that the enemy would exploit it was to prove correct, but at that moment they were not in any strength near Persano, nor were they to be reinforced for another twenty-four hours. As for Clark's impression of the state of the 45th Division, it is reasonable to conclude that it was based more on the timidity of its senior officers than on the physical condition of its soldiers or its casualties. Except morally, it cannot have been hurt, let alone "badly bruised", by what had been no more than a little skirmishing. The rank and file may have been confused, even depressed, by these inconclusive manoeuvres, and the division may have been disorganised, no more.

If General Clark is to be criticised for his decision on the 12th it can be said that he "took counsel of his fears", he did not follow the logic of his analysis to its conclusion and he failed to discharge his proper responsibilities as the commander of an army. If he was so certain that a counter-offensive was about to be unleashed against his left–centre, it would have been prudent to call off the plan to recapture Altavilla, and strengthen his left by shortening and drawing in his right. As it was, the 6th Corps was spread out in a thin cordon of battalions some twenty miles long. The situation cried out for closer coordination between the two corps, so lacking on the 11th, but Clark, who had good reason to be dissatisfied with the progress of the 10th Corps, once he had assisted McCreery by shortening its front, left him to fight a separate battle, while he himself, virtually abdicating his position as army commander, personally directed the 6th Corps.

The position in 10th Corps was not dire, but stagnant. McCreery's hope of gaining a foothold in the exits of the mountain passes had been foiled, the airfield although clear was still dominated by the enemy and unusable, and he had lost his grip on the key area of Highway No. 18. The Scots Guards entered the "British" tobacco factory, only to be thrown out again, so it and Battipaglia were once more in enemy hands. On the 11th the 167th Brigade of 56th Division on the extreme right of the 10th Corps had repulsed the attack by KG von Doering, but in the evening part of KG Stempel after a brief but violent artillery bombardment fell on the remaining units of the 201st Guards Brigade still holding a stretch of Highway No. 18 west of Battipaglia, putting first a company of 3rd Coldstream and then a company of the 6th Grenadiers to flight and sweeping with undiminished momentum into the 6th Grenadiers' position. For a time it seemed as if it was about to be overrun, and the battalion headquarters staff burned their marked maps and code books. However, the remainder of the Grenadiers and Coldstream stood fast and then counter-attacked, to discover that their assailant was a single battalion, which upon being challenged disappeared as suddenly as it had arrived. The brigade commander nonetheless thought it prudent to withdraw half a mile or more to a position more suitable for defence. This short withdrawal had a significant if misleading influence on the plans the Germans were to make in the next few days. The 10th Corps had by the 12th suffered not severe but significant casualties, including the greater part of the 1,500 prisoners captured in the bridgehead, and it was everywhere on the defensive. It might be thought that this is where the presence of an army commander was urgently needed, but Clark was now obsessed by his premonition of an impending attack on the left of the 6th Corps, and determined to run that battle personally. In any case, rightly or wrongly, he considered that he could only advise and request a British commander, and not drive him as he would a subordinate in his own army.

He took steps to establish his command post ashore, not wishing to be shanghaied again, and made fresh dispositions to meet the threat of attack. General Walker was ordered to relieve the battalion from the 45th Division on the La Cosa stream and replace the two battalions in Persano with one of his own so as to free the 179th RCT to join the 157th north of the river, thus concentrating General Middleton's two formations. To Middleton's left an engineer battalion acting as infantry was posted to hold Bivio Cioffi, so as to meet a second request from McCreery to move the inter-corps boundary north in his favour. General Walker now had a front of fourteen miles to cover with seven battalions, having already lost one to reinforce the US Rangers in the Sorrento peninsula, and one other destroyed at Altavilla.

"On the other side of the hill" von Vietinghoff and his corps commanders were making their plans to strike west and south from their embattled centre, when an extraordinary piece of intelligence or, rather, a rumour reached them that the invader was preparing to re-embark. The scene was now set for the stirring events of the next two days, the so-called "crisis" of the Battle of Salerno.

VON VIETINGHOFF SHOOTS HIS BOLT

On September 12 the time had come for the Tenth Army to prepare for a final effort to drive the invaders into the sea, or retreat. There could be no half measures. Allied strength was growing every day, the German counter-attacks on the northern sector withered under tremendous cannonades from land and sea and the holders of the ring, the tank crews and panzer grenadiers of the 16th Panzer Division, were tired out. Protracted defence could only end in the immolation of the defenders under a sustained artillery bombardment cruel even by the standards of the Russian front. By this time, Sieckenius, whose soldiers had so far faced four times their number with great gallantry, was a disillusioned realist. General Herr, 76th Corps, was beginning to pick up the threads of the battle, and was devoid of false optimism, but his strong sense of what was practicable in a military sense was overruled by the insistent demands for success from von Vietinghoff at HQ Tenth Army, remote from the realities of the battle. Herr had hoped to launch his part of the *Gegenangriff*, the full-scale, coordinated counter-attack of complete divisions on the 13th, but as the remainder of the 29th Panzer Grenadiers could not arrive until after dark on the 12th, and the infantry of the 26th Panzer on the 13th and subsequent days, he decided to postpone it until daylight on the 14th. (In fact, only four out of six battalions of the 29th Panzer Grenadier Division fought at Salerno. The Reconnaissance Battalion of 26th Panzer Division took part in the attack towards Persano on the 13th, one battalion of its 9th was at Eboli that day and the other on the evening of the 14th. One company of tanks reported in from the north to reinforce the 16th Panzer Division on the 13th. The 67th Panzer Grenadier Regiment of 26th Panzer Division, the rearguard facing Eighth Army, did not fight at Salerno at all.)

The experience of the *Blitzkrieg* and the rapidity with which German commanders reacted to a sudden threat, to say nothing of the elan displayed by the troops as they threw themselves into the attack, like Meierkord on D-day, have led to the false impression that the German Army dashed into action like so many berserkers. Nothing of the kind. Its operations were carefully reconnoitred, the plan carefully made, units briefed, all in an orderly sequence. The German secret was simple: a combination of system and speed. Not a minute was wasted.

The direction of the counter-offensive of the 76th Corps front was left, by German custom, to Sieckenius, for he was already gripping the battle and knew every inch of the ground. His outline plan was to use the left wing of his division (basically KG von Doering, reinforced by the 2nd Battalion, 9th Panzer Grenadier Regiment and the Reconnaissance Battalion of 26th Panzer Division) to capture the bridge over the Sele near the tobacco factory, cross the river and establish itself at Persano. When that operation was complete the 71st Panzer Grenadier Regiment together with other elements of the 29th Panzer Grenadier Division and any elements of the 26th Panzer and the 1st Parachute Division that had arrived would strike due west towards the coast and if this prospered turn right, or north-west up the coast into the rear of the British 10th Corps. At the same time the 64th Panzer Grenadier Regiment (KG Stempel) was to attack along Highway No. 18, clear the remaining enemy lurking in the western edge of Battipaglia and open the road as far as Bellizzi. Simultaneously the 14th Corps would attack south from Ponte Fratte and San Mango, so that the British would be squeezed on both flanks.

At this point in this extraordinary battle the immensely experienced German General Staff fell victim to an inexplicable attack of self-deception. Beginning with von Vietinghoff they came to believe that the invaders were about to abandon the bridgehead and re-embark. How this came about has never been satisfactorily explained. It was certainly not based on a systematic evaluation of battlefield information. We can only conclude that it was partly due to the dynamics by which rumours spread, especially if welcome to men who, however hard-headed, had been for sleepless days and nights subjected to the stress of command in battle, and partly due to over-hasty deductions from fragments of information coming from the various battle-groups. The trigger appears to have been a propaganda broadcast from Berlin announcing that the defeated Allies were preparing to throw in the towel and take to their ships. Intended presumably to depress the morale of the Allies, this was seized upon in Tenth Army (never properly in the picture of the Salerno battle) as a fact. More or less by coincidence this flight of fancy was lent credence by reports from the lower echelons. At 10.45 a.m. on the 13th HQ 76th Corps reported that in the southern

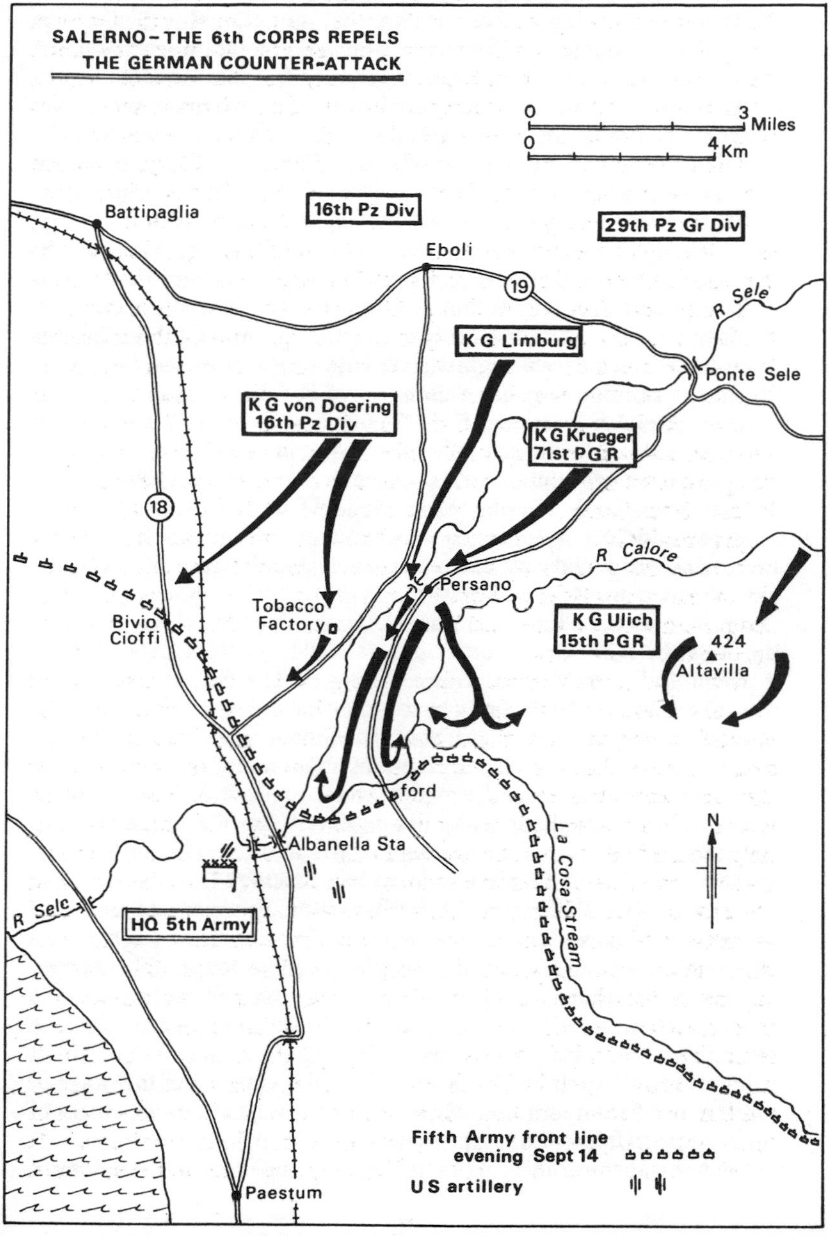
SALERNO – THE 6th CORPS REPELS
THE GERMAN COUNTER-ATTACK
0
3 Miles
0
4 Km
Battipaglia
16th Pz Div
29th Pz Gr Div
Eboli
19
R Sele
K G Limburg
Ponte Sele
K G von Doering
16th Pz Div
K G Krueger
71st PG R
18
R Calore
Persano
Tobacco
Factory
Bivio
Cioffi
K G Ulich
15th PGR
424
Altavilla
ford
Albanella Sta
La Cosa Stream
N
R Sele
HQ 5th Army
Fifth Army front line
evening Sept 14
US artillery
Paestum

sector (that is, the US 6th Corps) the enemy had withdrawn from a number of points. This, certainly, was the "situation report" after the débâcle of the 11th/12th, when the attacks so thoughtlessly launched on Clark's orders had been repulsed. It added that the invaders' "will to resist pressure" may not be counted on, adding "we must stick to the enemy", and referring to "commonly heard" radio reports that the British were evacuating Salerno town. At noon Dornemann, whose battle-group was still in that area, reported that "five cruisers" had moved inshore and were bombarding targets in his sector, adding, without giving any reason, "we are holding on as we get the impression that the enemy is going to re-embark".[1] The 64th Panzer Grenadiers reported that the enemy facing it, south of Highway No. 18 between Battipaglia and the "British" tobacco factory (from the 6th Grenadier Guards) had withdrawn slightly. HQ 76th Corps repeated the wholly erroneous information that Salerno town had been recaptured, and ordered the 64th Regiment (KG Stempel) to stand fast, as the 14th Corps was about to attack south-eastwards and drive the defenders of the northern sector into its arms. Coincidentally, and deceptively, the ever-active massed batteries of the invaders fell silent.

Of these indications only two were factually correct: that in two areas the enemy had withdrawn a short distance, and the guns had temporarily stopped firing. They may simply have been replenishing their ammunition stocks. During the attacks on the right and right–centre of the 56th Division one artillery regiment fired forty-three defensive fire missions and the total expenditure of 25-pounder shell was 10,000 per day. There were two reasons why the idea that the invaders were about to embark persisted, or at least was not refuted. The first was that the news would be a spur to the tired troops about to be launched into the counter-attack, the second was that were it true it was an excellent reason to attack without delay before the enemy's arrangements to cover so difficult an operation could be put in train. This in turn was made more urgent and was amplified by a message from no less than Oberkommando Wehrmacht (OKW), that the Fuehrer demanded an immediate success for political reasons. So, any faint-heartedness about the success of the attack or scepticism about the rumour seemed disloyal, even impious. One thing that is certain about this curious episode is that German Intelligence had no hint then or later that the opposing commander, Clark, had in fact gone so far as to instruct Admiral Hewitt to draw up plans for re-embarkation, but this was not until twenty-four hours later when he had been shaken by the events of the 13th/14th in the 6th Corps sector.

Such was the prevailing mood in the command and staff echelons of

Tenth Army when at 10.45 a.m. on the 13th Sieckenius assembled his officers to work out the details of the plan of attack already described. He himself appeared to be somewhat sceptical. He stated that ten ships had arrived in the anchorage and were probably landing another enemy division. He considered that the first move should be to collect the scattered fragments of the 16th Panzer Division and its reinforcing units and establish a firm defensive line as the base from which to launch the attack the following day: standard tactics. What he lacked was up-to-date information about his opponent. Accordingly he ordered a *Funkspaehtruppe* – an armoured car patrol with radio – to move out from Battipaglia immediately and probe down Highway No. 18 as close to the coast as it could get and report exactly what was taking place there.[2] Colonel von Doering was summoned to report on the situation on the lower reaches of the Sele river. Meanwhile the conference resumed, with von Doering in attendance, and all those practical soldiers agreed that despite the rumours of evacuation of the bridgehead, a full-scale attack would play into the hands of the enemy: "It saps morale, uses up men and ammunition and gives the enemy the chance to land further north." (A prospect that was to remain an obsession of the German commanders.) At 11.30 a.m. Lieutenant Mueller, the reconnaissance troop commander, not an officer who allowed the grass to grow under his feet, reported that he was four kilometres south of Battipaglia and had met no enemy. He added that it appeared as if there were none between his present position and the bridge over the Sele at Albanella railway station. Sieckenius immediately ordered all units to reconnoitre to their front and the main bodies to halt and conserve petrol.

The conference was then joined by Colonel Fritz Ruenkel, chief of staff to Herr in HQ 76th Corps. His intervention was fateful and to understand why it is necessary to remind the general reader of the unique position of the German General Staff in the command system of the German Army. In the US and the British armies it would be unthinkable for a commander to send a junior staff officer with anything more than a personal message or instruction to one of his subordinates if its tenor required more tact or more emphasis than could be conveyed in a written signal. (At that very moment General Alexander's chief of staff was visiting HQ Eighth Army to impress on Montgomery the urgent need to speed up his advance and take the pressure off Clark at Salerno.) He could be forceful, he could be candid, he could listen to objections, he could make offers of extra assistance, but his authority derived from his commander-in-chief and his duties were limited to conveying his commander's views. By contrast, the German Ruenkel had full, delegated powers, inherent in his membership of the General Staff. He knew what was required – that there should be no faltering in the 16th Panzer Division. He could demand to have the full situation explained and then give out such orders, if necessary overriding those of the commander on the spot, as would achieve his chief's, von Vietinghoff's, aim. This was to gain at least a success that could be politically exploited, to administer a psychological shock to the invading army and enable the Tenth Army to withdraw in good order. He himself was whole-heartedly in favour of the aim and personally stage-managed the whole operation. He declared that the "American army should be cut in half by exploiting the existing gap and striking towards Albanella station".[3]

Ruenkel's determination to force Sieckenius into immediate action was fortified by another report from the energetic and inquisitive Mueller. He was, he signalled, now four miles from Battipaglia having arrived at the road fork on Highway No. 18 at Bivio Cioffi and could see no enemy in the area. Ruenkel countermanded the decision to wait for the rest of the 26th Panzer and 29th Panzer Grenadier Divisions and launch an attack in strength on the 14th, and ordered Sieckenius to thrust forward with the troops already available and as soon as possible.[4] What resulted certainly gave the 6th Corps an unpleasant shock and so alarmed the Fifth Army commander that he never swerved from the idea that his whole position was endangered. This gave birth to the legend of the crisis at Salerno averted by the courage and personal intervention of General Mark Wayne Clark. There is no question about his courage, or that his intervention in the battle was effective, for he was a man who always rose to an occasion. It could be said of him as it was of Massena, that "his faculties redoubled amid the roar of cannon", but crisis there was not. Ruenkel's attack was made from weakness. It was more of a raid in force, exploratory and opportunist in character, launched without proper reconnaissance or time to combine units from several divisions, and it failed.

The attack of the afternoon of the 13th included a half-baked thrust made with the 2nd/64th Panzer Grenadier Regiment and about one and a half battalions of parachute infantry to clear an enemy mistakenly regarded as "weakened" in the Fosso–Bellizzi–Point 210 area. This ran into the 167th Brigade on its left and the 201st Guards Brigade on the right, and met with disaster. The 56th Division had been able to shorten its line further, thanks to General Clark, and had pulled back to better defensive positions and was able to fight the sort of battle the British were good at, a sturdy defence supported by their incomparable artillery. Between the defensive barrage and the controlled small-arms fire of the infantry this limb of the attack withered away. (The Grenadiers recorded that they loosed off no fewer than 55,000 rounds of rifle and machine-gun ammunition on that day.) McCreery's front was still over-extended and his tired battalions were subjected to some determined attacks on either flank, but they proved staunch and their line barely dented. The 76th Corps made better progress on its left against the Americans.

The revised plan was for the weak battle-group KG Kleine Limburg accompanied by those of KG von Doering's tired and depleted units still capable of a serious effort after five days of continuous fighting, to advance southwards along the north, or right bank of the Sele, cross it by the bridge near the tobacco factory and attack the American battalion believed to be in the Sele–Calore pocket. It would be followed by a parachute battalion to take over Persano village after it was captured, and the 2nd Battalion, 9th Panzer Grenadier Regiment, the first contingent to arrive from the 26th Panzer Division's 9th Panzer Grenadier Regiment, to cover the right flank of the advance. KG Kruger, made up of the 71st Panzer Grenadier Regiment and the Reconnaissance battalion of the 26th Panzer Division, part of 29th Panzer Grenadier Division in position at the Ponte Sele, was to drive down the left bank of the Sele on to Persano, thus squeezing the defenders front and rear, after which Ruenkel intended a somewhat ambitious "internal envelopment" by KG von Doering and KG Kleine Limburg moving once more south along the right bank of the Sele, recrossing it by the bridge at Albanella and taking La Maida, M. Chirico and rolling up the American defence line behind the La Cosa stream from west to east. All this appears to a British or an American officer a terrible muddle, better suited to a war-game board than a real battlefield, but the German Army was immensely skilled at rapid manoeuvre by groups formed *ad hoc* and quick to move to the aid of each other or seize on any mistake by the defence. The weakness of this final throw was the weariness of the units, the lack of tanks, the 16th Panzer having lost over half its strength already, and a total absence of ground support from the Luftwaffe; two vital ingredients of *Blitzkrieg*-type tactics.

General Clark's fear of an attack on the left–centre of the 6th Corps was, therefore, not unjustified, based though it may have been on intuition. What is difficult to understand, even with all the advantages of hindsight, is why he made no attempt to correct the weaknesses of its current disposition, and even aggravated them by ordering that another attempt to secure Altavilla be made on the 13th. As a result of his generous, but entirely necessary extension of the 6th Corps front in favour of the 10th the American sector had been not only over-extended but its units fragmented and mixed together. The front of the 45th Division was extended again to the left of the engineer battalion of the 36th Division at Bivio Cioffi by a battalion of the 141st RCT, from the same division. The attack to recapture Altavilla had to be made by separate battalions from the 142nd and the 143rd RCTs. The orderly arrangement of RCTs under the infantry regimental commanders had in fact disintegrated, and General Walker had to resort to employing three brigadier-generals to coordinate the sectors of his front: his own deputy commander, the redoubtable O'Daniel and one borrowed from the staff of Fifth Army. Owing, perhaps, to the fact that Clark, by virtually usurping the command of the corps from Dawley, was blurring the spheres of responsibility, no one had coordinated the defensive arrangements at the junction of the 36th and 45th Divisions, or noticed that the right flank of the battalion at Persano was open, just where Ruenkel's blow was about to fall.

It will be recalled that after the fiasco of the offensive on the 11th initiated by Clark, the 2nd Battalion 143rd Infantry had been sent to Persano to relieve the 179th RCT which side-stepped to its left and joined its fellow, the 157th, concentrating General Middleton's command north of the Sele. Slipshod staff work by the two divisional staffs, unnoticed and uncorrected by 6th Corps HQ, resulted in the 2nd/143rd being dangerously isolated. There was a yawning gap between its left-hand company and the forward battalion of the 157th RCT covering the tobacco factory, and the bridge over the Sele had been left unguarded by either division. Its right was completely exposed, because after the repulse on the 12th General Walker's line of forward localities followed the south bank of the Torrente la Cosa. To make matters worse, the battalion commander himself adopted a faulty disposition. The terrain between the two rivers was ideal for tanks; hard, dry, whale-backed in section, falling away to the two river valleys. (It was an Italian Army exercise ground and firing range.) Persano village was overlooked by rising ground a mile to the north-east, so that the battalion commander, correctly, took up a position there with three of his companies, but for no apparent reason pushed out the fourth 2,000 yards up the range road. The divisional artillery had not been told the exact positions of the battalion, nor do there appear to have been attached observers, which inhibited its defensive fire. When KG Kruger came rolling down the range the battalion commander gave his troops the ridiculous order to lie low instead of engaging with every weapon available. All these errors combined to give Ruenkel a temporary success and General Clark an unpleasant shock.

The German battle-group commanders had not been able to complete their preparations until the afternoon of the 13th. KG von Doering, or what remained of it, then found the defences south of Bivio Cioffi too strong for it, so it sheered off and joined KG Kleine Limburg in its attack on the 1st Battalion 157th RCT at the tobacco factory. Hit front and flank this battalion's position was rapidly overrun; it broke and the survivors fled to the rear, rallying on the 3rd/157th. Part of KG Klein Limburg motored then with great verve across the unguarded bridge at Persano and attacked the luckless 2nd/143rd Infantry in the rear at the same time as KG Kruger, basically a battalion of the 71st Panzer Grenadier Regiment and a handful of tanks, drove through the isolated company "G" and fell frontally on its main position. Like two or three of the British battalions in the 10th Corps, the Americans were overawed by their first experience of a German attack delivered *à outrance*, every weapon blazing, tanks shooting up the defences while the grenadiers, shouting, leapt from their armoured carriers to follow their officers and under-officers in a charge made at the run, firing their sub-machine guns and flinging grenades as soon as they came to close quarters. Their morale broke, they offered little or no resistance and 500 out of a total strength of 834 surrendered, the rest fleeing to report that they had been attacked by a full panzer division. Meanwhile, the 71st Panzer Grenadiers scored another success over at Altavilla. The 3rd/142nd Infantry, following its orders, was preparing to capture Point 142, and was actually assembling on its start line when it was beaten to the punch and driven back in disorder, leaving one company surrounded. The 1st/142nd Infantry, sent up to support the attack, never arrived, having been caught by intense artillery fire when jammed in a defile, and cut to pieces.

The time was now 5.30 p.m. with about an hour of daylight remaining. The view from HQ Fifth Army was bleak. General Walker had already suffered the loss of three battalions reduced to cadre, good only for puttying up small gaps in his defensive front. In the 45th Division the 1st/157th Infantry was more or less in the same case. The sound of battle was only too audible at HQ Fifth Army, located three miles south-west of the Sele–Calore confluence behind the 45th Division's gun line. There seemed little to protect it from being overrun, and it went to panic stations; understandably, for the political consequences of its loss and the capture of the army commander would have been even more dire than the military. A scratch force made up of headquarters staff and employed men was hastily assembled for its local defence. General Clark put it at ten minutes' notice to move if necessary, and ordered a fast naval craft to stand by to take him to 10th Corps, where the situation was more stable and where he could retain a toehold in Italy, if the worst came to the worst. More questionably he gave what he surely intended to be a secret and confidential instruction to Admiral Hewitt to make contingency plans to re-embark the 6th or possibly both corps. This was wholly impractical, but Hewitt, following the strict discipline of the US armed forces, complied with his orders, and his staff went through the motions of the exercise, but it was abandoned as abruptly as it had been started.* Hewitt himself, although unshaken, was not in the happiest of positions, as the air-naval conflict had reached the highest pitch during the battle. Two of his most valuable units, USS *Philadelphia* and HMS *Uganda* had been hard hit and were *hors de combat*. Fortunately for the invaders, the danger of the Germans cutting through to the sea was averted, partly by a misfortune to the right wing of KG Kruger, now thrusting deep into the Sele–Calore pocket, and the instant reaction of the well-trained and well-commanded artillery of the 45th Division.

A military road ran south from Persano through low ground to a point a quarter of a mile east of the confluence. It may have seemed reasonable to assume that no one built a road leading to nowhere, and that at its end there would be a bridge, but there was not. It was purely a road serving a training area. The only ford, near S. Cesareo on the Calore, was overlooked from the high south bank and difficult to find. There was no ford over the Sele. Having rounded up his prisoners the German commander, following the German principle of exploiting success, remounted his grenadiers and belted south at full speed, only to find that he had stuck his head in a bag. He was hardly to blame, for being part of the 29th Panzer Grenadier Division fresh up from Calabria he did not have the same detailed knowledge of the ground as the 16th Panzer Division. (The Italian maps were inaccurate, not having been amended since 1939, and gave both sides trouble.) He paid dearly for his mistake. In the 26th Panzer Reconnaissance Battalion every senior officer became a casualty. KG Kruger was immediately engaged by the observers of two field artillery battalions deployed south of the pocket, their fire reinforced by an armoured field battery sent up to join in the bombardment, together with some tanks and tank-destroyers. The field artillery fired 3,940 rounds in the next four hours and the panzer grenadiers, greeted by this rude welcome

* Apart from the tactical dangers of the withdrawal proving a rout and exposing the craft ashore to artillery fire, landing craft cannot easily beach and then load and haul off, as the additional weight increases their draught. Once aground they can only refloat by discharging their cargoes.

and failing to find an exit from the pocket after much milling around, withdrew to Persano.

Ruenkel was now faced with the question of what his next move should be. On the one hand the German soldier had once more given an impressive demonstration of the superiority of his fighting power, the leading troops were less than seven miles from the beaches and all Ruenkel's training as a German officer pushed him to the conclusion that now was the moment for the final heave that might dislodge an enemy already shaken by the day's fighting. On the other, he could count the odds, which were cruelly against him. Privately he might have agreed with the views of the corps commanders. Balck, who was making little progress against the British 46th Division, and his own chief, Herr, were at that very moment trying to convince the euphoric von Vietinghoff that the enemy was not in full retreat, and that though it might be possible to score a few more local tactical successes there was no hope of a strategic victory. The Allies were growing stronger, and to persist in the counter-offensive would only destroy the Tenth Army. However, Ruenkel had been sent by Herr with the mission of driving his divisional commanders hard, and he considered that it was his duty to persist. He scolded Generalmajor Fries, 29th Division, for the failure of his battle-group in the pocket to fight its way out (such was the authority of a mere colonel of the General Staff) and at midnight gave out orders for resuming the offensive on the morning of the 14th. In the 29th Division the group at Altavilla was to stand fast, and the one in the pocket was to cross the Sele by the bridge south-east of Persano, make for Albanella village and then hook south-westward for Paestum and the coast. KG Kleine Limburg was to cross the Sele using the bridge near Albanella railway station and try to roll up the American line south of the La Cosa stream, as before. Neither attack made any headway. Dawley and Walker, urged by Clark, shortened the line and plugged the holes in it. Clark played a general's part, touring the front, encouraging the troops and letting them see that he was cheerful and confident, and the troops, with characteristic American resilience, recovered their form, and grasping the fact that the way to deal with the panzers and panzer grenadiers was to stand firm and unleash their own formidable fire-power, shot them to pieces. By 3 p.m. they had repulsed every attack and their positions everywhere were intact.

Late in the afternoon Ruenkel conceded failure and ordered all the German units to halt wherever they stood and dig in. General Sieckenius toured the front and returned at 9 p.m. with a gloomy report. Of the one hundred odd tanks in his division fifty-four had been runners on the morning of the 13th. Now he was down to twenty-two. (His 2nd

Panzer Regiment was the major source of tanks for the various battle-groups formed in the whole of the 76th Corps.) As far as his own division was concerned, the men were worn out by their exertions and depressed by the enemy's relentless artillery fire. They could do no more. Ruenkel was forced to agree that the 16th Panzer Division was a spent force, but even then remained determined to make one more effort. He reorganised the 76th Corps front, giving the sector north of the Sele to the 26th Panzer Division (lacking its panzer regiment but reinforced by two battalions of parachute infantry from Apulia), and confirmed that the 29th Panzer Grenadier Division would command all operations south of the Sele. There was to be a pause all day while this reorganisation was completed and preparations were made for the resumed offensive on the 16th. The 29th Division was to continue on the same thrust line and objective as on the 14th. The 26th was to attack through Battipaglia and open the vital stretch of road to Bellizzi, still dominated by the British 56th Division. This, it could be hoped, would squeeze the British between the 76th Corps and Balck's Hermann Goering and the 15th Panzer Grenadier Division hammering away at the 46th Division in the north, and the 10th Corps position might crumble.

This was indeed a forlorn hope. On the 15th the Allied aircraft were for the second day in succession out in force over the bridgehead, and their bombing combined with the sustained battering by the guns on land and sea held up the regrouping until after dark. Battipaglia lay in ruins, its streets choked with rubble and impassable to vehicles. The German artillery observers had not been able to find the units to which they had been assigned in the dark, with the result that the fire-plans in support of the attacks were not properly registered by daylight and proved ineffective. On the 16th the 29th Division made no impression on the now tightly knit and confident defenders along the La Cosa stream and once more the attacks withered under the American fire. The assault units of the 26th Panzer Division were once more decimated by the British defensive barrage as they assembled on their start line, and had made only a few hundred yards' progress before they were thrown back to it by a powerful counter-attack by the tanks of the Royal Scots Greys who, displaying the true cavalry spirit, charged the attacking line from a flank and drove through it from end to end. They counted 200 German dead, and so the Scots Greys avenged the Hampshires. The remnants of the 26th Panzer Division were barely able to hold the position where it had assembled for its desperate stroke.

After this third failure Kesselring assessed his position. He was not dissatisfied. For eight whole days he had with his scanty resources forced the Anglo-American army on to the defensive despite its air-power and the support of the heavy guns of the Allied fleet; indeed he was sure he had its measure. He could repeat this manoeuvre indefinitely, and had proved his point that he could fight a defensive war in central Italy. On the 17th orders went out to Tenth Army to put his plan for withdrawal into effect, and as a first move Herr disengaged, unharassed by any pursuit, and began to pull away to the north.

So ended the great crisis – it could be called the great "flap" – of the Battle of Salerno. To be sure, there had been much hard fighting, setbacks and many anxious moments, but such is the very nature of war. When, however, all is said and done, the event that had so alarmed General Clark and led him momentarily to consider re-embarkation, and whose shock-waves reverberated as far as Alexander's HQ 15th Army Group in Sicily and Eisenhower's HQ in Algiers, was the attack on the 13th by no more than four battle-groups, each no more than a reinforced battalion; the whole little more than a British brigade or an American "regimental combat team".

By the 15th Clark had been reinforced by the first echelon of the British 7th Armoured Division, the third regiment of the 45th Infantry Division, and the dramatic if belated arrival of the 505th Parachute Infantry, dropped on the beach near Paestum, while an independent parachute battalion was dropped operationally at the same time behind the enemy lines near Avellino. By then the "crisis" of the battle was over.[5]

The plan for the withdrawal of the Tenth Army was for the 76th Corps to wheel back, pivoting on its right, while the 14th hung on like grim death to the gateways leading northwards out of the bridgehead. Both corps would then gradually withdraw behind successive belts of demolitions until they reached the Gustav Line.

It took McCreery's tired infantry ten more days to force their way through the mountain passes against the dogged resistance of Balck's equally tired panzer grenadiers, learning the difficult and to them unfamiliar art of mountain warfare as they went. At last on September 27 their vanguards emerged from the defiles leading to the plain of Naples. Those who had the opportunity to enjoy the pleasant prospect of orchard and vineyard with Vesuvius smoking peacefully in the distance, like the artillery observers perched on the last foothills covering the advance, then became aware of a strange phenomenon. There were no aircraft in the sky and the Allied artillery was for once silent, but as far as the eye could see the landscape was suddenly covered by a pattern of erupting plumes of brown-black smoke, followed by the muted rumble of distant explosions. Its significance became clear as the tanks and infantry advanced into the plain. The German engineers had fired their demolitions. Every bridge and culvert over stream, canal and irrigation ditch had gone up in the air; every crossroad and raised embankment had been cratered.

The pace of the victorious advance on Naples was to be determined by the speed at which the engineers could sweep for land-mines and bridge the gaps. That was to be the pattern of war in Italy until the bitter end.

6

SALERNO – THE POSTSCRIPT

Salerno had been truly an extraordinary battle. The low ratio of troops to space meant there were wide-open gaps not only between the corps and divisions but between battalions, and the result was "mobile warfare at the halt", as the British Field-Marshal Wavell once said of the middle period of the Battle of the Somme. The 16th Panzer Division gained the upper hand at first because it was a fully motorised and armoured formation and Sieckenius handled it as if it were fighting an action on the steppes of Russia painted on a small canvas. General Clark persisted in regarding it as a defensive battle, an affair of defensive lines. In staff colleges and academic institutions where strategy and tactics are studied Salerno can doubtless still provide many "lessons" in the art or science of warfare. There is no need to labour these. It is sufficient to say that its course underlined the morale effect of violent, offensive action, of the propensity of intelligent and able men on both sides of the firing line to become the victims of their hopes or fears in defiance of the evidence, and above all, of the ancient principle that a force given a difficult and dangerous mission against a formidable opponent must have the strength and resources to match.

Salerno was a decisive battle by virtue of being indecisive. Had Clark been provided with two full corps, strong in armour, able to burst out of the ring of hills and in the process smash the game but skeletal German divisions, Kesselring and his strategic arguments would have been discredited and the campaign in Italy have taken a completely different course. As it was, Kesselring concluded that one German soldier was worth three Anglo-Americans – they were soft, feared close combat and soon gave up – and given the topography of Italy he could prolong its defence indefinitely. The casualty figures support his view, bearing in mind that the Tenth Army was on the offensive, the costlier phase of war, as much as or more than the Fifth Army. The Germans inflicted 8,659 casualties and suffered 3,472; captured 3,000 prisoners and lost

630, most of them in the defence of the beaches on D-day. The superior performance of the Germans was at the root of the Allied commanders' conclusions too, although they were less objective.

In private the British and American commanders despised each other for lack of drive, attacking in insufficient strength and lack of appetite for combat. In this they resembled two whores upbraiding each other for lack of chastity. There were excellent, good, indifferent and downright bad units, both American and British, the real difference between them and the Germans being that many were green; hastily raised, from essentially unmilitary and on the whole reluctant populations. Their armies were what the Germans in a favourite but pejorative phrase used to call "militias". They had to be handled appropriately and that had been beyond the ability of some commanders and their staffs at Salerno. By contrast the German war-machine had been created for the pursuit by force of the national aim from a population long educated and indoctrinated in the martial virtues, and strictly trained and disciplined. German soldiers at Salerno had been easy to handle and their commanders had made mistakes without paying any penalty, taken risks and gained rewards. In fact, they had conducted the battle in a classical manner whereas their opponents had made elementary mistakes.

Salerno therefore was an important event in the Italian campaign, not only because it enabled the German soldiers to take the measure of their opponents, but unalterably fixed the attitude of the Allied commanders to each other. The private reports of the British liaison officers attached to HQ Fifth Army were very disparaging of the Americans, who had made a bad plan, failed to exercise control of the battle, and had been sufficiently panicked to plan for re-embarkation. Clark's vanity was badly scarred and he was convinced that the British as a matter of policy were determined to steal the publicity for victories gained by American valour. He took a strong dislike to McCreery which lasted until the end of the war; a "feather duster", as he called him in his private diary.

The British were alarmed and humiliated by an event unparalleled in their military history. On September 16 a group of replacements ("reinforcements" in British terminology) 700 strong disembarked on the beach and refused to join their designated units. Mutiny, a premeditated, collective refusal to obey orders, is the most heinous of crimes in all armies, and though unthinkable, fear of it is never very far from the surface of consciousness in the military mind. The better the commander the more clearly he understands the delicacy of the balance between good leadership, man-management and discipline on the one side and the fearful stresses and strains imposed by modern warfare on the other. Its causes are known and the early symptoms detectable. Mutiny can be averted, but once the bonds of discipline are broken it is not easy to restore them. The ancient remedy was to surround mutineers with loyal troops and artillery loaded with case-shot and offer them the choice of obedience or massacre, but such draconian measures were no longer appropriate in the armies of the Western democracies. (The sterner and more brutal Russians and Germans never hesitated to shoot down a soldier who flinched or refused to obey an order in action. The officer who failed to do so was himself liable to disciplinary action.) A sit-down strike by 700 men, therefore, presented the officers of the beach organisation and the military police with a problem for which the regulations offered no solution.

In the opinion of the authorities the basic cause of the mutiny was the failure to explain to the men concerned the grave emergency in the 10th Corps. The 9th Royal Fusiliers, for instance, had lost 300 all ranks at Battipaglia, a battalion of the Queen's Regiment 182 and the 5th Hampshires three-quarters of its strength, and all the infantry needed replacements to some degree. Had this been understood, it was argued, there would have been no trouble. The blame, in fact, was shifted to the staff and commanders of the base organisation. This was a contributory cause, but the trouble had deeper roots. Unlike the US Army, the British, who in any case were desperately short of man-power, had no well-organised flexible pool of replacements by which men trained in the appropriate skills – squad rifleman, machine-gunner, radio-operator – could be sent to any regiment or battalion. In the British Army, with its system of mutually exclusive regiments designed to reinforce group loyalty and *esprit de corps*, a Guards battalion could only be reinforced by Guardsmen, Highlanders by Highlanders, and so on. It so happened that when the urgent appeal for infantry replacements for the 10th Corps was received and the staff of the base organisations trawled for infantry, some 200 caught in the net were men left behind by two veteran Eighth Army divisions, the 50th Northumbrian and the 51st Highland, which had returned to England in preparation for OVERLORD. These men believed that they had been promised that they too would be sent home as soon as they could be released from "extra-regimental employment", or completed their convalescence from wounds or illness. The argument advanced in their defence, that being indoctrinated with the spirit of the regiment they resented being posted among strangers, was not so much the cause as the fact that they might be retained in Italy and altogether miss the chance of being reunited with their families. To this must be added the factor that the Scottish infantry, splendid fighters as they were, were given to riot and indiscipline, and took a pride in the fact that only their own officers and NCOs could control them.

The impasse on the beach was resolved by the corps commander himself, Richard McCreery. Hearing of the trouble he went to the spot and undeterred by violent barracking addressed the mutineers. He reminded them of the seriousness of their offence, explained that their own comrades, British soldiers, were hard pressed and in danger, that he understood their feelings, but if they went at once and joined the battalions to which they were assigned their offence would be ignored. Five hundred responded, and 192, all from the 50th and 51st Divisions, were disarmed and returned to Africa for trial by court martial. The three ringleaders, all sergeants, of what had been a carefully organised act of collective disobedience, were sentenced to death and the remainder to terms of imprisonment. All sentences were then suspended, and the offenders sent back to Italy to earn their cancellation by good behaviour, which they did.[1]

The moral of that unhappy incident was not lost on the British, and least of all on McCreery who, though no "feather duster", was an excellent man-manager. He realised that a British citizen army required very careful handling. The gut feeling of the Salerno mutineers was neither a refusal to face the dangers of the battlefield nor undue attachment to their regiments but that they had been treated unreasonably; it wasn't fair, a consideration counting a great deal with the British of all classes. The accusation that British commanders did not drive their men as did the Americans is, therefore, to a certain extent correct. Every British operation was carefully planned so as to save lives – to use fire-power and good tactics rather than an effusion of blood to reach objectives. As McCreery was to say when he became commander of the Eighth Army, "It was like an old steeple-chaser, good for one more race if it were carefully handled."

In contrast to the British commanders' acceptance of human frailty, American commanders were overtly romantic about the capability of their men and covertly disgusted at their actual achievements. The contents of a covering letter from Colonel William Martin, who commanded the 143rd Infantry in 36th Division, to Major-General Fred Walker with an after-action report was applicable throughout the 36th and 45th Divisions:

> Officers from replacement depots who are inexperienced and who are not familiar with their platoons are assigned just prior to combat.

All these vacancies should be filled much further in advance and also during the period of waiting for assignment these young officers should be given intensive training of the same type as units to which they are assigned are given. Most officers from replacement depots report soft and unprepared for the arduous task of leading a platoon in combat. The result is that they break down under stress and strain of battle and whole units become disorganised. Too many officers and as a natural sequence too many men are defeatists rather than determined fighters because they exaggerate enemy potentialities and report disturbing rumours of enemy strength and presence. This must be corrected and stopped and the spirit of confidence must prevail when men go into battle.[2]

Clark's perfectly correct reaction was to hound the inefficient who tolerated incompetence wherever they might be and to drive his Fifth Army remorselessly until they were hard, efficient and as professionally arrogant as the Germans. Casualties would not deter him and he would set an example in his intolerance of subordinates who did not drive their men in the face of the enemy as hard as he drove his army and himself.

An event contributing to the legend of Salerno was the drop of part of the 82nd Airborne Division into the bridgehead on the night of September 13. It was dramatic enough, but it achieved no more than to boost morale for its influence on the battle was hardly decisive. It only underlines the makeshift nature of the arrangements for the reinforcement of the bridgehead, and that the obvious flaws in the operational plan for AVALANCHE were the wide gap in the centre and the vastly over-extended front initially allotted to the 10th Corps. When McCreery asked for his sector to be narrowed by moving the inter-corps boundary north it was done at the expense of poor Dawley, thus robbing Peter to pay Paul. Yet the obvious remedy was not adopted by Clark until the morning of September 13 (D-day plus four): to use the 82nd Airborne Division. GIANT II, the Rome operation, had been stood down on September 8 only when some of the leading aircraft had taken off, and the division made available to the Fifth Army, but Clark, preoccupied with the battle (or, possibly, not informed by his chief of staff) did not become aware of this until the 11th. Understandably, following the theory of airborne strategy so vehemently propounded by its supporters, he first could only reiterate the proposals for distant objectives along the lines originally proposed and shelved in GIANT I; to drop them where they could most effectively interfere with the movement of enemy strategic reserves. This was the task given to the independent 2nd/509th Parachute Battalion which

Clark ordered to be dropped near Avellino on the night of September 14 with the mission of harassing the rear of the Germans attacking the 10th Corps. The operation was ill-timed and failed mainly owing to inaccurate navigation by the US Air Force. Not until the morning of the 13th did he arrange for a regiment to be dropped inside the 6th Corps perimeter that night where it was most needed.

The real significance of this affair is the light that it throws on the capabilities and characteristics of the commanders of the Fifth Army and the 15th Army Group. It showed that Clark lacked the instinctive grasp of tactics possessed by lesser but more battle-wise commanders. Alexander had let the unsound plan for AVALANCHE pass with no comment or objection, as he had the original plan for the invasion of Sicily, although objectionable on exactly the same grounds of dispersion. It does not require the advantage of hindsight to perceive that once the excellent 82nd Division was again available, Clark had in his grasp the quickest, best and most positive way to influence the battle at Salerno, by inserting it complete (plus some heavier artillery and tank-destroyers, not too difficult to supply) into the void between the two corps. Alexander, true to form, urged Clark to make use of it, but never gave the order. For what else do general officers commanding-in-chief exist? Instead, he wasted time in exhorting Montgomery to do what, if not completely impossible, was at least very difficult, and something that officer had no intention of doing. Here was seen the first indication of the flawed relationship between a strong-minded but tactically naive subordinate and a commander-in-chief who shrank from imposing his will; which was to bedevil Allied operations until November 1944 when Clark succeeded Alexander as leader of the army group.

This was manifested again in the Affair of the Adventurous Journalists, mildly comical but injurious to Anglo-American relations. We left the British 13th Corps in Calabria, toiling forward over crest and crag through as complete a belt of demolitions as hitherto seen in war. It is greatly to the credit of its engineers that by September 8 it had covered over 100 road miles in five days, when it had run out of bridging material. Montgomery, on the very day of the AVALANCHE landings, reported that he was halting for a few days to improve his lines of communications. His decision was not made solely from over-caution. Unless there are roads over which trucks carrying petrol can run a motorised army is stalled, and until the existing roads can carry bridging lorries they cannot be extended. Not surprisingly, on the 10th he received an anxious signal from Alexander, urging him to disregard administrative risks and hurry to Clark's aid. This having no effect Alexander sent his chief-of-staff to Montgomery on the 12th to re-emphasise the need for haste, and offering extra shipping to speed up the transport of stores. Montgomery replied that the best he could do was to send his light troops ahead, resume the advance of his main body on the 13th, and hope to pose a threat to the enemy forces surrounding the beach-head on the 17th. With this Alexander had to be satisfied, though it would seem that he felt anxious about the progress of AVALANCHE and even the safety of the Fifth Army well before Clark.

By the 14th the 5th Division Reconnaissance Regiment's leading troop was at Scalea, on Highway No. 18, without contact with any German outpost, and on the 16th it met a patrol from the 6th Corps at Vallo, some thirty miles south of Paestum. No one in the intelligence branches at Fifth Army or 15th Army Group should therefore have been in any doubt that the no-man's-land south and east of the bridgehead was occupied by no more than a handful of German troops observing the movements of the Eighth Army. Nevertheless, the arrival in the Salerno bridgehead of a party of journalists from HQ Eighth Army, announcing that they had seen no enemy en route, caused great astonishment. This enterprising band together with their conducting officer had been visiting the forward areas, where they were told that there was no sign of the enemy. Scenting a scoop, they decided to try their luck and push on to Salerno. With the advice and help of friendly Italian officials they were able to avoid German picquets and thread their way through a maze of demolitions, including a belt made by US engineers to bar the approaches to the right flank of the 6th Corps, arriving at HQ Fifth Army on the 15th. There they were interviewed by Alexander himself, who was visiting Clark, and were able to inform him that nothing opposed the advance of the Eighth Army.

This incident somewhat naturally led to a certain amount of derision on the part of the Americans. (Armies rapidly become jealous of their reputations. The British First took great exception to the vainglorious boasting by the Eighth whose members claimed to have come to its aid in Tunisia.) It would however have been no more than a minor irritation, had it not been for Montgomery's personal message to Clark that soon he hoped to have joined hands with him. More harmful were directives from the press relations department of Alexander's head-quarters, suggesting that the situation at Salerno should be played down and the advance of the famous Eighth Army should be played up. This may have been intended more for enemy than friendly consumption, but it illustrates the dangers of manipulating news. It deeply offended the publicity-conscious Americans and was in the political context crass to a degree.[3]

All hinged on personalities. Montgomery had made it clear in August that he considered the whole BAYTOWN project misguided and the distance between the two landings dangerous. One cannot help feeling that he enjoyed being proved correct. In any case his energy was expended in bursts, with lulls in between during which he did nothing but reflect, or bombard his seniors with advice on the future prosecution of the war. By September 12 he was beginning to rouse himself. He was about to deploy another corps and his eyes were turning not to Salerno but to major operations on the Adriatic coast, even the capture of Rome by an attack from the east. Martin Blumenson has suggested persuasively that a more enterprising or politically astute commander might have formed a sort of flying column and despatched it to Salerno. Such an improvisation was completely foreign to Montgomery's military philosophy and it is rather absurd to argue that it would have been anything more than a gesture and, moreover, open to misinterpretation. Montgomery could just as easily have been accused of trying to steal the credit of Clark's success.

Alexander had been wrong to believe or encourage the idea that the Eighth Army could reach the Salerno bridgehead in time to do any good. If he felt that only Montgomery could save the Fifth Army he should have spoken to him face to face, and made himself familiar with the true state of affairs on the 13th Corps' lines of communication. What Clark required was more infantry in the beach-head, and Alexander was, in the last analysis, responsible for wasting the British 1st Airborne in SLAPSTICK (where it achieved nothing of value) and not insisting on the 82nd being used to reinforce Clark as soon as GIANT II was cancelled.

All of this is summed up by the picture of Montgomery reaching *down* from a vehicle to shake the hand of Mark Clark when he visited Salerno on September 24. It signifies the myth that the Eighth Army rescued the Fifth – of which many senior officers of the former remained convinced – and provoked the counter-myth that the Fifth had survived attack by a superior force while Montgomery dawdled. It is the sequel to the Affair of the Adventurous Journalists. Behind the captions there is another story. Clark's inexperience was palpable but Montgomery's patronising manner which established that there was a pupil and master relationship and that there was an unbridgeable chasm between the experienced Eighth and the novice Fifth Army was insufferable. Clark knew that he had not gripped the battle, to use a term to which Montgomery was addicted. In fact he had muddled through in spite of favourable odds, but he was not one to admit it, yet until he did he was incapable of learning any but the wrong lessons from the battle. One of these was that he would follow Montgomery's advice not to take any notice of what Alexander told him to do because Alexander was a man of straw. Monty had known it for years. Another was that he would take a leaf out of Montgomery's book and become a celebrity at the head of a celebrated army. Like Montgomery he would thrive on deriding his rivals and his allies, but be much more circumspect than Montgomery about the way that he did it. He would keep his nose clean and avoid the pit into which Montgomery's arrogance was leading him.

The version of the battle as a near-run thing which he had pulled out of the fire served him well, and he himself believed it until the end, but it required a sacrifice and Dawley was sacked. On the 14th Clark received the Distinguished Service Cross for his leadership, and he thoroughly deserved it. But the complexity of Clark's personality is illustrated by his uncertain touch when dealing with unsatisfactory subordinates. Another general might have put Dawley on a ship for Africa at the first sign of not measuring up to his heavy responsibilities. Yet he wavered, as he was to waver over Dawley's successor, Major-General John P. Lucas, whom he also had to relieve, and over General Walker. It might have been thought that a man so determined to succeed might have demonstrated his force of character, and dissociated himself from failure by being a good butcher, but this he was not. When one of his staff boldly told him that he had sacked the wrong man and that it was General Fred Walker who ought to have gone after Salerno, he turned on him and rent him. It is true that when he was involved in building up the new US Army divisions he had earned a reputation for ruthlessness, but then he was acting for a powerful chief and was under his aegis. When the supreme authority was his, he was apt to falter. He only sacked Dawley when prompted by Alexander. When he relieved Lucas, Dawley's successor, he weakly told him that it was because he was under pressure from Alexander. He allowed General Walker to continue in command, in spite of the poor performance of the regiments for whose training he had been responsible. It is possible that Clark felt diffident because he had been appointed corps commander over men who were older than he and senior in army rank, although that does not match his reputation for ruthlessness. It is difficult enough to make the decision to sack a corps or division commander in mid-battle even with great experience, and Clark was new to the burden and solitude of an army commander. He was also a man who weighed his every action as it might affect his own position, and in the politicised US Army all his prospective victims had friends at court.

As regards his relations with his British ally, Clark was not an anglophobe in the sense that his famous contemporary "Vinegar Joe" Stilwell was, who hated them as ancient enemies and despised them as dudes and snobs. He was far too intelligent, although many intelligent Americans were irritated by the British habit of self-deprecation combined with an ineffable sense of superiority. Again, it was the slightest threat to his own position or reputation that alarmed and angered him. The root of his dislike for the British was partly jealousy and his conviction that they intended to exploit him and his American soldiers.

Clark bore one other grudge after Salerno. He felt that the air forces had let him down. They had not interdicted the German forces coming up from Calabria, who had remarked on the absence of fighter-bombers on the roads. Their bombing of the 14th Corps routes had been ineffective and they had not made their presence felt on his own battlefield until the 14th. His air liaison officer had been refused the missions that he requested time and again and when they were granted they had taken too long to fulfil. To a large extent events had simply confirmed what his American colleagues had told him was the form in Sicily. Here again, he laid the blame at the door of what he conceived as British procedures propagated by Air Vice-Marshal Coningham and Air Marshal Tedder, and on the lack of support from Alexander.

Unhappily, Clark learned neither tactical nor operational lessons from Salerno. He was not a man given to analysis or self-criticism. All he perceived was that in his ambition to play a grand role as the commander of an army he had been handed a mission beyond the resources that he had been allotted. He had been too bold at Salerno, he was convinced. Four months later, on January 22, 1944, when he visited his 6th Corps at Anzio, on the first day of the next major landing that his Fifth Army was to undertake, he observed to its commander, General John P. Lucas, Dawley's successor, "Don't stick your neck out Johnny. I did at Salerno, and I got into trouble." In one way and another the Battle of Salerno cast dark shadows a long way ahead.[4]

III

Interlude

7

MINES, MUD AND UNCERTAIN TRUMPETS

For if the trumpet give an uncertain sound, who shall prepare himself to the battle?

1 Corinthians 14:8*

When Kesselring ordered the Tenth Army to break off the Battle of Salerno he had good reason to be pleased with the way things had gone. It had suffered no irreparable damage, its withdrawal was proceeding smoothly and his arrangements for a protracted defence on his "winter line" were beginning to take shape. He did not regard Salerno as a defeat: far from it. He felt that he had taken the measure of his opponents who for all their vast resources and devastating fire-power were no match for German troops. When it came to close fighting a platoon of panzer grenadiers had proved a match for whole companies of American or British infantry. As well as his tactical and strategic success Kesselring had won another, moral victory: in the contest for the support of the Fuehrer. Hitler spent part of October and November vacillating between the advice of Rommel, who argued that Italy south of the line Pisa-Rimini was untenable, and Kesselring, who continued to press that he could hold the Allied armies south of Rome, for months if necessary, pointing as proof to the success of his operations so far. In November Hitler came down finally in favour of Kesselring, giving Rommel another appointment and disbanding Army Group "B". All the German troops in Italy were placed under command of a new Army Group "C", which included the Tenth Army and a new army, the Fourteenth, commanded by Generaloberst Eberhard von Mackensen.

This reorganisation freed Kesselring from the trammels of remote

* The Authorised Version, a quotation frequently on the lips of British generals who were great Bible readers. Americans may be more familiar with the Revised Standard Version: "If the bugle gives an indistinct sound who will get ready for battle?" In fact, the instrument used for military signalling in *c*. AD 47 was probably a horn.

control by Hitler and the Oberkommando Wehrmacht (OKW, the supreme HQ of the German armed forces), though Hitler remained incorrigibly addicted to telegraphing absurd orders on minor tactics. Nevertheless Kesselring still had to make provision for two inescapable dangers to his rear and his lines of communication. He had to retain garrisons in the industrial north, where the workers were strongly Communist and there was a growing risk of insurrection, and he had to guard his flanks against Allied amphibious assaults. Kesselring over-estimated the amphibious capability of the Allies, and since as an educated German officer he would always have sought to manoeuvre an opponent out of a strong position rather than attack him frontally, he naturally assumed that his enemy would act in the same way. Accordingly he held back, posted his reserve divisions near likely landing places and was loth to move them to a threatened point on his front until the last minute.

Hitler's first instruction to Kesselring, in October, was to establish a defence line across the narrowest part of the leg of Italy, from Gaeta to Ortona. Then, if the Allies did not press him but showed signs that they were using southern Italy simply as a base or stepping stone for an invasion of the Balkans, Kesselring was to consider launching a spoiling counter-offensive. In retrospect there is a degree of irony in the opposing views of the two sides. Hitler and his advisers feared an invasion of the Balkans more than an offensive in Italy because of the double threat to the supplies of oil from Romania and the encourage-ment that it might give to the anti-Axis and partisan movements in the area, real or potential. The Allied landings in Africa, Sicily and Italy had demonstrated the tactical and strategic initiatives made possible by sea-power. Yet these were the very moves that the US Chiefs of Staff were determined to circumvent, the first by direct opposition at the conference table and the second by the withdrawal of assault shipping from the Mediterranean. This is not to say that their policy was mistaken: on the contrary, it is probable that the Balkans might have swallowed more troops and resources than Italy. It is, however, a classic example of how opposing commanders, each in their own way, are apt to "take counsel of their fears" instead of considering how best to use their resources to inflict the maximum damage on their opponents. However, Hitler soon lost interest in a counter-offensive in Italy, for after all it was only a secondary theatre, where a defensive strategy was appropriate. The mission he finally gave to Kesselring was to hold the Allied armies south of Rome; Rome, because being essentially a politician, like Churchill and Roosevelt, he also attached the utmost importance to its value as a symbol.

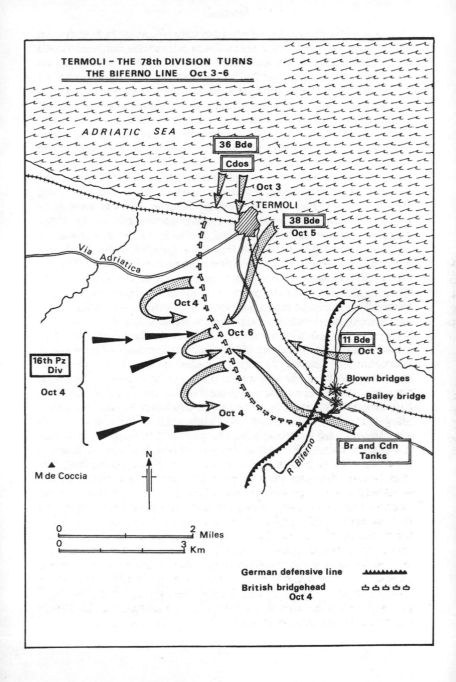

TERMOLI – THE 78th DIVISION TURNS
THE BIFERNO LINE   Oct 3–6

ADRIATIC SEA

36 Bde

Cdos

Oct 3

TERMOLI

38 Bde

Oct 5

Via Adriatica

Oct 4

11 Bde

Oct 3

Oct 6

16th Pz
Div

Oct 4

Blown bridges

Bailey bridge

Oct 4

R Biferno

Br and Cdn
Tanks

▲
M de Coccia

N

0   2 Miles
0   3 Km

German defensive line   ▲▲▲▲▲▲▲▲

British bridgehead   ♧ ♧ ♧ ♧ ♧
Oct 4

Kesselring's plan, well thought out in advance, was to fight a series of delaying actions beginning on a line south of Naples, and finally conduct a protracted defence on the strongest natural line in Italy. This ran along the southern slopes of the mountains looking down on the right bank of the Garigliano river from its mouth to the mountain mass whose summit was M. Cairo and south-eastern buttress Montecassino, commanding the Liri valley and the main avenue to Rome, and thence eastwards through rugged, mountainous country along the River Sangro from its source near Castel di Sangro to its mouth on the Adriatic. Along this he ordered his engineers to construct a deep belt of fortifications, the *Gustav* Line. An enemy advance up the Adriatic coast would meet a succession of natural barriers in the shape of deep mountain valleys through which ran rivers magnified into torrents by the winter rains, and so was the least attractive axis for an Allied offensive. Kesselring deduced correctly that it was the western sector which was more likely to be threatened, for though its natural defences were formidable, the two main routes to Rome ran through it, Highway No. 7, the Via Appia of antiquity, along the coastal strip between the Tyrrhenian Sea and the Auruncan mountains, and Highway No. 6, the Via Casilina, through the Liri valley. To give the Gustav Line in this sector more depth two defensive belts were added to it; the *Bernhard* Line as an outpost and breakwater forward of the Garigliano river, taking in the natural bastions of Ms. Camino, Difensa and Sammucro, and behind it a "switch" or stop line, known to the Allies as the *Hitler* Line, barring the north-western exit from the Liri valley and ending at Terracina on the coast. Between the Gustav and Hitler Lines some discontinuous fortified lines were prepared and improved as time allowed. Such, in outline, was Kesselring's "Lines of Torres Vedras", his "Hindenburg Line", on which he prepared to fight all the winter. To give the German engineers time to complete their task Kesselring decided to fight four delaying actions: south of Naples, along the line of the Volturno and Biferno rivers, from M. Massico to the River Trigno and finally on the Bernhard Line itself. This masked the strongest section of the Gustav Line and he intended to make the Allies fight very hard before he yielded it.*

* To avoid confusing the reader we will refer only to the Bernhard, Gustav and Hitler Lines as above. The term "winter line" was used loosely referring to all three, the Hitler Line was also called the Senger Line and the various delaying lines were also given names. The whole front of the Gustav Line from the foot of Montecassino to the sea was barred by a deep, fast river. In the north where it flows in a loop round the east side of Cassino town it is the Rapido. Below the town it is joined by the smaller Gari, and takes its name, becoming the Garigliano downstream of its confluence with the Liri. In Allied accounts, however, it is called the Rapido as far as that point.

The total force available to Kesselring in Italy fluctuated between twenty and twenty-five divisions, but a division is not a satisfactory measure of strength when assessing the German armies because the value of even those of the same type varied a great deal from time to time. There were elite divisions of parachute troops, SS divisions, mountain divisions, Jaeger (light infantry) divisions, panzer and panzer grenadier and ordinary marching infantry divisions, all with different scales of men and weapons. The official scales of tanks and artillery were seldom maintained owing to losses on the Russian front and the shortcomings of German heavy industry. Hitler complicated matters further by his fad of playing at being the director of the war on his maps, using a "division" as a sort of chess piece of fixed value. He never allowed weak or wrecked divisions to be broken up to reinforce others, and one of the traps Allied Intelligence staffs had to avoid was crediting a "division", once located, with its official strength. (The other, into which at least the British fell repeatedly, was reporting such and such a unit as being low in morale; estimates regularly disproved by the British troops who met them in battle. This was the consequence of accepting too readily the information volunteered by deserters, many of them non-Germans, who habitually condemned their officers and NCOs to justify their desertion.)

It is no reflection on the hastily trained citizen soldiers of the United States and Britain to say that, as Kesselring believed, the German soldier, the genuine article, was superb. How far, outside the ranks of the parachute regiments and the SS, he was a fanatical believer in the total wisdom of the Fuehrer and ultimate victory is impossible to say. He was, however, strictly disciplined and thoroughly trained, the two being essentially interdependent, and indoctrinated to follow, if not the Fuehrer, at least his officers, not blindly, but with obedience and intelligence. The definition of a well-disciplined soldier as one who understands the logic of the orders he receives, and has the skill and courage to carry them out correctly exactly applied to them, but this was reinforced if necessary at the slightest sign of flinching by the pistol of his officer. Yet, paradoxically, the relationship between ranks was easier and had more camaraderie than in the British or US armies. The dictum that the backbone of an army is its NCOs was especially applicable. The under-officers, *Feldwebels* (sergeants) and corporals carried more responsibility and exercised far more authority than customary in the British or US armies. They habitually led in combat, leaving the comparatively few commissioned officers to plan and direct operations, although of course as in all armies, the officers were expected to take personal command and to place themselves at the head of their troops in an emergency or in moments of danger. (In the British and American armies the drain of good NCO material into the service corps and to a lesser extent into the special forces such as the Rangers, Commandos and airborne troops led to too great a dependence on commissioned officers, with the consequence of severe wastage and often the complete paralysis of a platoon or company bereft of their leadership.)[1]

Good as the genuine article, the *echt* German soldier was, the German regiments, judged by their own high standard were, except for the elite and fanatical parachute troops and the SS, growing gradually weaker, because the appalling casualties on the Russian front had led to their dilution by freed prisoners of war from the Red Army. Some ethnic groups, Russian Cossacks for instance, who hated their Soviet masters, volunteered wholesale to serve under the Swastika after they had been captured, and in Italy were used in complete units to relieve German regular troops of the duty of hunting down Italian partisans. Others, known as *Hilfswilligeren* ("willing helpers"), shortened contemptuously to "*Hi-Wis*", had turned their coats to avoid a slow death by starvation or overwork and were employed in German regiments; sometimes on combat duties, but more often in ancillary or menial tasks. This dilution, however, did allow the German regulars to concentrate on fighting, and fight they did, long after any hope of victory had evaporated. Like the legendary soldiers of the French Foreign Legion they were prepared to "march, march, fight and die" until their world fell in ruins, and they accepted this grim, Wagnerian fate with fatalism.

The soldiers of the half-dozen different nationalities fighting in the Allied armies might not have been as hard-bitten but they were well led; confident that they could win the war and then go home. They applied themselves to the task in hand with good humour and stoicism, encouraged by the fact that their front was continually advancing. To them the sound of the trumpet was clear: it was their generals whose ears were afflicted by discordant notes.

In December, after two and a half months of bitter fighting, the Allied commanders were scolded by Churchill for lack of progress, and had the strategy of a major amphibious operation foisted on them, with the aim of breaking the Gustav Line in ten days, capturing Rome and consolidating these gains by the first week of February. In view of the geography of Italy, the severity of the Italian winter and the fighting quality of the German soldier, that this was so much military moonshine should have been apparent before the end of ninety-nine days of fighting between the Battle of Salerno and mid-December, when at last the Allied armies came hard up against the Gustav Line.

The responsibility of sorting all this out was primarily Eisenhower's and, if he did not act, Alexander should have tackled him. There was an opportunity and motive for action in early November when Eisenhower received confirmation that Kesselring had been ordered to defend the Winter Lines. That information and the nature of the fighting in the Bernhard Line made it obvious that the Allies were not simply following a retiring enemy. However, as nothing positive was done by their superiors until December the two army commanders were left to fight almost separate campaigns with the inconvenient mixture of American and British units which they had inherited from Salerno. Clearly, then, the costly and indecisive nature of operations in the last three months of 1943 flowed from the initial failure to analyse the Allied aims in Italy in a logical way and to make a master plan of how operations should be developed before the invasion was launched. Warfare has its own blind momentum. Clark and Montgomery could not simply sit still and consolidate, so both men honestly strove to direct their respective armies at goals consistent with their respective missions. Also, it is not unfair to either man to say that they felt, albeit subconsciously, that they were pursuing a beaten enemy, or at least an enemy who had no intention of fighting a protracted defensive battle. The notion that the defection of the Italians from the Axis might lead to Hitler abandoning the greater part of Italy lingered and was to influence Allied thinking into 1944. In such circumstances what Haig had said long ago in the summer of 1918 seemed a good guide: that manoeuvres formerly regarded as risks to be avoided should now be accepted as a matter of course – and it was duly followed.

After Salerno, then, Montgomery was given as his first objective the airfields at Foggia, and then the mission of advancing up the Adriatic coast as far as Pescara, wheeling left across the mountainous central spine of the country and liberating Rome provided that the Fifth Army did not get there first. (It was formally allotted to Montgomery by Alexander, but Montgomery mentioned it in conversation to Clark in September when he visited the Salerno bridgehead. In view of the relationship between the two men Alexander may as usual have simply ratified Montgomery's intentions.) This was the most difficult axis of operations so far traversed by a British army since Wellington had scaled the *Tras os Montes* or Roberts had set off from Kabul to Kandahar, but at least those two generals commanded armies that marched on two or four legs and did not require to build scores of bridges strong enough to carry tanks, and supplies of petrol and ammunition counted in thousands of tons.

The tasks facing Clark were hardly less severe but his correct course of operations and his immediate objectives were obvious. On September 18 he summoned his two corps commanders to his HQ in the Salerno bridgehead to receive fresh orders. McCreery was to follow his original mission and break out along Highways Nos 18 and 88 through the narrow defiles leading through the mountains to Naples, secure the port, and then line up along the Volturno river between its mouth and Capua preparatory to crossing it. Major-General John P. Lucas, who was to relieve the luckless Dawley in command of 6th Corps on September 20, was to send the US 3rd Division by the mountain tracks to Avellino and then extend eastwards from McCreery's right along the upper reaches of the Volturno, with the US 34th Division to the right of that again, while the US 45th Division (made up to full strength by that date) advanced via Eboli along Highway No. 91 to Benevento.

Had anyone in the 45th Division ever wondered what had delayed the Eighth Army's march to relieve Salerno he would have had the answer by the end of the first fifteen miles of the division's advance, as it waited for the divisional engineers to replace twenty-five bridges blown up by the retreating enemy. Nor was this the only obstacle. At every position suitable for a delaying action an enemy rearguard might be found in position, supported by artillery observers shelling the bridge site and its approaches. This could only be driven off by a properly organised attack. At Acerno, ten miles from Battipaglia, the US 3rd Division had to deploy a complete regiment to remove riflemen and machine-gunners dug in on the far side of a deep and wide gorge. Near Oliveto on Highway No. 91 a lieutenant and a corporal of the 45th Division won Congressional Medals of Honour for separate actions when single-handed they attacked and silenced enemy machine-gun posts, but normally the enemy rearguards did not fight to the bitter end. Their object was to delay their pursuers for as long as possible and live to fight another day, moving off as soon as the enemy threatened to get around behind or above them. On rare occasions a glimpse of them could be had through binoculars; a few gaunt, unshaven men in shabby grey uniforms slinking away defiantly to repeat the same tactics a few miles back; the machine-gunners carrying their much-feared MG42 "Spandaus"* over their shoulders and swathed with cross belts of reserve ammunition, each rifleman similarly decorated and a stick-grenade thrust handily down the leg of a muddy jack-boot.

---

* A "Spandau" was the German machine gun No. 38, with a cyclic rate of fire of 1,000 rounds per minute, called a "burp-gun" by the US infantry and much feared by all who came under its fire.

The unsung heroes of this and every other advance in Italy were the men of the US Engineers and the Royal Engineers, whose work had to go forward while others fought. No soldier would pretend that it was enjoyable to be shot at, or to fight cooped up inside the hull of a tank that might burst into flames and roast its occupants alive, but the "sappers", as the British called them, had to display a different and more cold-blooded courage. They had to carry out tasks requiring cool thinking under fire without being able to take cover or being able to shoot back, conscious that their personal enemies, the German engineers, were determined to break their nerve or kill them, as the Germans well knew that such skilled men could not be replaced easily. Road-mines (the flat, cylindrical "Teller" mines) were fitted with anti-handling devices or booby-trapped; one fiendish device being succeeded by another as soon as the trick of the first had been discovered. The whole Allied advance depended on the nerve and skill of relatively few men engaged in this lethal battle of wits, scrabbling about in the mud feeling for tell-tale protrusions and wires, only too aware that a wrong guess would be punished by their being blown to pieces.

The 10th Corps after a rough introduction to the art of mountain warfare in the passes met the same sort of resistance in the plain of Naples. As in Calabria, combat degenerated into a slow advance, traffic jams, and waiting for the sappers to clear a route. McCreery began his break-out on the 23rd, and it was not until 9.30 a.m. on October 1 that the armoured cars of the 1st King's Dragoon Guards reached the centre of Naples, abandoned by the enemy but still subject to sporadic bursts of rifle-fire as the citizens settled outstanding scores with the Fascisti.

The occupation was marked by a mildly comic episode throwing a small but not insignificant shaft of light on the enigmatic character of General Clark. A task force composed of the British 23rd Armoured Brigade to which the US 505th Parachute Infantry Regiment was attached had been formed to clear Naples, and on the morning of the 1st the parachute commander, Colonel James M. Gavin, later famous as General, was up in front with his leading troops as they approached its suburbs when one of his staff arrived with a message too important to be entrusted to the radio. Gavin was to halt his advance until the Army Commander, no less, arrived to make a "triumphant entry". This was a manoeuvre for which there was no "standard operating procedure" and one for which Gavin's previous training had not prepared him. Besides, the responsibility for General Clark stopping a bullet from a stay-behind German sniper or some trigger-happy Neapolitan would be his, but orders were orders and parachutists were expected to cope with any emergency. Gavin formed a column with General Clark in an armoured half-track followed by a battalion of his regiment mounted in trucks, placed himself at its head in his Jeep, and set off to find the Piazza Garibaldi where, the Fifth Army staff was confident, a large crowd would be assembled all agog to see their liberator. Disappointingly the convoy drove through deserted streets to an empty square, as the citizens had prudently decided to stay indoors behind closed shutters until the shooting stopped. Gavin heard later that a crowd had in fact gathered, but in the Piazza del Plebiscito where, as he put it with pleasant irony, "conquerors traditionally were received".[2]

Meanwhile, on the other side of Italy Montgomery, his mental energy restored now that he was faced with a task suited to his capability as an army commander, applied himself to two preliminary and extremely important tasks. First he sent off a task force based on the 4th Armoured Brigade to secure the airfields in the Foggia area, which it did without meeting any serious opposition. Next he had to organise and reanimate a new Eighth Army. Few of the old Desert hands "with sand in their boots" remained in the new incarnation. There were the staffs of Army HQ and HQ 13th Corps, the 4th Armoured Brigade (scheduled to return to England) and some of the army artillery. The 2nd New Zealand Division with its new organisation of two infantry and one armoured brigades commanded by the heroic Bernard Freyberg, which had been re-forming in Egypt, was not ready for battle in Italy until early November, and the veteran 4th Indian Division did not arrive until December. (The New Zealand Division had previously had a British armoured brigade but had formed a New Zealand one in Egypt.) Montgomery would have liked to have recovered his 10th Corps together with its three British divisions, but that was out of the question until the Fifth Army could be reinforced by the same number of US divisions. In any case the 7th Armoured Division, the oldest serving unit of the Desert War was due to return to England for OVERLORD, where the 50th (Northumbrian) and the 51st (Highland) Infantry Divisions had already gone. Montgomery, a "regimental" soldier to his fingertips, had come to regard the old Desert Army as a sort of extended regiment, "his" army, understandably as it had won the battles which had made him famous. He refused to believe that any part of it was not perfect, but in fact these units were no great loss. The two infantry divisions had fought a long time with great self-sacrifice and they were burnt out morally and physically. Both required to be completely restored from rifle companies upwards. As for the 7th Armoured Division, the kindest thing that can be said of it is that its high opinion of itself was not shared by independent observers outside the mystic circle of the old Desert Army. The new team that lined up for the autumn battles on the Adriatic coast was far better, indeed, with hindsight, too good to fritter away in the bloody and unprofitable little battles that were to follow. They were the 1st Canadian, the 2nd New Zealand, the 5th British, the 8th Indian and the 78th Infantry Divisions.

The other essential task was to build up the Eighth Army's logistic backing. As no long-term strategic plan for the Italian campaign had been made, it had not been possible to make a preliminary administrative plan, which was much more difficult than operational planning. If an army is to have freedom of movement it must be made well in advance and put in working order as soon as possible. Now it had to be done as the Adriatic advance actually began. Neither military writers nor line soldiers concern themselves greatly about administration because it is complicated and dull, though they are the first to allocate blame if the operational plan fails through maladministration, soldiers starve, die for lack of medical attention, the guns cease to fire for lack of ammunition or the tanks to roll for lack of motor-fuel. Montgomery is sometimes condemned for refusing to take administrative risks but he, like all British regular officers, had been brought up on the lessons of the administrative failures of the Crimea, South Africa and Mesopotamia. Moreover, he could not move physically until his communications had been restored, as we saw in Calabria. Only one good trunk road led up the Adriatic coast and that was unsuitable to carry the traffic of a modern army. It had been systematically wrecked together with the rest of the road and railway network. The base area and all the apparatus for supplying a modern army in the field had yet to be set up: transportation units, dumps of petrol, ammunition, food, ordnance and engineer stores, hospitals, workshops for the repair of weapons and vehicles, camps to hold reinforcing units in transit and replacements, and all the arrangements essential for the well-being of the troops such as a postal service, rest or holiday camps, welfare organisations and the service the US Army called the Post Exchange and the British the NAAFI.

Seen in distant historical perspective the fighting in the last three months of 1943 seems no more than an entr'acte between the excitements of the landings in September and the sequence of long-drawn-out and bloody battles to breach the Gustav Line in 1944, but that is not how they appeared to those who took part. Veterans of the Western Front declared that – though the scale of events was far smaller and battles did not last as long, between the intensity of the fighting, mud, and the severity of the winter – Italy was almost as unpleasant as Flanders or Picardy. To quote the experience of only one unit, by Christmas the total casualties in the 1st Canadian Division were 176 officers and 2,613 NCOs and rank and file killed, wounded and missing, 1,617 sick, of which 323 were diagnosed as "battle fatigue", and therefore as effectively out of action as those physically injured. These figures, confirming the rate of loss of the 10th Corps at Salerno, revealed the degree to which the British had underestimated the need for infantry replacements. The growing gap between demand and supply taxed the ingenuity of the British, Commonwealth and Polish commanders until the end of the war in Italy. Unlike the Americans who, in the person of Clark, considered that a commander had failed who did not continue to press his attack as long as he had a reserve to throw in, the British were forced to rely on fire-power and battle-craft, and to take their time to secure an objective. Nevertheless, when fighting the German soldier, who defended each ridge and river line with remarkable economy of force and turned a key position like Ortona into a miniature Stalingrad, the price of most objectives was a long infantry casualty list, however skilled the tactics employed. This was seen at Termoli.

When the Eighth Army reached the German defence line along the River Biferno Montgomery decided to use his few landing craft to turn its seaward flank by amphibious assault while the main force attacked frontally. By capturing Termoli, a small town two miles north of the Biferno, he would effectively cut off the German line of retreat along Highway No. 16. Termoli was only lightly held by a detachment of railway construction engineers stiffened by a platoon of parachute troops whose parent battalion covered the Biferno river further to the west. The initial attack was made by two British commando units acting as spearhead for the 78th Division. The plan was to land the Commandos in front of the town before dawn on October 3 while the 11th Brigade, the 56th Divisional Reconnaissance Regiment and six Sherman tanks of the 3rd County of London Yeomanry* crossed the river and joined them. The few landing craft available would then go back and pick up the 36th Brigade (reduced of course to "assault" scales) and put them ashore at Termoli during the night of the 3rd/4th. The 3rd Army Commando and the 40th Royal Marine Commando cleared the enemy out of Termoli, those not captured being rapidly scattered. The Germans had blown the road bridge over the Biferno but the

---

* "Yeomanry" was the ancient title of volunteer cavalry, later incorporated in the Territorial Army, converted in the 1930s to Royal Artillery or armoured units.

engineers though short of equipment built a bridge of boats by which the anti-tank guns and some fighting vehicles of the divisional reconnaissance regiment were able to cross while the infantry waded through the shallows. Then "General Mud" took a hand. On October 3 it began to rain heavily, the Biferno rose to a height which prevented fording and reduced by-passes round demolitions on the approach roads into a gluey swamp in which the vital tanks, field artillery and ammunition vehicles stuck. Inside the bridgehead it proved impossible to move anti-tank guns up to the defensive perimeter, where they were badly needed, for General Mud had been joined by General Sieckenius.

The 16th Panzer Division had been pulled back to a rest area north of the Volturno to refit and reorganise after the battering it had received at Salerno, but being the only reserve unit available, and as OKW had ordered that Termoli was to be held "at all costs", it was sent there hot foot. Two battle-groups already known to the reader, KG Stempel and KG von Doering arrived on the 4th after a ninety-five-mile march over the mountains and threw themselves into the battle. For a short time the British position in Termoli looked desperate. The artillery of the 78th Division was down to 200 rounds per gun* and pumping them out as fast as possible in an attempt to hold off the panzers. The only hope of reinforcing the bridgehead by land was a bridge strong enough to carry tanks over the Biferno, but all the Bailey† equipment had been withdrawn from the divisional park to repair the lines of communication. The Royal West Kents had been overrun and the perimeter contracted to the outskirts of the town when there was a dramatic change of fortune. Bridging equipment was rushed up and the Royal Engineers working at high speed under fire put a bridge across the Biferno strong enough for the Sherman tanks of the 12th (Three Rivers) Canadian Armoured Regiment to join the fight. On the 6th the whole force counter-attacked and drove off the German battle-groups, the good shooting of the Canadian tank gunners being particularly admired. The moral of this action is that attractive as it may seem to turn the enemy flank or land in his rear the issue still has to be decided by ordeal by battle.[3]

* Say, two hours' expenditure at normal rates of fire.

† The "Bailey bridge" was the invention of a British engineer of that name. Essentially it was made of standardised components suitable for carriage in ordinary transport, and bolted together to form as long and as strong a bridge as was required, like a giant version of Meccano or Erector toy kits. The simplest of the launching drills was to construct a bridge of rather more than double the length required to span the gap, so that it would not overbalance, and push it forward on rollers until the end hit the far bank. It was one of the great war-winning inventions, and adopted by the US Army.

All that the "end-run", as the Americans called the manoeuvre, achieves is to shift the scene of combat momentarily to a site more advantageous to the attacker. If, however, he falters or is in insufficient strength to defeat the enemy reserves or is pinned by a determined counter-attack, then he has lost the advantages of surprise and the initiative and the tables may be turned on him. It used to be said in Burma, where the British were continually subjected to Japanese infiltration and encirclement, "Don't forget that when the Jap is round behind you, you are also round behind him" – something equally clear to the German commanders. Faced with a determined opponent the attacker who does not succeed in an envelopment or an attack on the rear outright may be at worst cut off, at best be thrown on the defensive and so become an embarrassment to his own side instead of a threat to the enemy. This was to be seen on a large scale at Anzio.

On the Volturno front General Clark's hopes of a rapid advance and a crossing of the river on the run over a broad front were dashed by October 9. To force the passage of a large river is a difficult enough operation when the attacker has every advantage, but on the lower reaches of the Volturno where the 10th Corps had to cross, the river was one hundred yards wide and six feet deep, and flowed at four to five miles an hour, and the approaches, soon converted to deep mud by the passage of vehicles, were sown with mines. Clark's disappointment that the formal assault crossing had to be delayed until the 13th showed in his impatience with McCreery, when the latter's right division, the 56th, gained only a toehold on the far bank, and McCreery refused to press its attack. By then the 46th Division, which was making the main corps thrust on the left, had a good bridgehead on the coast. The 7th Armoured Division, whose initial crossing was only a diversion, also had a bridgehead and, next day, built the only thirty-ton bridge across the river – albeit one that led into muddy terrain unsuitable for armour. But the main Fifth Army thrust was supposed to be astride Highway No. 6 from Caserta towards Rome at the town of Capua and upstream where the 3rd US Division was to cross in the vicinity of Triflisco. So Clark was angry at the 56th Division's failure there and compared its effort with the excellent performance of the 3rd Division on its immediate right. Von Vietinghoff described their operation as "very cleverly planned and forcefully executed" by its commander General Lucian Truscott. He observed that the division avoided the mistake made at Salerno by advancing regardless of the threat to its flanks. To protect the 3rd Division's flank Clark handed over its thirty-ton bridge, constructed in six hours under fire, to the 56th Division and shifted the corps boundary to allow the British to use it to cross the Volturno. But he made another black mark in his record of British failures and American successes. The 3rd Division was, indeed, a consistent achiever for Clark, but on this occasion McCreery was right not to insist on the 56th Division repeating its attack and Clark's decision saved both lives and time.

Assault river crossings cost time, men and materials, as Clark discovered. It is not enough simply to cross a river, one also has to have the means at hand to follow up the enemy without delay and in sufficient strength to prevent his standing again a few miles up the road. Montgomery has often been charged with slowness when in fact he was building up the means to enable his army to "fight through" an objective. On the Volturno, it was not until October 24 that the advance could be resumed along the whole front because the Fifth Army had not the means to press the enemy closely. Then exhausted infantry had to forget about rivers for the moment and think about mountains. At last, in November it came up against the Bernhard Line.

On November 6 McCreery ordered the 56th Division to drive the enemy from the great feature overlooking the confluence of the Liri and the Garigliano from the east, M. Camino: a tangled mass dominated by three peaks, each descending slowly to the south in bare ridges, the whole very broken and extending some six miles from east to west and three from south to north. It was held by five battalions, against which Major-General Gerald Templer, who was by then commanding the division, could pit only four British, the 6th Grenadier, 3rd Coldstream and 2nd Scots of the 201st Guards Brigade reinforced by the 7th Oxfordshire and Buckinghamshire Light Infantry; the largest force he considered could be maintained by porters and 100 mules with Italian muleteers, but supported by 168 guns. The Panzer Grenadiers and the Guardsmen contested the possession of the heights from the 6th to the 14th, when McCreery with considerable courage advised Clark that he wished to break off the action and bring the survivors down, which was agreed.

Perhaps it was then that Clark's slowly festering Anglophobia was aggravated by disillusion with McCreery's determination and British fighting power. The 56th Division was the one which could not carry out its assigned mission at Salerno and had caused him to over-extend the front of the 6th Corps. The 10th Corps as a whole had taken two whole days to prepare its advance to Naples, and then he had to give it the 505th Parachute Regiment to help it along. The 56th Division had failed on the Volturno and had to cross via the 6th Corps sector. And now it had given up on Camino. The "poor, dumb British" he called them. However much he did to help them they never seemed to get on any better. What Clark did not know (and it would not have moved him if he had) was that by the third week in November the infantry battalions in the 10th Corps had suffered an average figure of 409 casualties, never to be completely replaced, and that the first Battle of Camino, for instance, cost the 6th Grenadier Guards 220 out of 483 and one of the Scots Guards companies 51 out of 108.

East of the Rapido river, Highway No. 6 is overlooked by M. Lungo from the south and M. Sammucro from the north; at the foot of the latter the village of S. Pietro Infine was fortified and strongly held. This was another of those positions which the Fuehrer ordered to be held to the last man. The task of clearing it was given to General Walker and his 36th Infantry Division whose fate it was to have some of the more unpleasant assignments; first Salerno, now S. Pietro, and later an ill-fated assault crossing of the Rapido. Walker, reinforced by the 504th Parachute Infantry Regiment, a Ranger battalion (equivalent to a British Commando) and tanks, mounted attack after attack between November 8 and 16, when the defenders of S. Pietro, a battalion of 29th Panzer Grenadier Division, withdrew. By then he had lost 150 killed, 800 wounded and 250 missing, and still had to go on and try to take the next village, S. Vittore, where the next layer of the Bernhard Line was anchored to the western foot of M. Sammucro. (Inside S. Pietro 300 Italian civilians died out of the 1,000 or so who refused to leave their homes and tried to weather the storm in their cellars or in nearby caves.) Martin Blumenson, in his *Salerno to Cassino*, devotes a whole chapter to this action, which, taken with Camino, provides a revealing contrast in the styles of warfare employed in the British and US armies. The British simply could not afford to lose 1,200 men in a single action of secondary importance.

At the beginning of December McCreery launched a second attack to clear M. Camino, using a brigade of the 46th Division on the night of the 1st to secure a good jump-off point for the 56th Division, supported by a short but intense artillery programme designed to blast the enemy defence posts and stun their garrisons. Clark added every gun in range belonging to the neighbouring US 2nd Corps to the 256 guns of the 10th Corps. In the opening fire-plan that carried the troops of the 56th Division on to their first objectives, 1,329 tons of ammunition were fired in seventy-five minutes, and in the subsequent bombardments 3,000 tons more. On December 6 Kesselring agreed that it was profitless to feed any more valuable reserves into this furnace and the Tenth Army withdrew to the forward edge of the Gustav Line.

On the Adriatic coast the Eighth Army succeeded in crossing the Sangro and breaking into the Gustav Line at its seaward end, but its rate of advance had slowed down to half a mile per day and its losses had become more than it could bear. The New Zealanders fought a long and costly battle to capture one of the strongest of the enemy bastions, the hilltop town of Orsogna, once actually entering the streets in a surprise attack, only to be ejected after a fierce fight. Orsogna could have been captured, at a price, but it was not a price that New Zealand could afford, unless a whole division written off was worth the exchange. Nearer the coast the Canadians cleared the enemy from another key area of the defence near the village of S. Leonardo after eight consecutive attacks, and they were faced with a German parachute battalion determined to defend the coast town of Ortona. The resourceful Canadians worked out the tactics of street fighting as they went along, and their clearance of the town still remains a model for anyone who is forced to engage in that peculiarly unpleasant form of warfare.

At one moment Montgomery dared to hope that he might break through, but the weather tipped the balance. Movement on the Adriatic coast was difficult and sometimes impossible, but north of the demolition belt the defenders were free to move in any direction over undamaged communications and move reserves to every threatened point in turn. The weather grew worse week by week. On December 5 Montgomery recorded in his diary that the Sangro, over which his vital communications now ran, had risen eight feet and all the bridges built by the engineers were under water or had been washed away. Operations had to stop while every company of engineers concentrated on replacing them. By mid-December he was clear that it was futile to persist, and closed down the offensive. He and his new army had failed, but failed with honour. Neither his methods, his determination nor the valour of the troops of four nations could be questioned, but the whole operation had been launched at the wrong place and at the worst time.

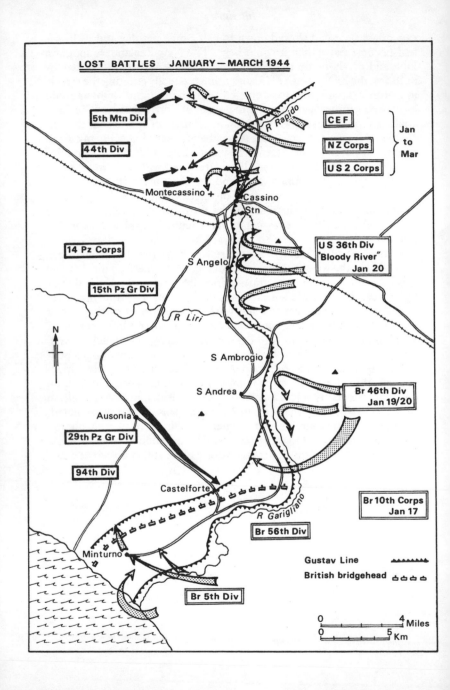

LOST BATTLES   JANUARY — MARCH 1944

5th Mtn Div

44th Div

R Rapido

CEF

N Z Corps

U S 2 Corps

Jan
to
Mar

Montecassino

Cassino
Stn

14 Pz Corps

15th Pz Gr Div

S Angelo

U S 36th Div
"Bloody River"
Jan 20

R Liri

S Ambrogio

S Andrea

Br 46th Div
Jan 19/20

N

Ausonia

29th Pz Gr Div

94th Div

Castelforte

Br 10th Corps
Jan 17

R Garigliano

Br 56th Div

Minturno

Gustav Line

British bridgehead

Br 5th Div

0   4 Miles

0   5 Km

IV

Lost Battles

8

AN ODOUR OF GALLIPOLI

*This whole affair had a strong odour of Gallipoli and apparently the same
amateur was still on the coach's bench.*

*Major-General John Lucas, commander US 6th Corps,
diary entry, January 10, 1944*

No doubt General Lucas was tired when he came out of the line on
December 31 and was shown the plan for the amphibious "end-run" at
Anzio that he was to command. That might explain why he was so
sceptical about it. However, the more he looked at the plan in the next
week the less he liked it, and he was particularly irritated at the way it
was being foisted on him by Alexander's and Clark's staff officers, who
seemed to him to know very little about fighting battles. It reminded
him of Gallipoli and the similarity became closer when he heard that
Winston Churchill was its instigator.

Lucas had replaced Dawley in command of the 6th Corps. After
Salerno he had fought his divisions over the Volturno in October and
through the mountains of the Bernhard Line in November, when two
weeks of unrelenting rain made mud "the consistency of good, thick
bean soup and about the same colour".[1] In November and December
his 3rd, 36th and 45th Divisions were replaced by French divisions and
on December 31 he handed over the French troops on the corps front
to the newly-arrived French Expeditionary Corps headquarters of
General Alphonse Juin, and on the left to Major-General Geoffrey
Keyes' 2nd (US) Corps, which had been in the line since mid-
November. The 2nd Corps now absorbed Lucas' remaining division,
the 34th, and Lucas' headquarters withdrew to take over the two
divisions destined for Anzio, the fresh 1st British, newly arrived from

North Africa, and the rested 3rd US that we last met on the Volturno, commanded by Lucian Truscott.

Lucas was a down-to-earth practical soldier, by then experienced in fighting Germans and the logistics of warfare in the mountains of Italy. Although a sympathetic and understanding man he was not considered soft. Retaining no lingering illusions about the capabilities of infantry relying on their own weapons and an artilleryman himself, he had made his artillery support effective and fearsome. It had been the saviour of the lives of his infantry every day since Salerno. He had also created, from scratch, a system of mule transport, without which neither his infantry nor his artillery could have sustained the fighting in the mountains. His pack train of about 500 mules, ponies and asses used whatever equipment could be scrounged from the ordnance or "liberated" from the countryside. "The result was the most peculiar collection of little jack asses, pack saddles, ponies and gear of all descriptions that I have ever seen," he wrote, "but it worked. It had to work." As for the handlers, men who had the knack and acquired the knowledge emerged from unexpected places. Often the despair of weapon training instructors, useless on the square or "boot camp" and incorrigibly scruffy, they enjoyed their independence and worked around the clock, usually on their own, toiling up narrow tracks where shelling could panic heavily loaded animals into a gadarene descent to the bottom of a ravine.

Even if fatigue may have coloured Lucas' judgment of the Anzio plan, his experience qualified him to criticise it. Careful, and sceptical of get-rich-quick methods, he was allergic to over-sanguine believers in the triumph of will over reason, there being too many of them at Fifth Army and the other higher headquarters in the rear, he believed. Indeed, had he known the full story of the plan's provenance he might have extended his critical comment – "I am amazed at the ignorance of war displayed by the leaders of a people who have been at war for so many years" – which condemned his own countrymen as well as Churchill and Alexander at whom it was directed.

Indeed, Eisenhower had allowed the campaign to drift in the three months since Salerno. His mind had changed too often. Although he had received contradictory, sometimes impracticable, instructions from Washington and London he did not play the part of commander, demanding clear directives so that he could make decisions, because he preferred the status quo. He was not used to taking responsibility, and continued, in spirit, Marshall's staff officer. As Alexander was under Montgomery's influence, because he had been a student of his at the Staff College, so Eisenhower, as one of the Marshall ring, was under

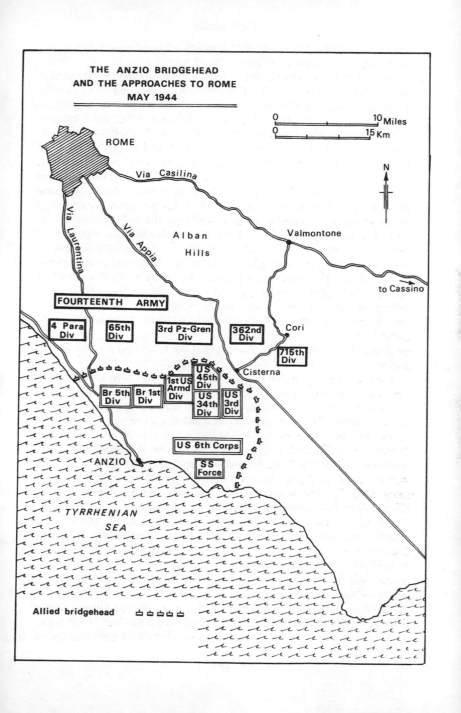

THE ANZIO BRIDGEHEAD
AND THE APPROACHES TO ROME
MAY 1944

0 _____ 10 Miles
0 _____ 15 Km

N

ROME

Via Casilina

Via Laurentina

Via Appia

Alban Hills

Valmontone

to Cassino

FOURTEENTH ARMY

4 Para Div

65th Div

3rd Pz-Gren Div

362nd Div

Cori

715th Div

Cisterna

1st US Armd Div

US 45th Div

Br 5th Div

Br 1st Div

US 34th Div

US 3rd Div

US 6th Corps

SS Force

ANZIO

TYRRHENIAN SEA

Allied bridgehead ☖☖☖☖☖

Marshall's spell. Alexander was a courageous battle soldier; Eisenhower an excellent staff officer. Unfortunately what both men lacked
was experience in directing large-scale operations. Both were attractive
to politicians because they were malleable. They suited each other
because each found the other easy-going and understanding. In fact
they were too alike and, although the Alliance benefited from their
personalities, operations suffered. Neither could make a military plan
and stick to it through political and military vicissitudes. Alexander
lacked a strong staff officer to make him do it until General John
Harding arrived in 1944, and even then he slid away from any firm
decision. Eisenhower had Bedell Smith, but he was a politician too, and
the rest of his huge staff did not command much respect from field
commanders who found its grasp of operations palpably deficient. The
Allies were desperately short of experienced operational staff officers,
for most of them were in fighting divisions. So Eisenhower fell into the
hands of staff planners and, being inexperienced himself, was too easily
blown off course by opinionated and persuasive subordinates whose
qualifications were questionable. The reputation of Eisenhower as an
admirable coalition leader will endure only if we recognise the effects
that his two personality flaws, inconsistency and inconstancy, had on
operations.

Just before Salerno, Eisenhower told the CCS that German resistance would force the Allies to "advance methodically" in Italy. A
euphemism for a series of stiff battles between short advances, it
described Montgomery's view rather than his own which, presumably,
was to be reflected in the dispersed landings and optimism about the
result of the Italian surrender. During the "crisis" at Salerno he
declared that any advance after the battle would be too difficult for the
troops he had, but when the battle ended without disaster he cheered
up, declared that the Germans would not stand south of Rome and
forecast the fall of the capital in a month. In early October he returned
to his first opinion, saying that the Germans would withdraw, pacing
themselves, to the Pisa–Rimini line.[2]

Had Eisenhower reflected soberly on events since Salerno he might
have concluded that whatever their ultimate intentions, in fact the
Germans had resisted so strongly and withdrawn so slowly that by
October 9, when Clark reached the Volturno, a review of his strategy
was timely. Hitler, who had vacillated while Kesselring carried on his
dogged resistance, came to that conclusion about then. News of the
change of German strategy – to stand firm on the Gustav Line –
reached Eisenhower from his chief intelligence officer, Kenneth
Strong. Eisenhower's moods had been influenced by Strong's com-

forting opinion that the Germans would withdraw, despite evidence from the field that they were not doing so except under extreme pressure. Both men paid too little regard to field conditions and too much to the current indulgence in what one staff officer called the "annual 'collapse of Germany' predictions" which were greeted with derision and cynicism in the field. Eisenhower was too much addicted to Ultra,* from which this information about German intentions originated.

Ultra was a destabilising influence on Eisenhower because he had no consistent plan – no master plan as Montgomery put it. In the field, Ultra could seldom be the principal source of intelligence for commanders fighting battles. At the highest level its importance was greater, of course, but even there it should not have been the foundation of strategy, but its guide. Yet Eisenhower's perceptions were "startlingly changed" about October 7, by information from Strong about Kesselring's intentions.[3] On October 4 Kesselring had persuaded Hitler to let him make a prolonged stand south of Rome and on the 9th Hitler had referred to the Bernhard Line as of decisive importance. Reinforcements were traced moving south to bring Kesselring's strength to nine divisions. On the 25th Hitler sent for Kesselring and reversed his intention to appoint Rommel to command all the German forces in Italy. Rommel had favoured a withdrawal to the Pisa–Rimini line and, eventually, to the Po. On November 6 Kesselring's appointment in his place marked "the end of the withdrawals" and on the 23rd Kesselring assumed supreme command with instructions to hold the front south of Rome indefinitely.[4]

This information set in motion one of the train of events that sent Lucas to Anzio in January. Eisenhower perceived that an advance to the Pisa–Rimini line, let alone the Po, was too tough an assignment unless the Germans could be dislodged by an amphibious landing on the west coast behind the Winter Line. Nevertheless it was still necessary to reach Rome with its neighbouring airfields, and the Pisa–Rimini line to cover them. Consequently, although it was always possible that Hitler might change his mind again, on October 13, the day that Clark crossed the Volturno, Eisenhower asked the CCS for more landing craft. Washington was unmoved and adhered to its conviction that the Germans would not stand until they reached the three lines in the north – the Pisa–Rimini, the Po and the Alps. There would be no more resources and no change in the decisions made at

---

* "Ultra": code-name for the British intelligence source based on radio-intercept provided by the station at Bletchley, England.

QUADRANT in Quebec City in August that 7 divisions, 170 bombers and troop-carrying aircraft, assault shipping and landing craft would leave the Mediterranean for England at the beginning of December.[5]

It had been assumed by the army commanders that amphibious end-runs were essential if the campaign in Italy was to proceed, so Eisenhower's request was not innovative but was the only way the purpose of the campaign could be achieved without excessive loss of life. At Termoli, Eighth Army had mounted a comparatively small operation on October 3. At about the same time Clark ordered General ('Iron Man') O'Daniel to form an amphibious operations section to plan landings on the west coast. He made a number of proposals in October. All were frustrated either because the navy found that those planned close to the front used unsuitable beaches or those further afield, for which the army needed a larger force to ensure that it could survive longer, required too many ships.

Nevertheless, from O'Daniel's work emerged the conviction that Anzio was the place for a landing to unhinge the Winter Line and take Rome, provided that the main front of Fifth Army was advancing and it had reached the vicinity of Frosinone. The size of the landing force obviously depended on the ships available and there the outlook was bleak. To find out how bleak, Eisenhower's staff undertook a study at the end of October, primarily to determine whether even the planned build-up of forces in Italy could be completed before the landing ships and craft required for it left for England. The conclusions were discouraging. If fifty British LSTs and twelve US craft were retained for an additional fifteen days, until December 15, the build-up of ground forces could be completed and there would also be sufficient for an amphibious landing by one division. The air force units, whose maintenance would eventually require as much shipping as the whole of the Eighth Army, could not be accommodated. However, if these craft were retained until January 5 the whole build-up could be completed and the amphibious landing mounted.[6]

All this must be taken with a pinch of salt. The CCS was bound to offer a reprieve on behalf of the air force because its members agreed that the unqualified purpose of the campaign was to establish it in Italy, but the bill for its maintenance, the equivalent of one whole army, had not yet been presented for payment. In effect, the paper gave notice that the resident fleet that remained after December 15 would have to be larger than the CCS had envisaged, whether or not amphibious operations were undertaken. However, in such calculations variables were disguised as constants; they were "cockshies", more assumption than fact. At this comparatively early state of the art a few of these variables were the methods of loading craft, their turn-round time, serviceability and repair, the endurance of their crews and the casualty rate of ships. The staff figures were, naturally, conservative as the very successful supply of Lucas' force from January until May, maintained in the teeth of naval complaints that the ships were being driven too hard, was to demonstrate.

Bedell Smith was the sponsor of this study. An astute man, although not a very military one, he was nobody's fool and was playing the game of politics on behalf of his own campaign as, he well knew, were the staffs in Washington and London on behalf of their own special interests. At about this time, he was required to answer a CCS proposal at the QUADRANT conference in September on the merits of a landing in the south of France to divert German divisions from OVERLORD in the spring of 1944.[7] He poured cold water on the idea. Its feasibility, he argued, would depend on the Pisa–Rimini line having been reached by then. In that case there might be better ways of engaging German forces and of employing shipping. He suggested three: an end-run around the Pisa–Rimini line, a land thrust into southern France or one into Yugoslavia. Bedell Smith was a consistent opponent of the invasion of southern France which was shortly to be given the code-name ANVIL, unlike his master who wavered, unable to comprehend its military shortcomings. But it was Bedell Smith who established the principle that as ANVIL depended on the progress being made on the Italian mainland, the CCS would have to provide adequate shipping for the latter if it wanted the former. Thus ANVIL would serve Italy by compelling the CCS to leave more shipping in the Mediterranean which might be available for Anzio and subsequent operations and also for the general maintenance of land operations.

This marked the beginning of ANVIL as a bargaining chip in a strategic tug of war between the air forces and the armies and between OVERLORD and the Mediterranean. When Eisenhower was appointed Supreme Commander for OVERLORD in December, taking Bedell Smith with him to England in January, he changed sides on ANVIL, adopting the CCS view that it ought to be mounted, but he still wavered between the political wisdom of pleasing Marshall and the military logic of Brooke, Montgomery and Bedell Smith, who were against it.

ANVIL seemed an ally to the commanders in Italy when Eisenhower, provoked by Ultra intelligence and realising that shipping, time and the weather were all pressing him for action, called the commanders to a conference at Carthage on November 3. The outcome was a rehash of the ambitious scheme for the Eighth Army to attack towards Pescara and then to effect a right hook through Avezzano to threaten Rome from the east. The Fifth Army would take advantage of the east-coast offensive to thrust northwards and then land a force at Anzio when its main front reached Frosinone. None of this was new and all of it fanciful: Rome and the Pisa–Rimini line were still the objectives. But it served as a dish to set before the CCS to tempt it to relent over landing craft. Even then Eisenhower played his cards like a politician. Having received the blessing of the CCS on his "plan" on the 6th, he then gave them the bad news about shipping and asked for an extension until December 15, on the grounds prepared by Bedell Smith's study. Having received that bonus on the 8th he asked for a further extension until January 15 as his amphibious plans would take rather longer to prepare.

The politics of ANVIL and the Italian landings was made the more Byzantine when Clark was named to plan and command the former, if and when it were mounted, on the assumption that that would not be until the Fifth Army reached the Pisa–Rimini line. In this appointment there lay a potential conflict of interest although Clark's immediate concern was to resume the advance that he had halted in mid-November to regroup his forces. Then his aim was to break through the Gustav Line, reach Frosinone and mount the Anzio operation. On December 10, when it was clear to him that without more troops he could not even reach the Gustav Line, Clark proposed that the force for Anzio be enlarged from one division to two in order to panic the Tenth Army into a retreat on the main front and to give the landing force additional security as it would have to hold out for longer than was originally intended. The proposal assumed that the troops for it would come from North Africa. At this time the Eighth Army was fighting desperately at Orsogna and Ortona, beyond the Sangro river but short of Pescara. In fact, Montgomery was about to close down his operations on the east coast. By December 18, after he had been advised that he had to make a final decision about Anzio and Montgomery had called a halt on his front, Clark wisely and naturally recommended that Anzio be cancelled.

By this time the CCS had agreed to extend the date for the return of Eisenhower's landing craft to January 15 in accordance with decisions taken in Cairo and Teheran where Stalin, Roosevelt and Churchill had conferred. One of these decisions led to the restoration of Anzio, although it was restored without taking into account factors that had caused Clark to recommend its cancellation.

The heads of state and their chiefs of staff went to Cairo towards the end of November and on to Teheran for a summit meeting with the Soviet leaders. Afterwards they returned to Cairo to wash up the dirty dishes, as it were. It was at Teheran that Joseph Stalin put the question to Roosevelt, "Who will lead the cross-Channel attack?" Roosevelt had procrastinated over making that important decision and was caught on the wrong foot. "That old Bolshevik is trying to force me to give him the name of our Supreme Commander," he whispered to Admiral Leahy, "I just can't tell him because I have not made up my mind." Actually, Stalin's point reiterated the one made by Montgomery to the point of tedium about every Allied operation from HUSKY onwards: that commanders, not staff officers, ought to make military plans. Until a commander for OVERLORD had been appointed there could be no plan for it, and with no commander's plan how could Stalin be anything but sceptical of the Allies' intention to attack across the Channel? Stalin had a very good point, quite lost on Roosevelt, who believed that "planners" made plans and commanders simply carried them out. Montgomery was very soon to show that the commander was the boss from the beginning of the conception of a plan and that the planners were simply his hired help.

While the iron was hot Stalin struck again. He persuaded the Americans to place OVERLORD, ANVIL and Italy in strict order of priority. Since all of them could not be pursued equally, and ANVIL was confirmed as part of OVERLORD at Teheran, to be simultaneous, Italy was doomed to be milked at ANVIL's expense. ANVIL, in effect, became the Mediterranean branch of OVERLORD with the same priority. May 1944 was the target date for both. The Americans were pleased to have Russian support in preventing the British making Italy into a major campaign, and ANVIL was an insurance against that happening, as Marshall knew. For their part the Russians were happy to prevent the British using Italy as a springboard to the Balkans, where they intended to pursue their own, expansionist policies. As a consolation prize Churchill received an assurance that the capture of Rome should precede OVERLORD and that the Pisa–Rimini line ought to be attained before ANVIL. As shipping had to be allocated for the purpose, the date for its return to England had been postponed until January 15 – a concession that did not seem to be of great moment as the Italian front was not expected to break open by then. That conclusion discounted the ability of Winston Churchill to exploit the slightest toehold to argue for his own favoured policy were anyone rash enough to offer it.

At Cairo, after the party left Teheran, Roosevelt was goaded into naming a supreme commander for OVERLORD and he appointed Eisenhower. The news reached Algiers and became official on December 10. Consequently when Churchill recovered from a bout of pneumonia, which kept him in bed for some days after his arrival in

Tunis on the 11th, and began to rekindle what he called a dying theatre of war, Eisenhower, destined for greater things, stood on the sidelines. He was unwilling either to oppose Churchill's proposals, so much like those he himself had put forward in November, to anticipate the opinion of his successor, General Maitland Wilson, who was to assume the post on January 8, or to reveal himself as an interested opponent now that he was the commander designate of the rival OVERLORD. "Jumbo" Wilson, as he was known, was no stranger to the political problems of high command and was a shrewd, even cunning operator who had to strike a cautious balance between the wishes of his prime minister and his position as an international commander.[8] Further-more, the general-post that had been set in train by Eisenhower's appointment took Bedell Smith away with him and brought General Jake Devers from England, where he had been the supreme American commander, to be Wilson's deputy. Devers was Marshall's choice as an officer who would see that US interests were upheld in Wilson's HQ. Montgomery was told on December 21 that he was to command 21st Army Group in the invasion of France. Oliver Leese, one-time commander of 30th Corps in the Eighth Army, was brought back from England to command the Eighth Army. Clark and Alexander were to remain in their posts.

With the supreme commander neutral, whether he was Eisenhower or Wilson, the decisions were made by Alexander, weak, compliant and eager to please Churchill, whose protégé he was, and the ambitious and impatient Clark, also a favourite of Churchill's. Churchill's intention was to disinter Anzio and capture Rome before the landing craft were removed to England.

On December 19, when Churchill had recovered from his pneumonia sufficiently to despatch telegrams energetically the body was still warm, for Clark had cancelled Anzio only the day before. The stagnation of the whole Italian campaign was "becoming scandalous", Churchill informed the British Chiefs of Staff. No use had been made of the landing craft in the theatre since Salerno, he asserted (inaccurately). Obligingly the British chiefs agreed that use ought to be made of existing craft. With this neutral admission in his pocket Churchill took the game a stage further. He announced that Rome must not be sacrificed today for the French Riviera tomorrow. Churchill had never liked ANVIL and the "French Riviera", and intimated that he envisaged the stalemate continuing until the following May, by which time it would be too late to take Rome. Something had to be done quickly. On these grounds he lobbied vigorously among senior officers at Tunis and uncovered a solution that appeared to satisfy everyone there. In principle, Anzio, which became code-named SHINGLE, was possible with two divisions if the requisite craft were held in the Mediterranean until February 5. So Churchill cabled Roosevelt to ask for his agreement before moving on to Marrakech to convalesce.

Churchill had breathed new life into the campaign at just the right moment for Clark. In the long December evenings, after a gruelling day of visits to units and of office work, Clark often looked at the calendar and pondered his future. His hope of taking Rome and later taking his own Fifth Army to southern France, where it would be part of the great adventure of OVERLORD, had receded. It looked as though he was to remain in what was becoming a backwater while others went on to new adventures. Montgomery was leaving the Eighth Army to command the landing phase of OVERLORD. Omar Bradley, who had commanded the 2nd Corps in Sicily and was junior to Clark, was to command the First US Army under Montgomery and would then command the 12th Army Group in which Patton would command the Third Army. Patton had been the commander of the Seventh Army in Sicily until his unfortunate behaviour over the slapping incident, but he had been too valuable not to forgive. Patton was no friend of Clark's, but Devers he neither liked nor respected and certainly distrusted. Clark found it depressing that Devers was to have an influential position as Wilson's deputy where he would have time on his hands to get into mischief. Alexander, it appeared to Clark, was being left on the shelf in his present post and as long as he remained in it there would be no promotion for Clark. Indeed the tide had seemed to be ebbing under both men's keels and Clark noted in his diary that Alexander looked depressed. Both men therefore welcomed Churchill's initiative not only for their own sakes but also because it would raise the spirits of their troops.

The men of the Fifth Army had had a miserable time, as we have mentioned, attacking range after range of mountains that dominated the two roads leading in the right direction: to Rome. They had captured the ruins of bleak, stone villages smelling of dung and perched on ridges at the ends of mule tracks. They had crossed and re-crossed the sinuosities of the tributaries of great rivers which flooded and swept their bridges away overnight, leaving them without food or ammunition. Carrying ninety-pound loads 1,500 feet up stony re-entrants with the occasional steep pitch had made them disinclined to take on the enemy waiting for them at the top. Squads and platoons fought isolated actions miles from any road; hot food was a rarity. Wet clothes, hardly noticed in the activity of daylight, froze at night and made the soldier shake when he was sleepless, hungry and nervous.

There was a high and increasing incidence of battle fatigue. Perpetually wet feet produced "trench foot" if socks were not changed regularly. It was a nasty ailment that many junior officers at first ignored because they believed it to have been peculiar to the Western Front. It could cripple a man, however, unless attended in its early stages and it added to the long list of sick and wounded.

Physical isolation from friends was a new and unwelcome experience for most men, and harder to bear at night when a line of rocks easily became an enemy patrol in the imagination. A post on some craggy knife-edge would be held by four or five men, all that was left of a full "squad", as Americans called the basic unit of infantry. If one of them were wounded he would have to remain with the squad or find his own way down the mountain to an aid post. It was Hobson's choice. If he stayed he was a burden to his friends and would freeze to death or die from loss of blood. If he tried to find his own way down the mountain it was all too easy for him to succumb to the temptation to rest in a sheltered spot where he would fall into a bemused sleep from which he might never waken. It was also easy to lose his way when his mind was not too sharp, and die of exposure. Shelling was a severe test for isolated men, particularly at night when shells made a louder and more frightening noise and sounded closer than in fact they were. Often the fate of being wounded again on the way to a dressing station deterred men from making the attempt.

A steady drain of casualties and simultaneous losses from sickness and exhaustion reduced units to shadows of their original effectiveness in a couple of months at most, without their engaging in any large battles. Their rapid replacement by trained men was essential but the American method of doing so was severely criticised in Italy. Although American battalions were larger than British ones they often became less effective because they were kept in the line until they were what the Germans called "used up": their fire-teams having been disrupted by casualties, the rifle companies simply went through the motions of attack, making a lot of noise but moving very little. Yet it was impossible for the G1 staff – the branch responsible for personnel – to sustain divisions in continuous fighting trim when there was usually no more than one at a time out of the line resting and refitting and infantry replacements were not arriving in the theatre, for the Fifth Army was at the mercy of a reinforcement and training system in the United States over which its staff had no control. As we have mentioned, the basic problem for British, American and Commonwealth staffs was that as the strain of casualties fell overwhelmingly on one part of the division, the "infantry strength", relatively few casualties – expressed as a proportion of the total divisional strength – rendered the division ineffective. The point to note is that it is the "fighting strength" and, still more, the "infantry strength" of the division, that indicated the sharpness of its cutting edge. A few figures will illustrate this point.

29th Panzer Grenadier Division, (strength on July 2, 1944)[9]

Fighting Strength i.e. infantry, armour, artillery and engineers
5,217

Infantry Strength i.e. 6 battalions less heavy weapons
1,734

Total Strength i.e. including staff and supply
12,889

2nd New Zealand Division (Average strength, 1944)[10]

Fighting Strength 5,400

Infantry Strength i.e. 6 battalions including heavy weapons of the infantry
1,800

Total Strength *14,000*

In reading these figures remember that 90 per cent of all casualties were suffered by the infantry which comprised only 13 per cent of the divisional strength. When a division undertook a set-piece attack and suffered, say, 800 casualties in a week's fighting, it could not remain efficient. Compelled to perform when 700 of its infantry were missing from the line, its actions were unlikely to inconvenience the enemy greatly. In defence, provided morale held up, units at half strength could give a good account of themselves provided that they were well supported by their heavy weapons units, in which casualties were seldom high. Hence the Germans enjoyed an advantage even though their units were weak.

There are some related points to make before we leave this subject. Mark Clark, and virtually every senior American with the exception of Dwight Eisenhower, expressed the opinion that the British were less determined in attack than Americans. Although, they observed, British infantry was as brave, or even braver than American, it performed less well. They attributed this to British commanders' need to conserve manpower and their recollections of the Somme and Passchendaele deterring them from driving their men. They believed, too, that the British junior officers were poor tacticians. While there was some truth in this it was based on a false premise about performance, for the Germans ranked British infantry above American although they thought their tanks were inferior. And while it is true that Sir Ronald Adam warned commanders in Italy that infantry reserves were running out when he visited them in October 1943, there is a more fundamental explanation for the way the British spared their infantry and for the way American commanders drove theirs. It is illustrated by the difference in their replacement systems, a subject already mentioned in connection with the mutiny of British reinforcements on the beach at Salerno. In the British system the unit was treated as an organism to be preserved. It was a complex of human relationships, a team, like the Montreal Expos, Manchester United or the New York Islanders, liable to be completely disrupted by heavy casualties unless properly trained and acclimatised reserves were available. When fire-teams were destroyed or replacements outnumbered original team members, their efficiency and that of the whole unit in the line was reduced. The American system, described as brutal by more than one American, had replacements arrive in units as complete strangers. Furthermore, it did not train them to perform all the skills that would be required of them in battle when there were casualties to key men. It certainly produced large numbers of uniformly trained men but they were drafted into units like spare parts into an automobile. The system was industrial in conception, not organic as was the British.

Like industry in the 1930s, the American system was heartless and bore heavily on newly arrived replacements, who were thrust into combat without time to settle in. As a result they suffered heavy casualties. The best human material was consigned to the technical arms and services so that the US Infantry was starved of good NCOs, who had a key part to play in conditioning new arrivals, and junior officers, often inexperienced, had to do their work. The pressure on them was great, as the US commanders were taught to drive their infantry hard, but the result was the junior leaders resorted to deception to cover up the fact that the system was not working. By contrast the British private soldiers were far less amenable, contrary to the received idea, and if they were to submit to authority required careful handling by their company officers and NCOs, who were taught that their first duties were not so much tactical as leadership and man-management.

This brings us back to the earlier reference to the cutting edge of units and our comment that American commanders were tougher-minded than their British colleagues. Alexander believed that Clark was too tough on his divisions and ran them into the ground. In the forthcoming battles of Cassino he told him so, in connection with the 34th Division. Clark disagreed; he thought British commanders were soft. He often criticised his 10th Corps commander, Richard McCreery, for not pushing his divisions harder. McCreery thought that Clark was unrealistic about what could be achieved – indeed about what Clark's American units were actually achieving. The observation of the New Zealander, Howard Kippenberger, who commanded a brigade in this and earlier campaigns, a much-respected and very experienced soldier, although not a professional, puts this matter in a sensible light:

> All through the Italian campaign we find elaborate planning and preparation, tremendous bombardments and then attacks succeeding or failing with sometimes only some scores of casualties. The cutting edge, though, was thin.[11]

In contrast, Mark Clark, in his diary and amongst his staff, held the view that an attack that failed with few casualties was a poor performance. The British had discarded such a view after their experience on the Western Front. In their book a big butcher's bill indicated bad tactics, not steely resolve. What was more, in the modern battalion, the number of specialists had increased and the strength of the rifle companies decreased, so the cutting edge – the infantry strength – wore out faster, as it had in the Fifth Army after it had driven in the Bernhard Line. The Fifth Army was exhausted.

The cancellation of Anzio (SHINGLE) would have been a blessing for the Fifth Army, which needed a breathing space sorely; its restoration found it jaded. Although his own divisions were fresh, Lucas well understood how tired were the troops on the main front on whose performance his personal survival as a commander, let alone his success, was going to depend. He could not comprehend the almost insanely optimistic belief prevailing at Clark's and Alexander's headquarters that the Fifth Army could break through the Gustav Line barely a week after it had reached it when the Bernhard Line battle had been so tough.

> Army has gone nuts again . . . Their general idea that the enemy is fleeing in disorder. The only reason is that we have been able to advance against them with comparative ease and to advance a few miles [to the Gustav defences] . . . We are not (repeat not) in Rome yet.[12]

Admiral Cunningham also seemed to be infected. He assured Lucas that the Germans would fold up and that there would be little to oppose him. "The chances are seventy to thirty that by the time you reach Anzio the Germans will be north of Rome." "Apparently," Lucas noted in his diary, "everyone was in on the secret of the Germans' intentions except me."

Lucas' mission was to land with the 1st British and 3rd US Divisions, reinforced by an armoured regiment (battalion) with each division. In support he had an armoured infantry and a tank battalion from the 1st (US) Armoured Division (Combat Command A), a Royal Marine Commando and an Army Commando, the 504th Parachute Infantry Regiment and the 509th (Independent) Parachute Infantry Battalion and the 1st, 3rd and 4th (US) Ranger Battalions. D-day was January 22. Naturally Lucas' first concern was to ensure that he had enough shipping to get to Anzio and to maintain his corps there. He found that that was not the case at the beginning of January.

An answer to Churchill's telegram to Roosevelt from Tunis had reached Marrakech on December 22. Roosevelt had agreed subject to certain conditions of which the meat was that OVERLORD and ANVIL should not be prejudiced. When Clark's and Lucas' staff examined the shipping capacity allotted to them and compared it to the force that it was intended to send to Anzio they saw that the operation was not possible. Lucas' G4 (chief supply staff officer) told him that the navy intended to dump them on shore with seven days' supplies and leave them to their fate:

> No build-up, no maintenance, Fifth Army would catch up in that time. Lucas launched a protest which was the origin of Clark's demand for more shipping and for its retention. The Navy was depressed because only two days in the week were suitable for beach landings so that they could guarantee only 450 tons of supplies per day, whereas the requirement was for 1,500.[13]

In consequence Churchill had to be asked to obtain extra landing craft and he sent another telegram to Roosevelt on which the President again replied affirmatively. On January 8 a conference was held at Marrakech at which this news was announced and orders were given for SHINGLE to go ahead.

Next day Lucas attended a conference at Alexander's headquarters.

> Sir Harold started the conference by stating that the operation would take place on January 22 with the troops as scheduled and that there would be no more discussion of these points. He quoted Mr Churchill as saying: "It will astonish the world" and added, "it will certainly frighten Kesselring". I felt like a lamb led to the slaughter but felt entitled to one bleat so I registered a protest against the target date as it gave me too little time for rehearsal . . . I was ruled down . . . many reasons being advanced as to the necessity for this speed. The real reasons cannot be military. [His staff reported upon

their return from Marrakech that the high command obviously had information that had not been imparted to him or to them. There must have been very definite indication that the enemy intended to pull out and move his forces north of Rome. If so all the more reason for making this end-run strong and well-equipped so that the withdrawing forces could be intercepted and destroyed.] This whole affair had a strong odour of Gallipoli and apparently the same amateur was still on the coach's bench . . . General Alexander, in addition to his remark as to inspiring fear in Kesselring, said in great glee that Overlord would be unnecessary.[14]

The logistics of SHINGLE having been settled Lucas considered his operational plan on the 12th, 13th and 14th. On the main front Clark intended to attack across the Garigliano with the 10th Corps on the 17th so as to draw in the German reserve divisions 29th and 90th Panzer Grenadiers, both of which were within easy reach of Anzio. The 2nd Corps, with the 36th Division and the 1st Armored Division's Combat Command "B" would attack across the Rapido at S. Angelo and thrust up the Liri valley on the 21st towards Frosinone. Then Lucas would land at Anzio at dawn on the 22nd. He was to undertake three tasks in succession, namely, to seize and secure a beach-head in the vicinity of Anzio, to advance and secure Colli Laziali – the Alban Hills – and to be prepared to advance on Rome. Colonel Brann, Clark's G3 (chief operations staff officer), gave him a slightly different version of his mission on the 12th, which indicated a difference of opinion between Alexander and Clark, and that Clark intended that Lucas follow his instructions, not Alexander's. His primary mission, as Lucas now understood it, was to secure the beach-head. "Much thought had been put into the wording of this order so as not to force me to push on at the risk of sacrificing my corps. Should conditions warrant, however, I was free to move and to seize Colli Laziali," he noted in his diary. The Rome mission was dropped.

Historians have made much of the precise wording of Lucas' orders, but whether Lucas was ordered to advance *at once* "to" the Alban Hills, as Alexander intended, or "on" them, as Clark intended, and whether he was to make himself secure first before advancing, is beside the point. Commanders are not intended to follow the letter of their orders but the spirit of them. What matters is whether, when the time came, Lucas conducted the battle sensibly in the light of circumstances, whatever he was told to do before those circumstances could have been known, and whether he pursued the spirit of his orders. And that poses the question whether Lucas had been clearly told what was the general operational idea of the Fifth Army?

There was a difference of opinion between Alexander and Clark that had already surfaced in Brann's visit to Lucas to change the 6th Corps mission. It concerned which of the two fronts, Fifth Army's or 6th Corps, was to assume the initiative in persuading von Vietinghoff's Tenth Army to withdraw. Alexander wanted the 6th Corps to act boldly and to seize the Alban Hills. He believed that only then would the Germans relax their grip on the main front and be caught in an envelopment between the 6th Corps' blocking position astride the Alban Hills and the advancing Fifth Army. A supine 6th Corps would not have any effect on the main front where the Germans were very strong.

Obviously the Germans would hold on to the strong Gustav Line for they could turn and deal with the 6th Corps in their own time when they had gathered units from the north of Italy and the Gustav fighting had died down. In view of the tough and effective resistance that they had offered in the Bernhard Line it was unlikely that they would be easily dislodged. Nevertheless Clark's idea was to break the main front, as we have seen. That required Lucas to play a waiting game at Anzio, timing his break-out to coincide with the advance of the Fifth Army up the Liri valley.

Lucas was sceptical of the 2nd Corps' ability to break the Gustav Line and so he was convinced that Clark must have some special information up his sleeve about German intentions or capabilities that encouraged him to think it could. The comments of Cunningham and the optimism of Alexander pointed to that as well. Later, Clark railed against "British Intelligence" – a cover-word for Ultra – for giving him "all the wrong gen" on this and earlier occasions. Certainly the situation at the front before the operation began cannot have given him much encouragement. The operation was at best a "calculated risk", the title that he gave his book about the Italian campaign, and he was doubtful, for good reasons, whether within the constraints of time and resources, it had a reasonable chance of success. In the end it was the overoptimistic intelligence reports that tipped the balance of his opinion and led him to accept the risk.

Later Clark said that had he known the truth he would not have proceeded. That was surely hindsight. He had weighed the risk against the fact that success would further his natural and legitimate ambitions to attain and prove himself equal to the highest levels of command. He had considered his relations with Churchill. To reveal his doubts about SHINGLE might damage an excellent rapport. Churchill, he knew, disliked ANVIL, and it was a point in Clark's favour when he asked to be relieved of his appointment as commander designate of that operation.

He was refused, but by making the gesture Clark had shown that he was at one with Churchill. Churchill's eye was fixed on Rome and Clark, too, had irrevocably chosen that as his goal. For a different reason, therefore, he too felt that ANVIL ranked second to its liberation. He could, however, cherish the hope that if Rome fell quickly he might have the command of ANVIL as well.

Lucas had none of these compensations to comfort him. He was not ambitious and did not relish what he called "these battles of the Little Big Horn". "They aren't much fun," he mused, "and a failure now would ruin Clark, probably kill me and certainly prolong the war. Disagreeable contingencies, particularly the second which has no appeal for me at all."[15] Lucas retained his sardonic humour through the period of the landing rehearsals which had gone badly. The final one, on January 19, resulted in the loss of forty DUKWs (2½-ton amphibious trucks) and nineteen 105-mm howitzers. "All because the Navy did not close on the beach; which they admit", and that had been because they had not swept the mines in the area and had changed the venue at the last moment.

> I stood on the beach in an evil frame of mind and waited. Not a single unit landed on the proper beach; not a single unit landed in the proper order; not a single unit was less than 1½ hours late. A discouraging beginning . . . I figured that at least the [actual landing] could not be any worse.[16]

Lucas' worried state of mind was, to say the least, inappropriate in the commander of a great and dangerous enterprise, although his doubts about its success were well founded and ultimately justified. For a brief moment, though, the omens were auspicious. On 17 January the British 10th Corps successfully crossed the lower Garigliano and established a large bridgehead. On the 22nd the Royal Navy put the 6th Corps ashore at Anzio and nearby Nettuno without a hitch. It was one of the most complete surprises in military history. But though Lucas may not have heard the bad news, operations on the main front had gone badly wrong by then. The British 46th Division and the US 36th Division had both been brutally repulsed in their attempts to cross the river higher up.

Clark and Alexander visited Lucas at Anzio on the day that he landed. Neither referred to the disaster on the main front, nor did they suggest that he should retrieve the situation by aggressive action: on the contrary. Clark's warning, that Lucas was "not to stick his neck out" – as he, Clark, had at Salerno – were his last words as he re-embarked for Naples. They reinforced Lucas' mood of caution and ensured that the great enterprise was to become a great siege.

THE SOLDIER'S ART

Think first, fight afterwards, the soldier's art.
Robert Browning. "Childe Roland to the Dark Tower Came",
stanza 15

In January 1944 Kesselring pondered the options open to the Allies. He concluded that their best course would be to attack in the Cassino sector with the aim of opening the Via Casilina where it ran through the Liri valley, in combination with an amphibious operation to turn the western end of the Gustav Line. Here his military judgment was sound, for that was the plan eventually approved by Alexander. However, what are hypothetically the best options are not necessarily the ones adopted by an opponent. Kesselring's own staff assured him that there was no evidence of a build-up in front of Cassino, and Admiral Canaris (head of the Abwehr, the Wehrmacht intelligence service) that he had detected none of the signs of an impending landing – naval reconnaissance, concentrations of landing craft or rehearsals. Kesselring accepted the assurance that an offensive was not imminent. He was soon disillusioned, on both counts. On January 17 McCreery opened the Fifth Army offensive with an attack across the lower Garigliano, and on the 22nd Major-General John P. Lucas and his US 6th Corps disembarked unopposed at Anzio. Both achieved complete surprise.

The first attack of the Fifth Army was made by the 10th Corps on the lower Garigliano. McCreery took the greatest care to conceal his concentration in an area dominated by observers on the commanding heights north of the river. (The guns were brought up battery by battery as near to the eastern bank as possible and left unmanned.) On the night of the 17th the 5th Division attacked in complete silence near the mouth, sending one battalion embarked in DUKW amphibians to capture a beach to the north of it, while the 56th Division, supported by one of the massed artillery bombardments favoured by the British, successfully crossed the river higher up. By the 19th Minturno was in McCreery's hands and he had a bridgehead two miles deep.

Clark had made an outline plan early in December 1943. The magnet that attracted him was Rome, and he hoped fervently that the honour of liberating it would fall to the soldiers of the United States. Accordingly he chose as the axis of his main thrust the Via Casilina (Highway No. 6), through the Liri valley, as it was the most direct route between his objective and the northern sector of his front, where his US 2nd Corps was deployed. His general idea was to use the British 10th Corps on his left next the sea to draw in the German reserves, and the 2nd to drive through to Frosinone. When, and only when Frosinone had fallen would SHINGLE be launched, but Churchill's intervention had forced a change of timing. SHINGLE was now to take place on January 22, by which date Clark had to break open the Gustav Line.

His general idea remained the same. The Fifth Army was to attack in succession from the left: first two divisions of the 10th Corps towards Minturno on the 17th, then its 46th Division at S. Ambrogio on the 19th, followed by the US 36th Division of the 2nd Corps at S. Angelo on the 20th. The 2nd Corps was to open the road to Frosinone and join hands with the US 6th Corps emerging from its bridgehead at Anzio. Clark held Combat Command "A" of the US 1st Armored Division (the equivalent of an infantry RCT or a German *Kampfgruppe*) and the 2nd New Zealand Division in reserve ready to exploit.

The commander of the 14th Panzer Corps holding the front opposite the Fifth Army was Generalleutnant Frido Senger und Etterlin, an outstanding soldier and master of defensive tactics, but he was surprised by the opening thrust of Clark's offensive. McCreery's attack came in a sector where he least expected it and had penetrated a position he could not easily reinforce from the Liri valley. He had to call for help. Kesselring was for the moment at a loss. His own HQ had mistakenly placed the US 3rd Division in the centre of the line and believed that the 1st Armored Division had been reinforced, whereas in fact the first was elsewhere rehearsing for Anzio and the second had detached its CC"B" to the 6th Corps. Should he now commit his immediately available mobile reserve, relying on the Abwehr assurances that the amphibious landing in his rear which he feared was not imminent and lend immediate aid to the 14th Panzer Corps, or trust in his own judgment and keep his reserves in hand? In the event he had little choice. Von Senger had decided that the right flank of his long front was naturally the strongest and entrusted it to the low-grade 94th Infantry Division, now shattered by the unexpected 10th Corps attack. Kesselring without delay ordered forward the 29th and 90th Panzer Grenadier Divisions, resting and coast-watching in the area of Rome. They came under command of von Senger on the 19th and 20th. By the 21st he had halted the 10th Corps and pushed it back in some places. McCreery, without his 46th Division, which according to the Fifth Army plan was committed to a separate attack, held his ground with difficulty and was unable to develop his potentially valuable bridgehead at Minturno. The attack on S. Ambrogio failed. On the 20th and 21st the 36th Division was repulsed bloodily at S. Angelo. With these defeats one of the two interdependent limbs of Clark's plan had been amputated the day before Lucas landed. The new conditions demanded a review of the respective roles of the 6th Corps and the main body of the Fifth Army. Rightly or wrongly Clark had decided to retain his original plan, which intended that Lucas should be cautious, and that the initiative should come from the main front. He was not going to adopt Alexander's conception of making the 6th Corps take the initiative. He now had to mount a costly and ultimately vain offensive (the First, Second and Third Battles of Cassino) to take the pressure off the 6th Corps, or to reach it as originally planned. He had, in fact, lost the strategic initiative when he told Lucas on the quayside at Anzio on the 22nd to be cautious.

Why did Clark act as he did in January? The answer is that he was under severe pressure to unlock the main front and he was not general enough to sit down and unravel the quandary in which he found himself and so arrive at the best course of action. He chose the less risky course, militarily and politically. To explain the first and basic element of his problem we have to refer back to the strenuous argument over landing craft, implicit in the whole question of future strategy in Italy. The Combined Chiefs of Staff had, in a final move, consented to delay the return of the landing craft required to sustain the 6th Corps in its beach-head to February 5. If rigidly interpreted this meant that by that date a land line of communications had to be open to Anzio. Such rigidity was nonsense, for complex plans can be expected to miscarry, and their projected timetables and phase lines are never more than targets. The craft reserved for ANVIL would still be in the Mediterranean, and in any case the 6th Corps could not be abandoned to its fate arbitrarily on the 5th. We can assume that Alexander's staff understood this and did not take the terminal date as seriously as they appeared to, but this locked Clark into an unalterable time-frame, between January 22 for the launching of SHINGLE, fixed irrevocably by the factors of naval preparation, logistics and training and bringing the operation to a successful conclusion a fortnight later.

There was another time factor affecting the main front: the date on which the 10th and 2nd Corps could close up on the Gustav Line, which in turn affected any redeployment across the front and the close reconnaissance of the approaches to the river and the enemy defences. The right wing of the Fifth Army in fact only reached the line of the Rapido on January 17 with all the major units in the same order from the sea on the left to the Rapido on the right as they had advanced from the Volturno to M. Camino and S. Pietro. With his painful experience at Salerno still vivid Clark judged it correct to attack on his land front first to draw away the enemy reserves from Lucas. This left him with two tactical options. One was to try to "bounce" the river line as soon as his leading troops arrived in the hope that the Gustav defences were as yet not fully manned and then as one or other of the crossings succeeded reinforce success. The other, taking into account the difficulties of a river crossing in the face of the enemy, however weak, the natural strength of the Gustav Line and the exhaustion of his troops, was to mount a deliberate attack concentrated on the most promising *Schwerpunkt*. Clark chose neither. Instead, he combined the most unfavourable features of both courses.

The fatal flaw in Clark's plan was that *he had decided in advance that the bridgehead he intended to exploit was to be won by the 36th Division at S. Angelo*. This was reasonable enough if deduced from the terrain. The coastal route along the Via Appia ran along a narrow corridor between the sea and the southern slopes of the mountains, and was easily blocked. Further inland the Auruncan mountains were virtually trackless, with one good but narrow road leading to Ausonia. The least difficult axis was along the Via Casilina through the Liri valley and so to Rome. It was an obvious deduction to make that the Fifth Army *Schwerpunkt*. (The same conclusion was later reached by Alexander's future chief of staff.) Here Clark's thinking, hitherto sound, was inhibited by another flaw, his irrational dislike of McCreery and his lack of faith in the fighting power of the "poor dumb British".

He was determined not to place US troops under a British commander, not because they would be misused, but because a British commander would not drive them hard enough; nor would he even have US and British troops closely associated in the same operation. Von Senger was surprised that Clark did not immediately exploit McCreery's success. The fact was that he had no intention of doing anything of the kind. Both his corps commanders, McCreery and Major-General Geoffrey Keyes, US 2nd Corps, expressed their doubts about Clark's plan for successive crossings, but Clark remained unmoved. The role of the 10th Corps was to draw in the German Army Group reserves, and no more. The role of the 46th Division was simply to secure the left flank of General Walker's crossing place. After that the Gustav Line battle was to be an all-American show.

The reason for this was not military but emotional. There was another factor exerting a strong influence on Clark. When on December 8 President Roosevelt had pinned on to Clark's blouse the medal of the Distinguished Service Cross which had been awarded for his service at Salerno, Roosevelt had charged him, rhetorically perhaps, with the task of liberating Rome.[1] Clark seized upon the goal and it became his obsession. Being the man he was he began to read in every move of Alexander's the British intention to cheat him out of such a triumph.[2] The first of these moves was the transfer of the 2nd New Zealand Division from the Eighth Army which came under Clark's command on January 20 as an exploiting force for the 2nd Corps. It was to circumvent such a plot that Clark arranged his scheme of manoeuvre to be a breakthrough at S. Angelo followed up by his own US Army divisions, the remainder of 1st Armored and the 34th Infantry.

So much for the "grand tactics" of the affair, lying between strategy and the hurly burly of the battlefield. An army commander may, or may not, confirm the feasibility of his goals by closely examining the ground and the detailed plans in person. It is more usual, having taken the measure of a subordinate and delegated the execution to him, to trust him, but the corollary is that the superior commander must listen to his objections or recommendations. Clark, as at Salerno, was guilty of what Napoleon called "making pictures". No one who had examined the approaches to the Rapido or the Garigliano from the south-east and the mountains looming over the right bank could have been in any doubt about the formidable nature of the operation. Serious military operations require something more than arrows drawn on the map and the sublime confidence that only the will-power of the commander is needed to carry the troops to their objective. The Fifth Army staff ignored the fact that the 46th Division had only enough assault boats to carry one brigade, and that so narrow a front invited the enemy to concentrate his fire. In the event most of the boats were lost or overturned in the strong current and only the 2nd Hampshires secured a toehold on the far bank. Next morning General Hawkesworth ordered it to be withdrawn, fortunately without further loss. McCreery agreed, as did Clark, although it strengthened the latter's poor opinion of the British when McCreery refused to order a fresh assault at the same place.

The attack by the 36th Division proved a disaster that was to haunt Clark the rest of his life and injure his career. By the 20th the sector the 36th Division was to attack was securely held by the grenadier regiments and the reconnaissance battalion of the 15th Panzer Grenadier Division, well dug in and stiffened with tanks and assault guns. Unlike the dejected US infantry, the panzer grenadiers patrolled vigorously on the left bank and mined the approaches to the river, conveniently marked for them by the tapes put in position by the US Engineers before H-hour. The US Engineer commander, having complained about the lack of basic engineer stores, recorded his opinion that "an attack through a muddy valley that was without suitable approach routes and exit roads and that was blocked by organised defences behind an unfordable river [would] create an impossible situation and end in failure and great loss of life". Both Keyes and Walker thought that it would have been better to go in through the 10th Corps bridgehead, or at Cassino, but neither took a firm line for fear of appearing defeatist or cared to argue with Clark when his mind was made up.

The 36th Division itself suffered from three handicaps. Its commander Walker was defeated before the operation began, committing his doubts to his diary:

> We might succeed but I do not see how we can. The mission assigned is poorly timed. The crossing is dominated by heights on both sides of the valley where German artillery observers are ready . . . The mission should never have been assigned to any troops with flanks exposed. Clark sent me his best wishes . . . I think he is worried over the fact that he made an unwise decision when he gave us the job of crossing the river under such adverse tactical conditions. However, if we get some breaks we may succeed.

The division itself was in poor shape. Only one half of the 1,000 infantry casualties suffered in the December fighting had been made good and the replacements, coming as they did in the US Army to strange battalions, had not been given time to settle down and form new fire-teams. The veterans were all tired and lacking in enthusiasm. This was not beyond the power of the regimental officers to put right, but the third handicap, the inefficiency of the divisional staff, could only have been corrected by action by a higher commander long in advance. An assault river crossing is not simply a matter of getting into boats and paddling across a river. It is an intricate set-piece operation requiring thorough reconnaissance, meticulous staff work and close supervision of the preparations. It is an engineer operation to the far bank, where the infantry take over, and an artillery operation from start to finish to protect both arms, so as to give the engineers a chance to build the bridges, for until they are open for tanks and heavy weapons to cross the bridgehead is not safe. It is also essential for the infantry and engineers to have complete mutual trust and understanding based on association and combined training.

It would be tedious to provide a catalogue of the mistakes and omissions that led to the débâcle later known as the "Bloody River". All the basic rules were ignored. The assault strength was only four battalions, the infantry and engineers were all unknown to each other, the infantry had to carry heavy assault boats two miles over boggy ground, H-hour was set for 8 p.m. so preliminary movement alerted the enemy artillery and machine guns, and from the first the approaches and crossing places came under so intense a fire that many of the infantry threw down their loads and quit. The most amazing omission was any concerted artillery fire-plan. The American guns remained silent until daybreak for lack of previously registered targets.

After a grisly night of sunken boats and smashed footbridges, newly discovered mines, lost units, shouting and disorder amidst terrifying concentrations of *Nebelwerfer** bombs and heavy shells falling in smoke and darkness, the leading companies had been driven into isolated pockets on the far bank and could not be, or were not, reinforced. The organisation of boats and bridges, never adequate, had collapsed. Walker decided to withdraw what men he could. Keyes, however, was under pressure from Clark to make Walker try again. Walker reluctantly ordered the battered regiments to assault again on the afternoon of the 21st. The renewed effort was pressed through the second night. A combination of mud, muddle, enemy shelling and lack of will-power prevented the vital Bailey bridging reaching the river. Many believed that in the conditions it was senseless to try; that it would have been impossible to assemble and launch the bridge under direct fire. All the light bridges had been smashed and the only way to reinforce the squads a few hundred yards beyond the river was for men to swim over.

As the miserable night gave way to the misty, smoky and noisy morning of the 22nd, the defensive fire on the far bank slackened. Walking wounded accompanied by "helpers", shock cases and simple deserters who had had enough, trickled back in large numbers. The 36th Division had shot its bolt. Its heart had not been in it. During the afternoon the operation was officially abandoned. The total casualties

---

* Five-barrelled rocket launchers known to US troops as "Moaning Minnies", from the discouraging sound of the bombs in flight.

were 1,000 killed and missing and 600 wounded. After the last shots had been fired Generalmajor Rodt, 15th Panzer Grenadier Division, simply reported that he had "prevented enemy troops crossing at S. Angelo". The Tenth Army had no idea that it had scored so important a defensive victory. It seemed to its staff that the attempted crossing had been part of the curious Allied plan to attack in sequence all along the line with the object of holding the German reserves on the main front, a view confirmed when Lucas landed at Anzio on the morning of the 22nd.[3]

It was now clear that the situation had changed out of all recognition to that envisaged in the original plan, and that Alexander and Clark needed to agree on a radical reappraisal and give Lucas positive orders. We have already emphasised Alexander's weakness in this respect. He made a fatuous suggestion that the 6th Corps should push out mobile battle groups which was unreal as Lucas only had marching infantry divisions neither constituted nor trained in such manoeuvres. Clark, though he saw the danger now that his main attack had collapsed and Lucas was on his own, was too cautious to issue a firm order running counter to the original, vaguely offensive concept of SHINGLE. The Combined Chiefs of Staff would hardly be pleased to learn that the resources they had allotted had resulted in a defensive stalemate. (What the incensed Churchill called "a stranded whale".) He determined to be imprecise. Lucas, the reverse of dashing, deeply pessimistic but basically sound, could see that as the Germans were now able to concentrate their whole attention on his corps it would be rash to go marching off into the wild blue yonder towards the Alban Hills leaving his base uncovered. When therefore Clark told him "not to stick his neck out", as he had at Salerno, and "get into trouble" Lucas took it as Clark's expressed wish, and interpreted it as an order, to be translated into action. He sat down and established a firm defensive perimeter.

Throughout the 22nd the German commanders hourly expected the news that the Allied amphibious force had moved quickly to the area of the Alban Hills and was astride the line of communication of the 14th Panzer Corps. That evening von Vietinghoff telephoned Kesselring, suggesting that he should pull back from the Gothic Line, only to receive a flea in his ear and the firm order to stay put. Kesselring, always stalwart in adversity, had been busy all day. Immediately he heard the news he ordered the only local reserves he had, the 4th Parachute Division, in the process of forming and the Ersatz (replacement holding) Battalion of the Hermann Goering Division from the Rome area to block the roads leading from Anzio to the Alban Hills. As early as 8.30 a.m. he ordered von Vietinghoff to send HQ 1st Parachute

Corps to Anzio to take charge of the units as they arrived; battle-groups from the 1st Parachute, 3rd Panzer Grenadier and 26th Panzer Divisions from the Adriatic front, and part of the hard-worked 29th Panzer Grenadier Division back from the right of the 14th Panzer Corps. Von Mackensen was to send the 65th Infantry Division from Genoa, the 362nd Infantry Division from Rimini and elements of the new 16th Panzer Grenadier Division from Leghorn, and to organise a new infantry division, the 92nd, in northern Italy from replacements and other oddments. To back these up the 715th Infantry and the 114th Jaeger Divisions were called from the south of France and Yugoslavia respectively. Finally von Mackensen was to come down with his Fourteenth Army HQ to take over the Anzio front when it had initiated these moves.

At 5 p.m. HQ 1st Parachute Corps was in position and in control, and by nightfall a thin containing cordon had been thrown around the 6th Corps. Kesselring was therefore once more his cheerful self. His plan was first to strengthen the containing force and then, when the time was ripe, use his battle-hardened parachute and panzer grenadier units for the *Gegenangriff* to throw the invaders back into the sea. On the 23rd, when Lucas had still done nothing, Kesselring felt that there was no immediate danger of the Allied perimeter expanding or of a break, confirmed later by more accurate intelligence of Lucas' real strength. On the 26th von Mackensen arrived to establish a proper chain of command and tidy up the "multifarious" jumble of units composing the cordon round Lucas. Kesselring had given the Allied commanders and, indeed, students of the art of war a lesson in clear thinking, sound appreciation and rapid reaction.

By contrast the Allied force was in an unhappy position, due to the failure of Alexander and Clark to think first and then issue clear orders. As we have said, the original instructions issued by HQ AAI to HQ Fifth Army were for Lucas to advance "to" the area of the Alban Hills, and Clark had altered this to "on", i.e., "towards", them. Neither was satisfactory, and after it became clear that by the 21st the Fifth Army had failed to break through the Gustav Line on the Garigliano front Lucas was in even greater need of clear and unequivocal orders. Without the immediate prospect of linking up with the 2nd Corps he was in a dangerously exposed and isolated position. The courses open to him were three: (a) to establish a strong defensive perimeter around his bridgehead until his build-up was complete and his only fully mobile force, CC"B" of the 1st Armored Division had arrived; (b) to make a dash for the vital ground using his infantry supported by the tanks of the armoured battalion that had landed with the assault force;

(c) using such groups, assisted perhaps by the independent parachute infantry unit and the US Rangers, to conduct an aggressive mobile defence. (This appears to have been the tenor of the comment made by Alexander, but if "mobile battle-groups" were to have been the order of the day, then Lucas should have been told earlier, so that he could train them before ever his troops were embarked.) The only other course was to delay the landing until the Fifth Army was ready to make another attempt to break through on the Garigliano front, but this was impossible.

Alexander and Clark were in an acutely difficult position, but it was of their own making. To have called off SHINGLE on the 21st after all the fuss and the concessions made by the Combined Chiefs of Staff would have been impossible: it would have cost both their heads. Nor was a SHINGLE on the defensive any good, so instead of rethinking the situation after the collapse of the Garigliano offensive they acted blindly, gave no fresh orders to Lucas, other than Clark's advice to him to be cautious. Then, leaving Lucas to take the hint and dig in, Clark went back to his own HQ to revive his offensive, for without it he thought that Lucas might not survive, let alone be able to exploit his position behind the Tenth Army.

What we have not so far mentioned is the arrival of the Corps Expéditionnaire Français in Italy, equipped by the Americans and organised on the same pattern as US Army divisions and therefore logically placed under command of the US Fifth Army. This fine formation will be fully described in a later chapter. Here it is sufficient to say that its divisions were in all respects regular infantry, "Free French" and native North Africans, and that its North African colonial troops were skilled in mountain warfare. Two divisions, the 2nd Moroccan (2e DIM) and 3rd Algerian (3e DIA) were already operating in the bitterest of winter weather in the massif north of Montecassino. On the 24th Clark ordered Juin to direct his effort into a left hook swinging through Belmonte and Terrelle to Piedimonte, a little mountain town perched on the escarpment overlooking the Liri valley from the north. (It was to be a key objective in the battles for Cassino and the Liri valley as it was the northern or anchor of the reserve line giving depth to the Gustav position.) Juin's thrust was to be reinforced by Major-General Charles Ryder's 34th Infantry Division operating inside his hook and on his left. Ryder jumped off on the 25th, one RCT with Cassino as its objective and the other on the high ground immediately behind the great and famous Monastery of Montecassino: a fortress-like building with magnificent command which was to hypnotise every commander involved in Cassino battles.

Meanwhile Alexander and Clark agreed to reinforce Lucas and spur him to take offensive action. CC"A" of the 1st Armored was due to land on the 28th. One RCT of the 45th Infantry Division was rushed to Lucas on the 25th, and the rest of the division, by this time commanded by Major-General W. Eagles, was ordered to follow CC"A". Alexander and Clark paid Lucas separate visits on the 25th. Alexander congratulated him on the organisation of the bridgehead, but offered no operational guidance or advice. Clark seemed to be on edge as if, Lucas thought, Alexander had communicated his impatience to him. Having cautioned Lucas against a rash advance on the 22nd he now urged him to use his reinforced corps to attack and suggested that he begin by expanding his perimeter to include Cisterna and Albano. Clark could not reveal his long-term strategy, because he had none, unless it was the Micawberish expectation of a dividend from the Cassino operation. Lucas could not understand why Clark was vacillating in this way, for though his corps would be much stronger by the 30th, so would the enemy. The fact was that Clark was hunting with the hounds while he ran with the hare, a safe policy for him, but unhelpful to his embattled corps commander.

Lucas, still in two minds, adopted a policy cautiously offensive instead of cautiously defensive; of piecemeal nibbling along the front. The British 1st Division was to take Aprilia and then Campoleone, the 3rd US Isobella and then Cisterna. The 3rd lost a complete Ranger battalion and failed to take Cisterna, while the 1st got as far as the railway station at Campoleone, and there its trouble began.

Lucas had a fair share of the soldierly virtues; he was clear-headed, methodical and a sound if unenterprising tactician, but he was an insular American, unable to enter into the minds of soldiers as idiosyncratic as the British or as exotic as the Brigade of Guards. At first he was impressed by their smartness and efficiency, noting in his diary: "I think they will be all right but they are sometimes a little hard to understand. They are, however, splendid soldiers. No braver in the world." He soon changed his tune. "I had lost confidence, at least to some extent, in the British division and its commander. They seem unable to make even the simplest recce without getting into trouble. They would advance with the greatest possible bravery but always with heavy losses which could not be replaced, and always on a narrow front that gave the enemy opportunity for his pinching off tactics." On February 4 when the 3rd Panzer Grenadier Division with the aid of elements of four other divisions was indeed "pinching out" Penney's salient at Campoleone: "The British are in serious trouble . . . they have occupied an advanced position for days and are now in danger. I ordered General Penney to withdraw but due to enemy pressure he has been unable to do so. I hope it is not too late."

There is a certain irony in this complaint, because it was to be the constant gripe of the Americans that the British refused to accept casualties, but it was Lucas who was to blame. He had missed the bus (if ever there had been a bus to catch) on the 22nd, the 29th was far too late for the sort of operation he had launched, and it was he who had ordered Penney into an impossible position just as the Germans were about to strike back. He was still talking about offensive action on the 6th, though by then he had already been warned by Clark to change over to the defensive, on the basis of Ultra information that the Fourteenth Army would attack on the 7th, which it did.

By the time the brigade at Campoleone had extricated itself with heavy loss Penney was back on the defensive line Buono Riposo ridge–Carroceto–Aprilia, though over-extended with gaps in his front that the Germans were not slow to exploit. On the 7th the Germans struck as predicted and forced him off his three main positions to a far less suitable line further back, among the infamous "wadis", deep water-courses subjected to flash floods and covered with thick scrub on the left, and the Anzio wetlands of canals and irrigation ditches on the right. There both sides paused to reorganise, for the British had made the Germans pay dearly. Clark relieved Penney and put the 45th Division in the line.

On February 16 von Mackensen launched his deliberate counter-offensive, FISCHFANG (catching fish) straight down the Via Anziate, the Anzio–Albano road. He made one deep penetration, but by the 19th halted after some of the bitterest and most costly fighting in the Italian war. The British contingent had been reinforced by Major-General Templer's 56th Division, from the moribund Garigliano front. One of its brigades had taken over the defence of Aprilia on the 4th, and another the defence of the wadis on the 11th, where British and Germans were to play a lethal game of hide and seek until mid-May. The sector was further reinforced by the US 504th Parachute Regiment, after which the remnants of the 1st Division went out of the line. On the 19th, when the German attacks had died away, CC"A", the 30th RCT of the 45th Division and the 1st Division, in the line again and still full of fight, counter-attacked. They threw the Germans back, taking hundreds of prisoners, and then to their astonishment, white flags began to go up in front of them. The Germans had had enough. They had shown incredible determination, but the weather was terrible, the ground soggy and unsuitable for their heavy tanks and from beginning to end they were subjected to the unceasing and overwhelming Allied fire-power until even German nerves snapped. The casualties on both sides were brutal, each side lost some 19,000. German bodies were found behind their front line stacked up like cordwood awaiting burial. On the 28th von Mackensen attacked again and kept on until March 3 but with no other result than more losses.

By February 20 the 6th Corps had won a decisive defensive victory. The German attack had been pressed on Hitler's orders because he wished to demonstrate that an Allied invasion force could be thrown back into the sea, and that that would be the fate of attempting the Channel crossing. It had failed signally. No counter-attack on such a scale was ever again launched in the west, except in the Ardennes in December 1944.

It had been a "soldier's battle", decided by the stubborn fighting of the British and United States infantry and the leadership of the battalion commanders and their officers. In a narrative which is all too often concerned with bad blood and inter-Allied resentment at the top it is pleasant to record the camaraderie between the fighting troops. The divisional commanders, concerned only with winning the battle and not rivalry, acted together. In fact they were forced to by a total lack of grip shown by Corps HQ. It is not the way to run a battle, but Truscott, Harmon, Templer (of the 56th Division) and Penney assisted by Evelegh (the British deputy and liaison officer at Corps HQ) seemed to have run the defence and counter-attack against FISCHFANG as a sort of syndicate.[4]

The cement of the Allied troops was lower down. British and Americans were deeply involved (British artillery supported the Americans, US tank-destroyers the British) and the leaders of both armies displayed that cheerful sangfroid and elementary, sardonic humour that cheers soldiers up. Men like Webb-Carter, commanding the 1st Duke of Wellington's Regiment, always immaculately turned out, "treated parlous situations with total composure and a kind of disdain that was highly comforting", and was imitated by his subordinates. Andrew Scott, Irish Guards, affecting an American accent, would greet his neighbour, Lesley Freeman, 3rd/504th Parachute Infantry, with "Hi ya, Colonel, what d'ya know?" to which the ritual reply ("English"?) was "Morning, Colonel, not a goddam thing!" This is the description of a British battalion HQ after four days of fighting, the companies down to thirty effectives each:

> Occasionally an air-burst from an 88 mm gun arrived over our heads and everyone mechanically ducked rather like worshippers at some strange rite . . . Battalion headquarters was in a culvert driven into

the embankment . . . It was knee-deep in water and crowded to capacity. The Regimental Aid Post was there and a few wounded men were being treated. A heterogeneous mass of officers and men were milling about, all talking a trifle hysterically. Looking tired, but utterly unmoved in the babel was Colonel David Wedderburn, the commanding officer of the Scots Guards . . . surrounded by Americans, Sapper and Gunner officers all of whom were under his command in the composite force which had been scraped together to hold the position . . . seated in a corner and smoking a singularly evil cigar was an American officer. He was the liaison officer from the tank destroyers . . . A large tank was firmly stuck in the mud outside . . . very successfully rendering it practically impossible to get in or out. A few signallers huddled on the steps and tripped up everyone who had achieved the manoeuvre round the tank.

The battle was won, in the old phrase used by countrymen in Somerset in hard times, "by keeping on keeping on".[5]

Lucas' reward for successfully steering a course between military realities and the conflicting wishes, vaguely expressed, of his masters was the sack. This "solemn, grey-haired man who smoked a corn-cob pipe [and] looked older and smaller than he actually was" had preferred to wait for the enemy, for he was a counter-puncher by temperament. His diary reveals how he kept his force well balanced, his reserve intact and his logistics tidy. In February he had counter-punched to some purpose and had won a defensive battle. However, this was not the whole story. That he lacked charisma was not his fault, but that he seldom visited the front and that his staff remained entombed in an underground HQ, "the catacombs under Nettuno surrounded by the macabre and cheerless relicts of early Christians", was his own choice. His divisional commanders all complained that they were never given adequate information about current operations, the enemy or Lucas' future intentions. They had carried him to victory. Left to himself he would have hesitated totally to commit his armour to the clinching counter-stroke. He had to go.

The dismissal was necessary, but it was not well done. Clark told Lucas that it was not he but Alexander who had insisted on the change. This was disingenuous, to say the least, for Clark himself had noted that Lucas tended to dither. Both Clark and Alexander were under pressure from London and Washington from the moment that the deadline of February had passed without any strategic gain to show for the diversion of precious military resources. Churchill, following his needling practice of searching for damaging statistics, obtained the figures of 70,000 men and 18,000 vehicles shipped to Anzio. "We must have a great superiority of chauffeurs," he said. It was this sort of enquiry that had presaged the dismissal of Wavell and Auchinleck, and though Alexander was Churchill's protégé he did not feel entirely secure. Clark recalled that during the German attacks on the beach-head Alexander had said to him: "The position is serious. We may be pushed into the sea. That would be bad for both of us and you would certainly be relieved of your command." Alexander may have offered this thought in a phlegmatic and semi-humorous British manner, but to Clark, always worried about his position and his growing suspicions of the motives of everyone around him, it was no joke.

Clark had cause to be worried, although it is not known whether he was aware that he was under scrutiny. The US Chiefs of Staff were deeply dissatisfied, and not soothed when in reply to their enquiries of General Sir Maitland Wilson, the British Commander-in-Chief in the Mediterranean, he explained the difficulties on the main front, but suggested that at Anzio an opportunity had been missed. Marshall then asked Major-General Jacob Devers, Wilson's US deputy, to find out if "any or all the US commanders had failed". When General Sir John Dill, the British representative on the Combined Chiefs of Staff, observed that perhaps Clark, not Devers was the man to ask, Marshall replied, "Clark may be the man to go". Lucas was therefore a perfect scapegoat, especially as he had no "constituency" and was the sort of officer who accepted his fate without complaint, except to his diary.

During this period, fraught with operational setbacks and difficulties of every kind, Churchill offered Alexander excellent advice that he should neither advise nor urge his subordinates but order them to do what he wanted:

> American authorities . . . say their Army has been formed more on Prussian than on the more smooth British lines, and that American commanders expect to receive positive orders which they will obey . . . I trust that you are satisfied with leaving Lucas in command at the bridge-head. If not you should put someone there whom you trust.

Unfortunately Alexander was psychologically incapable of following Churchill's advice, and whether it would have worked with Clark is conjectural. Perhaps not, as Clark, set on a predetermined course and under severe stress, was probably unmanageable.

Clark never spared himself, physically or mentally. The burden of command of an army in the field is a very heavy one and it bore heavily on Clark. Every visit to Anzio was a risk. His light aircraft was twice involved in accidents, and once when travelling by sea his naval patrol boat was fired on and Clark had to prop up the wounded skipper while he steered to safety. In Anzio he rescued a British driver from a blazing ammunition truck under shell-fire. For this a Bronze Star was added to the DSC he had won at Salerno, but while commanding generals should not lurk in deep dugouts or remote chateaux they should as far as possible be spared such experiences. (The opinion of General William Slim. After he had given a rousing pep-talk to a British battalion a soldier called out, "We'll be right behind you, sir, never fear!" "Oh, no you won't," replied the General, "I'll be a long way behind you.") All this is only to Clark's credit, but temperamentally he nursed his anxieties. He was unable to relax and detach himself from the immediate present, or believe that "Quiet, calm contemplation will unravel every knot". As his diaries reveal he was in a constant state of agitation, as worried about the way the high command was about to treat him as about the enemy. There is not a line of self-criticism, or consciousness of having made an operational error. His failures were the fault of others, usually the British. Worse, he suspected every British move as designed to frustrate him, reduce his span of command and eventually rob him of the goal of liberating Rome with American arms.

He complained to Devers about the British military hegemony in the Mediterranean; Wilson in Algiers, Cunningham at sea (there is a long complaint about Cunningham's high-handed alterations to naval support and maintenance for the bridgehead, by no means unjustified). What Clark lacked was a sage adviser, like Eisenhower. Devers, damagingly, played Iago to Clark's Othello when he revealed his anxiety to him. He told him of Alexander's proposal to relieve Clark of Anzio so that he could concentrate on the Cassino–Garigliano front which, in the event, he discarded in favour of shortening the Fifth Army front, later giving the Eighth Army the Liri valley–Cassino sector. In January (as we shall explain later) Alexander was given a new British chief of staff, and following his advice he decided that the true centre of gravity of operations was west of the Apennines. At first move he had already transferred the 2nd New Zealand Division, and the 4th Indian Division followed in the first week of February. He was undecided for the moment whether to group them under Clark, to alter the inter-army boundary or command them directly from HQ AAI. This greatly upset Clark, as did later moves to rationalise the composition of the Fifth Army with its all-US 2nd Corps, mixed-US 6th Corps, British 10th Corps and the French Corps. He wrote in his diary:

I have been so hamstrung and jockeyed by higher headquarters that the Fifth has lost a great deal of its power to control its own tactical operations but I will insist, as long as I am commander on presenting my views and demanding their execution as far as possible.

It is a measure of Clark's confusion that in his diary he never had a good word to say about the British Army, but strongly resented any move to remove his British divisions. It is also a measure of the man that he never revealed his resentments by anything more than momentary outbreaks of irritation, when he took advantage of Alexander's monumental calm.[6] He poured it all out in his diaries.[7] Perhaps it would have been better if the two men had had one good blazing quarrel, but neither man was built for such a solution. As the fighting in Anzio died down Clark turned his attention to the problem of breaking through at Cassino, enough to try the best of generals.

10

FEAR, HOPE AND FAILURE

After Walker's Texans had been defeated on the Rapido Clark decided to attack Cassino town itself. He had rejected that course earlier for the good reason that its defences were so formidable. Indeed, Italian staff studies and exercises over the years had concluded that it was impregnable from the south. Were Clark to succeed, and to go on to take Rome, he would join a very small band that included Belisarius, the Byzantine, in 536, and Garibaldi, who had conquered the Eternal City from that direction, none of whom, however, had found a defended Montecassino blocking his way.[1]

Cassino sat astride the Via Casilina which crossed the Rapido before entering the town. In the centre of the town the road turned southwards through a right angle, skirted the foot of Montecassino (Monastery Hill) with the huge stone abbey on its summit, and then curved north-westward up the Liri valley towards Piedimonte. Monastery Hill and the town were a single defence unit; the hill rammed into the town like the bows of a huge ship, its prow a ruined castle. From the castle you could drop stones down the chimneys of the houses below. South and east of the town and the Via Casilina the flat lands on either side of the Rapido were wet and had been deliberately flooded. Huge lakes of water made that approach impracticable, even to tracked vehicles. The railway entered the town on that quarter by a series of bridges and viaducts over the main stream, its tributaries and some small canals. All of them had been demolished.

A glance at the ground was enough to persuade Clark to cross the river north of the town. He would then advance under the port side of the ship, as it were, on a road paralleling the river's west bank, and enter the town from the north. He would, at the same time, climb the hills above the road and make a short right hook to occupy the summit of Monastery Hill and to cut the Via Casilina west of the town. This assignment he gave to Ryder's 34th Division.

Time was still Clark's enemy. Ryder's operation would not start until the 24th, and, unaided, it would take him a week to clear the Germans who were blocking the Via Casilina in the Cassino position. Needing to bring more pressure on the Germans facing Ryder, Clark decided to use Juin's CEF on a thrust line that threatened Cassino more directly. The CEF had been engaged on a wide hook deep in the mountains and making towards Atina. Clark now persuaded Juin to shift his thrust to the southern side of M. Cairo with objectives Terelle and then Piedimonte. The Frenchman was not keen on it for he believed firmly in the old military adage that sweat saves blood; his interpretation was to advance where the Germans did not expect him, in the higher mountains. Clark's new directive still required his units to climb mountains, to depend on mule trains for their supplies and to live on scanty rations and go short of water, as before, but also to run head-on into tenacious resistance to his attempt to outflank Cassino within sight of the town. The immediate objectives M. Belvedere and M. Terelle were bound to be tough ones, for which reason he wished Clark had ordered the 34th Division to attack on his flank or left him to pursue his original objective, Atina. He did not approve of Clark's tendency to give single divisions or corps separate and loosely coordinated tasks; the CEF and 34th Division ought to attack side by side. A key to the fighting in the mountains was observation. M. Cifalco had been within his grasp but would now be abandoned. From it the Germans would look into his rear as he attacked towards Terelle, on to the Rapido where Ryder was to attack, and be able to observe most of the American and New Zealand gun areas behind M. Trocchio.

Juin started his new operation on the 25th and Ryder on the 24th. Like the 36th, Ryder's division had had a tough time getting to the Rapido. His operation report for January, issued on about February 3 when two of his regiments seemed on the eve of a great victory up in the clouds behind the Monastery, included this passage:

> Fighting was the bitterest met to date; casualties from all causes were high; replacements were slow in arriving and were inadequate in number. Nevertheless, with 33 days of front line duty behind them, 28 of which had been spent in sanguinary conflict, the period ended with the 135th Infantry attacking through the 168th Infantry to capture the high ridge which dominated the valley and barred further progress to the northwest.

The 34th Division's operations staff had not exaggerated their experience in January, although had they known what was in store for them in the first ten days of February they might have worded it

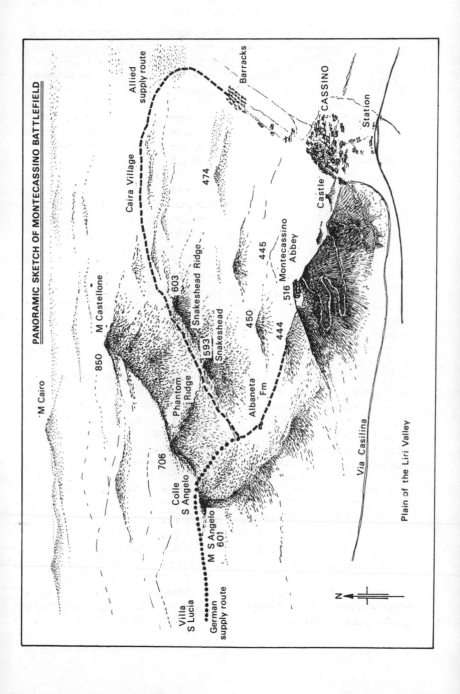

PANORAMIC SKETCH OF MONTECASSINO BATTLEFIELD

M Cairo

850 M Castellone

Allied supply route

Caira Village

Barracks

603 Snakeshead Ridge

706

Phantom Ridge

593 Snakeshead

Snakeshead

Albaneta Fm

474

445

450

444

516 Montecassino Abbey

CASSINO

Station

Castle

Colle S Angelo

Villa S Lucia

M S Angelo 601

German supply route

Via Casilina

Plain of the Liri Valley

N

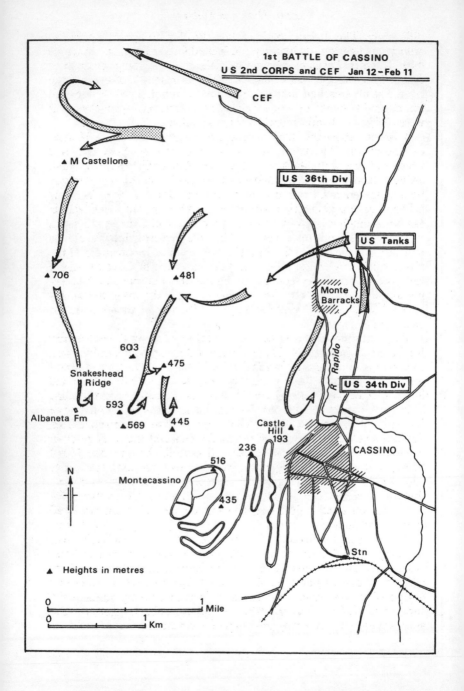

differently. The division had reached the Rapido opposite Cassino after bitter fighting. Its infantry had inched forward against tenacious 44th Infantry Division rearguards. When the leading companies reached the valley it was a quagmire. The Germans had diverted the river. Patrols splashed forward and found it running swiftly between steep, muddy banks or stone walls. The promising approaches to it were blocked by bands of barbed wire and mines.

Towering above the Rapido was the formidable bulk of the Montecassino massif. The Colle Maiola spur rose steeply above the road which was one of the divisional objectives. Astride the road an Italian artillery depot at M. Villa, called "the Barracks", seemed to be strongly held by the enemy. From it a re-entrant, or "draw" as the US Army called it, ran up to the high ground. A northern spur of Colle Maiola ran into a much larger valley in which the village of Caira guarded the twisting road leading up to Terelle. The valley led on up into the clouds to M. Castellone, one of the 34th Division's probable objectives. If the direct route to Cassino above the Barracks were blocked the Caira valley would offer a back door to Montecassino. Detached and hovering above everything and only visible on clear days was the snow-covered mass of M. Cairo, 5,500 feet. It, too, was a vantage point for observant German eyes.

The Barracks was the first objective of the assaulting 133rd Infantry Regiment on January 24. Having taken it the regiment would attack southwards into Cassino. Behind it the 168th would cross and attack into the hills. But the mud near the river, even more mines than had been expected, fierce small-arms fire and heavy mortaring and shelling brought the attack to a halt on the near bank. In the early morning of January 25 Ryder shifted the attack further north to avoid the fire from the Barracks. Attacking with three battalions abreast and every gun that could bear pounding the Barracks and the hills behind, the 133rd hacked out a shallow bridgehead. But they had not done enough to allow the 168th Infantry to pass through them and had temporarily lost the will to move forward themselves under the German fire. The battalions remained in their wet and shallow holes being hammered all through the 26th.

For the operation to succeed, it was essential to seize a bridgehead of sufficient depth that enemy anti-tank guns could not dominate the river crossings. If tanks could cross into the bridgehead they might be able to eliminate the strongpoints holding up the 133rd by direct fire, but it was not possible. The valley bottom was so soft that twenty tanks of the supporting 756th Tank Battalion were so badly bogged on the approaches to the river they could not be recovered until the battle was over, and routes by-passing the boggy ground were covered by German anti-tank guns.

After a company of the 135th, the remaining regiment in the 34th Division, crossed on the left of the 133rd and was pinned by fire, Keyes pressed Ryder to commit the 168th, as Clark was in turn pressing him to hurry and get armour moving through Cassino. Clark, bad as the going was, still believed that it was possible to launch armour up the Liri valley, and the Via Casilina through Cassino was the bottleneck that he was determined to clear. Consequently the 168th was ordered to cross the Rapido on the right of the 133rd. With six companies of engineers building tracks four tanks at last were able to join the forward infantry on the 27th and help them carve out a shallow bridgehead. Although all were knocked out by the early afternoon, and others were prevented by the collapse of the tracks leading to the river from crossing, the infantry made progress alone. Their principal objectives were a grassy hill above the barracks called Point 213 and a knoll nearer Caira village, Point 56. With these captured, they might attack the barracks and then advance down the road to Cassino and in the other direction to Caira.

That night of the 27th a company reached the top of Point 213 and occupied it. And then in one of those moments of stress caused by fatigue and isolation its commander lost his nerve. He ordered his men down again. A panic started and soon two other companies retired. The regimental commander then decided to withdraw his remaining companies which had been isolated.

The French had made progress on the right of the 34th Division by this time. Attacking on January 25 they took the Colle Grosso. By the end of the 26th they were on Belvedere above the top bend of the hairpin road to Terelle. They could not reach M. Abate, from which they would have overlooked Terelle, until the Americans had made some progress, but from Belvedere they were able to harass the German positions in Caira village.

With the German defence on his right so loosened by the French, Ryder recommitted his 168th Infantry further north to attack across the lower ground and take Hills 213 and 56. On January 29 his tanks found a way across the river. Their appearance on the far bank proved decisive by the afternoon, although the night was far advanced before the two objectives fell. That night also, the 142nd, brought over from the 36th Division to reinforce Ryder and provide a link with the French, started working across the slopes behind Caira and below Belvedere in the direction of M. Castellone. On January 30 Caira fell to a platoon of infantry and tanks of the 168th.

With the 133rd still held up by the Barracks and unable, for the time being, to advance on Cassino, Ryder's next move was to commit the 135th and 142nd through the breach at Caira to exploit into the mountains between Monastery Hill and Castellone. The clouds which commonly descend from M. Cairo enveloped the advance of both regiments. The 135th occupied much of the Colle Maiola and the first and highest ring contour of the Castellone feature, while the 142nd reached the Mass Manna feature, only a kilometre from Terelle. Both objectives were seized on February 1 almost unopposed. In the narrow passage between the Rapido and the hills the 133rd attacked and cleared the Barracks after bitter fighting on the 1st and 2nd but when tanks and infantry tried to exploit towards Cassino they were halted by anti-tank and machine-gun fire.

While the 135th was continuing its thrust towards the back door of the Cassino defences and the 133rd was held up at the front, von Mackensen was beginning his counter-stroke against the British 1st Division at Campoleone. Churchill, watching "his" force at Anzio with disgust which was now turning into apprehension, urged Alexander and Clark to keep attacking the Germans at Cassino. "We have a great need to keep continually engaging them, and even a battle of attrition is better than standing by and watching the Russians fight."

The French and the 34th were certainly doing all that could be expected of them and it had been touch and go for the Germans. January 26 in particular had been a day of crisis for them. The 132nd Grenadier Regiment of the 44th Division had halted the Americans in the marshes opposite M. Villa, but the two battalions of the 191st Grenadiers from the 71st Division which lost Belvedere and the entrance to the Secco valley leading to Belmonte had been hard hit. A small number of French tanks tried to break through to Belmonte but were stopped by artillery fire. HQ 14th Panzer Corps was convinced that an armoured formation was working with the French. The 2nd/191st and some engineers, held in reserve near Terelle, went forward to retake Belvedere but failed. To Schmidt von Altendstadt, the new Chief of Staff of 14th Panzer Corps, it appeared that the French would take Terelle within hours, thus "causing the Cassino block to cave in from the north".

Von Altenstadt combed the southern front for reserves. But the 10th Corps was attacking again and on the 27th it forced the redoubtable 29th Panzer Grenadiers off M. Natale and M. Rotondo. Colle Ceracoli was also under attack in the 15th Panzer Grenadiers' sector. Consequently, only two of the battalions of the third regiment of the 44th Division, the 134th, could be spared to move north into corps reserve in the Belmonte area. The 1st/134th went into action there on the evening of the 26th, but was halted by artillery fire. The 3rd/134th reinforced two battalions of the 191st and one of the 131st which was sealing off the French salient. The 94th Division's reconnaissance battalion was sent to the Atina area from the south.

The pattern for German tactics at Cassino was already taking shape. Kesselring personally controlled the use of reserves because he had to balance the needs of the Fourteenth Army at Anzio with those of the Tenth at Cassino. He milked divisions elsewhere, unit by unit, to reinforce the two threatened sectors. As a result the Germans held the front with small *Kampfgruppen* not divisions, but as they fought against single Allied divisions, whose activities were not closely coordinated or reinforced and consequently grew weaker by the day, these piecemeal defence methods into which they were forced by necessity became a virtue. They also confused the Allies' Intelligence staffs which found, for example, regiments of the 3rd, 29th and 90th Panzer Grenadiers at both Anzio and Cassino.[2]

On the 27th, the 15th Panzer Grenadier Division had to extend its left boundary to cover the positions vacated by the 134th Grenadiers and the Germans still expected an attack on Cassino town from the east. Kesselring visited the 44th Division and 14th Corps on that day and calmly announced that the Allies were not strong enough to break through north of Cassino. He had been encouraged in this belief when the 2nd/191st chased the French off M. Abate on which they had gained a foothold, and the 1st and 3rd/134th retook the top of the road from Caira to Terelle. Caira itself was still firmly held. It looked to both the Tenth Army and Army Group headquarters that the French had been brought to a standstill, for which von Vietinghoff was "deeply thankful".

The man responsible for the whole German front from the sea to the watershed of the Apennines was Frido von Senger, a gentle hero, far from the Hollywood stereotype of a stiff, monocled, arrogant German general. He had neither the charisma of Rommel nor the forceful personality of the two men who were to defend Cassino against all comers: Ernst-Guenther Baade, commander of the 90th Panzer Grenadiers,* and Richard Heidrich of the 1st Parachute Division. He

---

* The 90th Panzer Grenadier Division was the resurrected "90th Light", lost in Tunisia and the renowned and respected opponent of the Eighth Army in the Desert War. It had been the first of the Afrika Korps divisions to arrive in 1941 when it was called the 5th Light Division.

was a man of intellect, a Rhodes Scholar at the outbreak of the First World War, as his son was to be after the conclusion of the Second.

> His face once seen was not easily forgotten: his high forehead, under black hair receding at 53, bisected by a prominent vein, and his great beak of a nose between deep-sunken dark eyes, gave him in profile the look of a hawk. In repose his face was austere, but when he smiled, as he often did, the effect was attractive; and his hands with their long fingers, with which he gestured eloquently, were those of a pianist. His daughter remembered especially the way her father carried his trim, athletic frame: "He was quite different from the Prussian image. You would have to see him move, with that gentle grace, not at all stiff – more French really than Prussian."[3]

Von Senger was a Bavarian, a career soldier, who had not been involved politically on behalf of or against the Nazi Party, although he was unsympathetic towards it. By 1940 he was commanding a motor brigade in the great armoured advance across northern France in May. After France was defeated in June von Senger stayed on to enjoy two years in association with the rural aristocracy of France, which he found similar to his own in its sympathies, and then became chief liaison officer to the Franco-Italian Armistice Commission in Turin. There, too, he found himself in an environment that he enjoyed and understood. In 1942, though, he was plunged into the Russian slaughter-house when the division that he commanded was one that attempted to rescue von Paulus at Stalingrad in the winter of 1942–3. Returning to the west he was assigned to evacuating the German troops, in particular the 90th Panzer Grenadiers, from Corsica. In October he took command of the 14th Panzer Corps in the Bernhard Line. After Stalingrad he knew that his country would be defeated and he prayed that its leaders would make peace. In the meantime he fought on from his headquarters in Roccasecca (where, as he noted, being a devout Catholic, Saint Thomas Aquinas was born) juggling his units and encouraging them with his visits, usually on foot for their positions were often hundreds of feet up a mountain.[4]

Von Senger was never given to premature optimism and reminded his superiors of the casualties his units had suffered from artillery fire. In future daylight counter-attacks might have to be replaced by night raids. The worst was yet to come, he thought. And he ordered the 2nd/361st Panzer Grenadiers of the 90th Division from the Garigliano front across to Arce, twelve miles up the Liri valley, and sent the 2nd/134th, the last reserve behind the 15th Panzer Grenadiers, to M.

Castellone. An Ersatz (field replacement-holding) battalion* and a company of German Air Force ground troops were hurried to the M. Abate area. Kesselring himself could only offer to send an element of the 90th Division fighting at Anzio, KG von Behr, to Cassino "within the next few days".

It was as well that von Senger acted, for on the 29th the French were again attacking at M. Abate and in the Belmonte valley and were threatening to take Terelle by an advance up the road. He took the 3rd/131st out of the line south of Cassino and sent it to M. Castellone, and he extended the front of the 5th Mountain, then in the central Apennines, on whom the pressure had been eased, to include the Belmonte valley.

At a conference at his headquarters that day von Senger told General F. Wentzell, von Vietinghoff's chief of staff, that he believed that the Terelle thrust was the most dangerous. Even though the Allies seemed to be employing no more than two French regiments there, and a third US one was reported to be coming forward, the artillery concentrations were so heavy that he believed they realised its importance. The British in the south were systematically destroying the units of the 94th Infantry and 29th Panzer Grenadiers, and although they were no longer believed to be intending an operation "in the grand style", they were preventing him from pulling out any more units of the 90th and relieving the 211th/71st for use in the Castellone sector. Von Senger was losing men at the rate of a battalion a day in the north and the 29th Panzer Grenadiers' casualties for the period 21–31 January were even heavier.

Wentzell clarified a number of points about the future. The Cassino block had to be held until the Anzio bridgehead had been eliminated by the Fourteenth Army. When that was done, he could expect to be reinforced and he might take the offensive. On the other hand, if von Mackensen failed, a new situation would arise. Von Senger cited the inadequacies of the Hitler switch line through Piedimonte and declared that the Gustav Line was more economical in man-power. If a withdrawal became necessary, he thought that the 14th Corps ought to go right back to the area of the Alban Hills, but Wentzell told him that no withdrawal from Cassino was contemplated at the moment. Von Senger would have to take risks in other sectors to find the men to hold it.

Once the Germans had made up their minds to hold the Cassino block at all costs, they thinned out their line elsewhere even more

---

* Ersatz Battallionen were frequently used to defend the line in an emergency.

ruthlessly. On the 31st, the 3rd Battalion of the 3rd Parachute Regiment was ordered south from the Adriatic and a battalion from the 200th and another from the 361st Panzer Grenadiers arrived, both from the 90th Division. Their division commander, General Baade, was appointed to command the Cassino sector on the same day.

January 30 had been another bad day at Caira village and along the Rapido. A large force of American tanks, having forced their way over the river the day before, shot up the bunkers of the 1st/132nd Grenadiers, one by one, forcing the survivors up on to the Colle Maiola behind. Thirty-five men of the 191st, all that were left, were pushed off M. Abate by the French that night. On their right the 2nd/134th, with only thirty men remaining, withdrew towards Terelle. The remnants of the men from Caira, together with the 2nd/132nd and the newly arrived 2nd/361st Panzer Grenadiers, began to prepare a makeshift switch line between M. Castellone and Villa S. Lucia on the 31st. The three battalions of the 131st Grenadiers moved to cover the road to Terelle on either side of Massa Manna. But by the time they got there the US 142nd Regiment had forced the handful of defenders from the 134th back into Terelle. (The 142nd had been detached from the 36th Division to reinforce Ryder. On February 6–7 the rest of the division was relieved on the Rapido by the New Zealanders and joined in the battle on the heights.)

The 142nd were slow to follow up and there was time for the 1st/8th Panzer Grenadier Regiment of the 3rd Division to arrive at Terelle on February from the 5th Mountain Division's zone on the left. An alpine battalion from the 76th Corps also started on its way from the Adriatic. But the 14th Corps was now sure that the French were exhausted and that the Americans intended to switch the main thrust southward round the back of the Monastery towards Villa S. Lucia.

The new danger sector was between Castellone and Colle Maiola. Castellone itself was reported to have been occupied by two American companies in the mist on February 1. A counter-attack by the 15th Panzer Grenadiers' engineer battalion failed to dislodge them, but two companies of the 2nd/361st Panzer Grenadiers prevented the 135th Infantry from advancing over the col towards M. Caira. The rest of the battalion blocked the Americans on Colle Maiola.

Baade arrived on February 1 and at once began to reorganise the Cassino defences. A flamboyant, stormy figure, he demanded fresh troops, and made them a condition for stabilising the front. As a start, the 3rd Parachute Battalion arrived to throw the Americans off Castellone, which Baade considered his main task. His own 1st/361st Panzer Grenadiers were pulled out from the Garigliano front and anti-tank, field artillery and engineer battalions from the 94th. The 3rd/8th Panzer Grenadiers followed their 1st Battalion from the 5th Mountain's front.

The activities of the 34th Division on February 2, however, gave Baade no time to mount a counter-attack and he found that he had to use the parachutists to plug holes in his front. Von Senger was not much concerned at the US 133rd Regiment's attack in the valley from M. Villa towards Cassino town, but he was determined to reinforce behind the Monastery until the massif was safe. He told Baade that he was to have another parachute battalion from the Adriatic and even the division's machine-gun battalion from Anzio. The 2nd/200th Panzer Grenadiers of his own division would reach him on February 4. The wisdom of thinning out opposite the 10th Corps was confirmed when it was learned on the evening of February 2 that the 56th Infantry Division had left the 10th Corps for Anzio.

By the evening of February 2 the US 2nd/135th Infantry had occupied most of the area of gullies and spurs called Colle Maiola. They had shelled the 2nd/132nd Grenadiers until they were "pulverised" and the 2nd/361st Panzer Grenadiers until they "melted like butter in the sun". Only thirty-two men survived the ordeal and they scratched some shelter in the area of Point 593, hoping to hold out until the 3rd Parachute arrived to stop the rot. Battalions caught in the open on those rocky hillsides were quickly destroyed. If the Americans could maintain their momentum it seemed that they must sweep Baade's men off the south-western edge of the Cassino massif.

But during the night the parachutists counter-attacked from the area of Point 593, and although they lost the Point 475–Point 476 spur after recapturing it, they retained the ridge that included Points 450 and 445 opposite it, which was separated only by a deep gully from the Monastery. On Castellone the US 3rd/135th pushed on to Point 706, while two battalions of the 142nd held the higher feature behind them against attacks from the north. The 1st/361st Panzer Grenadiers arrived to take over Point 593 and the parachutists were moved back to the Albaneta area as a reserve behind the 1st Alpine Battalion, who now faced the US 3rd/135th Infantry. The fighting had already reduced the parachutists to 130 men.

When the Parachute Machine Gun Battalion and the 1st Parachute were on the way to Cassino, von Vietinghoff decided that the whole of the Parachute Division should be brought in by degrees from the Adriatic and that Baade's 90th Division should replace them there. The shattered 2nd/361st was the first to be pulled out. But instead of going to the Adriatic it found itself helping to relieve units of the 44th

Division Group so that they could be reorganised. The other battalions of the 361st Panzer Grenadiers suffered the same fate. By February 4 the nine battalions of the 44th, two of the 8th Panzer Grenadier Regiment and an alpine company numbered less than 1,500 men.

February 4 and 5 were wet and stormy days on which a lull in American activity seemed to indicate that they were at last tiring. Baade's position, on the other hand, was improving. The 1st Parachute Division celebrated its arrival by pushing the 3rd/135th Infantry off Point 706, but lost it soon after to a counter-attack. In what was to be called the Snakeshead Ridge area, the German positions along the ridge containing Points 445 and 450 and around Point 593 began to harden. The 1st/200th Panzer Grenadiers, part of the Behr group from Anzio, reached Roccasecca and, soon after, went into reserve behind the Colle S. Angelo. Some of the parachute machine-gunners took up positions near the Monastery and others joined the hard-pressed 211th Grenadiers in the northern outskirts of Cassino town, where they were located on the mountainside near Point 175, at Point 165 and on Castle Hill.

The US 133rd Infantry took up the running on the 5th. Having previously reached the outlying houses of the town on the road from M. Villa, they sliced through the machine-gunners on Point 175 and briefly occupied Castle Hill. The Castle, separated by a deep gully from Point 175, was to be a tactical position of great importance in the struggle ahead, but the Americans were not strong enough to hold it.

The lull on top of the hill was required to allow the US 168th Infantry to relieve the 135th opposite the Point 450–445 ridge, six or seven hundred yards from the Monastery itself. The 135th would then concentrate on the thrust from Snakeshead to Point 593 and Albaneta after its 3rd Battalion had been pulled off the Castellone ridge. The weak 141st and 143rd had been relieved by the 5th Brigade of the New Zealand Division on the night of February 5 and would reinforce the 142nd. The 36th Division would then be concentrated in the area from Castellone to Massa Manna.

The remoteness of the battlefield up in the clouds from staff and commanders must be stressed for, as we shall see, it was to cause serious errors of judgment, and even ignorance of the exact location of the front-line troops. Battalions took three hours to climb to the forward positions and several days to become oriented to a new type of fighting and new terrain. From their caravans miles away on the other side of the Rapido, the divisional and corps staffs could easily lose touch with the conditions of battalions which had been "up there" a week or more. They knew, as a staff statistic, that the turn-round time of a mule column was about fourteen hours, but not, perhaps, what proportion of the food, blankets, batteries and ammunition was lost on the hillside on the way up, and what the loss entailed for attacking battalions. The commanders, daunted by the length of the journey on foot and the time it took, did not often visit battalions and regiments. In consequence, they were inclined to plan operations from the map without properly grasping the importance of particular features or the peculiar nature of the terrain. Only a close and detailed examination on the ground could reveal that the tangle of features identified by spot-heights constituted a single tactical system, articulated by the skilled German tacticians into a web of strongpoints supported by mutual cross-fire and local counter-attack. It was useless to try to nibble at it: only a strong simultaneous attack could succeed. This is the key to understanding the whole battle on the heights.

Loss of communication with the fighting units led rear staffs to look at the short distance on the ground which separated their men from the edge of the Montecassino massif and to assume that they were as close to victory. Yet their divisions were growing weaker while Baade's original battalions, tired and almost decimated too, were being continually reinforced by fresh units. The US Army at this time was short of reserves in Italy and was traditionally reluctant to break up organisations in one part of the front to provide fresh battalions in another as the Germans had done. The employment of British troops from the 46th Division was a possibility, although it raised many administrative problems and the touchy question of the employment of troops of one nationality under the divisional command of another. But when all is said, there is no indication that Keyes or Ryder was prepared to lay down the torch or to accept help from outside the corps to carry it further. By the time they did so, it was too late.

The reinforcement by the 168th Infantry did little to relieve the plight of the men of the 34th Division, worn out by lack of hot food, exposure to damp and extreme cold and unceasing bombardment. Attacks were repeatedly arranged and then postponed because the infantry were physically incapable of movement or so demoralised that they refused to leave their fox-holes and sangars. The full story of that last week of hell behind the Monastery has never been told. All coherence and direction of the battle was lost. Operational reports written at divisional HQ record attacks that may never have been launched although planned, and certainly placed the forward troops in locations that had been lost to the enemy. The staff in the valley below did not recognise, or would not admit what the battalion officers knew full well, that their men had reached the absolute limit of their endurance. The fact was that the regimental commanders had to order officers to man the police posts behind the front line to turn back "stragglers" – deserters – who joined the steady flow of walking wounded and litter-bearers moving to the rear.*

It does not seem that attacks along M. Castellone were ever pressed to the col connecting it with the Colle S. Angelo feature. But the 142nd almost reached Albaneta on the 11th and only the intervention of Oberst Schulz, who committed a platoon of engineers until he could organise a force from his 200th Panzer Grenadier Regiment from behind Points 505 and 575, saved the position. Meanwhile, the terrifying *Nebelwerfers* from the 71st Regiment caught a company of the 142nd on the forward slopes of Phantom Ridge and on the open ground in front of the buildings called Albaneta. Few of them returned.

Castellone was a sinister feature – scrubby trees and bushes grew on the three ring contours, but elsewhere there was little shelter. Daylight movement brought immediate retribution from the artillery observers of both sides. The rocks splintered and had as much power to kill and maim as the metal of shells and bombs. Yet it was a highway to the Colle S. Angelo ridge, and if sufficient strength could have been found it provided a route straight to the rear of the German positions.

Baade recognised the threat and had been waiting to mount a two-pronged counter-attack, operation MICHAEL, since February 5. The left thrust was to cut through to Terelle and bring the reverse slopes of Snakeshead and Maiola under direct fire. The right was to retake Snakeshead and roll up the Point 475 ridge from the north. Early in the morning of the 12th, Baade at last had a battalion of the 200th Panzer Grenadiers ready for the left thrust, but he had to forego the other. The Grenadiers, it seems, got right to the end of the ridge, meeting little opposition, but they were so heavily shelled all the way that the battalion lost 8 officers and 160 men and had to be pulled back. From then until May, when the Poles used this route with initial failure and final success, Castellone saw no important fighting.

More bitter and continuous was the fighting for the positions immediately behind the Monastery. The German defences on Points 569, 593, 450–445, Monastery Hill, and 444 were arranged round the rim of a bowl. When one position was lost it could be counter-attacked from another point on the rim. The strongpoints were not reinforced

---

* The American historians often use the term "stragglers" for men who deliberately leave the ranks to escape from the battlefield. The British term is "deserter", a small but important distinction, as in British usage a straggler is a man separated involuntarily from his unit, e.g., in a night attack, or when a column is bombed.

by concrete or panther turrets, as were the ones in the town, but caves in Monastery Hill, right under the walls of the Monastery itself and behind Point 593 provided shelter for reserves and aid posts.* Anti-personnel mines were used effectively, particularly in front of the Point 450–445 ridge. The defenders learned from experience to cover every dangerous approach with machine-gun fire. Gradually, they strengthened their sangars, as the number of their dead and wounded mounted from incessant mortar and artillery fire and strafing fighter-bombers, of which they complained bitterly. But they did not measure their casualties in hundreds like the attackers. It is remarkable that although "the head" of Snakeshead Ridge was higher than Point 593 by a few feet, and the other American firm bases were higher than Point 450, the German defences were hidden on the reverse slopes. In contrast the forward American positions were exposed. The Americans could take only two routes to the German positions. They could move along the narrow and closely observed ridge of Snakeshead to Point 593, the highest point on the rim, and by Points 569, 476 and 444 to the Monastery; or from the 475–474 ridge, across the grain of the country to Points 450–445, and from there across a deep gully to the Monastery.

The 135th won and lost the summit of Point 593 several times between February 6 and 9 and ultimately American sangars were built within forty yards of the Germans on the top. So close were the two sides that it was not possible to shell Point 593 with safety. In the spring of 1944 green shrubs grew among the boulders and screes – an oasis in a sea of death and brown destruction.

The 168th launched three great attacks by the other route to the Monastery. They held Point 450–445 only briefly and had to be content with some uncomfortable platoon positions in the gully below it. One of their attacks flowed over Point 445 and down to the foot of Point 516, the hill on which the Monastery stood. A patrol winkled some prisoners out of the caves up on the road but fierce machine-gun fire from Points 444 and 476 in the rear, as well as from further along Monastery Hill, prevented them from mounting a heavy attack on that line of approach.

By the end of the 9th, both sides were already exhausted. Rain and snow storms on the 10th added to the misery of the men. In one last effort Ryder used the 141st and 142nd in an attempt to clear Point 593 and Albaneta, but in vain. By the evening of the 11th the 2nd Corps had

---

* Both sides built *sangars* (Urdu), or breastworks of loose stones where the ground was too rocky to dig.

to admit that it could do no more. The 135th, with rifle companies down to an average of thirty, were still losing men from shells and sickness even in reserve. The 168th companies may have averaged sixty. The 36th Division had started the battle in a weak state. By the end its battalions were little more than a hundred strong. Down in the Rapido valley, the 133rd Regiment had been attacking the 211th Grenadier Regiment incessantly. It, too, was exhausted.

But statistics are inadequate to describe the condition of these divisions. Shells are not respecters of individuals. The brave men and the key men seem to receive more than their share of wounds and death; companies are demoralised by the removal of experienced and trusted officers and NCOs. Battalions are unbalanced when companies have to amalgamate because of casualties. They will recover with rest and reinforcement, but only if an experienced nucleus has survived and with it the sense of having fought stoutly and effectively.

Frightful though their casualties were, the 34th did leave the hill with honour. Fred Majdalany, a company commander in the British 78th Infantry Division which fought at Cassino later, wrote this of them:

> The performance of the 34th Division at Cassino must rank with the finest feats of arms carried out by any soldiers during the war. When at last they were relieved by the 4th Indian Division fifty of those few who had held on to the last were too numbed with cold and exhaustion to move. They could still man their positions but they could not move out of them unaided. They were carried out on stretchers.[5]

A few days later, the National Guard Division we saw at Salerno, the 45th, was earning the grudging respect of the Germans at Anzio for its stubborn defence of the Via Anziate between Aprilia and the Lateral Road at Anzio. There it was the Germans who were massacred, stopped by the same excellent artillery which had held them on the Sele in September 1943.

11

THE TORCH IS THROWN

On the evening of February 11 "Al" Gruenther, Clark's chief of staff, phoned Freyberg and told him: "The torch is thrown to you." Alexander and Clark had agreed on the 8th that if the 2nd Corps had not broken the Cassino position by the end of the 11th the New Zealand Corps would take over the offensive at dusk on the 12th and complete the task. Gruenther had just heard from the 2nd Corps that its final effort had failed and Freyberg was ready with a plan dated February 9th. (For reasons that seemed good at the time a British corps HQ was not introduced into the battle, nor were the reinforcing divisions placed directly under Keyes. Freyberg was ordered to form a corps HQ, *ad hoc* and untrained, to command the 2nd New Zealand and 4th Indian Divisions responsible to HQ Fifth Army. It was a bad arrangement and led to the complex of errors in formation and decision that are associated with the Battles of Cassino.)

The reader may compare the action set in motion to passing a baton in a relay race: or, in reality, he may visualise incoming teams of well-fed and rested officers receiving information from exhausted incumbents and the silent files of their men slipping into slit trenches in the dead of night, taking over marked maps, target lists, code-words and the rest. Fresh muscle and full ranks joining the fray – one good heave and over she goes! But it was not to be like that at all. Neither Freyberg nor his corps staff expected that their takeover would be straightforward.

Put simply, Freyberg's orders were to place the 4th Indian Division behind the positions occupied by the 34th and 36th Divisions in the Snakeshead and M. Castellone areas and carry on the attack that had stalled so close to its goal. At that moment the 4th Division's leading brigade, the 7th, was in position around Caira village, but the others were still east of the Rapido. As soon as possible the Indians were to renew the attack westward beyond Castellone to cut the Via Casilina

176

below Villa S. Lucia, and attacking from Snakeshead, seize Monastery Hill and descend its slopes to cut the road on the western outskirts of Cassino. The New Zealand Division was to cross the flooded fields to the Rapido, repair the railway bridges and causeways over its tributaries and seize the railway station on the south side of the town. New Zealand tanks and more New Zealand infantry would then clear the town and break out of it into the Liri valley. CC"B" of the US 1st Armored Division would join the advance and, possibly, the British 78th Infantry Division from the Eighth Army, due to come under Freyberg's command on about February 17. The 133rd Infantry of the 34th Division would hold the enemy in front of its present positions in the northern outskirts of the town.

This was the latest of several plans for using Freyberg's divisions. Alexander had briefed Freyberg as early as the first week in January, as soon as he realised that Clark would need reinforcement, and Freyberg had taken pains to visit every part of the front before his division crossed the Apennines to come under Clark's command as early as the 20th. The first assignment given the division was to exploit the 36th Division's crossing of the Rapido at S. Angelo. After that had failed it was warned to be ready to pass through the 34th Division at Cassino. When the 133rd Infantry was held up in the northern outskirts of the town while the rest of the division were making progress, the 5th New Zealand Brigade replaced the battered 141st and 143rd Infantry on the Rapido – one Maori company taking over from two battalions of the 143rd – to allow the Americans to join the rest of the 36th Division in the mountains. On February 4 Freyberg was planning to use the 4th Indian Division in a wide movement beyond Castellone in conjunction with the French while his 6th Brigade went over M. Maiola to attack through the Americans. It is strange that Clark made no use of the 2nd New Zealand Division as soon as it was available, for at that moment the attack by the US 2nd Corps was close to success. (Indeed, give or take a few hundred yards its forward localities were to be the jump-off line for the Second, Third and Fourth Battles of Cassino.) On February 8, when the 4th Indian Division had completed its move from the Eighth Army and was assembled under Freyberg's command, he made a fresh plan. The New Zealanders were to clear Cassino town, attacking through the positions held by the US 133rd Infantry, while the Indians captured the Castle and supported the attack into the town. This was cancelled on the 9th, when Alexander weakly agreed that Keyes should be given one more chance to capture the Monastery unaided. By the evening of the 11th he had failed completely, and Gruenther made his dramatic telephone call to Freyberg.

177

The records of this sequence of plans made and discarded reveal that previous histories are in error when they suggest that it was the *Second* Battle of Cassino for which the New Zealand Corps was formed, and that Clark could not have employed the New Zealand Division earlier. Why did he not do so? The real reason was Clark's objection to the progressive dilution of the Fifth Army by "foreign" divisions. Both Clark and Keyes understood that the reinforcement by Freyberg's corps was necessary, but felt its entry into "their" battle was an evil that should be postponed. New Zealand reconnaissance parties, which had insinuated guns and thousands of vehicles into crowded and muddy fields earmarked for Americans, in some cases without permission, were resented as the vanguard of the much vaunted Eighth Army come to conquer where they had failed. Keyes had no intention of playing second fiddle to the newcomers or even fighting alongside them. The Americans were also apprehensive that they would be expected to give the New Zealanders special privileges – as the British did. Freyberg, who had fought in the Mexican Civil War and had commanded a brigade in operations over a quarter of a century before, was a formidable figure. Clark warned Keyes that he was virtually an independent commander who had to be handled with kid gloves. Clark himself greeted Freyberg cordially and Gruenther was charming and helpful as usual, smoothing out the numerous difficulties that arose when a strange corps from a foreign army took over in his area. But behind the façade of "dear and darling" there lurked the danger that relations could deteriorate into "snap and snarling" unless both sides compromised when there were disagreements.

Alexander compromised with Clark and Keyes on February 8 in granting the 2nd Corps more time, although he knew that its divisions were very tired. General Lemnitzer, Alexander's American deputy chief of staff, told Alexander, who had sent him to find out the facts, that the Americans were almost mutinous.[1] Ryder denied it and said that they were eager to continue. As a result, when the torch did pass to Freyberg on the 11th it was already extinguished.[2] Blumensen suggests that as Alexander wanted to keep the New Zealand Corps to exploit, it was he who kept them back on the 8th. That is not the case. On the 12th, as we shall see, he told Freyberg not to attack until he was ready and that he intended him only to gain a bridgehead and not to exploit towards Anzio as well. It was Clark who was still impatient, he who wanted to break the Rapido front at once and he who kept the New Zealand Corps out of the battle on the 8th because he thought that their participation in the battle would slow it up.[3] However, Alexander could and should have imposed his will on Clark and his failure to do so was a fatal error. No better example could be found of the disadvantages of coalition warfare which handicapped the Fifth Army in Italy time and again. Had the 4th Indian Division and the 6th New Zealand Brigade been committed as intended on February 9, the battle for Cassino could have been won then and there. Instead, an exhausted 2nd Corps held on too long and a hiatus occurred while ally relieved ally on difficult ground far from any roads. The momentum was lost and the new brooms resorted to the bombing and destruction of the Benedictine Monastery above the town in a vain attempt to regain it. To describe the events that led to that sad event as a continuous chain of cause and effect would be inapt: rather, it was a matrix of national pride, of which Clark's stiff-necked attitude to the British, and the concern with the danger to the 6th Corps at Anzio causing him to leave the Cassino front to Keyes and Gruenther, are the axes.

Freyberg's two battles for Cassino were failures, or at least partial failures; stages in the long process of breaking the Gustav Line. They would have attracted little attention had heavy bombers not been used to destroy the Monastery. The enormity of the act, however, and the accusation that Freyberg was to blame, that it achieved nothing, combining stupidity with vandalism, offended New Zealand pride.

In 1950, before the Korean War claimed his services, Clark published *Calculated Risk*, an account of his career until he entered Austria in 1945. Lord Freyberg, as he had become, was then the Constable of Windsor Castle. Major-General Sir Howard Kippenberger, one of the most distinguished New Zealand officers, and a highly intelligent and experienced combat officer who had commanded the 2nd New Zealand Division at Cassino while Freyberg acted as a corps commander, had been appointed Editor-in-Chief of the New Zealand official history. Newspaper reports of Clark's remarks at a press conference to launch his book reached Kippenberger in Wellington. It appeared that Clark had blamed Freyberg for the destruction of the Monastery. He had been against it, himself, he said, but Alexander had taken Freyberg's side and he had had to give way. Freyberg was asked by Kippenberger to give Neville Phillips, author of the volume on the Italian campaign, the details of his part in the decision but he declined to be involved in what he considered a political issue. His conscience was clear, he said. Phillips should try to place the events in context and tell a straightforward story from the documents available in the archives. However, Freyberg was persuaded to talk to Fred Majdalany who was writing *Cassino, Portrait of a Battle*, and in 1957, the year Phillips' volume appeared, Majdalany's well-researched but controversial account of the battle and of the circumstances in which the

Monastery was bombed was published. He had this to say of the passages that Clark wrote about his own opposition to the bombing:

> ... Clark, who gave the order for the bombing, disclaims responsibility for the decision. If he had confined himself to a military reappraisal of the bombing, there could have been no objection to his being as outspoken as he liked. In fact he ignores the special circumstances, conditions, and pressures prevailing at the time. He ignores the important psychological impact of the Monastery. He ignores the fact that two Commonwealth divisions were now being required to tackle a task that had just knocked the heart out of two American divisions. He makes little attempt to recreate the context in which the difficult decision had to be taken. He merely devotes himself to an angry apologia – disclaiming responsibility for an order which he himself gave, and blaming it on his subordinate commander, General Freyberg.[4]

In fact, Majdalany was wrong in saying that Clark gave the order. Clark, sensitive to the political risk in attacking such a target, passed the responsibility to Alexander who decided that, if Freyberg felt it necessary, he would agree. Clark was aware that if he authorised the bombing on the grounds that the Monastery was a military objective, and yet the ground attack failed, he would be called a vandal. On the other hand, were he to refuse Freyberg's request and the ground attack failed bloodily, he would be blamed for the loss of lives. Clark had to make the kind of decision for which, it has been justly said, army commanders are paid. He pleaded, as one reason for passing the responsibility to Alexander, a recent instruction from Eisenhower that warned commanders against doing wanton damage on the spurious grounds that it was going to save lives. For another, he said that he was unwilling to refuse a Commonwealth commander what he would certainly have refused an American. Finally, Clark pointed out that Freyberg had right of appeal over his head to the New Zealand Government if he believed that his division was going to be endangered by his orders. On these grounds he had no other option than to ask Alexander to adjudicate between himself and Freyberg.

There is no doubt that Clark was against the bombing. He asserted that the Germans were not occupying the place but that if it were bombed they could justifiably use its ruins. It was an axiom that ruins were easier to defend than standing buildings. The basis of his belief that the Germans had not occupied the Monastery was that they had given a guarantee to the Vatican that they would not, except to liaise with members of the Benedictine order. They had also undertaken not to take positions closer than 330 yards from the walls. Clark's intelligence reports on the first point were inconclusive but the evidence that the Germans had broken the second agreement was provided when prisoners were taken from a cave in the hill under the wall of the Monastery. The 34th Division reported seeing Germans firing from positions well within the 330-yard limit. Such evidence might have been confirmed by air photographs, perhaps, but the use of tunnels and caves by civilians and soldiers could not easily be distinguished, for there were many refugees sheltering near the building. Common sense, though, told the practical soldiers that their opposite numbers would not deny themselves any advantages that the hill itself offered, even if the building, useful as a hospital and rest area, was only a defence position of last resort. We know now that von Senger, himself a practical soldier, had ordered that the 330-yard limit be ignored in December and that afterwards the Germans occupied positions all round the building.[5]

At the Vatican, suggestions had been made that emissaries should be sent to inspect the ground so that the Monastery could be declared neutral by common consent, but the proposal was tacitly dropped.[6] Politicians at the Vatican, the diplomats and even members of the Benedictine order resigned themselves to their feeling that nothing could save the Monastery from serious damage once it became "an integral part of a physical feature that was not only occupied but to a high degree fortified". The question whether the Monastery itself was occupied was a red herring. We now know that it was not; at the time that was not certain. It was perverse of Clark after the war to emphasise that it was not occupied by soldiers, in which he was correct, while ignoring the tactical fact that it dominated a feature that was a legitimate objective.[7] Indeed, once the Germans had abolished the 330-yard zone – which their diplomats denied they had done – and the Allies had decided to attack the Hill, the Monastery was doomed to be destroyed by shells alone. They had started their work in January and continued it, finishing what the bombers left undone in February, until the Monastery was captured by the Polish Corps in May.

We can be sure that Clark was perfectly aware of these tactical points – except the formal abolition of the 330-yard zone of which his units had, nevertheless, given him sufficient evidence. His motives in emphasising what Majdalany called a "red herring" were ideological and political. He wanted to save the building – the Mother House of the Benedictine Order – and he was absolutely right in that. But his motives, and those of Alexander and even Freyberg, were also political. Allied civil and military leaders were susceptible to the opinion, widely expressed in the press of the time, that soldiers must not be asked to shed their blood for a building, however sacred or venerable, particularly when all the soldiers involved believed it to be defended, as was the case at Cassino. They also knew that parents of young front-line soldiers put the safety of their Bert – or Hank – before that of Saint Benedict's, or any other shrine. They were equally aware that on the other side of the hill Nazi propagandists had already made a successful exercise out of the rescue of the art and archival treasures in the building by members of the Hermann Goering Division in December. The Germans were saying that the Allies were cultural barbarians much less concerned about the European heritage than themselves.[8] If the Monastery were destroyed by American bombers, particularly if the soldiers failed to take the ground on which the ruins stood, German propagandists would effortlessly score a valuable political and moral success, on a plate. Clark wished to deny the Germans this propaganda victory which he thought was inevitable if the bombing went ahead. When all turned out as he had feared, he was resentful against Freyberg. He was still resentful in 1950, indeed, even more so when the morality of wartime bombing was no longer unquestioned, and he was prompt to blame his subordinate.

Clark's fury over the Monastery incident is quite understandable: he lost the tactical battle when Freyberg's corps did not take the Monastery and he lost the political battle when it was destroyed. Two important but unanswered questions bear on these points. The first is how it came about that a request by Freyberg for fighter-bombers, which it was within Clark's authority to grant without reference to Alexander – other than to inform him, perhaps – became a mission by 135 heavy and 87 medium and light bombers, which had to be authorised by Maitland Wilson and his chief airman, Lieutenant-General Ira Eaker, in Algiers.[9] The second bears on the failure of the ground attack. Why did the bombers strike about sixty hours before 4th Indian Division attacked the Monastery? Had the Monastery been captured immediately after the bombing on February 15 its destruction might have been excused even if subsequently it had been found to have been unoccupied by German troops. The act appeared wicked as well as inept because the ground attack failed and the means used were disproportionate and inappropriate to the end desired, for the bombers were inaccurate. Proportionality, the principle on which Eisenhower had based his instruction about wanton damage in December, was ignored. The same criticism may be applied to the destruction of the town of Cassino on March 15.

The reader may have had his fill of fighting after following the fortunes of the US 2nd Corps in the first battle of Cassino that died away on February 11. It will therefore be enough to say that in the two operations that comprised the second and third battles the New Zealand Corps succeeded by the end of March in adding a small bridgehead in the town (too small to provide a springboard for an advance into the Liri valley). The first of these was called AVENGER and opened with the bombing of the Monastery on February 15. The second, DICKENS, exactly a month later, opened with the destruction of what remained of Cassino town. Instead of offering an account of AVENGER, which resulted in no gains, we shall attempt to answer the questions that we posed above, namely how the heavy strategic bombers were committed and why the 4th Indian Division was unready to exploit their mission. First, though, it is necessary to introduce the two divisions on whose behalf the Monastery and the town were destroyed.

The New Zealanders had been in the Mediterranean since 1940. They had fought in Greece and Crete, in Syria and in the Western Desert. Their role at Alamein had been prominent and after it the New Zealanders fought across North Africa, their Government bowing to Churchill's appeal to keep them in the Mediterranean and to the compelling argument that shipping could not be spared to send them home, as it wished. But when Montgomery wanted the 2nd Division for the invasion of Sicily because it was his most experienced and highly trained formation which worked, in Churchill's words, "with unsurpassed cohesion", Mr Fraser, the Prime Minister of New Zealand, demurred until he had consulted the House of Representatives.

The question before the House was whether or not to reinforce the Pacific, as had the Australians. By 1943, however, the Japanese threat had receded from the South Pacific and with it some of the enthusiasm of New Zealanders for fighting there with their 3rd Division. In the long run it was a question of retaining either the 3rd in the Pacific or the 2nd in the Mediterranean and disbanding the other, for the economy also had to be maintained. It was decided to keep both for the time but to recall the 3rd and use it as a pool of replacements for the 2nd. The reasoning was both sentimental and hard-headed. There was a surge of public feeling at the time that enough had been done for the Allied cause by a country of only a little over one and half million and that fighting in both the Pacific and Europe was too much. Affection for Britain was strong even if the military tradition celebrated on Anzac Day was not, so New Zealanders were readier to fight in Europe than against the Japanese in "America's war". Moreover, by 1943 the 2nd Division had attained a place in public esteem that could not be ignored. At the time that the House decided to renew its mandate, and to allow it to fight in Italy, glowing pride in its deeds was fanned into flame by Freyberg's account of its operations up to the Axis surrender at Tunis in April 1943. Freyberg's bulldog expression staring out from the pages of the newspapers had more appeal to New Zealanders than the words of wishy-washy politicians. But it was Winston Churchill who "set the magic of his style in the service of a cause". Instructed by a true reading of New Zealand history, he sounded the strain of Imperial unity in "sentences resonant with the cadences of Gibbon and ornamented by a reminiscence of Tennyson" – which naturally impressed a House unfamiliar with eloquence, and it decided to continue the war in the Mediterranean.[10]

Unlike Canada, whose wily Prime Minister, W. L. Mackenzie King, had promised "conscription if necessary but not necessarily conscription" and then introduced a dubious scheme by which only volunteers were sent overseas, New Zealand conscripts went where they were told. But the first three "echelons" or brigades sent to Egypt in 1940 had been volunteers who had enlisted before conscription was introduced when the supply of volunteers dried up. They had been overseas since then and it was time to replace them. So the summer of 1943 saw a general-post in the division in Egypt. Six thousand men went home in leave drafts in exchange for new men who came out in the returning ships. It was hoped that most of the veterans would return after taking their leave but as only 20 per cent did so the division lost all but a cadre of experienced men. Their replacements were also refreshment; for too much experience of battle takes the edge off the best and makes men unduly cautious. The New Zealand Division crossed to Italy to rejoin the Eighth Army in October, and in November and December fought the gruelling battles, Orsogna in particular, of which we have already written.

By February 1944, after three and a half months of winter fighting, all the armies in Italy were suffering to a lesser or greater degree from disillusionment and lack of enthusiasm. Among the Allies, desertion was becoming a problem. Men were sometimes charged with it, although cowardice in the face of the enemy was the crime, because it was less difficult to prove in law but bore the same penalty. Desertion – real desertion – in the Western Desert, or even in North Africa, had had few attractions. In Italy it had many, for there were farms into which men were welcomed with open arms and warm beds as replacement for husbands and sons who were prisoners, refugees or dead. In the cities it was not difficult to hide and a thriving black market provided a living. In the prevailing circumstances it was discouraging for New Zealand soldiers to hear that 30,000 Grade 1 soldiers were retained at home, that miners were exempted from service and that many contemporaries had been released from the home army for extended periods. When the 3rd Division returned home from the Pacific in February, many fighting in the 2nd at Cassino asked why they should not go too. The sense of purpose that had been universal in the desert and in the first months in Italy was eroded, not to be recaptured until the final months of the war when men from the New Zealand 3rd Division arrived as reinforcements.

Discipline became a concern of divisional officers in both of Alexander's armies in February 1944, although the two divisions in Freyberg's corps were the least affected by the prevailing mood, to judge by statistics. Freyberg was always sensitive to the spirit – "the feel" – in his division. Alexander, another soldier with an excellent regimental record in action and a sixth sense about morale, was increasingly worried as the year 1944 wore on. The figures in the table overleaf are extracted from those collected for Alexander by his staff and by Freyberg's.

General Freyberg attributed the low rate of crime and high morale in his division to date to the good type of man who had been sent overseas, to medical services that dealt with cases of shock before they reached a point of no return, and to sufficient reinforcements to allow sick and wounded time to recover. Everyone knew that he could return to his own unit and his own friends. Most of all, the high state of training and the care that Freyberg took to ensure that his operations were successful, and that lives were not wasted, gave everyone confidence in the management. The junior officers were largely selected from men who had been proved in battle while serving in the ranks. Many of the rest had joined with the first echelons and had fought in many battles. But Cassino proved to be a strain on the morale of all ranks, particularly Operation DICKENS, a failure which could be attributed to no other division. Long afterwards soldiers were outspoken against the way that it had been handled, to an extent that would have been unacceptable in any other division. But the 2nd was like a family business run by a lot of cousins who were shareholders. Criticism was a natural right.

The New Zealand of 1939 was still a rural country and most of the men came from small communities where they were used to being close to the boss and to righting grievances by speaking directly to him themselves. Even the Prime Minister was accustomed to being hailed in the street or phoned by complete strangers, including private soldiers. The government and corporate structure was unpretentious – as befitted a small country in which wealth was very evenly spread and real poverty or conspicuous wealth were rare. Living in an uncrowded

TABLE

1. The ratio of Battle Casualties to Battle Exhaustion cases is an indicator of the morale of "the cutting edge". In the 2nd New Zealand Division the ratios are shown below during peak periods of battle in 1942–4 per thousand of divisional strength.

		BC :	BE
June/July 1942	Matruh – Fuka and 1st Alamein	50	7
November 1942	2nd Alamein	48	0.5
November–December 1943	Orsogna and the Adriatic	30	2.5
February–March 1944	Cassino	25	9
1944 as a whole		98	32

Note: A similar table in the War Diary of the 5th Canadian Armoured Division (ADMS) shows figures for the infantry battalions of the Canadian 1st Infantry Division. The ratio of BE : BC shows that 23 per cent of casualties were battle exhaustion, almost the same as for the New Zealand Division in 1944.

2. Another indicator, one that requires more explanation since it does not specifically concern the "cutting edge", is the record of courts martial for offences such as Cowardice, Mutiny, Desertion and Absence Without Leave on Active Service.

	Mutiny	*Desertion*	*AWOL*
4th Indian Division	–	13	4
2nd NZ Division		–73–	
		including two cases totalling 25 men in December 1943 and July 1944 of refusing an order in the face of the enemy.	
46th Division	–	256	22
56th Division	31	162	47
1st Division	–	106	48

Source: Freyberg Papers, New Zealand Archives, Wellington.

country (it is a thousand miles from the North Cape to The Bluff) in a natural environment second to none where bananas, oranges, grapes and peaches, fine livestock, cereals, timber, fish and fowl could all be raised in one area of the country side by side, New Zealand soldiers considered that they had a natural right to enjoy life wherever they were, including the battle zone, or be told the reason.

If there was a characteristic that Freyberg's men had in marked degree it was sensitivity to unfair treatment and unwillingness to put up with it. They would not stand for "side" or class and rank privileges, but they were not "pushy", being unspoiled by hectic life in big cities where the need for a man to stand up for his rights leads to a chip on the shoulder. With their throw-away humour and unhurried ways, so exasperating to the city-bred, they resembled the Canadian Maritimer and his American cousin from the State of Maine.

Freyberg was soft-hearted in dealing with his men, sometimes over the objections of his superior officers. "Don't your fellas salute any more?" asked Montgomery as he rode around the Division with Freyberg when it had just arrived in Italy. "Oh well!" replied Freyberg, "if you wave at them they'll wave back." It was true, and Freyberg probably was waving to a soldier whose name he knew, particularly if he was one of those who had behaved outrageously out of the line. Like Wimberley of the 51st Highland Division with his "Jocks", Freyberg treated his Kiwis like unruly children of whom he was unspeakably proud, even when they misbehaved. "Bernard, you really must do something about it," said Oliver Leese when he had been offered bottles of Chianti by soldiers hanging out of the back of a truck in front of his staff car. "That's nothing," said Freyberg, "they filled a whole water bowser with wine and ruined it."

Freyberg's paternalism took the form of manipulating his immediate subordinates, a practice at which most successful generals excel. His conferences were run as democratic assemblies where relaxed pipe-smokers, like Kippenberger, had their full say, but in the end it was Freyberg's plan that was adopted even if someone else proposed it and was allowed to believe that it was his own. But sometimes there remained a doubt as to what had been decided and as Freyberg's staff tidied up the details they found it difficult to know what private arrangements their general had made.

His formidable physical presence, his medal ribbons attesting to his survival through many battles, and his unquestioned devotion to New Zealand and New Zealanders were assets to those around him that far outweighed his equally obvious limitations. Fifty-four years old, English born, raised in New Zealand, he had fought with Pancho Villa in the Mexican Civil War before he fought in the British Army in the First World War, at Gallipoli and on the Western Front. He was a brigade commander in 1917 and 1918 in the 29th Division and the Naval Division. Awarded the Victoria Cross – a decoration that confers unique prestige on general and private alike – he won the Distinguished Service Order three times and was wounded nine times. He was to emerge from the Second War with another DSO and more wounds, and as a Grand Commander in the Order of Saint Michael and Saint George, a Knight Companion of the Bath, and a Commander in the Order of the British Empire. In February 1944 he was streets ahead of his fellow divisional and corps commanders in experience. Had he not been the chosen instrument and trusted servant of his government he felt that he would have been a corps commander in his own right. Instead, he had a special position as a very senior divisional commander with that right of appeal, which he did not need to use but which allowed him to minimise his casualties. It made him potentially a prickly subordinate. Within the British system, where his position was well understood, he could usually criticise without causing offence, at least in principle. Indeed, he had criticised General Auchinleck's methods in the final months of his command of the Eighth Army in June and July 1942 which did cause offence, but was saved by the arrival of Montgomery, with whom he saw eye to eye.

Freyberg was not a noted tactician, nor was he an intellectual soldier. His forte was steadiness and experience at the divisional level. He was neither quick on the uptake nor a clear thinker and certainly not at his best when he had to conceive and conduct an independent operation by more than a division, still less by a mixed corps in a difficult operation under an American commander whom he neither liked nor trusted. That was the position in which he was placed at Cassino. Alexander had thought hard and long whether to take over the battle himself, move the army boundary and give it to the Eighth Army, then commanded by Oliver Leese, who knew his Freyberg, or send Sydney Kirkman with his 13th Corps headquarters to run it. But he had left the operation in Clark's hands. Politics had decided him to do that, not confidence in Clark's judgment.

The New Zealand Division resembled a panzer grenadier division in that it had two infantry brigades and one armoured brigade. It lacked armoured infantry but its organisation was suited to the roles that the Germans had given their Panzer Grenadier Division – plugging gaps, restoring the front by a limited counter-stroke and end-runs round the enemy flank. The latter had been its task on occasions but Freyberg and his staff were not at their best in that kind of operation. Rather they excelled in the use of their concentrated artillery, which was exceptionally efficient, with infiltration by the infantry to bring about the collapse of German positions. They liked space and naturally opposed battles of attrition. Freyberg had only six infantry battalions and therefore had strictly to limit their casualties. Clark already had the reputation for being an attrition general and Freyberg's sophisticated nose told him soon after he arrived that Cassino had the potential for becoming such a battle. It stank of the Western Front.

Freyberg's other division was the famous 4th Indian, which had built up its reputation in Abyssinia, the Western Desert and the long pursuit to Tunisia. Though one of its most brilliant feats had been the escalade of the Jebel Fatnassa by night at the Battle of Wadi Akarit, it was not a "mountain" division, nor were any of its units except the Gurkhas natural mountaineers. Unfortunately, by the time it arrived in Italy it had lost some of its cutting edge, having suffered heavy losses in Africa, including a complete brigade in the débâcle at Tobruk in 1942. The replacements, including the new 11th Indian Infantry Brigade, though fit and eager, had not yet had the time to be welded into battle-hardened fire-teams.

Indian Army divisions differed from other Commonwealth formations both in organisation and the basis of their morale. Commanders, senior staff officers and most of the regimental officers were British. (Although by 1944 "Indianisation" was producing a steady flow of excellent Indian officers they were still a minority.) The artillery was British – "Royal Artillery" – the engineers Indian "Sappers and Miners", and one battalion in each infantry brigade was British. The soldiers were drawn from "martial races" as distinct from each other as Germans are from Spaniards – Punjabi Mussulmans, Sikhs, Rajputs, Dogras, Jats, Mahrattas and Gurkhas from Nepal – all volunteers and men of good social standing, recruited from smallholders and yeoman farmers. Their morale was based primarily on their collective identity as members of an honourable profession subscribing to a code of courage, fidelity and devotion to duty, expressed in the Urdu word *izzat*,* literally "honour".

This unusual morale, centred on personal honour, the army and the regiment rather than patriotism, was reinforced by the special relationship between the Indian troops and their European officers, recruited in peacetime only from those who were high on the passing-out list from Sandhurst. They were supported by native captains (subedars) and lieutenants (jemadars) promoted from the ranks,

---

* Equivalent to the German *Soldaten Treue*.

189

roughly equivalent to the under-officers in continental armies. Those unfamiliar with the Indian Army are apt to consider the British view of it exaggerated and sentimental, but its regiments were very professional as well as closely knit, paternal family groups, very durable, and capable of brilliant feats of arms.

Something of the feeling of officers for their men can be understood from a passage in a letter written to General Freyberg by the divisional General, Francis Tuker, who was taken ill just before the battle and forced to relinquish command:

> I am ever so thankful my division is being looked after by yourself. With you there, I know that no single life will be squandered and that those that are spent will be well spent.

Tuker was an unusual man. Intense, introspective, artistic, scholarly and devoted to India, Indians, his service, his division and his men, he was a very different personality from Freyberg, but the two had in common devotion to their men and an obstinate determination to save life if possible. Both were obsessive about their commands and tended to do too much themselves. Together, they represented what Clark and other senior Americans liked least about the British service, its paternalism and its refusal to accept casualties.

Unfortunately Tuker, prostrated by arthritis, was unfit to command but unwilling to hand over to his deputy, his artillery commander, Brigadier H. W. Dimoline, a Territorial officer. Tuker remained brooding in his command caravan, giving advice from time to time. Dimoline also listened to two of his brigade commanders, O. de T. Lovett of the 7th Brigade, who played the main role in AVENGER, and the strong-willed A. Galloway of the 5th Brigade who was predominant in DICKENS. In effect, the division was commanded by a committee; always a recipe for failure, militating against the speed and boldness which were essential if Clark's aim to break out towards Anzio was to be attained. It was not, however, the only factor operating against it.

A HATEFUL TAPESTRY IN THE SKY

> Earth opens where the squandered bombs fall wide
> And all our view's a burning countryside.
> Only the sudden metal weight of fear
> Brings back the platitude that life is dear,
> Keeps us awake while we sit staring out
> With Reason pounding, "what's it all about?"
>
> *Denton Welch, 1915–48*

The stage was now set for the Second Battle of Montecassino, a bloody fiasco, whose central incident, the destruction by air bombardment of Montecassino, reverberates to this day. The planning of the battle is a complicated story of accidents, of misunderstandings piled on misunderstandings, of complicated and conflicting evidence, and of suppressed evidence. The proceedings of a court of enquiry would run to a whole volume; indeed, volumes have already been written on the subject. Here we attempt only to provide an account of events in the order they took place, using some sources so far neglected.[1]

When General Clark at last decided to commit the New Zealand Corps his intention was to use it to preserve the momentum of the US 2nd Corps attack from the general direction of the Snakeshead and Point 593 on to Montecassino.[2] Essentially the mission of the 4th Indian Division was to thrust through the American positions in two directions with the aim of cutting the Via Casilina; southward past the Monastery and down the mountain slopes into the town of Cassino, and from M. Castellone to Villa S. Lucia. At the same time the 2nd New Zealand Division was to establish a bridgehead over the Rapido in the town, link up with the Indians and drive through into the Liri valley. There was to be no regular "take-over" from the US 34th and 36th

Divisions on the heights: the Indians were simply to form up behind the forward American positions and attack through them. For various reasons this proved impractical. The New Zealand attack was delayed by the Rapido river bursting its banks in the winter rains and flooding all the approaches, so that the route to Cassino was temporarily impassable to infantry and tanks. The US troops on the heights had shot their bolt, were paralysed by exposure and fatigue, and the arrival of the leading battalions of the 4th Indian Division, delayed by Clark's late decision to commit them there, coincided with the spoiling counter-attack called MICHAEL which the Germans had seized the opportunity to launch.

The terrible muddles which attended the mounting of the battle can be accounted for partly by the unwieldy command structure. The general in effective command was Clark, who was trying to control two widely separated operations at once – the battle for the Anzio bridgehead, which by mid-February was reaching a crisis and demanded all his attention, and Cassino. Above him was Alexander, and above him again Maitland Wilson, and his air commander, General Ira C. Eaker, USAAF, Commander-in-Chief, Mediterranean Allied Air Forces, who were to become involved in negotiations to provide air support. Clark's plan, avoiding a straight takeover, superimposed one corps upon another from different armies with different command procedures. The New Zealand Corps HQ was an *ad hoc* affair, without a proper staff, trained and accustomed to working as a team. Both its divisions were commanded by deputies. Howard Kippenberger, an outstanding infantry officer, substituted for Freyberg, who commanded the corps. Brigadier Dimoline, acting divisional commander, was a talented artillery officer, but not the man to drive a team of battle-hardened infantry brigadiers from so famous a division, or to stand up to the formidable Bernard Freyberg, VC.

To explain the course of events we have to unravel two interwoven skeins. One is the planning sequence for the battle on the heights, the other the great debate about how to deal with the Monastery, the great fortress-like building sitting four-square on Montecassino – the "hateful tapestry in the sky", as the New Zealand official historian called it, rather fancifully. All soldiers hate being overlooked by the enemy, and from Tuker and Freyberg down they were convinced that from its superbly commanding position the enemy was watching their every move. In fact, General Frido von Senger, a devout Catholic and a highly civilised man, had put it out of bounds to all German troops, except wounded in an emergency, but nobody was to know that, and the Americans had already, and correctly, located enemy positions on the

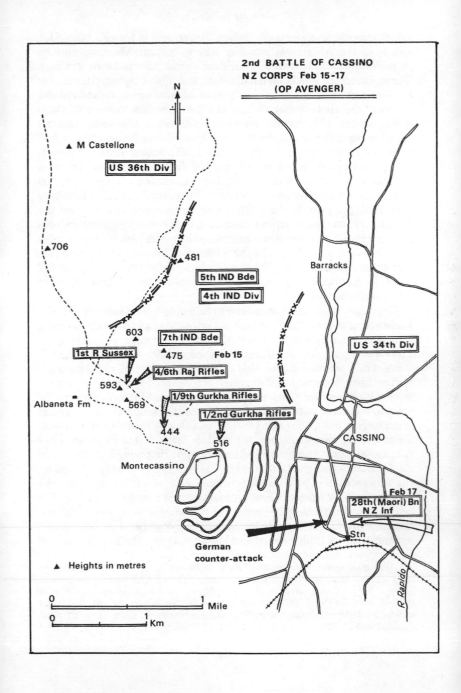

2nd BATTLE OF CASSINO
NZ CORPS Feb 15-17
(OP AVENGER)

N

▲ M Castellone

US 36th Div

▲706

▲481

5th IND Bde

4th IND Div

603
▲

7th IND Bde

475
▲   Feb 15

1st R Sussex

4/6th Raj Rifles

593 ▲

1/9th Gurkha Rifles

Albaneta Fm

569 ▲

1/2nd Gurkha Rifles

444
▲

516
▲

Montecassino

German
counter-attack

▲ Heights in metres

Barracks

US 34th Div

CASSINO

Feb 17

28th (Maori) Bn
NZ Inf

Stn

R. Rapido

0 _____ 1 Mile

0 _____ 1 Km

slopes close beneath its walls. When Tuker, still in his HQ but on his sick-bed, learnt that his division was to assault Montecassino he immediately decided that the building would have to be neutralised. Three American attacks on it had failed, and Tuker thought it futile "to hit one's head against the hardest part of the whole position and risk the failure of the whole operation". A book found for him by one of his staff in Naples revealed that the masonry walls of the Monastery tapered from twelve to five feet at the top. He decided that the best plan would be to use fighter-bombers armed with 1,000-pound bombs to breach them, the infantry racing in before the defenders could recover from the shock. Tuker had a deservedly high reputation as a tactician, and Freyberg readily took his advice. On February 9, the day Freyberg presented his plan to the Fifth Army, he asked Clark to have the Monastery attacked by fighter-bombers, Clark argued against the idea but observed that if bombers were used he would ask for the heavies and destroy the building. On the 11th, after Gruenther had told him that the torch had been "thrown" to him, Freyberg ordered his G2 (Air), Robin Bell, to submit a formal request for a fighter-bomber mission on the 13th.

There are two important points to be made here. One was that the Eighth Army as early as 1942 had put into action a joint army–air force staff and signal system for controlling direct air support and by early 1944 it was both fast and flexible. Freyberg did not grasp that the US Fifth Army was using the old, cumbrous system of requesting air strikes through normal staff channels. He seemed to think that as fresh information arrived from the heights behind Montecassino or the situation changed radically the USAAF could respond as rapidly and as sensitively as the RAF. (The USAAF was shortly to overhaul its system for providing ground support for the US Army, but in February 1944 that lay ahead.) Another consideration not discovered by the New Zealand staff until the last moment was that the US Army insisted on the demarcation of a "bomb safety line" at least 1,000 yards from the nearest friendly troops.* The second point is a technical one, highly relevant to the decision to prefer heavy bombers to fighter-bombers, taken on the 13th. In simple terms, a fighter-bomber does not "drop" its bomb. It flies at high speed and low altitude in a shallow dive, and at

---

* With good reason. Apart from ballistic probable errors, target identifications were often faulty. The authors have certain knowledge. The USAAF bombed the town of Souk-el-Arba in Tunisia, well inside the Allied lines, and the administrative echelon of the 74th Medium Regiment, Royal Artillery, 10,000 yards from the intended target and one of its battery command posts (FDCs) during the third Cassino battle, killing all the occupants.

short range "throws" it in a trajectory like an artillery shell. It is, compared with a bomber, very accurate. Medium and heavy bombers, flying at several thousand feet on a level course, in those days used optical sights and compensated for the spread of effect dictated by the laws of ballistics by flying in close formation and releasing a pattern of bombs simultaneously on the order of the "master-bomber".

From the 9th onwards Brigadier Dimoline was grappling with the difficulties of moving and maintaining his division along an inadequate route ending in six miles of a mountain path fit only for goats. He was so short of pack-mule transport that he was forced to use his 11th Brigade complete as porters, leaving only the 7th and 5th, scheduled to arrive in that order, for the operation. The 7th Brigade was already on the heights when the enemy upset his plans. Early on the morning of the 12th, a day on which a great deal of importance was to happen, Generalleutnant Baade's 90th Panzer Grenadier Division counter-attacked. Two of the 7th Brigade's battalions, the 1st Royal Sussex and the 4th/16th Punjab were approaching M. Castellone on the way to Snakeshead when the panzer grenadiers assaulted the exhausted and shaky battalions belonging to the US 36th Division holding that feature. Both were drawn into the fight, which they helped to stabilise with the assistance of some good shooting from the New Zealand artillery. So great was the confusion that at one moment they were ordered to attack Terelle, secure in French hands. Both battalions were stuck for the rest of the day in the open under artillery fire and suffered casualties. The fact was that it was extremely difficult to exercise command and control over a battlefield invisible from the plain below, where all the HQs were sited, with radio failure and telephone cables cut by fire, so visits had to be on foot and could take all day. On the 12th Dimoline was up in the combat area all day, and out of touch, until he returned at 6 p.m. to report the situation to Freyberg.

The 12th was also an eventful day for Freyberg. In the morning he was told by the Fifth Army that his request for a fighter-bomber strike on the Monastery had been turned down. He then attended a briefing at HQ 2nd Corps, where he discovered that Keyes and his commanders and staff were alarmingly ignorant about the true situation of his troops or their location. On being closely questioned "It was plain that none of them had been forward or was at all in touch with his men."[3] The exception was the assistant commander of the 34th Division, Briga-dier-General Frederic Butler, who contradicted his corps commander's statement that the Castle, on a feature overlooking the town, was in American hands. He provided the useful information that there was no evidence that there were German troops in the Monastery, but that fire was certainly coming from the slopes below it, and added that in his opinion the key points in the operation were Point 593 on one side of the Monastery and the Castle on the other. (This was an important point, which only became apparent to Butler, and Dimoline along with his brigadiers and battalion commanders who had actually visited the battlefield. The Monastery hypnotised all those who looked up at it from below. In reality the position could be compared to the siege of a medieval castle. The Monastery and Montecassino formed the keep, the last-ditch defence. The complex of ridges, subsumed under the title of Point 593 by Butler, and the Castle were the curtain wall, well furnished with bastions from which a deadly interlocking fire could be brought on the attacker.) Butler also broke the unwelcome news that the men were "out on their feet", that what had been reported as attacks by full regiments were in reality by weak companies, and that "there had been little movement forward for days".

In the afternoon Alexander and Harding called on Freyberg at his HQ to brief him on the operation instruction sent formally to the Fifth Army the day before. Its gist was that while he was anxious that the New Zealand Corps' operation should be pressed on as fast as possible, it was to be less ambitious and the mission to fit the means. (And military realities, it could be said.) Dimoline was to attack with both his brigades, ensuring that he was firm on the ground before he launched them. It would be enough to secure Montecassino and to advance down the hill to cut the road in the town. The thrust from M. Castellone could be scrapped. The 2nd New Zealand, as soon as it could move, should concentrate on establishing the bridgehead across the Rapido in Cassino town. All its strength should be employed in this task, and exploitation forgotten for the time being. Only when the bridgehead could provide a secure base line for further operations would they be attempted was the underlying implication of these fresh instructions.[4] (Curiously, there is no evidence of HQ Fifth Army formally communicating Alexander's instructions in writing or otherwise to Freyberg. HQ AAI's Operation Instruction No. 42 is certainly in its files, but whether this was due to laxity, the deliberate intention to ignore it or knowledge that Alexander informed Freyberg of its contents is unknown.)[5]

Freyberg raised the question of the refusal of the air-strike. Alexander gave him his full support and ordered Harding to take the matter up with Gruenther. This bore fruit at 9.30 that night, when Gruenther told Freyberg that a mission of fighter-bombers would attack the Monastery the next day, the 13th. By the evening of the 12th, however, there had been a significant departure from Tuker's plan of a coordinated air bombardment and infantry assault. When Dimoline had reported to Freyberg after his trip up the mountain they had discussed the air support question and talked about "softening up" the target in advance, as opposed to a closely coordinated breaching of the walls and an infantry assault. This process would continue while Dimoline completed the difficult business of putting his brigades in position and preparing the attack. Freyberg explained this to Gruenther when they spoke on the telephone late that evening. Gruenther made Clark's wish that he did not want the Monastery to be destroyed quite clear. He would permit the strike only if, in Freyberg's opinion, it was a military necessity. Freyberg, assuring him that it was, and that Dimoline, the commander who had seen the ground wanted it, added that in his own view a fighter-bomber strike on the scale envisaged would not demolish the building: "The thing was it would *soften the people who are there* . . ." (authors' emphasis), Major John White, Freyberg's military assistant, noted in his log.

Meanwhile the true situation on the heights was gradually becoming clearer, at least to Freyberg. At 5.15 p.m. on the 12th Keyes, having had a change of heart, rang up and told Freyberg that the physical condition of his men on the heights was so bad that he could leave them there no longer, and asked him to order the 4th Indian to relieve them first before mounting its attack. This suited Freyberg and Dimoline, and it was agreed, but it was to cause a series of postponements, difficult for anyone who had not ventured on to the actual positions to understand. The 5th Infantry Brigade, struggling up the slopes, was not to complete its takeover from the Americans until the early morning of the 15th. There was worse news to come. It was not until late on the 13th that Dimoline informed Freyberg of a much more serious snag: the Americans had lost the jump-off line from which he was forced by the configuration of the ground to launch his attack.

After dark on the 12th Lieutenant-Colonel J. B. Glennie (who was to write a professional account of the whole operation for a British Army study in 1968) took his battalion, the 1st Royal Sussex, up to Snakeshead. In his own words: "I was led up to the American sector by an American guide who led me up to the German positions until we were fired on. After a hasty retreat the American positions were approached from the enemy side! On arrival it was found that the sector was held by four US battalions (now each only 100 strong) from three different regiments of two divisions." When it was daylight the reason why the guide had taken him to the wrong location became clear. Like everyone on the staff at the 34th Division and 2nd Corps he believed that Point 593 and the ridge connecting Points 450–455 were held by the 141st and 168th US Infantry, whereas they had been driven off them by Baade's counter-attack, and were now crouching in gullies below the crest 200 yards short of it, and 800 yards from the Monastery on Point 516 at the nearest. The 142nd Infantry did not hold Massa Albaneta, Point 468, and never had.[6] The commander of the brigade saw at first hand that the lie of the land narrowed the front of any attack designed to restore these positions, now an essential preliminary to an advance on Montecassino. The Germans in their re-occupied positions were so skilfully sited in pairs of localities mutually supporting each other that only a broad-front attack had any hope of overcoming them.

Three misunderstandings arose from this. The first was between Freyberg and Dimoline. Dimoline had stated that he could not be ready to attack before nightfall of the 15/16th – the infantry brigadiers being adamant that they would have to attack under cover of darkness – and Freyberg agreed. When later it became apparent to Dimoline that a preliminary attack had to be made against Point 593 and that the main attack could not be mounted until the 16th/17th, Freyberg objected and insisted that he attack Point 593 *and* the Monastery on the 15th. A terrible misunderstanding was the result because Dimoline did not grasp that Freyberg had refused to permit his preliminary attack. The second misunderstanding occurred because Freyberg did not mention the loss of the vital Point 593 area to Gruenther, nor did he, on the 12th, point out that Dimoline could not attack the next day, as originally intended. No doubt he assumed, reasonably, that the 2nd Corps had told Fifth Army about the true state of affairs by the time that Gruenther phoned him about the air mission. The third misunderstanding was that General Ryder, 34th Division, himself did not know where his forward localities were. When on the morning of the 13th he was informed by the 2nd Corps that a mission was laid on to attack the Monastery that day, he invoked the 1,000-yard bomb safety line rule, protesting that if he withdrew for 600 yards the enemy would surely move up and re-occupy his hard-won gains. He demanded a veto on any air-strike because his troops held the sector and it was under his command. The mission was cancelled at 10 a.m. on the 13th and Fifth Army recorded that Freyberg was now interested in having the Monastery shelled instead. (A historical misconception was to arise from this.[7] It was thought that because the British insisted on the bombing of the Monastery, it was they who withdrew from Point 593, so permitting the Germans to move forward and block their attack. In fact the British never moved back, for reasons that will be explained shortly. When referring to the bomb safety line the 34th Division signal reveals that at its HQ it was still believed that its troops held the positions from which they had been driven two days previously.)

As it happened the fighter-bomber attack had been cancelled only to be replaced, almost at once, by one that was far more formidable. When Clark, then at Anzio, agreed to the revived mission against the Monastery late on the afternoon of the 12th, he told Gruenther not to allow it to take place before 10 a.m. next day. By then he intended to have spoken to Alexander in the hope of dissuading him from the project altogether. Bombarding the Monastery would not help the first phase of Dimoline's attack, as he wished to conduct it. If the air-strike had been arranged in its original specification, with fighter-bombers, and there had been a pause while the 4th Indian Division fought for its jump-off line, there might have been a faint hope that the true situation inside the Monastery could have been ascertained, although that did not answer the question of how to neutralise the enemy posts close to the foot of the walls without danger to the building. Neither Clark nor Alexander, however, had any first-hand knowledge of the tactical importance of the knobs and wrinkles of rocks over which the battle had to be fought, or indeed where the jump-off line actually was, except from a map, showing a horizontal advance of less than a quarter of a mile to the Monastery. In any case, Clark had no time for details that should have been the concern of battalion and brigade commanders: with the situation in Anzio in mind he wanted immediate effective action. What he had to do was to force or manoeuvre Alexander into taking the decision to bomb or not to bomb. He presented his argument skilfully.

Half-measures, like an attack limited to precision bombing by a few aircraft, he said, were no guarantee that the 4th Indian Division would secure a lodgement in the building, but if it were not in fact occupied by the Germans, such half-hearted action would give them ample excuse to do so. He suggested that there were only two courses: not to bomb at all, or flatten the Monastery with the biggest concentration of aircraft that could be arranged. Alexander unhesitatingly chose to bomb. For once he was positive. He agreed to approach Maitland Wilson without delay, his correct channel to General Eaker and so to Major-General Nathan F. Twining, USAAF, who commanded the Mediterranean Allied Strategic Air Force with its heavy bombers, while Clark's "own" airman, Brigadier-General Gordon Saville, 12th Air Support Command, took the matter up through air channels. Eaker and his people were equivocal about the suggestion on technical grounds. But as the Combined Chiefs of Staff, urged on by Arnold, had for some time been dissatisfied with the slow progress in Italy and considered that not enough use was being made of air-power to help the armies forward, Eaker decided to commit his heavy bombers for political reasons. They were ready to go on the 14th.

During the afternoon of the 13th Freyberg and his air support staff officer were called in by Gruenther to hear of a plan to use "700 odd tons in 1,000 and 2,000 pound bombs", and also keep up the bombardment on subsequent days. Nothing was said about the bomb safety line nor was any direct liaison between the ground troops and the bombers arranged. Freyberg did not point out that the 14th was a day too soon when he was told about the mission. When he returned to his own HQ his chief of staff came in with the news from the 4th Indian Division that the 5th Brigade would not be in position until the morning of the 15th. Freyberg phoned Gruenther to inform him and asked for a twenty-four-hour postponement. Gruenther immediately agreed subject to weather and the requirements of Lucas at Anzio, where the German Operation FISCHFANG was expected to start on the 16th. From then on things began to go badly wrong.

Freyberg had been ill-advised not to tell Gruenther the truth about the situation at Snakeshead. The consequence was that Clark thought that the Indians were being slow. Keyes had kept quiet and Gruenther never learned that the 2nd Corps had relinquished its forward positions. There was worse to follow. On the morning of the 14th Dimoline learnt that when the 1st/2nd Gurkha Rifles had attempted to take over the positions of the 142nd Infantry in the valley below Point 593 and on its north side, they too proved to have been abandoned by the Americans, and that the enemy was in them. Dimoline gave Freyberg this latest instalment in his tale of woe that afternoon. It meant that Point 593 could only be attacked on a one-company front as there was no way around it on the right. Dimoline said that he had to take the advice of his commanders on the spot that to attack the Monastery without taking Point 593 would be suicidal, since their right flank and rear would be completely open. Freyberg was very short with him. He would take no excuses for putting off the main attack. Dimoline was to stick to the date agreed: "We cannot go on putting it off indefinitely."

Dimoline sensed that he had failed to persuade Freyberg to allow a separate attack on Point 593 on the 15th, and now he had been rebuffed again. Yet his staff continued to believe that the main attack was to be on the 16th/17th and prepared a plan for withdrawal behind a suitable bomb safety line, assuming the bombing was to be late on the 16th. On the evening of the 14th Freyberg saw Clark at Fifth Army HQ and they "laid on terrific air attack on Monastery to start tomorrow". The word "start" meant that he had been promised mediums and fighter-bombers on the 16th too, although not heavies, which might be called to Anzio. The time of the attack was to be as late in the day as possible. Later that night, and precisely when is not clear, the air force looked at the weather forecast, which was generally good for the next three days, and decided that as cloud was expected to thicken in the mountains in the afternoon, they would advance the time of the bombing from about 1 p.m. to 9.30 a.m. As late as 2 a.m. the change of timing was not known by the 2nd Corps. In fact it was not until 7.30 a.m. that they sent a message to 34th Division: "Abbey will be bombed this morning 0930 and 1015." The vagueness and lateness of both reports does not say much for the staff work at Fifth Army HQ, which may have been under the impression that all Americans would be off the hill.[8]

Late that evening Dimoline called and learnt that the bombing was the next day. "A difficult situation arose. He did not realise the bombing was on tomorrow." Not only could he not attack the Monastery on the night of the 15th/16th, as he thought that he had explained to Freyberg, but the final relief of the 168th Infantry by the 5th Indian Brigade would only be completed in the early hours of the 15th and so the leading troops could not possibly withdraw behind the BSL. In fact, the takeover had been so difficult that he did not think that he could attack the Monastery until the night of the 17th/18th. Freyberg was very angry. If they cancelled the heavies they would never get them again, he told Dimoline. He refused to go to Clark "cap in hand", after all the fuss over the arrangements. After some arm-twisting Dimoline agreed to attack the Monastery on the 16th/17th covered by the mediums and fighter-bombers scheduled for the second day of the air attack. Dimoline said that he hoped that his forward troops would be safe.

At 9.30 a.m. on the 15th the bombing began and continued with long pauses until 1.30 p.m. One hundred and thirty-five B-17s dropped 500-pound bombs and incendiaries. They were assisted by forty-three Mitchells and Marauders. The bombing of the heavies from between 15,000 and 18,000 feet was inaccurate and it was only the final flights of mediums at 10,000 feet that were able to demolish the outer walls. Even then, the walls of the west wing remained standing, and the massive foundation, with its rabbit-warren of cellars, was untouched. The building was not reduced to powder but made into an admirable defence position which the Germans quickly occupied after dark. The 7th Brigade received only a few minutes' notice of the bombing and the units received none. "They told the monks and they told the enemy but they did not tell us," wrote Glennie, whose battalion received a few loose bombs. The division had twenty-four casualties.

201

Two attacks by Glennie's battalion on the 15th/16th and 16th/17th on Point 593 failed. Nevertheless, the division attacked the Monastery on the 17th and 18th. In three nights of hard fighting against the 1st Parachute Division, well protected by anti-personnel minefields and wire, the 4th Indian Division had nearly forty officers and six hundred men killed, wounded and missing.

On the Rapido flats, two companies of Maoris crossed the flooded fields and the bridges and causeways repaired under fire by the engineers, and fought their way into the railway station. Behind them the engineers failed to complete the last of several bridges to enable tanks to follow. Thousands of rounds of smoke shell concealed their work from German observers on the mountain but it was to no avail. In the late afternoon the survivors in the station were attacked by a few tanks. Their PIAT ammunition exhausted, they withdrew.

This brief mention of the fighting does not presume to do justice to the effort of the Indians on the heights nor to the superb fighting qualities of the 28th New Zealand Battalion in the Cassino station. The purpose here has been to determine how the Monastery was bombed on the wrong day using inappropriate aircraft.

So ended the Second Battle of Cassino, but Clark was not yet prepared to give up, and Freyberg wasted no time in preparing for the Third.

SCARCELY ANY GOAL

I have beheld the agonies of war
Through many a weary season; seen enough
To make me hold that scarcely any goal
Is worth the reaching by so red a road.
Thomas Hardy, The Dynasts, *111, 5*

When the Second Battle of Cassino died down on February 18, Kesselring sent his congratulations to von Vietinghoff. "Convey my heartfelt gratitude to 211th Regiment and to 1st Parachute Regiment not quite so strongly. I am very pleased that the New Zealanders have had a smack in the nose. You must recommend the local commander for the Knight's Cross." He felt that Oberst Knuth's grenadiers in Cassino had done a particularly good job in resisting the 133rd Infantry and then turning to beat the New Zealanders in their rear. It was they who had saved the day. Phillips wrote that "New Zealand hopes were dupes and German fears were liars", because only two companies of Maoris had been used against the station, but that the battle could have been won.[1] After deceiving the Germans into expecting an attack through the Americans on the Caruso road Freyberg had lost the initiative by not reinforcing the Maoris. A serious lack of drive and courage amongst the engineers, who admittedly came under heavy fire, had caused the bridging operation to be abandoned and the infantry to be withdrawn. Had the Maoris been reinforced the engineers would have had the time and the inducement to finish the job. The bridgehead at the station would have been invaluable when the battle resumed.

Freyberg drafted an outline plan for the new, third battle, operation DICKENS, on the 19th and took it to Clark that evening. (So called because someone recalled that Charles Dickens had once visited Montecassino.) Freyberg's problem was to find fresh ideas, since every variation so far seemed to have been already played; wide flanking movements, shorter hooks, direct river crossings and a drive into Cassino from the north down the Caruso road, where the 133rd US Infantry still held out in the outskirts of the town. Just before he saw Clark, Freyberg discussed the plan with Kippenberger and agreed with him that it was essential to enter the town from more than one direction and to get tanks into it, with the infantry, quickly. As the bottleneck between Point 175 and the Rapido restricted the rate at which infantry could enter the battle by the Caruso road, they decided to put only the Indians in there, while the New Zealanders entered by the bridge over the Rapido on Highway No. 6. The town would be taken in the first phase, and the Monastery heights would fall to the Indians in the second, while the New Zealanders exploited beyond the town, helping to dislodge the Germans above by outflanking them.

Clark's comment on the plan was that Freyberg had got it back to front; he did not think that Cassino could be taken until the Monastery heights had been secured. Freyberg, on the other hand, no longer believed that operations behind and beyond the Monastery could succeed. There were insuperable problems of terrain and logistics. The Indian Division could not attack on a broad front and it would be slaughtered if it attacked on a narrow one. The 7th Indian Brigade was exhausted, and most of the 11th was still required as porters. Only the 5th Brigade was reasonably fresh, but, even if reinforced by a battalion of the 11th, it was not strong enough to attack in two places. His own New Zealanders had to attack the town and exploit beyond it in conjunction with CC"B" of the 1st US Armored, also in two directions; southwards towards S. Angelo to enable the British 78th Division, which had moved into the line south of Cassino, to cross the Rapido, and along Highway No. 6. When Clark told him that he was "shocked" that he should repeat the mistake made at S. Angelo by attacking without first securing his flanks, Freyberg agreed to compromise. He would commit the 5th Indian Brigade against the Monastery. Its jump-off line would be from Point 445 at the top of the Hill on the right, through Point 236 above the top bend of the road from the town to the Monastery, to the Castle on the left. The 6th New Zealand Brigade would thrust into the town along the Caruso road. In short, the Indians would take the Monastery and the New Zealanders the town. The entry by Highway No. 6, and possibly by the railway line, would be opened up on the first night of the battle and used by the 5th New Zealand Brigade and CC"B" for the exploitation phase.[2]

204

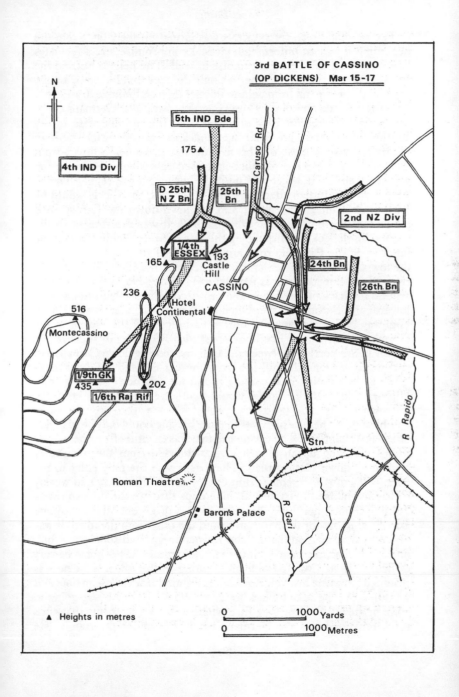

The modified plan for DICKENS was issued on the 21st. From the beginning it was an unfortunate tactical compromise and a few days later became a strategic compromise as well. The heights beyond the Monastery and the town formed a single defence unit linked by a gully that ran down the hill from behind Point 445, past Points 236 and 165, under the Castle on Point 193 and into the town. The Germans could use this route to reinforce the town from the Hill, and vice versa, if they continued to hold the line of strongpoints above and along its length. In theory the way to close off this avenue was to launch a broad-front attack against it, but it could not be retained unless Point 445 at the top was taken and held, which was unlikely, because it had repulsed many American and Indian attacks. At the other end, the Castle would be hard to hold unless the thrust into the town down the Caruso road penetrated beyond the Hotel Continental. It was the stopper in the second bottleneck, the first being the one between Point 175 and the junction of the Pasquale road and the parallel road at the entry into the town. This second bottleneck was between the Castle and the Gari river which ran southwards parallel to Highway No. 6 (Via Casilina) around the back of the station and provided an obstacle to an advance towards the Baron's Palace. Once the New Zealanders were astride Highway No. 6 at that point they would close off the escape of the Germans in the town. Freyberg's first idea had been to squeeze the enemy in this corridor between the Indians, coming down Caruso road and working along the hillside from the Castle, and the New Zealanders, with their tanks, coming round the southern outskirts from Highway No. 6. Both brigades would have stayed clear of the centre of the town.

The snag to the new plan was that the hillside could only be scaled at one place, Point 175. The Castle had to be taken either from there or by troops climbing up an almost vertical hillside from the town after advancing down Caruso road. The Castle was the only entry to the heights if Point 445 remained in enemy hands. Freyberg had weakly consigned himself to passing all his troops through the Caruso road–Point 175 bottleneck and then agreed to a divergent attack with one arm striking out for the Monastery and the other into the town. It was precisely the situation that he and Kippenberger had sought to avoid; one in which gaining and maintaining momentum was going to be very difficult. He had wanted to avoid fighting in the town. Now he was resigned to having his New Zealanders fighting from house to house. It was then that he asked Clark for heavy bombers. If he was going to commit the 6th Brigade into the town he would try to ensure that not a brick remained and the Germans would die under the rubble. He would have the infantry swiftly occupy the ruins before the German survivors recovered, and the tanks would accompany them, if possible. Behind the leading battalion the Indians would take over the Castle and assault across the hillside to the Monastery. However, bombing demanded the imposition of a bomb safety line, that irritating necessity, and the infantry would have to withdraw 1,000 yards before the bombing and advance again, a source of delay and confusion.

Why were not Freyberg's and Clark's conceptions both employed; namely by attacking simultaneously across the river into the southern part of town, down Caruso road into the town and after it had been taken from the Castle across the hillside to the Monastery? The reason was that Freyberg could only commit himself to two thrusts out of three because he had been told to reserve his second brigade, the 5th, to exploit. Clark did not want to use a brigade of the 78th Division for that role since it would have created a delay while it passed through the New Zealanders; he was probably right. He insisted on exploitation, impracticable though it was with so small a force, because the emergency at Anzio had reached a climax on the 19th and he wanted to draw German units to the Rapido front. In this dubious aim lay the source of the second, strategic, compromise in the plan.

In the days between the 19th, when the plan was conceived, and March 15, when it was eventually executed, Alexander's operational concept had changed radically. In January Lieutenant-General A. F. Harding had become his chief of staff and at once brought his strong intelligence and powers of analysis to bear on the subject of future strategy. His plan, to be later realised in Operation DIADEM (a codename adopted later) will be described in Chapter 15. Its bare bones were a rationalisation of the mixture of Allied divisions, the concentration of the main effort of the Allied armies on the Garigliano–Cassino front, and the postponement of a major offensive until the weather had improved, permitting full use to be made of the Allied superiority in the air and in tanks. As preliminary steps the New Zealand, the 4th Indian and the 78th Divisions were moved into the Fifth Army sector, and he proposed when the time was ripe to shift the inter-army boundary to the Liri river. Meanwhile, by February 22 Harding judged that FISCHFANG had been defeated and that von Mackensen's bolt was shot, so the 6th Corps was in no danger and did not require a rescue operation at Cassino. He recommended that Freyberg's aim should be restricted to securing a bridgehead big enough to serve as a springboard for the Eighth Army in the May offensive.

On February 22 Alexander sent an appreciation, drafted by Harding, to the British Chiefs of Staff. He envisaged three possible outcomes of the current fighting. First, the Germans might be driven back to the Pisa–Rimini line; secondly, the Allies might achieve a junction with the 6th Corps but be held south of Rome; thirdly, and this was the most likely, a bridgehead would be obtained at Cassino but the Germans would remain in the Gustav Line. His response to that would be to fight a decisive battle in the spring, starting in April and culminating just before D-day for OVERLORD, then scheduled for May. With that in mind there should be a pause in the fighting until then to gather men and materials, regroup and train. The 6th Corps would play a vital role and both it and the main front would have to be reinforced. Consequently, he asked them to postpone a decision about the removal of landing craft and divisions destined for ANVIL until March 20. Then they should decide whether ANVIL was the operation that would serve OVERLORD best or if it would not be better to have a resounding victory over the Germans in Italy in the month preceding it that would require them to reinforce to prevent a débâcle. This carefully worded proposal was calculated to receive support everywhere, except in Washington.

On the same day as this proposal was despatched, Maitland Wilson had offered his appreciation of the situation and had come to a different conclusion. He envisaged the battle to reach the 6th Corps grinding on and suggested that Allied air power ought to be applied in a double-barrelled discharge to help the armies. The left barrel would give direct support to the armies and the right, by a concerted interdiction programme to prevent the Germans supplying their troops south of Rome, would give indirect support. The Germans would be forced to withdraw without the armies having to attack at all. Churchill pronounced Wilson's paper "woolly", for it offered nothing new or promising. The airmen, who would be responsible, were naturally enthusiastic, for it offered them a decisive role. Wilson and Clark and Alexander talked over matters on the 19th, and the two British commanders with Freyberg on the 20th. They heard about the outline plan for DICKENS and blessed the idea of a break-out towards Anzio and the use of strategic bombers. Their concern for Anzio still obsessed them. Three days later, though, everything there had changed. Wilson was behind the times in not realising it perhaps, hence the difference between Alexander's and Wilson's proposals on the 22nd.[3]

On February 26 Churchill, Roosevelt and the Combined Chiefs of Staff responded to Alexander, giving Italy complete priority in Allied resources in the Mediterranean, i.e. over ANVIL, for the time being. Eisenhower, busy with OVERLORD in London, had supported Alexander because he wanted a larger assaulting force on D-day and, consequently more landing craft. The landing craft would serve him better in the English Channel, before D-day and immediately afterwards, than in ferrying two divisions to southern France. Furthermore, a resounding victory in Italy just before OVERLORD, followed by a postponed ANVIL (if he found by then that he could spare the landing craft) was the best solution for him. After this response Alexander expected that he would get what he wanted for the spring battle and that would not be affected by ANVIL. Therefore he was able to make positive statements about his future plans at a conference of army commanders on the 26th. When Clark heard what Alexander had to say he complained in his diary that splitting his front by shifting the army boundary south to the Liri was a low blow. It was another step in the plot to take over the highway to Rome from his Fifth Army. He argued that one more attempt should be made to rescue the 6th Corps while his Fifth Army was still in control of the Liri valley; urging that the original DICKENS plan with its exploitation phase not be changed. He won his point. Freyberg was left with the exploitation role; by March 15 when DICKENS began, Alexander considered the 6th Corps so secure that he was urging Truscott to take Cisterna and Carroceto as springboards for the future offensive. Wilson, who changed his tune when he received Alexander's proposal, accepted its premises and conclusions but insisted that the air element in his own proposal be retained.[4]

Freyberg also had made some conditions when he accepted Clark's modifications to his plan. He would not attack at all unless the bombing took place and he would not allow his division to suffer more than 500 additional casualties.[5] He also demanded that there be at least three consecutive fine days preceding the attack to allow the ground to dry for his advance into the Liri valley. Clark and Freyberg remained at odds about the aim of the operation, as did Clark and Harding. Freyberg went to see Harding confidentially on the 21st. Perhaps that visit led to Alexander's letter to Freyberg on the 23rd, the day before the battle was originally intended to start. Alexander had to be careful not to interfere and this passage was as far as he could go to reassure Freyberg:

> I put great store by this operation of yours. It must succeed as it is vital for us to gain control of the whole of the Monte Cassino spur and establish a bridge-head over the Rapido. If we cannot exploit this time, we must at least gain an exit into the plain for future operations when we launch our big offensive later – the all-out offensive to assist OVERLORD. I am quite prepared for you to employ the troops at your disposal which, of course, includes 78 Division.[6]

In this letter Alexander gave Freyberg the impression that the bridge-head was what mattered and not the break-out in the event that the larger aim adversely affected the lesser – as was clearly the case already. Furthermore he could use the 78th Division for either purpose.

When Freyberg held his conference with the airmen on February 21, Colonel Stephen Mack of the 12th Air Support Command warned him that the bombers could destroy the town in about three hours but that the infantry would only be able to advance with difficulty afterwards and that it would be impossible "to get tanks through the town for two days" because of debris. According to an officer who was present, General Freyberg "brushed aside" Mack's statement. If it proved that our side could not use tanks, neither could the enemy, he is supposed to have said. Nevertheless he expected his own tanks to be through the town in six to twelve hours. Information filed about the effect of bombing on built-up areas, for instance by the Germans at Stalingrad and the British at Battipaglia, was not shown to Freyberg. However, his reason for using heavy bombers was that he expected it to save lives, that the Germans would be stunned and that his infantry would be on top of them before they recovered. There was no controversy about the use of the bombers, as there had been before AVENGER. (The lessons learnt from Cassino did not prevent the use of heavy bombers at Caen, in July 1944, with much the same results for the same reasons.)

A number of preliminary moves were required before February 24, the earliest date for DICKENS. The 5th Brigade had to be relieved on the heights, where its positions faced the Point 445 ridge, by battalions of the 7th and 11th Brigades. The Americans on Castellone were to be relieved by the French, and the 133rd Infantry by the 6th New Zealand Brigade which was to carry out the assault. However, heavy snow on the 23rd delayed reliefs in the mountains and the 5th Indian Brigade was not back in Caira until the 25th. The attempt to secure Point 445 had failed on the night of the 22nd. On the Caruso road the New Zealanders took over a narrow wedge at the base of the mountains. On the right they took over Point 175, across the ravine from the Germans in the Castle. The front ran away north-eastward on the left of Caruso road along Pasquale road. At the point of the wedge they held houses round the junction of these two roads and a parallel road.

The snow and rain which started to fall on the 23rd continued day after day until March 7. Although fine days followed, and the tracks became fit for the armour again, the Foggia airfields were so saturated that the bombers could not take off. But at last, on March 15, the bombers were ready and the operation could start. The delay had not improved the corps' chances of success. Morale, raised to concert pitch by the prospect of immediate action, had sagged a little and the sickness rate, a good barometer, had risen. Security was imperilled because it was common knowledge that the town was to be bombed. Everyone had looked forward to the spectacle in February, but by mid-March the show had been running too long. Then on March 2 General Kippenberger, the much-loved and respected divisional commander, was severely wounded. His place was taken by Brigadier G. B. Parkinson, commander of the 6th Brigade.

Only the artillerymen, who never rested even when the units which they supported did, were able to use the interval to good effect. Their observation officers stared out on the desolate scene, day after day, and leaped to phone and radio at the appearance of even a single German minding his own business in a back area. When the rare target of importance appeared, hundreds of shells converged upon it. The landscape was soon indistinguishable from the Somme or Passchendaele. The area from which the 71st Nebelwerfer Regiment fired its hated rockets was like a ploughed field with shell holes almost lip to lip. Most feared by the Germans were the observation planes which fluttered over the river line and pounced on any German gun which dared to fire. The choice of gun positions was so limited that it was difficult to escape their notice. British gunners, who remembered the siege of Tobruk in 1941 and the Fieseler Storch, nicknamed "The Baron", which used to make their lives a misery, were glad that the tables had been turned. The German soldiers called the Air Observation Post "the orderly officer" because it flew up and down inspecting the front. One of poetic taste might have recalled a parody of Heine:

> Ich weiss nicht was soll es bedeuten
> Das ich so traurig bin
> Ein Aug das stets auf mich auf passt
> Folg mir wo auch immer bin.*

The 7th Brigade was losing about sixty men a day from the steady shower of rifle grenades and mortar-bombs and from exposure. Their positions were still not as well-protected as the Germans' and there were inadequate rear positions for reserves. Both sides fired propaganda pamphlets at each other recording the most depressing items of news, the German messages being printed in English and Urdu.

---

* Why am I so downcast
Oh, why so full of woe?
An eye above is fixed on me
Watching where e'er I go.

The isolation of the brigade was reduced a little by improvements to the track from Caira. By the time the battle began it was dignified by the name Cavendish Road and New Zealand engineers and Indian sappers had widened it until it was fit for tanks as far as a distribution point called Madras Circus. It was intended that a force of tanks should muscle up it, roll on between Castellone and the back of Snakeshead, go through the pass and surprise the defenders of Albaneta. From there a track led round behind Point 593 to the door of the Monastery.

The interval between AVENGER and DICKENS had been used to good effect by the 14th Panzer Corps to settle the 1st Parachute Division firmly in the Cassino sector, bringing Baade's 90th Panzer Grenadiers into reserve behind the front, where they could rest and absorb reinforcement. Baade was awarded the Oak Leaves to his Knight's Cross on the 22nd. Heidrich, the new commander, had been more fortunate than his predecessor in being given time to organise the defence. As the forward positions were under fire much of the time it had not been possible to provide the men with underground shelters. But in a second line, immediately in the rear, good progress was made in shoring up caves and strengthening cellars with concrete. Supplies were stockpiled in the town and on Montecassino. It was assumed that the Via Casilina would no longer be usable during the coming battle and that supplies would have to be run into the town from the mountain and vice versa. As supply parties had suffered many casualties, alternative routes were found avoiding areas which Allied artillery harassed systematically. To prevent the New Zealanders penetrating the southern outskirts of the town Heidrich established a switch line in the area of the Baron's Palace and the Roman Theatre. Medium machine guns and anti-tank guns were located there to prevent a thrust from the area of the station or the exploitation of a breakthrough in the town.

As usual, the Tenth Army had difficulty in determining what the Fifth Army intended. Wentzell had to make a search of prisoners' documents in the hospitals, for not one prisoner had been brought in from Cassino, which was "enough to drive one round the bend". German Intelligence could not discover the whereabouts of US 2nd Corps after its relief and on March 13 it was reported that the New Zealanders had been withdrawn from Cassino. An attack by the 15th Panzer Grenadiers on February 19, part of Kesselring's orders to keep 15th Army Group in a state of unrest and to take prisoners, cost it over one hundred casualties, including thirty-five prisoners. Prisoners from the new US 88th Infantry Division had been taken near Minturno on March 8 but they were so stubbornly reticent that it was not until the 16th that their captors could confirm it. When the Fifth Army had still made no move on March 11, Kesselring decided to go on leave. Although his field officers were becoming steadily more bemused by the uncertainty which shrouded Allied dispositions on the southern front, he believed that nothing "big" was intended until the spring weather started.

The final plan for DICKENS, which began on March 15, was almost the same as the original one agreed by Clark and issued by Freyberg, on February 21. The troops would withdraw before dawn to a safety line 1,000 yards from Cassino and the bombing would last from 8.30 a.m. until midday. Five hundred aircraft, medium bombers beginning and ending the performance, would drop 1,000 tons of bombs on an area measuring 1,400 yards by 400. In the afternoon fighter-bombers would be on call to attack prearranged targets. H-hour for the New Zealanders was midday. A barrage, lifting one hundred yards every six minutes, would lead A and B Companies of the 25th Battalion of the 6th Brigade through the northern part of the town to the line of Highway No. 6. On the right, D Company would advance from Point 175 to seize Castle Hill as a jumping-off point for the 5th Indian Brigade's operation on the hillside above the town. The tanks of the 19th Armoured Regiment would give close support to the 25th Battalion; the 5th New Zealand Brigade and CC"B" of the 1st Armored Division would fire into the town from the left flank. The first phase was to be completed by 2 p.m. By that time the 1st/4th Essex Regiment of the 5th Indian Brigade would relieve D Company on Castle Hill.

In the second phase the 6th Brigade would continue southward to the Baron's Palace where Highway No. 6 turns west round the foot of Monastery Hill. On the left they would take the station and the area of the hillock and then advance astride the Gari and its tributaries. Meanwhile, the 5th Indian Brigade would advance across and up the face of Monastery Hill to capture Point 435, called Hangman's Hill. The 7th Indian Brigade would demonstrate against the north side of the Monastery and take advantage of any German weakness. During the night of March 15 New Zealand and American engineers would bridge the river on both the railway and the Highway No. 6 entries to the town from the east. The 5th New Zealand Brigade would take over the station area and the tanks of CC"B" and the rest of the New Zealand armour would move into the bridgehead ready to exploit.

By the end of the first night the Indians should have seized the Monastery, but whether or not they had done so the exploitation phase into the Liri valley would begin at first light. In conjunction with the attack against the front of the Monastery a mixed force of American and New Zealand armour under the 7th Indian Brigade Reconnaissance Squadron was to advance from Madras Circus at first light on the 16th and arrive at the west side of the Monastery in time to support the 5th Indian Brigade's assault from the east.

The artillery fire-plan was on an enormous scale. A variety of unusual participants, including three Italian-manned railway guns and a few others which were supernumerary and were generally referred to as "Bush Arty", brought the total number of guns employed to about 900. The programme called for 1,200 tons of high explosive to be fired at the objectives and known hostile batteries in four hours. Although four or five tons of explosive had been allowed for every German defender, it was realised that this would not ensure success. While those in the town might succumb, the garrison of strongpoints further back had better shelters and might recover before the attacking infantry were upon them. There was also a danger that when the advanced sub-units withdrew beyond the bombline, the defenders would infiltrate forward into their vacant positions. The narrow front of the advance, which was overlooked from the hillside, prevented rapid and simultaneous engagement of the defenders who might have time to seal off the penetration. Finally the bombing might destroy all landmarks, and the rubble make the town impassable to tanks while it provided the surviving defenders with a continuous belt of concealed fire positions.

The bombardment was watched from Cervaro by Freyberg, Alexander, Clark and Lieutenant-General Ira C. Eaker. Tight formations of medium bombers were followed by more ragged ones of heavies. Half of the bombs landed on the target; most of the others fell outside because the dust and smoke obliterated the target from the sight of bomb-aimers. Those which fell as far away as Allied gun areas, transport lines and even on a hospital were less excusable. One complete group of heavies bombed Venafro which was over ten miles from Cassino. One hundred and forty civilians were killed or wounded. In terms of casualties the Germans suffered less than the Allies and civilians. As the last mediums droned away, Cassino was apparently laid waste. Not a building remained intact. Here and there a ruin remained unsteadily erect above what was now a shingle heap of rubble. When the guns opened up many of them subsided too.

The plan went well enough at first for A and B Companies of the 25th Battalion, which were making for the Hotel Continental and D Company, on its way to the Castle. Private E. H. Groves wrote his account of the D Company affair after the battle:

Before the attack the platoon officer told us that the attack was going to be merely a walk through the battered town. Objective the Castle feature. We had a good look at air photos. During the bombing in the morning most men were washing, shaving and brewing up. There was a lot of diarrhoea but the men's spirits were good. Pass-word was "Chota-Peg".

Moved up at about twelve o'clock in single file about five yards apart. Company commander stood as we passed by him. "How're you feeling boys?" Everyone was full of joy and good cheer. There was laughter and cracks like: "send me where the bullets are thickest". Our equipment was down to web and ammunition. Our company was below strength. My platoon had 24 men instead of 36 and my section 5 including the leader.

Up on the ridge we approached the town following B Company. Once there we slipped upwards leaving them to go on to clear the town. There was practically no fire. We got into a house on the hillside and found enemy in the lower storey looking down on the town away from us. The section leader and I killed four with a grenade and Thompson Machine Gun (TMC). We could not see if there were more. Found another house from which enemy was pinning down B Company men. We got round the house and killed three with TMC. We think we left enemy there too. But it takes time to clear houses and we had to press on. Ahead on the hillside were two dugouts or tunnels. My section leader stepped out from behind a wall to fire into these holes and was shot through the head by a sniper from below us. Our section now down to three men and I was section leader. We tried to move round the other side of the wall and a Spandau opened up so we were held on both sides. We waited for two hours. Then our own company appeared on our right going up the stone wall on to the ridge. We had got ahead by following B Company. We sang out to them and leapfrogged across. Joined them below the Castle. They were 17 Platoon and the remainder of my 18 Platoon. We moved up to the Keep and established ourselves round the broken walls. The enemy had moved behind the Keep in the quadrangle. Two of us moved through the archway but a Spandau round the corner got the corporal section commander. I moved back and found a hole through which to throw grenades down into the Keep. "Kaput! No shoot!" [was the welcome answer].

We were relieved in the rain by the Essex (5 Indian Brigade), about midnight. Our CSM had brought up the Essex. One company commander amused us by carrying a malacca cane. All day the only rations were emergency chocolate which is awful stuff . . .

By the morning of the 18th, when I had my first cup of hot tea, my platoon was down to four out of the twenty-four who started.[7]

A and B Companies of the 25th Battalion followed the barrage in along Caruso road with B Squadron of the 19th Armoured Regiment behind them. They passed their old positions and then the road running past the jail. A few hundred yards beyond they met resistance. There was brisk fire from Castle Hill on the right flank. Machine guns and snipers fired unexpectedly from the ruins of the buildings which they had entered and forced them into small infiltrating groups. The usually unreliable radio net between companies and battalion headquarters failed at 1 p.m. Snipers killed the runners who carried messages and the linesmen who were laying cables behind the advance. The tanks were unable to follow the infantry who by now were clambering over piles of concrete and girders and crossing sixty-foot craters. Smoke and dust still enveloped the ruins. It was hard to maintain direction. Even the loom of the hill on the right was not an effective aid because most of the fire came from the caves and ruined buildings clinging to its side and at its foot, and the infantry tended to swing off to the left to avoid it. The leading companies became intermixed. Control was soon lost and it was difficult to maintain forward momentum. Small pockets of Germans, continually on the move from position to position in the smoke, made the clearance of the town into an unpleasant game of cops and robbers. In the afternoon, German artillery joined in the battle from the Belmonte–Atina area, where it was protected by steep hills, and *Nebelwerfers* came out of hiding from beyond the Villa S. Lucia to make conditions even more unpleasant. By 3.30 p.m. A Company had advanced past the Nunnery on the left and a platoon had reached the convent on Highway No. 6. There they shared the remains of the large, sturdy building with Germans who prevented any further advance. Unsupported, the platoon withdrew. Another platoon turned right down the northern fork of Highway No. 6 with the intention of getting behind the Germans who were opposing B Company. But they were halted after a hundred yards. B Company met stiffer resistance in the buildings under the hill and could not reach its first objective which was Highway No. 6. The last line of the barrage along Highway No. 6 was fired twice more to help the companies forward in the evening and concentrations fell on troublesome mortars in the area beyond. But the real need was for more troops properly organised and these were not forthcoming. C Company, the 25th Battalion's reserve, went forward to the area of the jail and the Nunnery, not to press the attack but to maintain communications. It was midnight before B Company of the 24th Battalion arrived in A Company's area as the only paltry reinforcement.

What had gone wrong? The Germans thought that they had been let

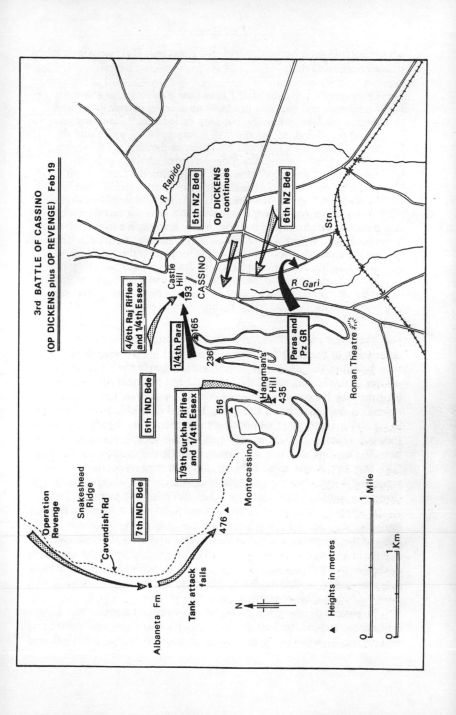

3rd BATTLE OF CASSINO
(OP DICKENS plus OP REVENGE)   Feb 19

off the hook. A member of the 2nd/3rd Parachute Regiment later taken prisoner revealed that:

> One part of a company of 2/3 Parachute Regiment was above the Continental and the other in a building near the Botanical Gardens (beside the Gari) when the bombing ended. No. 5 Company was round the church to the south of Route 6, No. 7 was round the School below the Castle and No. 8 was in the Castle. 7 Company was completely overrun. We formed a line of survivors with 60 men between the Telegraph Pylon on the hill below the Castle down to Route 6; eventually from the Castle to the Continental. We had had twelve Mark IV Specials in houses round the Continental and all but one were destroyed by the bombing. We sent out many men on patrol that night to give the impression of strength and to dig out buried men. We put the NZ troops on the defensive. On March 16th we had about 160 men in the town. On the night of the 16th/17th we got 80 fresh men. The New Zealand Infantry failed because they did not carry on past the Continental where there were no troops to hold them up. Our going back into the town was a bluff. There were only 40 men in the Continental in the afternoon of the 15th.

But that was more than enough to contain the survivors of two companies of the 25th Battalion. There had been a disgraceful delay over bringing the 24th and 26th Battalions into the fight. A private soldier of the 26th recalled that he had been told that the tanks would lead the way for his second wave, but when the tanks were halted by debris on the outskirts of the town, instead of pushing on alone they hung about waiting for something to happen. The steady movement forward intended by Kippenberger never took place and neither battalion commander nor the deputy brigade commander, I. L. Bonifant, was on the spot to sort things out. At a conference before he was wounded Kippenberger said that the infantry would have to double down the road to their start line when the bombing stopped. It was a mistake to suggest that tanks were going to be able to keep up initially and everyone should have been impressed with the need for speed. Instead the impression was that they were going to have a walk-over. So late in the war that was a surprising error, explained by Kippenberger's comment that by then too many units and sub-units in his division were commanded by understudies and that the 5th Infantry Brigade had a poor lot of battalion commanders.

The course of operation DICKENS was to prove a series of mishaps and heroic actions, by battalions, companies and platoons parried by equally small parties of the enemy, disconnected, failing, repeated, and eventually abandoned. As in AVENGER the basic cause was lack of troops. The German commanders were surprised, even perplexed that so huge an expenditure of fire-power was followed up by no more than handfuls of infantry and a few tanks.

As was predictable, the town itself was converted into an anti-tank obstacle of enormous craters, tangles of girders and roof-beams and masonry, from which a few parachutists with more than enough machine guns emerged. The best method of progress in such circumstances was to operate groups of infantry no bigger than platoons, each with a couple of tanks to cover them and each other. The infantry located an enemy post to be dealt with by the close-range precision fire of the tank gunners and their 75-mm cannon, after which they would rush in with grenades. The tanks, however, could not move until a route had been cleared for them, but the engineers, unprotected, were checked by the hot fire of the defenders, so there was an impasse, and the whole attack on the town was frustrated. Only four tanks, their commanders dismounted and choosing routes and the crews clearing with their own picks and shovels, contrived to work their way forward.

The attack on the Castle went better. A platoon of D Company of the 25th Battalion escaladed the couloir leading up to Point 165, and emerged from the scrub to eliminate the defence posts there. It took a company HQ and twenty-four prisoners, only to be pinned by fire from the Castle on Point 193 on one side and Point 236 above them on the other. The other two platoons of D Company took the Castle and another twenty-two prisoners, but this coup was not promptly followed up by the 5th Indian Brigade as called for in the plan. The 1st/4th Essex partly because of signals failures and partly through lack of enterprise did not reach the Castle until midnight on the 15th, by which time D Company commander had been forced to call in his exposed platoon from Point 165, where it was under attack. The 1st/9th Gurkha Rifles were supposed to be in possession of Hangman's Hill by dusk, but the 1st/6th Rajputana Rifles who were supposed to have secured the intervening features, had been shattered by an intense concentration of *Nebelwerfer* fire, losing two companies. Its attacks failed twice, that night and later the next day, when an unlucky hit wrote off battalion HQ including the commanding officer and the adjutant. The commanding officer of the 1st/9th, learning of the first disaster to the Rajputana Rifles, decided to hold two of his companies back at the Castle to wait for daylight, but relying on the skill of his mountaineers to move silently on a hillside in the dark, he sent the two others forward to sneak on to Hangman's Hill and hold it. One stumbled into an ambush, the other disappeared into the night.

Next day a New Zealand artillery observing officer reported men moving about on Hangman's Hill, and shortly afterwards a faint voice was heard on the C Company's radio reporting that they had taken the position and were in possession. Hangman's Hill was only 300 yards from the Monastery walls, but as the enemy still held Points 202 and 236 the Gurkhas' hope of rapid reinforcement was slight. However, the battered "Raj. Rifs", still good for a fight, took on Point 202, while the rest of the Gurkha battalion threaded its way in single file up to Hangman's Hill. The reader can obtain some idea of the pace of mountain warfare by looking at the apparently short distance from Castle Hill to Hangman's Hill on the panorama, and noting that it took eight hours to cover. By then parachutists and Gurkhas were already intermingled on the crag in close fighting; the company commander, his leg broken, was sitting with his back to a rock shouting encouragement to his men. He was awarded the DSO. When the rest of the battalion arrived the Germans prudently withdrew.

On the German side the conduct of the battle was dictated by the extraordinary Generalmajor Heidrich, 1st Parachute Division, who regarded the battlefield as his personal fief, would share its defence with no other troops and brook no advice or orders from above on how to run his battle. Von Senger was kept entirely in the dark about the situation. Heidrich's reports were deliberately vague, phrased to conceal rather than inform. Crises were only reported after they had been surmounted, or painted in such lurid colours that the eventual success of the parachutists appeared all the more heroic. Such exaggeration was unnecessary. Their ardour and self-sacrifice, pressed almost to the ` point of suicide, has become a legend. Heidrich was tolerated because he was successful. (When in May he was finally ordered to withdraw he refused to accept the order from anyone but Kesselring himself; this gasconade prompting Kesselring to observe drily that this was one of the disadvantages of having such strong-minded subordinates.) Von Vietinghoff and von Senger did not expect him to hold out if there were another big air attack, or that his supply dumps could last for many days of fighting. Heidrich was promised support from the Luftwaffe, but the general feeling was that rain would be better. More immediately, and more practically, Kesselring sent the 14th Corps two battalions of the 115th Panzer Grenadiers. They were used on the 16th to relieve the 4th Parachute Regiment on Colle S. Angelo to free it to reinforce the garrison of Cassino. At 6.30 p.m. the longed-for rain began to fall.

By the 17th such opportunity for success as had ever existed was lost and Operation DICKENS had stagnated. It had separated into three sub-battles. In the town and its environs the New Zealanders continued their nibbling, step-by-step attacks and the parachutists their fanatical defence. Both Clark and Major-General A. Galloway (who temporarily commanded the 4th Indian Division during March 9th –25th) favoured throwing in every available infantryman, but Freyberg, wisely perhaps, preferred the tactics of infiltration of small parties supported by a tank or two. It certainly kept down his losses. At the end of the battle the town was shared, and the two sides – separated in places by no more than the thickness of a wall – kept up a small, bitter private war until the May offensive.

The second bone of contention was the Castle, now firmly in the hands of the Essex and parts of the Rajputana Rifles, which commanded the covered way between the town and the summits of Montecassino. On 18th/19th, at the moment when the Essex were preparing to move up to reinforce the Gurkhas on Hangman's Hill, it was ferociously attacked by a group of parachutists who blew down a section of wall to gain entry. A terrific struggle ensued, resembling an eighteenth-century assault on a fort, rifles firing through loopholes, the attackers repelled by showers of grenades. The parachutists assaulted three times and were beaten off three times. The defenders were down to sixty men commanded by the one remaining officer, with three wounds, when the parachutists, under attack by Indian riflemen who had left the security of the wall and sustained an intense artillery defensive fire, finally gave up.

The third battlefield was the area of the Monastery itself. A converging attack was planned for the early morning of the 19th, from Hangman's Hill on one side and by a force of tanks from the direction of Snakeshead on the other. In fact the spearhead of one attack, the Gurkhas, was itself under siege, and the reinforcements who succeeded in fighting their way up to them amounted only to forty fit men and thirty wounded. Their attack from Hangman's Hill was called off. The tank attack, composed of American, New Zealand sub-units and some light tanks from the reconnaissance regiment of the 4th Indian Division, was a bold stroke which "for a few hours had the German radios crackling with excitement which almost amounted to panic". It was as mismanaged as any operation could be. Its commander, borrowed from the British artillery at short notice, had no experience of armoured warfare and had been given no clear mission, it had no accompanying infantry, did not contact the battalion from the 4th Indian Division on Snakeshead, and the commander, who made a long and fatal pause to obtain clarification of his instructions, finally withdrew up the mountain track by which he had arrived, to find that the enterprising parachutists had hastily sown it with mines. Fourteen tanks were lost in this fiasco.

These, it will be understood, are but three incidents in a chaotic operation in which some unit or other was desperately engaged almost every hour at some point over the whole area of operations. It was clear enough by the evening of the 19th that it was profitless to persist in DICKENS, but it was only recognised on the 23rd, when Alexander ordered the New Zealand Corps to stand fast and consolidate their gains, and Hangman's Hill to be abandoned. Elaborate arrangements were made to prevent alerting the Germans. Three volunteer officers were sent by separate routes with verbal orders for the withdrawal, each with a carrier pigeon to take back a message reporting the success of their mission. Two of the officers managed to slip past the enemy posts, and the evacuation was carried out without a single casualty on the night of the 24th.

The imaginative officer who composed Heidrich's battle reports wrote that the garrison on Hangman's Hill was still resisting desperately on the 26th and then that it had fallen on the 27th, 165 dead being counted and 11 prisoners taken. This was the only diverting item of news in a defeat redeemed by the courage and endurance of the troops, but none the less a defeat. Heidrich's victory was not cheap. Half of his 2nd/3rd Parachute Infantry disappeared during the bombing of the town, and of the four battalions defending it each could assemble only about two platoons on the 23rd. Von Senger, only too aware of how far the troops available to defend Cassino had been ground down by attrition, fully expected the Allies to resume their onslaught after a pause, for their artillery and tanks kept up a fire of such intensity after the 23rd that his rate of loss remained the same as during the offensive. His fears were unfounded, although he would not have been much easier in mind had he known that at last the Allied high command had resolved to wage war in more enlightened style than the one which had ensured the string of failures which had marked the past three months.

V

Interlude

Harold Alexander – C-in-C Allied
Armies, Italy – the air of steely resolve
concealed a lack of grip.

Albert Kesselring, C-in-C of the German
forces in Italy. Against odds he made the
Allies pay dearly for every mile.

Montgomery, commander of the 8th Army in 1943, meeting some of the Canadians he so admired.

Above: Mark Clark, right, whose great qualities as a commander were marred by jealousy and suspicion, with his trusted chief of operations, Donald W. Brann.

Right: Alfred Gruenther, Clark's cautious, diplomatic chief-of-staff throughout the campaign.

Heinrich von Vietinghoff, commander of
the 10th Army, who later succeeded
Kesselring as Commander-in-Chief.

Above: the unlucky Ernest J. Dawley, commander of the 6th Corps at Salerno, who fell foul of Clark.

Right: Richard McCreery, commander of the 10th Corps and of the 8th Army during its final victory. At once profane, puritan and highly professional.

Above: with Alexander, Oliver Leese, left, relaxed, wearing his usual quizzical expression; a disciple of Montgomery, he succeeded him in command of the 8th Army.

Right: "John" Harding, Alexander's chief-of-staff, a soldier of immense ability.

Right: Fred L. Walker, commander of the much battered 36th Division, who opened the road to Rome at M. Artemisio.

Below: John W. O'Daniel, the "iron man" of the Salerno beach-head.

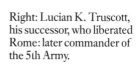

Above: John P. Lucas, commander of the 6th Corps at Anzio, talking to British commander V. Eveleigh. Like his predecessor, he was sacked after the battle.

Right: Lucian K. Truscott, his successor, who liberated Rome: later commander of the 5th Army.

Gerhard von Mackensen, commander of the 14th Army at Anzio, like his opponent Lucas, he was sacked after the battle.

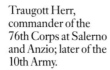

Traugott Herr, commander of the 76th Corps at Salerno and Anzio; later of the 10th Army.

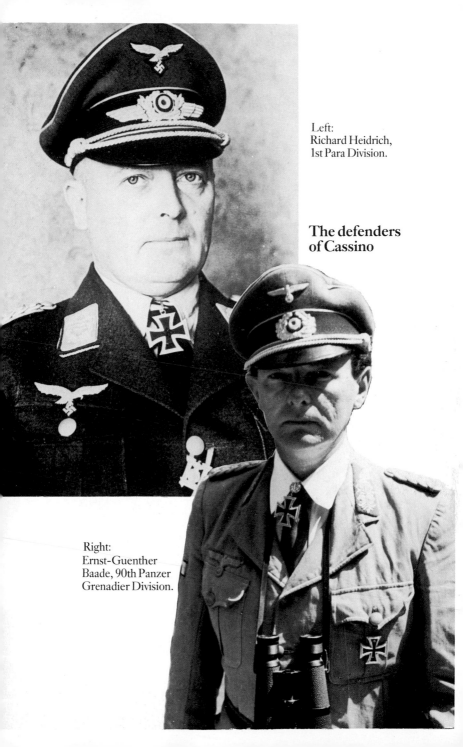

Left:
Richard Heidrich,
1st Para Division.

**The defenders
of Cassino**

Right:
Ernst-Guenther
Baade, 90th Panzer
Grenadier Division.

Left: Fridolin von Senger und Etterlin, commander of 14 Pz Corps, a master of defensive tactics.

Below: Geoffrey G. Keyes, commander of the 2nd Corps, right, receiving an honorary CB from Alexander.

Left: Wladyslaw Anders, commander of the heroic 2nd Polish Corps.

Below left: Alphonse Juin, master of offensive tactics: Commander of the CEF, saluting with his uninjured left arm.

Below: Bernard Freyberg VC, commander of the veteran 2nd New Zealand Division.

Strained relations

Above: A gloomy Clark, left, Alexander, centre, and right, McCreery, whose rare smile was a danger-signal.
Below: E. L. M. Burns, left, commander of the 1st Canadian Corps, talking to an unsympathetic Leese.

Two thrusting commanders:

Above: C. Vokes, of the
1st Canadian Division.

Right: B. T. Hoffmeister,
of the 5th Canadian
Armoured Division.

Sidney Kirkman, 13th Corps, who needed all his British phlegm to cope with Clark.

Charles Keightley, commander of the 78th Division and later 5th Corps.

14

ACHTUNG! JABO – "LOOK OUT,
FIGHTER-BOMBERS!"

And like a thunderbolt he falls.

The Eagle, *Alfred, Lord Tennyson, 1842*

In June 1944 a "landbound GI" scribbled off a few lines of appreciation to his air force friends of the past few weeks:

> I sometimes wonder if you guys in the Air Corps know how the
> landbound GIs feel about you. I heard that there was some jealousy
> and bad feeling between the branches. Nuts! The GIs in the
> armoured and the infantry worship the skies our Air Corps flies in.
> We never get tired of looking up when we hear our planes and
> shouting "give 'em hell boys!" When up front it's a grand feeling to
> see them upstairs – to see them clearing the way ahead. Every time
> we see one in trouble – or in an occasional dog-fight – we're pulling
> and pushing like a guy working a pin-ball machine. I've heard our
> top brass talk about the perfect support and cooperation we've had
> from the air!

A GI would never have given the US 12th Air Support Command
such praise a year earlier, for it was not until the late spring that the
USAAF was able to come to terms with the need to supply the ground
forces' vital requirement for close support, or to accept a safe method of
doing it.[1] Rather, when American aircraft came to support him his first
impulse would have been to take cover in his slit trench. Even as late as
the Battle of Normandy the troops used to say, "When the Typhoons
[RAF] come over the Germans take cover: When the Thunderbolts are
over we all take cover." As for the brass, when General Omar Bradley
was in Sicily he complained: "We can't get the stuff [i.e., close air

support] when it's needed, and we are catching hell for it. By the time our request for support's gone through channels the target's gone or the Stukas have come instead." So did General Ryder: "I noticed that in action when my tanks started rolling or my artillery opened on some target of real importance to the Germans the Stukas would be over in twenty minutes . . . failure of our air support is the weakest link in our tactical team today." After Salerno Clark had complained to Alexander that his requests for direct support through his air liaison staff had seldom been accepted, and when they were the air force response had been slow. It had taken the crisis of the battle, on September 13, to persuade the USAAF to come to his aid, when they had raised the daily mission rate from 66 to 587, and used their heavy bombers to wreck Battipaglia. The lesson should have been learnt, especially after it became clear that the USAAF policy of road interdiction had done little to prevent the move of the 14th and 76th Panzer Corps to Salerno.

But, as we have said, the air force commanders considered the air battle indivisible. They were governed by the doctrine that the US Army Air Force had acquired from the RAF and was enshrined in Field Manual FM 100-20, issued in July 1943. Close support for the army was low in their list of priorities. Their first task was to win air superiority, for without freedom to use the skies the other tasks were not feasible. Next came the interdiction of the land battlefield. The army was expected to provide its own close support and the air force would only attack targets beyond the range of artillery. After Salerno the first aim of the air force seemed to have been attained, except when the Luftwaffe made a special effort, as it did at Anzio. The tactical air force therefore devoted most of its energy to interdiction. In giving close support to the Fifth Army the 12th Air Support Command had not yet a system as effective as that of the Desert Air Force, RAF and Eighth Army in the final stages of the war in North Africa, for Americans interpreted FM 100-20 rather rigidly and the battle had not been sufficiently mobile, nor the weather suitable to give favourable opportunities to exploit its power on the battlefield often. Without opportunities and practice, techniques could not be tested nor the skills of the pilots perfected. Moreover, the American air commanders' view of the strategy of the war in Italy differed from that of the ground commanders. Indeed, they did not seem to be fighting the same war.[2]

The US Fifteenth Strategic Air Force was in Italy to wage the Combined Bomber Offensive (CBO) in company with the American Eighth and the British Bomber Command in the skies over Germany. When the Fifth Army was poised to enter Italy over the beaches of Salerno, the air war was entering a new phase. August 17, 1943, the day the Sicily campaign ended, was the anniversary of the US Eighth Air Force's first operation against targets in France and marked the start of its daylight penetration to more distant targets such as Wiener-Neustadt and Schweinfurt. Its losses during those long and largely unescorted flights were prohibitive and the replacement of lost crews and aircraft inadequate. Consequently, competition for air resources between the UK, the Mediterranean and other theatres, already acute, was sharpened. The Mediterranean commanders had to choose between ensuring that their air operations served the CBO just as their ground operations had to serve OVERLORD, or risk having aircraft and crews transferred to USAAF bases in England.

"Hap" Arnold, Chief of the Army Air Force and also deputy chief of staff to Marshall, was like a restless spider in his Washington office, driving himself to a heart attack and his subordinates in the European Theatre of Operations (ETO) to frustration and fury by his needling letters and goading. He and Marshall were as one in their support for the CBO, although Marshall did not share the opinion of Arnold and Carl "Tooey" Spaatz (Tedder's deputy in the Mediterranean until December 1943) that the invasion of Normandy might not be necessary if the CBO was given all the resources Arnold and Spaatz demanded. When Spaatz succeeded to overall command of the US strategic bomber forces engaged in the CBO he and Marshall were united in their resolve that the ETO, not the Pacific theatre, should have first claim on US air resources, and that the CBO should have priority over all other operations. Both men suspected that the British were not whole-heartedly committed to OVERLORD, and neither regarded Italy as a substitute for it, or even as a legitimate contender for resources required for the strategic aim. Another factor bearing on support for the army in Italy was that both the USAAF and RAF chiefs believed that given the necessary resources the CBO should obtain a decision unaided by the ground forces, and as a result they saw the ETO as a single front. The land generals saw Normandy and Italy as rivals.

Eaker, who had commanded the US Eighth Air Force in the trying early days of strategic bombing, went as commander of the newly formed Mediterranean Air Force in the great pre-OVERLORD shuffle at the turn of 1943–4. Subordinate to it was the Mediterranean Allied Tactical Air Force, and the strategic bomber force, the Fifteenth Air Force commanded by Major-General Nathan L. Twining, assigned to operate from airfields in Italy against the southern part of the CBO target area. So Eaker, as firm a believer in the supremacy of air power as any, was installed in the Mediterranean, with Spaatz as his direct superior in CBO matters in England. At the same time he was Maitland Wilson's chief air officer and adviser and commanded all the Allied air forces in the Mediterranean theatre.

In mid 1943 Eaker and his colleagues were satisfied that as far as Phase 1 of their doctrine was concerned they had achieved local air superiority, but the situation in the air war as a whole was horrific. At that time heavy bombers on long-range missions had to defend themselves against fighter attack with their own armament, which they proved unable to do. (And could not until the long-range P 51 fighter fitted with the Rolls-Royce Merlin engine and drop tanks came into service in December 1943.) On August 17, 1943 the Eighth Air Force lost 60 aircraft and over 100 damaged out of 380, and 600 aircrew killed, wounded or missing during raids on Regensburg and Schweinfurt. On October 14, 229 heavy bombers took off to attack Schweinfurt and its ball-bearing factories again and "the burnt out wrecks of *der dicker Hund* (as the Germans called the B 17 bomber) marked a trail hundreds of miles long", the prey of 300 Luftwaffe fighters. Sixty more aircraft and their crews were lost and seventeen aircraft so badly damaged that they were never repaired limped home with many of their crews dead or wounded.[3] Eaker's first aim in 1943 was therefore to conduct operations over German-held Italy calculated to bring the German fighters to battle and destroy them so that they could not be used to reinforce the CBO area. He had the added incentive that his own heavy bombers were about to join in the battle in the air over Germany and had already visited the Romanian oil fields.

The air strategy adopted with this aim was the interdiction of the German Army's lines of communication and in particular the Italian railway system, hoping simultaneously to provoke the German air defences and also assist the ground war by forcing Kesselring to shorten his supply lines by withdrawing to the line Pisa–Rimini. When evidence accumulated that Kesselring intended nothing of the sort it seemed to the air commanders imperative to take advantage of the long communication extending from northern Italy to the Gustav Line and plan a well-coordinated air programme. Honorary Group Captain Solly Zuckerman,* scientific adviser to the RAF, had analysed the effect of bombing on the Italian railway system during the spring and

---

* Lord Zuckerman, as he became, is a man of wide knowledge and formidable powers of analysis. The military were somewhat puzzled by his appointment at first, for he had so far distinguished himself as a zoologist and anatomist, with an excursion into a different field in the shape of his book *The Social Life of Monkeys and Apes*. He was scientific adviser at AEAF, MAAF and SHAEF in 1939–46.

summer of 1943, consulting Italian railway officials, aircrews and the air photograph interpreters. His report was used by Eaker when drawing up the interdiction programme for the late winter of 1943–4.

Zuckerman concluded that supplies could never be halted completely or permanently for there was too much surplus capacity in the Italian railway system, only 5 per cent of which was required for military purposes. However, it was feasible to bring it to such a state of chaos that road transport, which consumed much precious fuel and was less efficient, would have to be used over long distances, and kept standing by at potential bottlenecks in case of need. That had been the situation south of Rome in August 1943, according to Italian railway officials. The correct targets to bring about the desired effect were marshalling yards, not so much the tracks, although their destruction would be a useful by-product, as the rolling stock, engines, repair shops and the labour force from the area. By repeatedly disrupting the relatively important ones, the business of making up and despatching trains would have to be dispersed over many small sidings and rendered inefficient. Essentially Zuckerman's conception was strategic and not tactical. Over a long period it would create a condition of anaemia, not rapid death by starvation.

By contrast, the tactical method was to cut the lines at bridges, tunnels, embankments and cuttings. The Fifteenth Air Force had studied the bridge method and reported on December 11:

> The relatively small size of bridges makes them unsatisfactory bombing targets in that a large expenditure of effort is required to damage them. The question is whether the value of the expected results of attacking certain bridges will outweigh the expected value of dropping that tonnage of bombs on other targets.

They had hit one bridge in every 190 sorties. There was a marked variation in the construction of Italian bridges and hence in their susceptibility to damage. Most were small targets averaging thirty feet by three hundred and it might take ten missions of thirty aircraft to ensure an 82.2 per cent likelihood of a hit. Even then the bridge might remain serviceable. Naturally, Zuckerman concluded that tactical interdiction should be used only when a battle was in course and only near the battlefield.

It will be remembered that in the first two weeks of February the Combined Chiefs of Staff were impatient with the way the campaign was progressing. On the 10th Arnold wrote to Eaker suggesting that he should use the 2,900 planes at his disposal to blast a way into the Liri valley. Eaker retorted that even if he agreed the army could not make proper use of such support. The army staff had to have accurate locations for the forward troops and have passed them in good time to the air staff, and the assault units had to be ready to jump off the moment the air bombardment stopped, so as to take full advantage of its momentarily stunning effect. He was not in the least confident that the army staff could guarantee either. He preferred the conventional air force strategy, to isolate, or "interdict" the battlefield. Here he had the support of Maitland Wilson. On the 25th Wilson issued the general directive that conflicted with Harding's plan for a spring offensive. He observed that such an operation should be governed by the air factor; clearly a reflection of Eaker's ideas. Meanwhile the American Joint Chiefs of Staff (JCS), concluding that Eaker's interdiction plan would not produce quick results, supported Arnold's idea of using heavy bombers at Cassino. Churchill, who had poured cold water on Wilson's interdiction plan and approved of Harding's spring offensive, was not in favour of a pause at Cassino in the meantime. These conflicting ideas influenced the conduct of DICKENS, which was a battle emerging from a compromise.

Neither Eaker nor his deputy, Air Marshal Sir John Slessor, expected much from the bombing of Cassino. For his part, Alexander did not expect the air forces to strangle German supplies either, but as the JCS was anxious for territorial gains and yet averse to the battles of attrition in Italy that were absorbing men at a disturbing rate, and as Clark supported the JCS, Alexander agreed to the use of heavy bombers at Cassino and also to Eaker's new interdiction programme from March until DIADEM began. The bombing of Cassino was tentative and experimental, for the senior airmen had not much confidence in it. Alexander thought that it would save lives, as did Freyberg, who had a strong interest in not wasting them. In fact everyone thought that there was nothing to lose by trying it, and in any case that it would be unwise to resist the advice of Washington.

The mistake made by the staff of the Fifth Army was its failure to grasp the technical details involved and in not analysing the lessons which emerged from the bombing of Cassino a month earlier; something very much their business and which should not have been left to non-specialists in the *ad hoc* HQ New Zealand Corps. The after-action reports on the Cassino bombing suggested that even if technical failures and human errors had not occurred heavy bombers were too inaccurate for close support. Most of the errors, though, were laid at the door of the army. The target had not been marked continually by coloured smoke, mission leaders had not been briefed on the ground, the choice of flight paths had not been made to suit both the terrain and the location of friendly troops, and the army had not stated clearly the effect that they wished the air force to achieve. Above all, the army had not followed up quickly. In future bombing ought to be over a shorter span of time. Slessor and Eaker commented that they had no right to expect better results from the bombardment than had been obtained from much heavier ones on the Western Front, but the two cases were dissimilar. It had been shown conclusively on the Western Front that when bombardments were heavy, accurate, of short duration and were followed up closely by tanks and infantry they were usually successful.

At Cassino the bombardment of the enemy positions had been prolonged and woefully inaccurate, and the infantry follow-up delayed, so that the German defenders had been able to recover, emerge from their shelters and man their weapons. There were no procedures for coordinating the action of heavy bombers and the ground forces and no special communication network for making them effective, as had been developed between the ground forces and the tactical air forces.

Eaker's sensible conclusion was that the strategic bomber crews were not trained for close support and in future should be used only in emergencies as they had been at Salerno. The tactical air force, which had performed much better at Cassino, was the proper agent. To reinforce his point he took immediate action to improve liaison between the Fifth Army and the 12th Air Support Command. To strengthen his interdiction programme, which he had started on March 19 under the code-name STRANGLE, he added a tactical objective to the strategic one in the Zuckerman report, on the ground that medium bombers were more accurate than they had been at the end of 1943.

STRANGLE filled in the gap between DICKENS and DIADEM and merged into the interdiction programme for the latter. Exaggerated claims were made for its success at the time, and they were repeated in the US Air Force history, but if it is to be judged by its intention of making it impossible for the Germans to maintain their forces in the Gustav position it failed. Even the lesser claim that it forced the Germans to break off the battle south of Rome for want of supplies is unsubstantiated by the Germans. One motive for the exaggerated claims made for STRANGLE was to show that the air force was a decisive arm. Harris, Arnold, Spaatz, perhaps even Eaker, all believed that OVERLORD would not be necessary if the CBO were pursued to its logical end. The armies would land in Normandy to find that the air battle had been won and the Germans, starved of supplies, incapable of prolonged resistance.

STRANGLE had a third aim: to act as an operation test for a similar programme in Normandy. Its directors could monitor its progress by intelligence intercepts giving the details of damage repair and shifts to road and coastal shipping. Total interdiction seemed possible but Allied Intelligence had grossly overestimated the tonnage per German division consumed at "quiet" rates, and underestimated the amount already dumped close behind the front. Furthermore, the air force intelligence staffs underestimated the extraordinary ability of the Germans to organise emergency lifts and to use the hours of darkness to repair damage. Above all there was the spare capacity in the railway system, to which Zuckerman had drawn attention, and additional capacity in small coastal craft which supplied units within twenty miles of the coast through small harbours and over the beaches. Finally the weather did not improve very much in March and there were gaps of days in the offensive of which the Germans made good use.

The switch to tactical targets in April – to bridge-busting as well as marshalling yards – brought some successes but small targets were extravagant with crews and aircraft. Gordon Saville, the USAAF officer, told a friend in Washington on April 20: "Our waste of effort in trying to hit railroad tracks and bridges from high altitude is *simply fantastic*." In his opinion fighter-bombers were the most effective aircraft and their missions could be verified at low altitude. But they were unable to operate at night when medium bombers were not available either. This was a grave defect:

> We have neglected, and are neglecting, woefully night units for interdiction in close and direct support. The B-25 is a good airplane for this, but a unit cannot be both day and night.[4]

The interpreters of air photographs exaggerated the effectiveness of raids to support the optimistic reports of senior officers who favoured tactical over strategic targets.

Using the full range of German documents Eduard Mark has recently written an account of STRANGLE which balances the negative account of it offered here and the overoptimistic, and probably politically inspired expectations of the contemporary airforce leadership. He has discovered that the Germans made up divisional supply trains north of the alpine passes from Austria and unloaded them into road transport north of Rome, sometimes north of Florence and even north of the northern Apennine passes. The bombing of marshalling yards was, therefore, inappropriate except as a means of denying their use. Despite the titanic effort of the quarter-masters, the Germans did not restore significantly the level of ammunition holdings in the forward area after they had been run down in the February and early March battles. They remained at dangerously low levels through April and into the DIADEM battles in May. The Fourteenth Army attack against the 6th Corps at Anzio was not resumed in March because of ammunition shortage and von Senger's advice that his corps should be withdrawn from the Gustav position was offered because of the ammunition situation. It is evident that, while Allied soldiers may not have appreciated it, German shelling and mortaring might have been considerably worse but for STRANGLE. Unfortunately, there was a simultaneous dearth of ammunition in AAI, although not on the German scale, and it prompted Alexander to fly to the UK in April to obtain sufficient for DIADEM. Had there been a sufficiency German morale might have suffered more than it did from the Allies' gun superiority before DIADEM.

But when all this has been said, evidence has not been produced that German ground troops were handicapped in holding ground in DIADEM by shortage of ammunition. No doubt in retreat they were able to fall back on ammunition depots and avoid transporting it forward in daylight over roads watched by cab-ranks of fighter-bombers.

Not that STRANGLE was a wasted effort for German material was destroyed, fuel supplies and labour were expended. But the effort would have been better directed, in January and February at least, to stopping the movement of men rather than supplies, particularly the movement of units between the Gustav position and Anzio, the Plain of Lombardy and Anzio, and the Mediterranean fronts. These movements were slow and painful because of winter conditions but they were not prevented or made appreciably slower by air attack. As Zuckerman pointed out, interdiction was really effective only in close conjunction with ground operations, but there were none between the middle of March and the opening of DIADEM in May.

Slessor and Eaker kept in close touch with Spaatz in England who, with Harris, was trying to prevent his heavy bombers being used for Eisenhower's pre-OVERLORD interdiction programme in France. Spaatz found it useful to be able to point to STRANGLE as an example of an interdiction programme where tactical aircraft had been effective against bridges, contrary to Zuckerman's thesis, and to argue that the tactical air forces could provide for Eisenhower's needs while his strategic bombers were left to get on with their campaign against oil targets. It was a particularly appealing idea since tactical targets were usually further from civilian dwellings and the accuracy of tactical aircraft restricted the damage to houses.

Eaker's actions to improve the close support of Fifth Army by 12th Tactical Air Command* came to fruition in time for DIADEM, but the seeds were planted in January, when the Cassino battle was just beginning. Then a group of British air liaison officers arrived at Fort Benning, Georgia, to help the US Army conduct its first course on the subject. "We look upon ourselves as ambassadors," one of them remarked at the pre-course conference. His listeners thought, at first, that he was referring to the presence of British officers at an American school. But when he continued to explain that the British "found that the ground and air forces live in entirely different worlds and that liaison officers had come to regard themselves as ambassadors to a foreign power", one of those present thought that his words should be recorded. The RAF and the British Army were already separate services, wore different uniforms and had learned to respect each other's foibles, concerns and aims. Although all the Americans present were supposed to be in the same service, the airmen were still fighting for their independence and the soldiers to retain control. Good air support was the result of diplomacy and the recognition of the different and equal status of the Army Air Force by army officers.

In the British system, it had not been until the dogmatic separatist "Maori" Coningham had been succeeded by the positive, cooperative Broadhurst that the air support of Eighth Army had come of age. Clark and Saville, too, had to take the rough edges off the operational bible of the Army Air Force, FM 100-20, which categorically placed close support third and last in their priorities. The inferior rank of air officers working with the army, lower in the American system than the British, had to be disregarded and the arrangement between Clark and Saville, for instance, to become "less a system than certain practical arrangements which gave expression to a mutual understanding and close working relationship between the commands". The army had to say clearly what they wanted to achieve and the airmen had to decide how to do it. Aircraft had to be allocated for the use of army formations, even if they were not actually under command. It all amounted to a pragmatism that seemed un-American. But as in so many similar problems, once the Americans saw the need, they overcame the obstacles. Eaker wrote in April:

> There must be a thorough understanding on the part of the ground forces supported by such operations of the powers and limitations of the Air Forces engaged. A plan is now in operation in this theatre for

---

* The new name of 12th Air Support Command.

the exchange of personnel between the ground forces which will go a long way towards better education of both the air and ground elements on the other's problems.

All this was long overdue in the Fifth Army, but it was timely. April marked the beginning of better weather and of the pre-DIADEM planning and training. It was the first spring of the campaign in Italy, a time for new beginnings after the unsatisfactory experiences of the winter. The regrouping by which non-American divisions left the Fifth Army except for the French and the British in the Anzio bridgehead, facilitated air support. Furthermore, once the front started to move, strategic interdiction would give way to tactical interdiction and close support. The P 47 fighter-bomber – the Thunderbolt – carrying a 1,000-pound bomb, eight 50-calibre machine guns and, increasingly, rockets rather than bombs, came into service as the work-horse. The P 51, in its F 6 form, carried a K 22 camera for photography at from 6,000 to 8,000 feet. A P 38 without armament, called the F 5, flew at a minimum ceiling of 18,000 feet to undertake higher-level photographic reconnaissance. TAC also had medium bombers.

The key to success was to integrate observing and reporting agencies down to the lowest levels. In the early days a bomber safety line (BSL) was laid down by the army and was usually at least five and sometimes ten miles in front of the leading troops. At Cassino it had been a 1,000 yards. There were no forward controls to pass target information or to control bombing any closer. Support tended not to be "close" at all. Maturity had come too slowly, but by the great May offensive (DIADEM) a mature system had come into use. Forward controllers were established in the US 2nd and US 6th, and the CEF, both on the ground and airborne in light aircraft. A Close Support Line (CSL) was laid down inside the BSL and the previous embargo about taking on targets within artillery range was abandoned. It was recognised that not only had rockets and bombs a different effect and, often, a more salutary one than shells, but aircraft could see targets that were invisible to artillery observers. Formerly, German troops felt reasonably safe near the front if they were hidden from ground observers. Now they were liable to be shot at in daylight wherever they appeared above ground. Air controllers could summon aircraft from as far away as Naples. The result was that between May 16 and June 1 about 10,000 German vehicles of all descriptions were destroyed on the Fifth Army front. The cry *"Achtung! Jabo"* was often heard on German radio.

The CSL opened up a whole new area of activity and brought airmen and soldiers to see that they were fighting the same battle. An example was the introduction of "Horsefly", the appropriately named air force equivalent of the British "Air Observation Post", used by the artillery. The instigator of Horsefly was an artillery pilot flying a Piper Cub light aircraft (L 5) who landed, short of fuel, at the command post of the 1st Armored Division, fighting with 6th Corps. He had been engaging a horse-drawn battery at extreme range. Seeing Captain William Davidson, the chief air controller, he enquired why the air force had not established an L 5 airborne observer to bombard targets that were out of his range or were better suited to bombs and rockets than shells. Subsequently Brigadier-General Barcus, then commanding the 64th Fighter Wing, discussed the idea with Saville, procured the necessary aircraft, and on June 15 started to use Horsefly. Davidson, with an army observer beside him, inaugurated the scheme and it became standard practice for two pilots to be seconded to it for a month at a time. The aggressiveness of the earlier practitioners led them to operate up to twenty miles inside enemy territory. On several occasions pilots dived on their targets to indicate them to the Jabos which they had called up, no doubt praying that the Jabo pilots were quick in the uptake. One pilot, more eccentric and daring even than usual, fixed a bazooka to his aircraft and successfully joined in the fun when the target was a tank. There were casualties and at least one Silver Star, that awarded to First Lieutenant Ryland Dewey. Light aircraft were soon restricted to the zone between the BSL and the CSL.

Horsefly provided the finishing touch to a system that had seen the emphasis shift from Phase 1 in Tunisia and Sicily, to Phase 2 at Salerno and afterwards, to Phase 3 in the summer of 1944. By then the US practice bore a close resemblance to the British pattern, varying from it in detail and in style, perhaps, but very little in spirit. The USAAF had become wholly absorbed in its task of helping its friends on the ground.

In this way two important steps to ensure effective cooperation between the USAAF and the US Army had been taken between the landing at Salerno and the beginning of the battle for Rome in May 1944. First, the prejudices and suspicions of both sides were broken down. Second, command and control machinery on the same lines as the British had been created, with the added benefit that the two Allied air forces became interchangeable in terms of ground support. The third and equally important step was insistence on training. If they had a weakness, Arnold and Marshall (like Churchill) had a tendency to calculate battle-effectiveness by the numbers of guns, tanks, aircraft and men available. They seemed to have found it difficult to understand why not much more was achieved in 1943 when resources were lavish, than in 1942 when they were merely adequate. It was a question

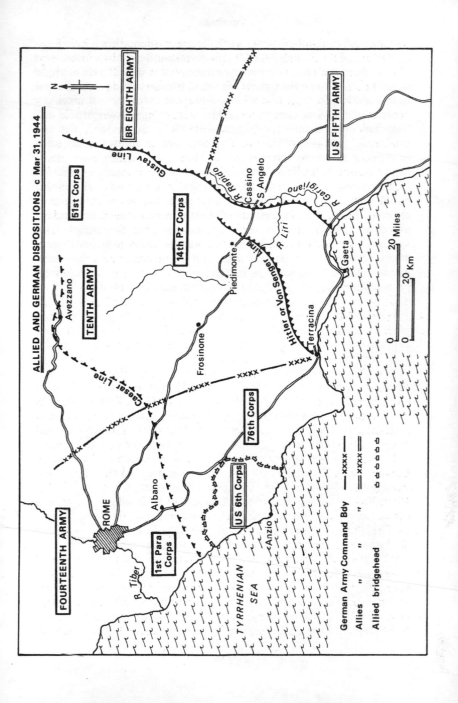

ALLIED AND GERMAN DISPOSITIONS c Mar 31, 1944

BR EIGHTH ARMY

US FIFTH ARMY

51st Corps

14th Pz Corps

TENTH ARMY

76th Corps

1st Para Corps

FOURTEENTH ARMY

US 6th Corps

Gustav Line

Hitler or Von Senger Line

Caesar Line

Avezzano

Piedimonte

Frosinone

Albano

ROME

Anzio

Terracina

Gaeta

Cassino

S Angelo

R Rapido

R Liri

R Garigliano

R Tiber

TYRRHENIAN SEA

N

German Army Command Bdy   ————— xxxx
Allies   "   "   ═══════ xxxx
Allied bridgehead   ᵔᵔᵔᵔᵔ

0   20 Miles
0   20 Km

of training, not simply in skills, but in battle-wisdom. When Eaker was commanding the Eighth Air Force his correspondence with Arnold was filled with appeals not only for more aircrews but time to train them. In peace he had had all the time in the world to train but few aircraft: now in the midst of war he had all that American industry and ingenuity could supply and no time to train. He tried to impress on Arnold and Marshall, who found it somehow difficult to understand, the vast difference between aircrew fresh from training units and after the experience of several operations. He had to resist the importunate higher commanders who pressed him to throw all his resources into the fray at once, for the veterans had to teach the newcomers things that could only be learnt in combat. This principle was not limited to aircrew training. It also applied to the whole machinery combining the efforts of the Fifth Army and 12th Tactical Air Force; the special pilots, special air liaison staffs, the ground forces themselves (who had to learn what the air force could and could not do in battle) and the senior commanders of both services. Its successful application was important in the continuing struggle in Italy and, indeed, in OVERLORD.

VI

At Last A Plan

15

A MAN OF RUTHLESS LOGIC

The ability to evaluate the situation objectively has always been a sign of true leadership.

General F. von Senger und Etterlin

Alan Brooke, the British chief of the Imperial General Staff, kept a watchful eye on every Allied operation from his desk in Whitehall. He sensed a lack of grip in Alexander's direction of the armies in Italy and suspected the competence of his command apparatus. This was no sudden perception. He had been aware of Alexander's shortcomings much earlier, during the concluding phases of the war in Tunisia and the battle in Sicily, but the responsibility then had been Eisenhower's and Brooke had not thought it proper to interfere. After Eisenhower left and was replaced by a British officer Brooke felt more directly responsible and decided to act. He could do nothing about Alexander's personality, but he could do something about his command arrangements. In the spring of 1943 Montgomery had written frequently to Brooke (the only mentor he acknowledged) urging that Alexander be given a first-rate staff and, what was essential, a chief of staff able to provide him with sound strategic advice who could also reorganise and invigorate his HQ. This, with its atmosphere, something between a London gentleman's club and the senior common room at an ancient university, may have faithfully represented Alexander's calmness, lack of urgency and distaste for vulgarly or ostentatiously imposing his will on operations, but it was not a powerhouse for energising armies.[1] In January Alexander's field HQ was at Taranto, he depended on an advanced HQ of AFHQ in Algiers for logistics, and he proposed to control the SHINGLE and Garigliano operations from a tactical HQ in railway carriages near Naples. Montgomery had once offered to send

Alexander an experienced officer from the Eighth Army. It so happened that there was just such a one in England, lately recovered from his wounds, who had proved in the desert to be a brilliant staff officer and a commander in the field. Brooke wasted no time. On New Year's Day 1944 Lieutenant-General A. F. Harding flew to Algiers to take up the appointment of Chief of Staff HQ 15th Army Group.*

"John" Harding, as he was always known in the British Army, was one of those rare British officers who reached high rank without being a member of the upper-class establishment, attending a public school, the Royal Military College, Sandhurst or the Royal Military Academy, Woolwich. His family sprang from the middle class, tough, hardworking backbone of Victorian England. His father was a solicitor's clerk at South Petherton, in Somerset, and his mother ran the stationer's shop. They brought their son up in their own tradition of strict religious observance and hard work. He received a good, basic education at Ilminster Grammar School and when only fifteen years old began work as a clerk in the civil service. The new Territorial Army provided interest and activity for just such as he, and fatefully he was commissioned as a second lieutenant in May 1914. Four years' active service ending with the temporary command of a battalion convinced him that the army should be his career. He applied for a regular commission, was accepted into his county regiment, the Somerset Light Infantry, and in due course commanded it. When he attended the Staff College at Camberley Montgomery was an instructor and Dick McCreery a fellow student, and he earned a reputation for application rather than brilliance. His true quality was to emerge in the wild, swirling desert battles of 1941, when he was Brigadier, General Staff of the 13th Corps. At one stage during operation CRUSADER, engaged with Rommel, the corps was scattered, its HQ cut off from its units by the panzers and the corps commander lost and out of touch. Harding took complete charge, issuing orders as if he were in command, restored the situation and brought that phase of the operation to a successful conclusion. He was twice awarded the Distinguished Service Order, usually reserved for gallantry in combat. The second citation described him as "that invaluable asset, a fighting staff officer". He went on to command the 7th Armoured Division, and was severely wounded when reconnoitring in the forward area at the end of the war in Africa.[2]

A "fighting staff officer", certainly, and also the possessor of a keenly analytical brain, but much as Brooke might have wished him to rule the roost, he could only exert influence. It is important to understand the

* Changed to Allied Armies, Italy in March 1944.

difference between the British staff system and the German, of which it was a pale imitation. The German general staff was a separate, united body, a caste rather than a corps, devised to serve, guide and even admonish generals who in the early days owed their position as much to their princely or noble rank as to their military knowledge. (Although, of course, in the twentieth century the German Army's staff-trained officers rose to high command.) If a commander was relieved for incompetence his chief of staff was dismissed with him, as he was also regarded as responsible. A staff officer was expected to initiate orders on behalf of his commander and virtually act as his deputy. (We have seen how Colonel Ruenkel intervened at Salerno, riding rough-shod over the divisional commanders.) In the German Army a general such as Alexander, chosen for integrity and diplomacy rather than brains, would by training and custom accept his chief of staff's guidance to the point of rubber-stamping his plans and orders.

Such a concept of staff responsibility was utterly alien to the British Army. In the first place there was, strictly speaking, no such appointment as a "chief of staff", nor was the staff a single body. The nearest to a chief of staff was the Brigadier, General Staff at Corps HQ and the Major-General, General Staff at Army HQ. The "general staff" was only a staff branch, concerned with operations, plans, training and organisation ("staff duties"). Personnel management with all its ramifications was the responsibility of the Adjutant-General's branch and supplies, logistics and movement of the Quarter-Master General's, whose subordinates were not "General Staff Officers" but the "deputies" or "assistants" of their chiefs, who had direct access to the commanding general. To be sure, the Brigadier (GS) or Major-General (GS) was the first among equals, and managed the staff as a whole, ensuring that it worked smoothly, but that was a far cry from the German system. As in the US Army, it was the commanding general who finally decided what the plan of battle was, and it was the head of the General Staff's duty to realise it and attend to the details.* As a result Alexander, who was on the best of terms with his valued chief of

---

* British staff nomenclature confused foreign armies. The US staff system was logically organised at all levels into four numbered branches: (1) Personnel (2) Intelligence (3) Operations (4) Logistics, with the letter "G" prefixing appointments at division HQ and above, "S" below. E.g., Brigadier-General Brann was Clark's head of operations "G3", the same appointment in a US regiment being the S3. In a British HQ a GSO3 (or General Staff Officer, Third Grade), shortened to "G3", was a lowly captain, concerned with keeping files and marking maps, the equivalent of the S3 was a "brigade major", and his colleague on the logistic side, S4, the "Deputy Assistant Adjutant and Quarter-master General" (DAAQMG).

staff, though repeatedly approving of his plans, often departed from them when he was faced with imposing them as orders on his recalcitrant subordinates, compromising when they could not agree. This was the root of Alexander's failure as a commander. "Harding was concerned with the loss of initiative, and decided that it was essential to sit down and have a hard, cool look at where they were really heading, which, in contrast to Montgomery's, was not Alexander's way of setting about things . . ." Alexander's system was to allow a plan to evolve through discussion with his army commanders. It was then the business of his chief of staff to translate it into order and action. The adequacy of the forces, the arrangements for command, logistics and so on were the concern of the staff.[3]

However well Alexander and Harding agreed, Harding could not possibly have controlled his vacillating chief as a German staff officer could his. Apart from the interpretation of the boundaries between their different responsibilities, Harding, like all British officers, had been indoctrinated with the tradition of absolute loyalty. To be sure, there are British examples of loyal staff officers addressing their commanders in forthright terms in the hope of keeping them on the rails (as de Guingand did once to Montgomery) or even having to call in the higher commander (as did Galloway on his own initiative when he summoned Auchinleck to HQ Eighth Army during the crisis of the winter battle in 1941) or, indeed simply taking charge, as Harding himself did during the same battle, but in the British Army such initiatives are rare and only possible in a dire emergency.

Harding could advise, but he could not alter Alexander's style. As Harold Macmillan (admiringly) noted in his diary: "He has the most effective way of giving not exactly orders but suggestions to his commanders. They are put forward with modesty and simplicity. But they are always so clear and lucid that they carry conviction. It is a most interesting (and extremely effective) method." (From whom, one wonders, did Macmillan – otherwise a shrewd, often a harsh judge of men – obtain such an impression? Or that it was Alexander, not Montgomery, who had reanimated the dejected Eighth Army in August 1942, and won the battles of Alam el Halfa and El Alamein?) It was precisely this flaccid system of command that was to prevent the full fruits of operation DIADEM being reaped in May and to botch the offensive against the Gothic Line.

These difficulties lay in the future, however. For the moment Harding had the full support of his chief and Clark, with a string of failures behind him, was in no position to be obstructive. He confided the bilious expressions of his grievances only to his diary. Harding first sorted out the question of command and staff and after "some difficulty" persuaded Alexander to allow him to organise a proper HQ for him in the great palace of Caserta, near Naples. That done he turned his attention to two other important matters. Strong as the Cassino–Garigliano front was, an offensive there was more likely to offer successful strategic development than the Adriatic front, so he recommended that the bulk of the Allied divisions should be concentrated there. To simplify logistics US Army and US-equipped French forces were to be grouped under the Fifth Army, and British Commonwealth and the British-equipped Polish Corps under the Eighth. Accordingly the New Zealand Corps was dissolved and its two divisions withdrawn to rest, the 2nd Polish Corps relieved the French troops in the mountains and the 13th Corps extended the Eighth Army front southwards to the confluence of the Liri and Garigliano rivers. From there the Fifth Army took over as far as the sea, the 2nd Corps on its left and the newly constituted Corps Expéditionnaire Français on its right, freeing the 10th Corps to rejoin the Eighth Army. This considerable redeployment occupied most of March and April. Next, because of the hoped-for timing for ANVIL and the question of surrendering landing craft, it was intended that the offensive would be renewed in April. Harding wanted more time to prepare it and also the advantage of dry weather, clear skies for the air force and hard going for the tanks. Mid-May was preferable, but to put back the date revived the conflict about landing craft and the surrender of the forces in AAI earmarked for ANVIL. This solved itself, as when the OVERLORD planners examined the problems of mounting it they advised postponement to June. May 11 was finally settled on as D-day for Alexander's offensive, code-named DIADEM.

Having arranged these moves Harding's next task was to embark on the rigorous analysis of the whole strategic situation in Italy; its bare bones are as follows. Alexander's mission was to attract the German strategic reserves to Italy for the benefit of OVERLORD. The Allied planners had, from time to time feared that Kesselring might slip away to the Pisa–Rimini line or a defensive position even further north, but this took no account of the fact that Hitler was temperamentally reluctant ever to give ground, at least without a fight, that the Gustav Line ran across the shortest and naturally strongest part of Italy and that immense effort had gone into fortifying it. Harding concluded that the Germans would conduct a protracted defence of the Gustav Line; from his point of view the best possible option, for he saw in the Allied dispositions the prospect of a battle of annihilation. If Kesselring was forced by Hitler to stand his ground until it was too late for him to disengage cleanly and stage an orderly withdrawal with an unbroken front from one defensive line to another, he could, in Harding's opinion, be trapped. "With ruthless logic [he] pointed out that neither pushing back the German line nor the capture of Rome would help to achieve the aim. That must be to destroy the German formations in Italy."[4] If that could be done, or even partly done, the liberation of a large part of Italy, the fall of Rome and the primary and overriding aim of drawing in the German reserves would follow.

The first calculation Harding had to make was the balance of strength. It is a military cliché that for a successful offensive a numerical superiority of four to one is desirable, but in terms of divisions (an inexact but convenient measure) the Allied armies could dispose of twenty-five, Kesselring twenty-three. It was not the true ratio of strength, because the German divisions varied a great deal in quality from the elite parachute troops and panzer grenadiers to ordinary marching infantry divisions, which were under-gunned, under strength and diluted with non-German personnel. The Allies had complete command of the air, and overwhelming superiority in artillery and in numbers of tanks. Harding's aim was to achieve local superiority by concentrating his forces at the vital areas. In the Cassino sector, the most important in his estimation, instead of companies and platoons he proposed to commit three corps, the 1st Canadian, the 2nd Polish and the 13th British, a total of six infantry divisions, three independent armoured brigades to support them and two armoured divisions with a third, the 6th South African, available. The Garigliano front was to be attacked by four and a half French divisions and the coastal sector by the US 2nd Corps with two. The 6th Corps in Anzio was to be built up to three US infantry divisions, two British, the Special Force of US Ranger and Canadian Commando units and the complete 1st Armored Division.

To keep the balance favourable at least during the break-in phase of the offensive Harding proposed an elaborate deception plan, DUNTON, to play on the German fear of another Anzio-scale landing in their rear. At the same time every precaution was taken to prevent German Intelligence from discovering the actual date of the defensive. All this, one of the cleverest and most elaborate deception plans made in the war before OVERLORD, was so successful that Kesselring was completely deceived, and on D-day both the commanders of the Tenth Army and of the 14th Panzer Corps were on leave in Germany.

Next Harding considered what the US Army aptly calls the "scheme of manoeuvre". The possible thrust lines were limited by geography to four: through the Liri valley to Frosinone (the Via Casilina); the very difficult route where McCreery had been checked, from Minturno up the Ausente valley behind the Auruncan Mountains to Ausonia; the narrow coastal strip along which ran the Via Appia to Terracina and Rome and northwards from the Anzio bridgehead. Having weighed the arguments for timings Harding decided on opening the offensive against the Gustav Line, and to launch the 6th Corps later as soon as it was clear how the battle was going and where the enemy reserves were engaged. Bearing in mind his aim of destroying a substantial part of the opposing force he saw that the key to such a battle was the articulation of the two fronts. The 6th Corps, far from being a stranded whale, was a cocked pistol pointed at the rear of the 14th Panzer Corps. The Liri valley, unpromising as it was (heavily fortified, cut up by streams and much of it covered with woods and tall crops, overlooked from the north), he decided would be the *Schwerpunkt*, for it was the only sector of the Gustav Line against which the Allied armour would be used in strength. Moreover it had to be held by the Tenth Army at all costs. It was a bottleneck, but if the cork blew out the Tenth Army would be cut in half. If, however, it was reinforced at the expense of the Fourteenth Army, and the 6th Corps broke out and began rampaging in the enemy rear, a commanding position would be gained for the battle of annihilation for which he hoped. He chose as the vital objective for the 6th Corps the town of Valmontone on the Via Casilina.

The next question, which could only be answered decisively when a full view of the situation was available, was how the battle should then develop. This was to become the subject of violent disagreement between Clark and Alexander and a bone of historical contention to this day, so a brief explanation of the nature of an envelopment in battle in modern warfare will not be out of place. The classical examples of envelopment ending with the victorious side establishing a sort of cordon round the enemy rear were outdated, owing to the purely technical developments. Tanks, mechanised mobility and increased fire-power enabled a threatened force rapidly to establish a fresh defensive front and also to strike back. It is true that in 1940 the Germans' *Sichelschnitt* – scything cut – cut off and liquidated the Anglo-French forces, and that the British served the Italians in the same way in the opening battles in North Africa, but in each case there was a great disparity in fighting power. To attempt such man-oeuvres against German commanders was as rash as trying to put a half-nelson on a grizzly bear. The classical examples, Cannae and Sedan, were often on German lips, but only as a sort of shorthand or symbol. They themselves were great practitioners of envelopment, but their real models were the annihilating battles of Tannenberg and the

Masurian Lakes in 1914, or their early successes during BARBAROSSA against the Red Army after the invasion of Russia in 1941. Their object *was to divide the opposing army or armies and crush the isolated portions in succession.* The later German phrase for such a manoeuvre was *Keil und Kessel*, literally the "wedge and kettle", "kettle" being used in the sense of "trap". (*Kesselring* is a sporting term, meaning to surround a wood with guns and drive the game outwards so none escapes.)

It must be understood that Valmontone, chosen as the 6th Corps objective, was simply the centre of gravity of a potentially critical area. It was not, as Clark seemed to argue, a spot where the 6th Corps would stand on the Via Casilina like so many traffic policemen ordering the stream of German fugitives pouring up it to halt. From there the whole front of the Army Group "C" could be disarticulated, by not only the 6th Corps but by all the Allied forces available.

Such was the outline plan for the great DIADEM offensive. As in all great operations there were many difficulties to be resolved besides the conflicting timings of OVERLORD, DIADEM and ANVIL. There was some alarm about the deception plan DUNTON, as it was felt that it might compromise ANVIL, if the false trails laid indicated the French Riviera as the site of the next great amphibious operation. The change of date settled that problem, and DUNTON was a brilliant success. Woven into it were the preparatory exercises for DIADEM (the Poles practising assaults on caves and dug-outs with flame-throwers, the 8th Indian Division the use of assault boats and the tactics of river crossings), false information for line-crossing agents that the expected offensive was timed for June, radio transmissions from simulated HQ for the German interception service to decrypt and misinterpret, and amphibious exercises by the Canadians and the US 36th Division in the bays of Naples and Salerno.

Alexander's most acute difficulties lay inside his own army group. The lesser arose from the existence of the 1st Canadian Corps. The Eighth Army front, extending from the foot of Montecassino and to the Liri river, was no more than seven to eight miles wide, not nearly enough frontage for the mass of British, Canadian and later South African armour that was going to be fed into it. One corps HQ was quite enough to control the battle, and the task had been given to the experienced British 13th Corps, commanded by Lieutenant-General Sidney Kirkman. It would be simple and convenient for him if the Canadian divisions and brigades could be placed under his command, but this was not agreeable to the Canadian Government or high command, who felt that Canadians should not be on a par with "colonial" troops like the Indians and used to reinforce British corps

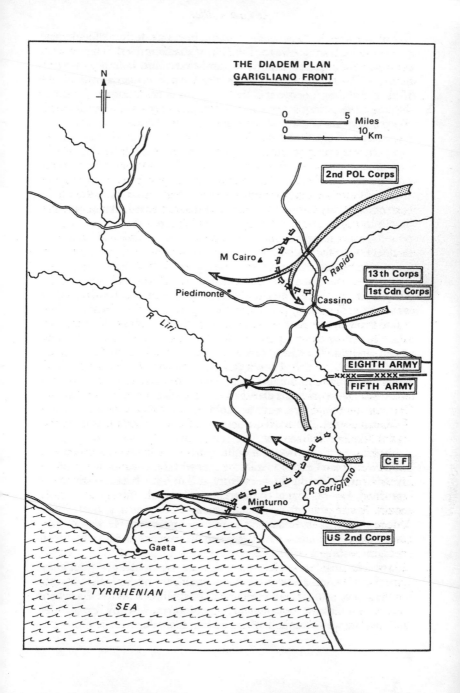

THE DIADEM PLAN
GARIGLIANO FRONT

N

0   5 Miles
0   10 Km

2nd POL Corps

M Cairo ▲

R Rapido

Piedimonte •

13th Corps

1st Cdn Corps

Cassino

R Liri

EIGHTH ARMY

xxx — xxxx —

FIFTH ARMY

CEF

R Garigliano

Minturno

US 2nd Corps

Gaeta •

TYRRHENIAN
SEA

and placed under British commanders. It was a question of legitimate national pride, but that was not all. The Canadians felt that their higher commanders required experience and that could only be gained in battle, which meant either putting the Canadian Corps through the 13th at some stage, or, what in the event was done, fitting the two corps into the Liri corridor side by side, leading to all sorts of complications. The correct answer would have been to have moved the inter-army boundary well south of the Liri, but that would have led to even more and vehement protests from the commander of the Fifth Army, who had taken the transfer of the Rapido–Cassino–Montecassino sector to the "British" as a personal slight.

Clark's mood during the preparations for DIADEM was one of anger, frustration and uneasiness, which was made plain to Kirkman when he paid him a visit. He made two insignificant requests. The inter-army boundary had not yet been moved, and he wanted to establish a small tactical HQ in the Fifth Army sector so that he and his operations staff and engineers could conveniently study the battlefield. A methodical and studious tactician, as soon as he had arrived in Italy he had formed small training teams to collate all the latest operational lessons, and he wanted two of his staff to be allowed to visit the British divisions in the Anzio bridgehead. Kirkman was kept waiting for some time before he was allowed to enter Clark's office, and then given a lecture on the Anzio landing. The gist of this was that for five days the German and 6th Corps build-up had run level, but then the Germans had pulled ahead. Kirkman did not understand what this had to do with current business. He wrote in his diary rather unkindly: "*Qui s'excuse, s'accuse.*" He noticed that Clark was very cold towards him and other British visitors at dinner. His two requests were refused. Puzzled, he consulted Major-General Richardson, the senior British liaison officer at HQ Fifth Army, and was told that quite apart from his dissatisfaction with the DIADEM plan Clark was still sore over what he saw as a British plot to rob him of the credit for his victory at Salerno.[5] Kirkman remained unruffled. He was one of those archetypal British officers who valued calmness and phlegm very highly, along with good manners, whose reaction towards bad ones was to remain impassive. He was going to have a close association with Clark and his patience and loyalty were to be highly tested.

The reasons for Clark's malaise were much deeper than these superficial causes. He was much too intelligent not to realise that the stagnation of SHINGLE and the operational failures on the Garigliano and around Cassino threatened his appointment as army commander, although he was incapable of seeing that his failures were of his own making. Being the man he was, he looked for a scapegoat and the British conveniently fitted the role. This was secondary. It seems unlikely that he knew that his relief was being discussed by the British, or that Alexander and Maitland Wilson had twice called in Harold Macmillan to advise them. (On March 29 and April 2, 1944.) Macmillan's sage advice was to exercise extreme caution. Alexander was due to visit London, and if it leaked out that the DIADEM plan or Clark's relief had been a *British* initiative it could have unfortunate results.[6] Clark's immediate worry was that although the DIADEM plan would put Fifth Army troops in the vanguard of the march on Rome the British were somehow planning to cheat him out of it. Rome was as important to Clark as his appointment to Fifth Army had been. It would be another step on the ladder to being recognised as a great soldier, and gaining the fame and recognition he craved, but now it was even more important. The general seen and extolled as the US general whose US army, alone, had liberated the Eternal City, would be unsackable.

Clark's plot was skilfully and convincingly laid. On the perfectly justifiable grounds of keeping his options open and planning for every possible variation of the situation when the 6th Corps broke out he ordered General Truscott to prepare four contingency plans. One was to go right-handed or south-east to join hands with the 2nd Corps, one to Valmontone, one north-east over the Alban Hills directly on Rome, and one to the left of the bridgehead, also towards Rome.

On May 5 Alexander, as was his perfect right, visited Truscott's HQ and was shown these plans. In his mild and non-committal way Alexander observed that only the thrust to Valmontone promised any strategic advantage. Truscott reported this to Clark, who became very agitated. He telephoned Alexander to complain of "unwarranted interference with Fifth Army command channels", and went on to pour cold water on Harding's proposed strategy and the possibility of cutting off any part of the Tenth Army. The Germans, he said, were "far too smart". Clark's understanding of grand tactics may have been imperfect or naive, but it is difficult to believe that he could not see the obvious rewards that envelopment of the German right wing would confer, or that he would be playing the leading part in a great victory. Rome in any case was to be his prize, whether the Tenth Army was manoeuvred out of its position, or whether it stood and fought. What he was doing was boldly testing how far he could go with Alexander. Valmontone was not open for bargaining, for it was integral to the whole plan. He had now at this late date made it clear to the Commander-in-Chief that they were totally at loggerheads, and it was at that moment Alexander should have dropped on Clark like the proverbial leopard from a tree but, alas, though Alexander was a lion, he was no leopard. As usual he soothed and temporised.[7]

In the meantime Keyes of the 2nd Corps and Juin, commanding the CEF, were girding up their loins for the impending battle, and the staff of the Eighth Army were assembling the great ram with which it was to batter its way past Cassino and into the Liri valley.

16

THE BATTERING RAM

There was no way round and no scope for cleverness, so I had to blast my way through.

General Sir Brian Horrocks, on his operation VARSITY, *to break through the Siegfried Line in February 1945*

When Alexander decided to entrust the task of breaching the Gustav Line at its strongest point to the Eighth Army he chose well. Mark Clark's nose may have been out of joint, but the supreme characteristic of American commanders and staff was their ability to mount very large operations at short notice and maintain their momentum. Once they had acquired the necessary experience they excelled in exploitation. By contrast the British were rather slow, not by temperament but because their experience had taught them that it was unwise to hurry or scamp preparations when attacking strongly entrenched positions, having attempted a round dozen since Alamein in 1942; five of them, like the Gustav Line, protected by fast-flowing rivers and overlooked by mountains. They were up to every trick of the game. Back in 1918 the Australian General Monash, a civil engineer, had compared his battle planning with the way he would tackle a construction project; a careful survey of the ground, assembling all the plant and material so that each item was ready to hand when it was wanted and setting about the actual work in a systematic manner. This was how General Oliver Leese and his corps commanders and their staffs planned the Fourth Battle of Cassino.

Leese was a Guards officer who had successfully commanded a corps under Montgomery, to whom he owed his promotion to command the Eighth Army, and for whom he had profound respect and admiration. He corresponded regularly with his old chief, giving news

253

of the army's achievements and old friends and discussing tactical and operational questions at length in letters that were full of good sense and sound military judgment. He even modelled his style of command on Montgomery's, not altogether wisely. Like him he set up a small, private HQ, where he lived in isolation from his staff with only his military assistant and aides-de-camp for company, and where it was not always convenient to visit him. General Templer (commander of the 56th Division in Anzio and later the 6th Armoured) was once much vexed at having to drive many miles to it over wretched Italian roads to discuss some trivial matter. Another visitor was surprised to find the army commander clad in the baggy plus-fours worn by infantry officers in pre-battledress days, shirt-sleeves and a straw hat watering the plants in the garden of the villa he occupied, and the starchy Canadian General Burns was shocked and offended to find that he was expected to discuss questions concerning his corps with a large, naked gentleman scrubbing himself in a tub of water in the open. Eccentricity must be spontaneous. Not every officer could successfully adopt Montgomery's "hail-fellow-well-met" system of chatting up stray private soldiers he met on his road journeys, and giving them cigarettes from the store he kept in his Jeep.

Leese soon after he took command found a Highland soldier sitting by the roadside and dutifully went through the routine. The "Jock" accepted the gift of cigarettes with good grace, and eyeing the large and burly figure with the baggy breeches observed amiably. "Ye're new tae this job, then? There was a wee bugger with a black beret dishing oot the fags a while back." *Non e vero e ben trovato.* No doubt the story was retailed by Leese himself, for there was no "side" about him. He gave the impression of a cheerful outgoing character, with not, perhaps, a lot of brain, always wearing a quizzical, amused expression, as if the world, even in wartime, was a comical place. Inwardly he was sensitive, highly strung and apt to overwork to the point of exhaustion. Later in his career he made a bad error of judgment* which marred it fatally, but his record in Italy was that of a somewhat slow and unimaginative but competent general.

The German defences between the Monastery heights and the north bank of the Liri river were known to be very strong, although the deadly

* Leese went to Burma as 11th Army Group commander, where in the course of a misunderstanding extraordinary in so senior and experienced an officer he relieved General Slim of the command of the Fourteenth Army after that officer had completed a victorious campaign, on the ground that he was tired out and in the belief that Slim had agreed. Leese was himself shortly relieved for exceeding his powers. It may have been that the accumulated strain of high command had told on him.

details of the Hitler Line were only disclosed when the Canadians attacked it. The northern heights were still securely in the hands of Heidrich's fanatical parachute infantry, whose lay-out and defensive fire-plan had been improved after every unsuccessful Allied offensive; the whole area being covered by an intricate cross-fire from mortars, machine guns and artillery, while the artillery observers could observe every movement between M. Trocchio and the Gari–Rapido. The Gustav Line was lightly held, with Heidrich's machine-gun regiment in Cassino town and four panzer grenadier battalions watching the river line and posted in depth. Nine miles behind them was the strongest section of the Hitler Line, where the fortified village of Piedimonte loomed over the valley floor past Aquino to Pontecorvo, with the Forme d'Aquino stream, its banks scarped to form an anti-tank obstacle and sown with mines, acting as moat. This section of the rearward defences of the Gustav Line (known variously as the Hitler, Senger and also the Orange Line) was a true fortress system of steel and concrete, designed to be impregnable. The bony skeleton, the "hardened" defences, consisted of deep underground bunkers where the garrisons could safely sit out the tremendous Allied bombardments that were known to precede an attack, rows of bottle-shaped machine-gun posts, the neck protruding just above ground fitted with a ring on which the gun in a steel cupola could revolve, interspersed with the turrets of Panzer Mark V tanks fitted with a long 75-mm gun capable of defeating any Allied tank's armour. In between, grouped round the Panther turrets, were trenches and emplacements for infantry and mobile anti-tank guns. Experience had shown that during the bombardment it was essential for company officers and under-officers to move about and encourage their men, and for local reserves to be moved without being destroyed by fire, so the whole system was interconnected by tunnels and communication trenches.

General Leese's outline plan for the breakthrough and exploitation was to consider the Gustav–Hitler–Monastery heights positions as a whole. General Kirkman's 13th Corps (three infantry, one armoured division, reinforced by Canadian and British tanks) was to cross the Gari under cover of a bombardment by every gun that could be mustered and deployed. Lieutenant-General Anders' 2nd Polish Corps was to drive the Germans from the heights and capture Piedimonte, so unhinging the northern part of the Hitler Line. According to the way the breaching operation went, Lieutenant-General E. L. M. Burns' 1st Canadian Corps would either go through the 13th or, as was decided in the event, come up on the left of the 13th and he and Kirkman would drive at the Hitler Line side by side. With the 5th

At Last a Plan

Canadian, the 6th British and 6th South African Armoured Divisions, the 1st (Independent) Canadian Armoured Brigade, the British 25th Tank Brigade and the Polish Armoured Brigade, Leese could dispose of more than 2,000 tanks in the Cassino–Liri valley sector, a concentration that even a Red Army general might have considered adequate.

This was all very fine, but the basic objection to the plan was the lack of space for manoeuvre. This great mass of armour was to be committed to a tiny battlefield, no more than seven miles wide from the foothills of the Cairo massif to the left bank of the Liri, with access only by the single main highway and a number of farm tracks and minor roads insufficient to carry the mass of tanks and supporting vehicles – engineers with their bridging trains, supply vehicles (an armoured division required 900 tons of fuel and ammunition at "intense", or combat rates) to say nothing of the field artillery forcing its way forward to keep in range as the advance progressed. Command and control at the tactical level would be hampered by mutual interference between the hundreds of radio sets crammed into so small a space.

It was also a mistake to make the Liri a boundary between the two armies, as it prevented flexibility of manoeuvre if one army uncovered the flank of the defenders facing the other. (Altering an inter-army boundary always requires firm control from the top, and Clark was very difficult to deal with over such matters.)

There can be no doubt that these objections were perfectly clear to every senior officer from Harding down, but soldiers are practical people if nothing else, and never expect ideal conditions. In any case, there was no time to repine. Everyone had to get down to the vast and complicated task of turning a plan of action into orders. As Monash has said, preparing a modern battle is like mounting an industrial enterprise. It requires both managerial skill and imagination, and while thousands of fussy orders on reams of paper must not be inflicted on the fighting echelons – "delegation of responsibility" is one of the unwritten principles of war – it is the duty of the staff to see that no detail, no missing horseshoe nail that might lose the battle, be overlooked.* At army-group level Harding and his staff officers had to arrange for two tired divisions to leave Italy for rest, reinforcement and re-training, and six new ones to be absorbed and accommodated. The French and three Eighth Army corps had to be moved up or across the front into the southern Cassino–Minturno sector, while the 10th (McCreery) side-stepped to north of the Montecassino–Cairo massif. As regards divisions, the 2nd New Zealand and the battered 4th Indian

* "For want of a nail the shoe was lost, for want of a shoe the horse was lost, for want of a horse the message was lost, for want of the message the battle was lost."

256

moved over to the northern sector, the 8th Indian, the British 4th Infantry and 6th Armoured Divisions moved into the Liri sector and over a thousand guns and the two divisions of the 1st Canadian Corps redeployed in suitable positions behind it.

All these moves had to be completed without arousing the suspicions of a watchful enemy, whose air reconnaissance could not be totally driven out of the sky, and whose Italian agents could easily pass between the opposing lines. A degree of concealment could be achieved by routine methods such as moving only at night and lying up in well-camouflaged hides by day, leaving dummy HQ behind in their old locations with their radio nets busy and so on. Training exercises, the Poles practising mountain climbing and the use of flame-throwers to attack strong points in caves, the British and Indian infantry paddling assault boats across rivers, the Canadian armoured regiments in-structing the Indian sepoys with whom they were to work in the techniques of infantry–armour fighting could be turned to good use by leaking real information as well as "disinformation" to suggest that no Allied offensive was likely before the first week in June. The German Intelligence staffs began to obtain a picture of Canadian troops and the US 36th Division engaged in amphibious exercises in the bays of Naples and Salerno, and of French and American divisions preparing to invade the French Riviera. All this helped to strengthen Kesselring's conviction that the Allied commanders were too intelligent to continue bashing their heads against the Gustav Line, and that they would try to outflank it by sea. His favoured landing areas were near the mouth of the Tiber for a direct thrust at Rome, Civitavecchia or Leghorn.

On the divisional and brigade levels there was also intense activity. The infantry, without giving the game away, had to allow as many junior leaders as possible to look by day at the ground over which they had to advance by night, study air photographs, familiarise themselves with the arrangements for artillery and tank support and brief their men. The engineers – the key arm in any river-crossing and breaching operation, and always fated to spend the longest time of any arm in the most dangerous zone, the actual crossing site – busily patrolled the river banks to locate minefields and where possible lifted them, reconnoitred the best bridging sites and concealed positions where their material would be assembled, and where, under their supervision, the infantry would "marry up" with their wooden assault boats and be routed forward to the river. After nightfall on D-day all the routes forward would have to be marked with white tapes and dim lights. A large engineer force, 1,500 strong with all the necessary vehicles and plant, was formed ready to cross the river as soon as possible and re-open Highway No. 6 through the ruins of Cassino, where the ill-considered use of heavy bombers had blocked it with rubble or it had disappeared in a series of enormous craters. The whole success of the 13th Corps attack would depend on the free use of Highway No. 6 as a main supply route.

The biggest single operation on the Eighth Army front was deploying the artillery and preparing the fire-plan. Following well-established British practice, every gun that was not required to give minimum cover to the inactive parts of the line and all the guns of reserve formations were concentrated and placed under central control. The assembly of 1,060 pieces of artillery with supplies of ammunition (600 rounds per gun for the 25-pounders in the 13th Corps and 1,090 for the Polish Corps, 350 r.p.g. for the mediums and 200 r.p.g. for the heavy artillery), together with the activities of signallers laying cable and survey parties mapping the gun areas had to be carried out with every precaution against being detected by the watchful German observers on the heights across the river. The batteries were brought up to the survey markers on their positions night after night and remained silent until the battle started.*

The plan itself was immensely complicated, for it had to be adjusted to the differing tasks and circumstances not only of assaulting divisions, but of brigades. It was in four parts. The first was directed at the enemy artillery, the second covered the assault crossing itself, the third was to look after unexpected targets appearing as the battle continued and the last – or rather one continuing throughout from the moment when the infantry and sappers emerged from cover and advanced to the river – was for smoke to conceal the sector under assault from the artillery observers on the heights to right and left. None of these plans could be imposed from above: the requirements of each individual division had to be taken into account, and the rival claims on artillery fire reconciled with the aim of using the artillery in the most efficient and effective manner.

Leese delegated the planning and control of the artillery to his chief artillery officer (Brigadier, Royal Artillery) Frank S. Siggers, and the magnitude of his task can be illustrated by the following statistics. Between April 4 and May 3 he held six coordinating conferences with

---

* At the battle of El Alamein in October 1942 the British had revived the complex artillery techniques developed on the Western Front in 1917, and used them in all deliberate attacks against strong defences. Mechanised artillery traction, the introduction of self-propelled field guns and the use of radio as a primary means of tactical control as well as fire-control conferred speed and flexibility to the artillery arm, and enabled it to use scientific gunnery in both set-piece and mobile operations.

one major-general, US Army, the Fifth Army artillery officer, and twenty-one British, Polish, Canadian and New Zealand brigadiers. Between the Liri and the Adriatic, including some welcome and valuable US artillery reinforcements, there were 124 regiments (or battalions) to deploy or redeploy, of which seventy-five, including heavy anti-aircraft batteries and eight US heavy or super-heavy battalions (155-mm guns, 8-inch and 240-mm howitzers), or just under 70 per cent of the total, were to be concentrated to cover the front of the 2nd Polish and British 13th Corps; total 1,554 pieces; engaged in the fire-plan, 1,087. The expenditure of 25-pounder ammunition alone for the battle was 1,220,000 rounds, the rest *pro rata*. The orders issued by the commander Royal Artillery of the 4th Indian Division for the opening phase with traces, appendices and schedules of fire (time-programmes) ran to 46 pages. The total number of artillerymen of all Allied armies employed was 3,700 officers and 70,000 NCOs and rank and file.

From dawn on May 12 (D-day plus one) until the bridgehead was secure and the enemy artillery observers forced back, a smoke screen was laid by generators across the whole front by the men of a complete light anti-aircraft battalion. This was monitored by a special observing officer on M. Trocchio (a height east of Montecassino commanding the Liri sector) who, if he saw a gap appearing, ordered smoke shell to be fired at the areas likely to be occupied by enemy artillery observers. This device was completely successful, but none the less considerable casualties were inflicted, especially on the devoted engineers during the crossing, mainly by close-range fire from mortars and machine guns on fixed lines. The German artillery fired a good deal, but blind (or "predicted") and casualties from shell-fire were but a fraction of what the enemy could have inflicted had the observers on the heights been given free play.

Brigadier Siggers was also given the task of coordinating close air support. The system employed was to establish a control also on M. Trocchio, connected through artillery signals channels to observers with the forward infantry and armoured units. Relays of fighter-bomber squadrons arrived over the battlefield ready briefed to attack pre-selected targets. If the Trocchio controller received requests for a target of opportunity or an emergency target he immediately rebriefed the pilots in the air who switched to it and the quickest recorded response was five minutes. If he had nothing for them they went on to bomb the targets already allotted.[1]

Some senior American officers scoffed at the British reliance on what they called "Ypres-style barrages" but then they had not been at

Ypres or yet encountered a defence system that could not be infiltrated or outflanked and had to be cracked open by brute force. They were to learn, but by bloody experience and not from the British experience. It is perhaps significant that among the team of artillery commanders assembled by Siggers twelve of the British brigadiers had, like he himself and the commander of the 13th Corps, all cut their operational teeth on the Western Front during the First World War.

Lieutenant-General Anders and Lieutenant-General Burns each had unique and difficult problems to solve. Anders' preparations were made difficult by the order that he was to refrain from close, active patrolling of Heidrich's defensive positions in case the loss of a prisoner or a dead man left behind enabled his opponent to identify the presence of the Polish Corps and so compromise the surprise value of the whole DIADEM plan. All the routes leading across the Rapido up to the heights above the Monastery were under close observation and the slightest movement subjected to accurate artillery harassing fire. The considerable tonnage of ammunition, food, motor-fuel and water – a cubic foot of water weighs sixty-two and a half pounds – had to be hauled up by night in four successive lifts; first in lorries, then in light vehicles, mule-pack and finally on the backs of the soldiers. As Anders said in his account, "The front burst into hectic activity as soon as dusk fell as if some giant ant's nest were working overtime." As Anders was determined to use his tanks his engineers had to work by day as well as by night to convert the goat tracks leading up the mountainside to roads fit for tracked vehicles and their supply lorries. Exposed sections of the route were concealed behind a framework supporting camouflage netting. Even with all these precautions the preparatory work was not completed without casualties Anders could ill afford. He had only two instead of three infantry brigades in each of his two divisions and being cut off from his native country had no reservoir of man-power on which he could draw for replacements. Discussing this with General Maitland Wilson he said that his best hope was a good haul of German prisoners of war, which could be combed for impressed Poles. He knew that Leese had given the Poles the post of honour in what would inevitably be a bloody struggle that might write his corps off altogether, but he was sustained by the knowledge that his soldiers were determined, in the awful and literal meaning of the phrase, "to conquer or to die".

Morale is too dry, too technical a word to describe the mood of the soldiers of the Polish Corps, while fanaticism implies a lack of rationality. Their attitude was rooted in the history of their unhappy country. In the eighteenth century it had been partitioned between Austrians,

Prussians and Russians, but they had resisted every pressure to alter their loyalty, or to change their religion, language and culture. The Polish state was re-established after the First World War, but fated to last a mere twenty years. The opening act of the Second World War was the invasion of Poland by Hitler, when Soviet Russia was quick to seize the eastern half of the country. The Russians herded a large part of the Polish Army and many civilians, including women and children, into captivity, where many perished. Anders himself was imprisoned in the Lubianka gaol and treated as a German spy. After Hitler invaded Russia, Stalin, after prolonged and difficult negotiations, persuaded some but by no means all of his captives to move to the Middle East. (He had no intention of allowing them to take part in the reconquest of Poland.) There under British protection and with British aid Anders was able to form and train the Polish Corps. The ardour of the Poles was not simply fuelled by an understandable desire for revenge. An intensely political people, even the humblest soldier perceived that if they helped to gain an Allied victory the road to a free and independent Poland might be open once more.

We must now turn to the Canadians, equal as soldiers to any of the Allies, though more relaxed in their approach, but reckoned formidable by the Germans. The Canadian Army was a militia of intelligent, adaptable, part-time soldiers controlled by a nucleus of no more than 6,000 regulars; too small a seed-bed to provide the number of competent senior officers required to command an army and staff the HQ of corps and divisions. That was the view, at least, of such senior British officers as Brooke, Montgomery, Alexander and Leese, and not an unreasonable one. What was crass on their part was to ignore the determination of the Canadian government to field a Canadian Army under Canadian commanders and not to allow Canadian units to be used piecemeal under the British commanders, and that they had to accept this political fact cheerfully and make their command arrangements accordingly. What was even more unreasonable was what the Canadians rightly saw as a circular or "Catch 22" argument; the British argument that Canadian commanders could not be trusted to conduct operations on the corps level because they lacked experience, and they could not gain experience because they were not trusted to command. The Canadian generals were too tactful to point out that this British attitude was hardly justified by previous British performance. The British Army had also suffered from a shortage of competent senior officers for very much the same reasons, and the performance of some of its corps and army commanders in the earlier stages of the war hardly gave them the right to feel superior to the Canadians or anyone else.

Their 1944 team had been arrived at by hard-bought experience and the elimination of the unsuitable by the harsh test of war.

A complicating factor in the equation was that though Montgomery had told General Crerar, the first commander of the Canadian Corps in Italy, that he wanted neither him nor his HQ in Italy, nor the 5th Canadian Armoured Division, he greatly admired the 1st Canadian Division, and made it clear that he did, a sentiment that was reciprocated. The Canadian Army resembled the British in that it was an assembly of disparate social groups each with a strong sense of identity: what in the British Army is cherished as the "regimental system". A population a quarter the size of Britain's was contained in a country whose vastness can be illustrated by saying the distance from coast to coast, from Vancouver to Halifax, is the same as from London, England to Sverdlovsk, in Siberia, or from Cairo to Durban. Geographical distance imposes social diversity. A "Maritimer" from Nova Scotia or New Brunswick has more in common with his neighbour in Maine, USA than with a man from Ontario in "Upper Canada".

The appropriate equivalent to, say the "Geordies" of the British Durham Light Infantry was the private of the Carleton and York Regiment from the Saint John River area, with his own peculiar outlook and regional dialect. The "Hasty Ps" (The Hastings and Prince Edward Regiment), the "Loyal Eddies" (Loyal Edmonton Regiment, from far-away Alberta) and the "Vandoose" (*Vingt-Deuxième*, the Royal 22e Regiment from French-speaking Quebec) cherished their difference with the same pride as the British Royal Sussex or the Rifle Brigade. This common institution of the "regiment" was a bond on the working level and made for mutual understanding. For instance the British 98th Field Regiment RA (The Surrey and Sussex Yeomanry), itself originally a Militia and later a Territorial unit, was on such good terms with the regiments of the 1st Canadian Armoured Brigade (Three Rivers, Ontario and Calgary Regiments) and other armoured units that when the whole Canadian Corps was transferred from Italy to north-west Europe in 1945 the 98th went with it. The pilots of the British "Air OP" squadrons attached to the Canadian Corps put up the red patch on their sleeves.*

There was another bond between the lower echelons of the two armies. The staff of the 1st Division soon found that the commanders and staff of the Eighth Army and its corps HQ were quite unlike their

---

* The Air Observation Post squadrons were a British innovation, part of the RAF equipped with light aircraft capable of landing on any short flat piece of ground and piloted by captains of the Royal Artillery, who controlled and directed artillery fire direct using normal artillery techniques.

stereotypes of superior, aristocratic generals with funny accents and staff officers *embusqués* in chateaux far behind the front line. "Monty" soon won them over, giving one of his typical performances when he first visited the Seaforths of Canada in Sicily, calling for the men to gather round his Jeep and addressing them, standing on the bonnet. "Who have we here?" he demanded, the reply being a roar of "The Seaforths!" "*My* Seaforths!" was his rejoinder, and he proceeded to the genuine flattery of telling them his future plans and their part in it. (Curiously enough it was this same battalion that back in England in May 1942 booed Montgomery when they marched home past him after Exercise "Tiger".) The Canadian units were a mixture of city or industrial workers officered by corporation lawyers, accountants, managers and business men, and men of the farms, prairie and woods from a large rural population, who were accustomed to looking after themselves and their own affairs without any state assistance. If something went wrong they repaired it, if they wanted something they made it; it is quite usual even today for a rural Canadian to build his own house. The military mixture made for adaptability; the townsmen better at the carefully organised modern battle, the countrymen at improvising when such structured operations were fragmented by the shifts and turns of warfare. They were all happy with the absence of bullshit, the informal efficiency, the use of Christian names, the cutting of paperwork and the use of standard operating procedures of the largely young, ex-civilian and immensely experienced British staff officers.

This made life difficult for General Burns and his regular staff. He himself was a reserved, even shy officer with the reputation of being an author and a military intellectual. The Canadian troops did not warm to him or to his staff who, compared with the British, seemed to be stuffily formal, bureaucratic, did things "by the book" and were apt to fuss about polished boots and blouse buttons being done up. Burns was faced with the double task of convincing both Leese and Alexander that he could command a corps in what was to be a severe test of any general's ability, and also his own battle-hardened subordinates; Chris Vokes of the 1st Division, Bert Hoffmeister a militia officer of the 5th, who had arrived at that appointment after commanding the Seaforths of Canada and the 2nd Canadian Infantry Brigade in active operations, or the equally experienced Brigadier W. C. Murphy. They were not to treat their corps commander with anything but respect, or indulge in what Montgomery used to call in his own brand of slang "bellyaching", but Burns was aware that neither they nor the British authorities had welcomed the establishment of a Canadian Corps, and he was too intelligent to be unaware that he was being silently appraised by his subordinates as well as by Leese. Burns was not temperamentally suited to such a psychological ordeal. For him the hardest part of it must have been waiting in the rear for the opportunity to prove himself while Kirkman swung the battering ram to open the road to the Hitler Line.

17

TIGER DRIVE

There is nothing special going on. Yesterday I called at the HQ of the two corps. Both commanders told me they did not yet have the impression that anything was going on.

Von Vietinghoff to Kesselring, 9.05 a.m., May 11

On D-day minus one, May 10, Generalmajor Friedrich Wentzell, chief of staff Tenth Army, who had just returned from leave, held a long telephone conversation with Colonel Beelitz, acting chief of staff to Kesselring. Wentzell was an able officer judged even by the exacting standard of the German General Staff, but even he was deceived, although as the record shows his fingertip feeling warned him of impending danger:

Wentzell: To my great pleasure everything is quiet. Only I do not know what is going on. Things are becoming ever more uncertain.

Beelitz: I told this to the Field-Marshal [Kesselring]. He looks very intently towards the coast. Yesterday there was another very interesting landing down there near Naples. The Marshal thinks that they have selected an area that typically resembles the Gaeta–Formia–Minturno sector.

Wentzell: Why that area in particular? One could well say that it is up there at Civitavecchia.

Beelitz: No. Up there it is different . . .

And a little later:

Wentzell: In past times one heard at least once in a while that such and such a division had left Africa, but now one hears nothing . . . since the 10th Indian Division appeared without any

265

warning I have become quite sceptical [i.e., of the performance of the German secret intelligence service, the 10th
Indian Division had only been located when it joined the
5th Corps on the Adriatic coast]. I think it not impossible
that things are going on of which we have no idea . . . but if
they do anything in the near future, it *must* be Rome.

Beelitz: In which case the question is: mouth of the Tiber, or
Civitavecchia? The Marshal thinks, however, that it will be
Terracina . . .

(Translation unedited by authors.)[1]

Although this is evidence of the success of DUNTON it does not
represent Kesselring's views quite correctly. On May 3, for instance,
he had attended an important exercise held to test the arrangements to
repel a landing at Civitavecchia in which the 29th Panzer Grenadier
and the 92nd Infantry Divisions took part but was reluctant to move the
29th to the Tenth Army front for some time after DIADEM had been
launched. Kesselring, like his army commanders and staff, suffered
from lack of information and so was reduced to deducing a possible
point of attack by imagined similarities between the exercise area and
the point threatened. He was also influenced by purely fortuitous
events, such as a sudden surge of traffic detected by German observers
on the roads in the Adriatic sector, or an unusual concentration of
shipping in Bari harbour. In his own mind, he was certain of only one
thing: that when the long-expected Allied offensive was launched, the
attacks on the Tenth and Fourteenth Armies would be no more than a
feint to draw his reserves away from the area chosen for an amphibious
attack designed to outflank the whole Gustav defence system.

As late as May 10 orders went out from C-in-C South-West to
complete the reorganisation of Tenth Army's front.

The 14th Corps became responsible only for the front from Terracina
to the Liri river; the 94th Infantry Division on the right and the
reinforced 71st Division on the left, with a depleted 15th Panzer
Grenadier Division acting as corps reserve and watching the coast
behind the right of the 94th Division. General Lemelsen, temporarily
in command, was to be attacked by two US divisions in the 2nd Corps
on the sector occupied by the 94th, while four divisions and 7,000
irregular mountain troops of the French Expeditionary Corps were
about to fall on the 71st Division. (This alteration displeased von
Senger greatly when he returned from an enforced holiday in Germany
to meet Hitler and receive a decoration, for he believed that the
Montecassino–Garigliano sector should be treated as a single tactical

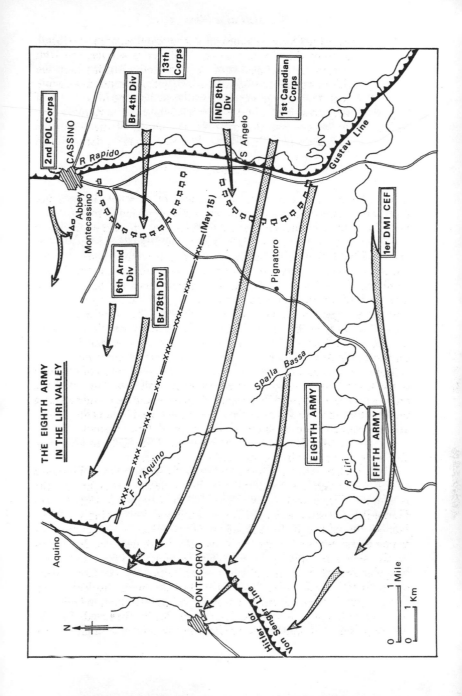

THE EIGHTH ARMY
IN THE LIRI VALLEY

N

2nd POL Corps

CASSINO

R Rapido

Abbey
Montecassino

6th Armd Div

Br 78th Div

Br 4th Div

13th Corps

IND 8th Div

S Angelo

1st Canadian Corps

Gustav Line

(May 15)

Pignataro

Spalla Bassa

EIGHTH ARMY

R Liri

FIFTH ARMY

1er DMI CEF

F d'Aquino

Aquino

PONTECORVO

Hitler or Senger Line

Von

0   1 Mile
0   1 Km

entity, where his corps reserves and his artillery could be concentrated on any threatened point.)

The 51st Mountain Corps (General der Gebirgetruppen Valentin Feuerstein), took over the northern half of the Liri valley to a point north of the central massif whose southern escarpment from the Monastery to Piedimonte glowered down Highway No. 6 (the Via Casilina) and the road to Rome. Its four divisions were disposed from right to left as follows: the grandiosely named 44th Reichsgrenadier-division Hoch und Deutschmeister[2] from the left bank of the Liri to a point one mile south of the Via Casilina; the indomitable infantry of Heidrich's 1st Parachute Division from there to the heights above the Monastery, the 5th Mountain Division on Heidrich's left and then the 114th Jaeger Division up as far as the junction point with Group Haucke. Group Haucke (an *ad hoc* corps), the 334th and the depleted 305 Infantry Divisions extended von Vietinghoff's left to the Adriatic where it faced the British 5th Corps, with only the 4th and 10th Indian Infantry Divisions in a holding role.

The outcome of the terrific battle that was about to take place between the 51st Corps and the Eighth Army was to be decided by a fatal divergence in opinion between two opposing commanders, whose analyses of the situation were, of course, completely unknown to each other. Harding, as we know, had concluded that the one sector where the 1,000 tanks and 1,000 guns of the Eighth Army could be used to the best effect was the Liri valley. Von Vietinghoff came to the opposite conclusion. He did not believe that the Allies would attempt another disastrous river crossing, but instead they would choose the Monastery heights as their *Schwerpunkt*, as he who held the heights held the valley. He was to be proved wrong. In consequence the Liri sector of the Gustav Line was held by a hotch-potch of units, some good, some inferior.

Cassino town was held by two under-strength parachute battalions, contained by the infantry of the British 6th Armoured Division, whose tanks were placed under command of the 4th Division for the assault on the Gustav Line. From Cassino to a point one mile south of the Via Casilina the front was held by the machine-gun battalion of the 1st Parachute Division. Between it and the left bank of the Liri the line was the responsibility of the 44th Division, but Ortner, its commander, had been ordered to surrender all his infantry and his reconnaissance battalion. Two of his regiments were detached to stiffen up the defence of the heights, and the other with the reconnaissance battalion to reinforce the 71st Division in the 14th Corps. In their place he was given a battalion of panzer grenadiers reinforced with part of another from the 115th Regiment of the 15th Panzer Grenadier Division, in 14th Corps, which he placed on his left next to the parachute machine-gunners. To their right he placed an *ad hoc* "blocking force" under a Colonel Bode (Sperrgruppe Bode)* consisting of two battalions from the 576th Grenadier Regiment, part of the low-category 305th Infantry Division in Group Haucke, and the other part of the 3rd Battalion, the 115th Panzer Grenadiers. The German Army was renowned for the ease and flexibility with which strange units could cooperate with each other in battle-groups, but this dispersal of a perfectly good division and robbing other corps to make it good was contrary to accepted German staff practice. These battalions, though in very strong and well-sited defences and supported by mortars and artillery, were to face an assault by two divisions deploying four brigades in the initial wave supported by 200 tanks and the main weight of the Eighth Army's artillery.

General Feuerstein was an experienced officer, sixty years old, who had only recently taken command of the 51st Corps, and though he had no inkling of what was about to hit him, or when, did not like any of these arrangements. They went against all his training. It is not too much to assume that a German commander of his generation might have in mind the surprise withdrawal of the German Army to the Hindenburg Line on the Western Front which completely dislocated the offensive planned by the French General Nivelle and had such momentous consequences. When Kesselring visited his HQ on May 10 Feuerstein suggested a withdrawal to the Hitler Line, at present unmanned. This, he argued, would be a shorter line to defend and he could create a reserve from his own resources, which at the moment was totally lacking. Kesselring refused, on the ground that it would be contrary to the Fuehrer's strictest orders, that no position was to be abandoned without a fight to the bitter end, but his decision might also have been influenced by his conviction that the main blow would not fall on Feuerstein's front.

It is instructive for the student of war to observe how, in this operation, generals of varying ability and widely different characters became the victims of what, in some, amounted to obsessions. Apart from Kesselring, General Alphonse Juin was convinced (with some justification) that the only way to break through the Gustav Line was along the least likely approach. The previous French experience in the mountains above Cassino had persuaded him of the folly of attacking

---

* A *Kampfgruppe* was a mobile, tactically self-contained group of all arms. A *Sperrgruppe* was only intended to dig in and fight a defensive battle.

bille en tête – bashing a brick wall down with one's head – a view shared
by Anders, who had secret doubts when he was ordered to attack on
that terrible battlefield, though he loyally accepted the task assigned to
him. Harding was as orthodox as a German or Russian, and applied the
principle of concentration, pure and undiluted. Alexander was the
victim of the delusion he had created for himself, that he could only
coax and cajole but never command. Clark was obsessed with the
capture of Rome, come what may.

What the critics of Harding's plan did not understand, and von
Senger and now Feuerstein did, was that in modern warfare it was not
concentration of numbers that counted so much as concentration of
fire-power by land and air – tanks, guns and bombers. Had Feuerstein
been allowed to shorten his line he would have been able to concentrate
the fire of his relatively few guns, and had the withdrawal he suggested
been carried out without giving the game away, the Eighth Army's
opening bombardment would have hit nothing but a few outposts, the
whole ponderous mass of cannon would have had to be moved forward
to within range of the Hitler Line and all Frank Siggers' careful
preparations would have been wasted.

The Allied Intelligence and Counter-Battery staffs had correctly
estimated the strength and location of the German artillery, as shown in
the table opposite, totalling 385 pieces, faced by 1,050 on the Eighth
Army sector, 400 on the CEF and approximately 200 with the US 2nd
Corps.[3]

If the reader is to follow Leese's development of his operations in the
Liri valley he must grasp the significance of this preponderance of the
Allied artillery, and also its potential. Effective artillery fire was possible
in darkness or bad weather, and its response time to calls for support
measured in minutes not hours.* Furthermore, the narrowness of the
Liri front, though it inhibited manoeuvre, was a positive advantage
when it came to concentrating the whole weight of the artillery on the
front of one attacking division or the other.

The Eighth Army's part in DIADEM was code-named HONKER, which
presented no difficulty in interpretation to officers who served in
India and who had hunted big game. The verb "to honk" is slang,
derived from the Urdu *hankna*, to drive game, but not in the sedate
manner used to bring partridges or pheasants up to a line of guns in the
English countryside. It was the sport of the Mughal emperors, who
used their troops to beat out game in the huge battues they enjoyed,

---

* Relatively speaking, compared with tanks or fighter-bombers, depending on
purely visual target identification and fire-control.

using the powerful Turkish bow on the then immensely rich fauna of India: rhinoceros, tigers, leopards and deer of every kind. A later generation of rulers, the English, used to "honk" the wild boar out of cover and ride them down armed only with a six-foot spear, but the acme of the art was to start an often very angry tiger out of the jungle and bring him to a hunter perched in a tree who, if he only wounded it, was in honour bound to climb down, follow the blood trail and finish it off on foot. The Eighth Army staff had met the formidable German soldiers too often to choose a punning or allusive code-name in a spirit of arrogance or frivolity. If the officer who chose it had in mind that the object was to drive the Tenth Army on to the muzzles of the tank guns and artillery of the US 6th Corps when it emerged from Anzio it was

---

German Artillery facing or able to intervene on the Eighth Army front

(Source, Lecture by Brigadier F. S. Siggers, Proceedings of the Royal Artillery Historical Society, Vol. II, No. 5 (January 1969); "heavy", 170-mm gun or 210-mm howitzer; "medium", 105-mm gun or 150-mm howitzer; "field", 105-mm howitzer; "AA", dual-purpose 88-mm; "RL", 150-mm five-barrelled rocket-launcher, or *Nebelwerfer*.)

German Formation	facing	*Allied*
Left sector, 51st Corps, 5th Mtn Div. and regt of 44th Div.; 2 heavy, 24 medium 36 field		10th Corps
Centre sector, 1st Para. Div.; 12 medium 25 field, 4 RL		2nd Polish Corps
Right centre sector, 44th Div., SG Bode 8 heavy, 14 medium, 65 field 8 AA, 40 RL (one complete Nebelwerfer regt)		13th Corps (Total Eighth Army covering Cassino–Liri sector, 1, 050)
Left sector, 14th Corps 71st Infantry Div.; 9 medium, 84 field (of which one group of 36 pieces was within easy range of the 13th Corps assault frontage)		Corps Expéditionnaire Français and US 2nd Corps (Total Fifth Army, Liri to sea, 600)
Ungrouped and listed as "miscellaneous" 2 heavy and 54 AA		

entirely appropriate. Officially code-words were intended to conceal rather than hint at the purpose or nature of an operation, but recondite as the choice was it is a clue to the thinking of HQ Eighth Army.[4]

Kirkman's private diary provides an illuminating account of how a corps commander spends his time before a great attack. His position is delicate, even ambiguous. He cannot, like an army commander, issue his orders, tour round the units to cheer up his troops and retire to his caravan to write letters or read books, leaving the details to his staff; resigned to the fact that he cannot usefully interfere until the battle reaches the crisis from which he hopes to pluck his victory. Divisional and brigade commanders are all busy with the minor tactics, techniques and mechanics of the battle they are about to fight and control from hour to hour. The corps commander has to ensure that all is going forward satisfactorily and that his divisional commanders are in his mind and can anticipate his moves, but without nagging them or "breathing down their necks"; too close control may only serve to irritate or be interpreted as lack of confidence. The corps commander's position is very like that of the managing director of a firm. He is the executive who realises the army commander's aim and plan. He is personally responsible for the conduct of the battle. The detailed plan is his. The army artillery fire-plan, the mission given to the army engineers and the priorities given to the tactical air force have all been adjusted to meet his requirements.

Kirkman was a rather dry, strong-minded highly capable officer from Montgomery's stable. He was an artilleryman specially selected by Montgomery to organise the fire-plan at Alamein and later successfully commanded the 50th (Northumbrian) Division in Sicily. On May 7 he attended the Sunday service in his HQ, reading the lesson he himself had chosen from Deuteronomy, Chapter 9: "Hear, O Israel: thou art to pass over Jordan this day . . ." the stern warning given by Moses to the backsliding Hebrews that the Lord alone conferred victory in battle, not because they deserved it but because He wished to exalt the righteous and subdue the wicked. (British generals were churchgoers without any undue piety – which was bad form – but all had been well grounded in the Authorised Version of the Bible at their public schools, predominantly Anglican foundations.) Then he went off to watch some "first class training" in river crossing by the 1st Battalion of the 6th Surreys on the Volturno river. On the 10th he visited all his divisional commanders to make sure that they understood exactly how he intended the 13th Corps offensive to develop once they had established a bridgehead on the far bank. British higher commanders attached far more importance to establishing this rapport than to the issue of detailed orders handed down to be rigidly obeyed, a system they had tried and found wanting in the First World War.

To "Pasha" Russell, 8th Indian Division, Kirkman explained that if his initial attack went well he was to take every risk and try to rush the Hitler Line, which he correctly believed to be virtually unmanned until the Gustav Line garrisons could fall back and occupy it. His orders to Dudley Ward, 4th Division, attacking on the right, were that once he had firmly established his bridgehead he was to wheel right, isolate Cassino and the Monastery from reinforcements and join hands with the Poles. Charles Keightley was to have one brigade of his 78th Division ready to cross from the 12th onwards, and he hoped later to insert his whole division between Russell and Ward with the Via Casilina as his centre line. He, too, was to go as fast as possible and try to "bounce" the Hitler Line. Once the 78th Division was fairly on its way, he told Ward, and Evelegh (whose division was split between supporting Ward and keeping the parachutists in Cassino in play) that he hoped to withdraw both their divisions into corps reserve ready for exploitation.

At midday on the 11th Kirkman assembled the whole staff of HQ 13th Corps and explained all this to them, so they could understand exactly what he intended and be able to anticipate his requirements by forward planning. In the evening he drove up the Via Casilina towards the river, noting with satisfaction that all the troops and vehicles seemed very well concealed, but later was made rather anxious by the noise the tanks and engineer vehicles made moving down to their assembly positions after dark. The day's entry ended with the weather forecast – "fine and dry" – and the reflection that though all river crossings in the face of a determined enemy were hazardous operations "the chances of success were greatly in our favour" and that he doubted whether "the Bosh [*sic*] had any idea of what was coming to him". There he was right, but then, nor did his troops, who were to be upset by a hazard from an unexpected quarter. Kirkman's opening sentence of the entry for D-day plus one reads, "We got across all right, but nevertheless a rather disappointing night and day." That was exactly the case, no more, no less. If that once-vaunted British characteristic, phlegm, is a prime requisite in a general, "Kirkie" had it in full. So did Leese, Alexander, Clark and Juin. They needed it, for though the 13th Corps attack had started as badly as Juin and Clark had predicted, it was firmly lodged on the far bank and so far had defied any attempt by the Germans to throw it back in the river, while the Poles, the French and the Americans had all completely failed in a dismal and costly fashion.

273

One of the traps into which a military historian can fall is that by trying to convey to his reader a clear and coherent account of what is invariably a confused and complex tissue of events he can fail to convey the true nature of combat. It is only too easy with hindsight to look down on the battlefield as if it were a chess-board, and the errors and lost opportunities revealed by the historical record, whereas in reality the impression of even a successful battle on the fighting soldier is one of a ghastly, bloody muddle. As for the commanders, they are more often than not blinded by the "fog of war", which at 11 p.m. on May 11 was not metaphorical at all, but literal – and thick. The night had started fine, the sky clear and star-lit, the early darkness turned into day by cones of searchlights providing "artificial moonlight". All that had remained was for the gun-position officers to make their last calculations to adjust the sight-settings in the gun-programmes in light of the latest details of wind and weather, and with the single order "Fire!" unleash the first of Frank Siggers' thunderclaps on the enemy batteries, while at the same moment the infantry and the engineers began their march from their concealed assembly areas down to the near bank of the river. Nature then defeated the meteorologists and the staff alike. The Garigliano valley was always subject to mist, though not usually as late as May, but when on that night it suddenly began to form, it was thickened by the smoke of the hundreds of bursting shells – British and German; mist turning into dense fog as Colonel Wilkinson and his anti-aircraft gunners began to ignite their smoke generators in good time to produce a satisfactory screen of the whole battlefield by dawn.

As a result battalions lost their way, the drivers of the engineer vehicles carrying the vital bridging material missed their routes, halted and were set on fire, and confusion reigned from one end of the 13th Corps front to the other. The opening barrage had been timed to dwell for a given length of time on the forward posts of the Gustav Line so as to give time for the assault troops to close up and eliminate them, but they arrived too late and the barrage, its timings rigidly dictated, began to creep forward before the attackers could reach them. The German garrisons, emboldened, poked their heads up, manned their weapons and brought a murderous fire of mortars and machine guns down on the crossing places. The misadventures of D Company, the 1st Battalion, 5th Royal Gurkha Rifles on the night and day of the 12th provide an epitome of infantry fighting in a night attack.

The 1st/5th were the reserve battalion of the 17th Indian Infantry Brigade, which was to land astride S. Angelo, that village of ill-omen, with the British 1st Royal Fusiliers to the right of it and the Indian 12th Frontier Force to the left. (The reader is reminded that the Indian infantry divisions were organised in the proportion of two Indian and one British battalion.) As soon as the Frontier Force had cleared the "bank", the raised embankment carrying the road between S. Apollinare and S. Angelo, the 1st/5th were to cross, D Company working with boats and acting as ferrymen, and follow A, B and C Companies when they had completed their task. Its commander, Major Maynard Pockson, had dispersed his men in cover in the vicinity of forward or "tactical" brigade HQ, sited in a convenient building, and went inside to await the radio message calling him forward. When it came he went outside, to be astonished by the fog and darkness. He "could not see his hand in front of his face" and could not find his men until his company runner fell into a slit trench occupied by two riflemen. All the paraphernalia used for a night advance, the white tapes, the hooded lamps, landmarks carefully noted by day, even the bursts of anti-aircraft tracer shell fired on a fixed bearing to indicate direction, were invisible. Pockson formed his hundred-odd men into a long snake, each holding on to the back of the belt of the man in front of him, placed himself at its head and peering at the tiny phosphorescent numerals in his pocket compass led them down to the river. To his great relief he hit the exact spot where he was to meet the second-in-command of the 12th Frontier Force, who told him that there were only twelve boats left. (In spite of all the rehearsals the current of the Gari proved so fast that boats in both divisions were swept downstream, made unmanageable by the casualties among the crews. Many more boats were damaged by enemy fire.) He worked all night until he was down to two, the return traffic bringing numerous wounded men, "whose moans and cries were not exactly a morale booster".

Nor were the still unburied bodies of the Americans and Germans, victims of the "Bloody River" affair. At dawn Pockson took his own company across, and on the far bank fell into the slit trench occupied by his commanding officer. "I thought you'd be forward under the 'Bank' sir!" he exclaimed, perhaps rather tactlessly. "What's happened?" "We can't get the tanks across, and everybody's held up," was the reply, and he was curtly told to go and disperse himself "over there", that being near the bridging site where the Indian Sappers and Miners were striving to build a bridge under a hot fire punctuated from time to time by large shells landing in the river and sending pillars of water fifty feet up in the air, and in full view of the windows of S. Angelo, bastion of the Gustav Line. A perfectly hellish day was spent by D Company in slit trenches that filled with water when dug down more than three feet, losing men one by one to a continual hail of shells and mortar bombs. Two attacks were arranged and then cancelled.

It was with a "feeling almost of joy" that the company was at last ordered to advance to the "Bank" at 5.40 p.m., assemble under its cover, and clear the enemy from a low bump or knoll in the plain some way to the right, commanding the rear of S. Angelo. On arrival Pockson became aware of a curious and unpleasant phenomenon. The "Bank" was so steep that it promised perfect cover from artillery, but a series of missiles rained down on the riflemen with an apparently vertical trajectory. "What can this be? Where is this fire coming from?" Pockson asked his second-in-command, his subedar, or Gurkha captain. He, a man of few words, pointed with the toe of his boot at a short wooden haft, the handle of a stick-grenade. The top of the bank had not been fully cleared by the Frontier Force, who had disappeared somewhere up the valley with their customary elan, and the men of the German 576th Grenadier Regiment were still in position and busy living up to their title of "grenadier", tossing an inexhaustible supply of them over the brink. This was too much to bear. "Immediately the leading sections were over the top with kukris* drawn. The occupants of the German posts . . . did not wait to greet Johnny Gurkha in person . . . [and] their booted heels were helped over the horizon with bursts of tommy-gun fire . . ."

Pockson now could turn his attention to the business of clearing the knoll, much encouraged by the arrival of three tanks of the 12th Ontario Armoured Regiment, however all became bogged in the marshy ground by the river before they could fire a shot. The Gurkhas went in alone and unsupported and soon ". . . the knoll could be seen swarming with Gurkhas throwing grenades and firing their tommy-guns into the mouths of the German bunkers. It was not long before the remains of the German defenders surrendered and some dozen or so enormous Germans – they always looked enormous with their large steel helmets and black knee boots beside their diminutive Gurkha escorts – were brought into my HQ." Pockson's next task was to tackle S. Angelo itself but ". . . before embarking on this adventure I felt I should take stock of my situation. Company HQ was becoming congested. The dead [Gurkhas] had been brought there, the wounded were waiting for stretcher-bearers and the German prisoners standing about in embarrassed silence. A quick check revealed that I had forty-five all ranks left, hardly enough to take on the village . . ." He reported to his CO, who told him to call off his attack, but to harry the garrison of S. Angelo all night and keep them jittery. (The place fell on

* "Kukri": a woodsman's slashing, lopping tool, leaf-shaped and about eighteen inches long, used for the same purpose as a machete or bolo. In Nepal it doubled as a weapon and was issued as a personal weapon to every Gurkha rifleman.

the following day to a full-scale battalion attack made by the other three companies with tank and artillery support.)

However, Pockson's troubles were not yet over. His forward platoons complained that they were being sniped from S. Angelo. He and his subedar turned their binoculars on to the village and agreed that one at least was ensconced in "the end house, left corner of the right hand bottom window. Yes, there it was, a distinct flash followed by a distant crack. My eyes turned to the FOO (the artillery forward observing officer attached to his company) . . . but my subedar read my thought: 'A tank would be better, saheb,' he said, pointing to one that was still sitting in the water meadows near the river." The question was who to send there across the open, fire-swept ground, and how to communicate with the crew. His subedar looked at him and said pointedly: "*You* speak English."* This, Pockson felt, was perhaps not the only language qualification required, for when training with the Canadians he had discovered that some of the crews spoke only French and among them were real "Red" Indians. (As exotic an addition to the Italian scene as his Mongolians from Nepal.) There was, however, no mistaking his subedar's meaning. Gurkhas were willing subordinates but also hard task masters. " 'All right, Subedar saheb,' I said, adding rather dramatically, 'Remember if anything goes wrong you command the company' . . . 'I know.' " Pockson, running and dodging, survived some bursts of Spandau fire, stopped on the safe side of the tank and hammered the armour with his kukri to attract the crew's attention, trying at the same time to construct a French sentence containing "bottom right hand corner". There was no reply. The tank, he now saw, was bogged up to the top of its tracks and empty, the crew having long since deserted it. Pockson, chagrined at having risked his life for nothing, made his way back safely to his company and broke the news to his subedar who, laconic to the last replied, "A pity, saheb."[5]

When Kirkman assessed his situation on the 12th he could well have repeated to himself the words of an equally phlegmatic corps commander, Douglas Haig, when he heard that his line had been broken at the First Battle of Ypres thirty years before: "Things are never as bad or as good as they appear in the first reports." Although in the 17th Brigade sector the 1st/5th were held up, the British battalion, the 1st Royal Fusiliers, was stuck for the time in a minefield upstream of S. Angelo

---

* All Indian troops were supposed to pass tests of proficiency in the English language, but in practice British officers made a point of using only the lingua franca, Urdu, in Indian regiments, or Gurkhali in the Gurkha Rifles. "Saheb" is the equivalent of "Sir", used mutually.

and relentless enemy fire had prevented the Indian Sappers and Miners from completing the bridge above S. Angelo, elsewhere things had gone better. Russell was able to tell Kirkman when he arrived at his HQ that he had two other bridges working and five squadrons of Canadian tanks over the river. One bridge had been built by his Sappers and Miners in the orthodox way, the other laid by an ingenious method invented by Captain H. A Kingsmill of the Royal Canadian Electrical and Mechanical Engineers, attached to the Calgary Regiment. He had adapted a Sherman tank to carry a 100-foot span of Class 40 Bailey Bridge (strong enough to carry a tank) on rollers on its deck, its rear end coupled to another tank. The two tanks drove down to the river with Kingsmill walking alongside carrying a telephone connected to the driver of the leading tank, which he positioned exactly on to its near-bank seat. The driver carried on boldly down the bank and into the middle of the river, baling out as his tank went under water, and the rear tank pushed the bridge forward until the front end rested on the far bank, disconnected and withdrew. (Kingsmill was awarded the Military Cross.)

A lucky hit by an enemy shell soon reduced the strength of Kingsmill's bridge, but not before a troop of four Calgary tanks had crossed. Its commander, unable to locate the infantry he was to support, with praiseworthy enterprise advanced 1,000 yards into the Gustav Line, and shot up any targets he could find. Five more squadrons of the 1st Canadian Armoured Brigade crossed by the other bridge. It was some of these trying to work up the river bank that had become bogged trying to support the 1st/5th, but the rest found firmer ground away from the river astride the S. Angelo–S. Apollinare road, and by 2.00 p.m. the Ontarios who had stuck when moving up to support Major Pockson had been dragged out of the mud by Canadian recovery vehicles and were once more operational. The combination of Indian infantry and Canadian tanks proved too good for the 576th Grenadier Regiment, as confirmed by the German staff report. Russell was poised for a considerable victory. In the next forty-eight hours he was to clear the "Horseshoe", the half-circle of foothills looking down on his crossing places where the depth positions of the Gustav Line were sited, and the way was clear for the Canadian Corps to enter the battle.

It was the performance of the 4th Infantry Division that gave Kirkman real cause for anxiety. He had already noted that one of its brigades was not properly trained, and he knew that the whole division had been left too long unemployed in North Africa after the end of the Tunisian campaign and had suffered what was all too often the fate of units in such a position; being treated as a pool for casual labour,

278

reinforcements and men for "extra regimental employment".* Dudley Ward, its newly appointed and dynamic commander, had not had enough time to restore the division to its former efficiency. The temporary disarray into which it fell on the night of the 11th/12th has been well described by General Sir William Jackson, who was present as an engineer officer. "It was," he says, "impossible to stifle the desperate feeling that the whole affair had grossly miscarried or, in soldier's language, it was 'an unholy balls up'." The causes were the same as had impeded the 8th Indian Division, fog, late arrival of the assault battalions, losing the barrage, and intense enemy fire as the enemy posts on the far bank came to life. The 10th Brigade, which successfully crossed on the right, had the added disadvantage of being pitted against the parachute machine-gunners, who were fully as aggressive as their infantry, and the 1st/115th Panzer Grenadiers. Many boats were lost in the unexpectedly fast current, some because of poor watermanship, some because the paddlers were hit, some capsized by the "passengers" jumping in down the steep bank in their haste to avoid the murderous Spandau fire sweeping the crossing places. In the 28th Brigade sector the leading battalion, the 1st King's Regiment, arrived thirty-five minutes late and had a bad time crossing, delaying the 2nd Somerset Light Infantry, who had to sit in the cleared lanes through the minefield on the near bank unable to disperse or take cover and losing men at a rapid rate to the incessant enemy fire; the morale was not improved by "stragglers and wounded from the King's [who] repeated and embellished wild rumours that the battalion had been virtually wiped out".

The most serious failure was in building tank-bearing bridges. By 1.00 a.m. the engineers were well advanced in the work of preparing the bank seats, but as soon as the heavy vehicles carrying the Bailey equipment began to move down to the riverside the noise of the engines

---

* As officers of those days can bear witness, unless the division and brigade commanders were sufficiently strong-minded, or "bloody-minded", battalions were subjected to a constant haemorrhage of junior officers, NCOs and men – always "the best" were demanded – for posts in training schools, clerks, storemen and quartermasters for establishments on the lines of communication and, worst of all – for no volunteer could be withheld on the grounds that he was essential in the regiment or battalion – for airborne troops, commandos, or the egregious "Chindits". The Canadian commanders very understandably complained to Alexander himself that having come all the way to Italy to fight, their men resented being detailed to run transit camps or unload supply ships. The inflation of special forces and the *bouches inutiles* on the lines of communication was one of the worst features of British man-management during the Second World War, not so much in numbers, although these were considerable, but because of the quality of men removed from the combat units.

attracted "defensive fire of such intensity that the Sappers were driven to cover and many of their vehicles set on fire". There was every possibility of a repetition of the "Bloody River" débâcle, but greatly to the division's credit the officers and NCOs pulled the operation together, and those natural leaders who pass unnoticed in barracks or when things are normal began to appear. Jackson gives as but one example the leadership of Lance-Corporal H. Granger, 2nd Battalion, 4th Hampshires. The battalion was, like Pockson's Gurkhas, acting as ferrymen, and the system adopted in the brigade was the sensible one of fixing lines across the river by which the crews could haul them across. Granger swam the river three times with ropes, and remained naked on the bank for four hours collecting stragglers and guiding them to the crossing points.[6] Through the efforts of many other similar but unremarked men of determination rallying their platoons in the bullet-pierced fog and darkness each brigade had by daylight won a foothold on the far bank, the 10th Brigade opposite Trocchio and the 28th about a quarter of a mile north of S. Angelo in the area defended by Bode's left-hand battalion. They had no tanks or heavy weapons, but with the aid of the artillery and their own rifles and light machine guns beat off a number of disconnected counter-attacks, but Kirkman after he had visited both divisions wrote in his diary: "They [i.e. the 4th Division] are however not in very good shape." He ordered Ward to commit his reserve brigade and build a bridge that night, "at all costs".

No sensible commander, and certainly not one so precise and given to understatement as Kirkman, uses such an expression except in the direst emergency and, as Jackson says, "It was meant literally and not as a figure of speech."[7] Accordingly at 5.45 p.m. on the 12th two field squadrons, Royal Engineers of the 4th Division, began work in the left–centre of the 10th Brigade's bridgehead (as far as was possible from the higher ground on the right), and by 4.00 a.m. on the 13th it was open for Ward's reserve brigade and the tanks of the 17th/21st Lancers, three squadrons in all, to cross. The price was 80 out of 200 Sappers working on the site. "This," said Kirkman, "alters the whole situation." He ordered three more bridges to be built, "gingered up Russell [and told him] to go faster tomorrow", and warned Keightley to have his leading brigade ready to cross on the 14th, strike north-west between the 4th and 8th Divisions, as already instructed, with the rest of his division to follow and join hands with the Poles on the Via Casilina on the 15th. He noted that the haul of prisoners, always a good indication of how a battle against the Germans was going, might be as much as 600, though the total casualties in the corps to date were 1,000, which was severe. All the same, Kirkman's final entry was "a most satisfactory day", but his hopes were soon dashed.

The advance of the 78th Division was held up by bad going, side roads collapsing under the weight of the tanks, clouds of dust reducing visibility almost as much as the fog of the 11th and "terrible traffic hold-ups". To make matters worse, the forward units of the 4th Division were not as far forward as they claimed to be nor had they mopped up the enemy completely, so the leading troops of the 78th had to fight their way forward to the area as the jump-off point for their attack.

Anders was ready to resume his attack southward to meet the 13th Corps but Kirkman, knowing that the Polish Corps was good for only one more all-out attack, had to ask for it to be postponed twice as Keightley, moving too slowly to suit Kirkman, gradually fought his way forward. Nevertheless, Leese felt that by the 15th his battle was beginning to go the way he wanted and that it should be accelerated. He ordered the 1st Canadian Corps to take over the front of the 8th Indian Division on the 16th. Major-General Chris Vokes, 1st Canadian Infantry Division, had been duly warned to relieve Russell, and had made the preliminary arrangements. The only obstacle to a smooth transfer was Lieutenant-General Burns who, Kirkman found, "lacked confidence in how to do it [i.e., the relief] and was generally suspicious". He quite firmly laid down that the normal procedure would be followed, which was that Russell would be in command of the sector and the operation until Vokes had his two brigades in action, and when he had his headquarters would take over control. A relief in the presence of the enemy is a complicated procedure, done by night and in complete silence, company by company, platoon by platoon and section by section, but both divisions were well trained and well disciplined and the Germans remained perfectly ignorant of the change, much to Kesselring's subsequent annoyance. One of the leading actors in the drama was now on stage, the battle had become an army battle, and it is time to look at it from the viewpoint of General Sir Oliver Leese.

18

THE BATTLE IN THE LIRI VALLEY

Then we have to give up Cassino!
Kesselring to von Vietinghoff, 5.25 p.m., May 16

Until May 14 General Leese had to be content with watching the progress of his battle and encouraging the reliable commander of the 13th Corps. He had one faculty essential if a commander has to be something better than *un bon chef ordinaire*: flair, or what the Germans call a "fingertip-feeling". When he decided to insert the Canadian Corps into the battle his timing was perfect. The indicators were not promising. To be sure, Russell's British–Indian infantry and Canadian tanks had reduced the fighting value of Bode's blocking group almost to zero, but Ward's division, its horns locked with the parachutists in and around Cassino town, was making only slow progress, as was the 78th Division, held up by the muddy banks of the insignificant Piopetto stream, impassable for tanks. There was fearful traffic congestion and Ward's leading brigade had failed to clear sufficient elbow-room for Keightley to make a tidy approach to his jump-off line. Leese knew that he could ask Anders to make an effort and that the Polish soldiers would respond with heroic self-sacrifice, but that would be profitless. Far better to wait until Kirkman and Anders could mount a simultaneous, coordinated attack. It is the business of an army commander at such a stage in a battle to decide on the right moment to invest his capital. Too early and he may clog the battlefield with troops and waste his precious assets against unshaken defences: too late, and opportunity has slipped through his fingers. It might have been prudent to wait until Kirkman had made greater progress, but Leese grasped what previous commanders had not, that possession of the low ground would make the heights untenable.

282

In fact, during what seemed to Kirkman an intolerable hold-up (and, as said, made him twice recommend to Leese that he should postpone the attack by the Poles) the 78th Division began to gain the upper hand in a series of disconnected, vicious little company and battalion fights as they bumped into the bits and pieces of what constituted Ortner's rearguards.

The 78th Infantry Division had in Tunisia established itself as one of the best in the British Army and had fought well on the Adriatic coast.* Rested and re-trained for six months after the Sangro battle its units were fully up to their old, aggressive form. On the 15th the 6th Inniskilling Fusiliers accompanied by a squadron of one of the best of the British armoured regiments, the 16th/5th Lancers, ran into trouble soon after they began their advance, coming under a hot machine-gun fire from German infantry hidden in a field of tall corn. Tanks and infantry charged immediately, and "after much tommy-gun work and tossing of grenades out of the turrets of Shermans" drove them off. They met stiffer resistance when they closed up to the lateral road to Pignataro. A model of a prompt battalion attack followed, supported by a hasty fire-plan by the artillery and the Lancers' tanks lined up to "shoot the infantry in". The Inniskillings captured sixty prisoners, five anti-tank guns, two assault guns and a Mark IV Panzer tank. On their right the 5th Northamptons, who had lost their supporting tanks in the early-morning Liri mist, bumped into a group of enemy, attacked off the line of march and captured 126 of them. These little victories were not cheaply won. The Inniskillings lost seventy officers and men, many of them to the intense fire the German artillery put down as a regular response to the loss of an objective.

On the German side the unwisdom of dispersing the 44th Hoch und Deutschmeister Division and replacing its organic units with inferior troops from high-number infantry divisions soon became painfully apparent. As early as the 4th General Ortner reported to Feuerstein

---

* The 78th Infantry and 6th Armoured Divisions were founder members of the short-lived First Army and there was a strong sense of divisional identity in both and an admirable rapport between them strengthened by an exchange of brigades, the 1st Guards going to the armoured division and the all-Irish 38th mechanised Infantry Brigade joining the 78th as infantry of the line, which paid off when their old friends in the 26th Armoured Brigade came to support them in the Liri valley. The 78th did not succumb to Montgomery's charm, and were scornful when he told them they had been promoted, in effect, by their membership of his Eighth Army. For a time the units displayed notices in bivouacs and elsewhere announcing that they had "no connection with the Eighth Army", to the amusement or annoyance of senior officers, depending on their previous loyalties.

that Bode's group was no longer effective and that without timely reinforcement by "strong reserves in close formation" (*sic*, meaning able to re-establish a continuous line of resistance) he could no longer oppose the British advance where he stood: the situation demanded withdrawal to the Hitler Line on the 15th/16th "at the latest". This statement, coinciding with what Feuerstein had felt from the first, required no elaboration by him, so he simply endorsed it with his bare signature and sent it on to HQ Tenth Army. This was not the only bad news reaching von Vietinghoff. Keyes' US 2nd Corps having recovered from its costly repulse on the 11th/12th was now fighting hard and was well on its way to Terracina. General Juin's Corps Expéditionnaire Français had surprised its friends as much as its enemies. Its North African colonial divisions had broken the Gustav Line in the mountains and the infantry and tanks of what had become famous as the Free French Division (now renamed the 1ère Division de Marche d'Infanterie) was driving along the right bank of the Liri. In spite of all this Kesselring clung obstinately to his convictions. He warned von Mackensen, Fourteenth Army, who was anxiously waiting for the Anzio front to explode in his face, to be ready to detach his only reserve, the 26th Panzer Division, to Gaeta to meet the imaginary threat of a landing between his left wing and the right of the Tenth Army, though on the 14th he gave way grudgingly to von Vietinghoff's appeals for reinforcements. He released the 90th Panzer Grenadier Division (Generalleutnant Ernst Gunter Baade), so its 200th Panzer Grenadier Regiment was sent to shore up the 14th Corps against French pressure, while the remainder, amounting to no more than a battle-group of the 361st Grenadier Regiment and a strong force of anti-tank and assault guns, went to the 51st Corps. It was hoped to use it to man the Hitler defences but instead it was drawn into the running battle in the Liri valley where it was to lose more than half its strength. Such was the situation when Vokes had completed his relief of the 8th Indian Division. The next phase of his offensive, for which Kirkman had been waiting so impatiently, could then begin.

This was made in the Eighth Army style, on a narrow front, closely supported by the tanks of the 26th Armoured Brigade and 400 guns. The defence included some of the best troops in the 51st Corps, for Feuerstein had risked thinning out on the heights to form a reserve from Colonel Schultz's 1st Parachute Regiment, composed of two battalions, a few field guns and eight 105-mm and twenty-three 75-mm assault guns. The fighting was bitter, but the 78th attacked with all their old combination of dash and infantry skill, and an offensive backed by such a weight of fire-power was too much even for the parachutists. The palm could have been claimed equally by the 2nd Lancashire Fusiliers and the 2nd London Irish Rifles, both of them exploiting the basic infantry rule that the best way of wearing down an opponent was to force him to counter-attack. Fusilier Jefferson won the Victoria Cross for his courage when tanks burst into his company position and he stood up in the open with his PIAT anti-tank grenade thrower and destroyed the nearest of them. The London Irish reached their first objective where they were subjected to a more powerful and formally organised counter-attack. Between their own weapons, the attached 17-pounder anti-tank guns of the Royal Artillery and machine guns of the Kensington heavy-weapons battalion they killed 100, destroyed 9 tanks or assault guns and captured 120 prisoners. The casualties on both sides were heavy. When KG Schultz arrived in the Hitler Line it had lost over half its strength, while on the 16th alone the Lancashire Fusiliers lost forty out of ninety in one company, and the London Irish five officers and sixty men, together with sixteen, all killed, of the Royal Artillery and Kensingtons. But the division had broken clean through the Gustav Line. "Quite a good day," Kirkman wrote in his diary.

That evening Kesselring and von Vietinghoff discussed the situation on the telephone:

Kesselring: I consider a withdrawal to the Senger position neces-
                  sary [i.e., the Hitler Line].
Von Vietinghoff: Then it will be necessary to begin withdrawal north of
                  the Liri. Tanks have broken through there.
Kesselring: How far?
Von Vietinghoff: To Piumarola. [He was mistaken. The 78th Division
                  did not enter until the next day.]
Kesselring: And how is the situation further north?
Von Vietinghoff: There are about 100 tanks in Schultz's area.
Kesselring: Then we shall have to give up Cassino.
Von Vietinghoff: Yes.[1]

That superbly laconic exchange with its final, plangent "*Ja!*" was the epitaph for the dead of seven armies in four battles.

The agony was nearly over. Leese saw the moment had come to order Anders to launch his long-prepared second attack to clear Montecassino. We have so far said little about the fortunes of the Polish Corps except to record that it had failed on the 12th with shocking loss, and it is time to give an account of those remarkable soldiers. Since the 12th Anders and his staff had been busy creating some infantry battalions *ad hoc* from his anti-tank artillery and service units, and in a careful analysis of the causes of their initial failure. The Poles have been romanticised for their reckless courage and by highly-coloured stories of Polish cavalry throwing themselves in kamikaze charges against the German panzers in 1939, but although their courage was unsurpassed the Polish officers were highly intelligent and thoughtful soldiers, as their adaptation to fighting in Italy was to show. Anders' conclusions were fourfold. In the earlier attack the assault had not been closely coordinated with the artillery bombardment. (This was Briga-dier Siggers' opinion also. He would have preferred both corps to attack simultaneously on the night of the 11th, so dividing the German defensive fire.) The ban on close patrolling had denied the assault units essential detailed knowledge of the enemy posts. The communications at that level were not proof against enemy artillery fire, and control was lost when it was most needed. These three had been compounded by a circumstance discovered later that was not likely to recur. H-hour had coincided with the relief of the troops in the line, and the parachutists being the good troops they were, instead of being thrown back into disarray ordered a general stand fast and fought at double strength.

Bearing these factors in mind the Poles set out to give Heidrich's troops a thoroughly rough time. They patrolled incessantly, keeping them constantly on the alert, and familiarising themselves with the details of the ground and defences. They tricked them into revealing the lay-out of their defensive barrages by real bombardment combined with mock attacks. They harassed the German positions continually with artillery fire stepped up by aerial bombardment. Even such troops as Heidrich's were not proof against such treatment. The noise alone causes lack of sleep, which in turn leads to irritability and slow reaction in an emergency. There is also a steady drain of casualties, for men become careless as they grow tired, they have to relieve nature, supplies have to be brought up, signallers have to go out to mend telephone cables and runners to carry messages, and at least one sentry in each post must keep a look-out. The loss in junior officers and in NCOs is more pronounced if they do their duty and move about seeing that weapons are kept clean and ready, and the men alert, while uttering words of encouragement.

Anders decided to renew his attack on the 17th, to coincide with Keightley's next drive in the valley below, but it had been anticipated by a brilliant patrol coup during the night, of a kind that is only possible to the most highly trained and opportunist infantry. During the night of the 16th a battalion commander in the 5th Kresowa Division sent out a patrol to have a final look at his objective. Its leader, perhaps exceeding his precise orders, "took out" a number of scattered posts on the so-called Phantom Ridge barring access to a key point in the German defences, the Colle (col) S. Angelo. From it a track led down to the Villa S. Lucia above the Via Casilina, and the reverse slope of Point 593, so long held by the Germans. Moreover, its possession was vital to the Germans if their troops in the Snakeshead area were to be withdrawn intact. On learning of the patrol's success the Polish battalion commander infiltrated his whole unit to reinforce it under cover of darkness. Next morning his brigade commander passed another battalion through it on to the col. The German reaction was immediate and ferocious. Counter-attack and attack alternated until nightfall, by when Anders had committed his last reserve and neither of his divisions had reached their final objectives. (Kirkman believed that he had failed completely and ordered Keightley to redouble his efforts and broaden his front to his left.) Nevertheless, Anders was not discouraged. As he wrote later, he felt that "The critical moment had indeed arrived, when both sides faced each other in complete exhaustion apparently incapable of making any further effort, and when the one with the stronger will, who is able to deliver the final blow, wins." He ordered an attack along the front to be resumed the next morning. That in fact the orders to withdraw had gone out from Kesselring's HQ on the night of the 16th does not detract from the achievement of the 2nd Polish Corps. It soon found that it was engaged only by the rear parties covering the retreat. At 10.20 a.m. on May 18 the 12th Podolski Lancers reached the ruins of the Monastery and hoisted the red and white flag of Poland on its walls.

There was still some murderous mopping-up to be done. Heidrich, a law unto himself by virtue of his reputation as a fighting soldier and who stood high in the Nazi Party, refused to accept the withdrawal order from anyone but Kesselring, and some of his fanatical troops not even from him. Both on the heights and in Cassino town when the 10th Infantry Brigade entered it on the same day snipers and diehards who had reserved their last round or grenade for an enemy had to be rooted out and killed. Such sporadic fighting was not over until midday on the 19th. By that time the task force of South African Engineers was busy restoring the Via Casilina through Cassino town over a wilderness of rubble and flooded bomb craters.

Leese went to Anders' HQ within the hour of hearing of the occupation of the Monastery to congratulate him and toast his success in champagne. His relationship with Anders throws further light on a complex character. Leese seems to have regarded anyone who spoke English as a sort of honorary Englishman, and made no concessions to him. A natural clash of personalities apart, he never reached any understanding or rapport with his colleague in the Fifth Army. When dealing with a sensitive foreigner he watched his step carefully, realising perhaps, that at heart they both belonged (as his hero Montgomery emphatically did not) to an old-fashioned if not obsolete school of good manners and chivalry. Leese was sensitive enough to visit Anders as soon as possible after the repulse of the 12th not to commiserate, but to assure him that the sacrifices made by his men had distracted his opponent from interfering with the 13th Corps river crossing. It was not that he spoiled his foreign corps commander. On the contrary, he was most forthright when the newly arrived Anders engaged in political controversy over the British Government's attitude to the future sovereignty of Poland ". . . in my capacity as Army Commander I have to point out to you how superfluous it is for any corps commander to express in public any opinion concerning the political situation . . ." he wrote, and it rankled until each man had taken the measure of the other and a warm mutual respect was substituted. Informally they conversed in Leese's fractured French. The healing process was accelerated by Leese's next order, which was without delay to clear M. Cairo, cover Kirkman's right flank and capture the hinge of the Hitler Line, Piedimonte. It was a mark of his confidence.

The Poles had suffered terribly. Said Anders:

> The battlefield presented a dreary sight. There were enormous dumps of unused ammunition and here and there heaps of land mines. Corpses of Polish and German soldiers, sometimes entangled in a deathly embrace, lay everywhere and the air was full of the stench of rotting bodies. There were overturned tanks with broken caterpillars and others standing as if ready for an attack, with their guns still pointing towards the Monastery. The slopes of the hills, particularly where the fire had been less intense, were covered with poppies in incredible number, their red flowers weirdly appropriate to the scene. All that was left of the oak grove of the so-called Valley of Death were splintered tree-stumps. Crater after crater pitted the sides of the hills, and scattered over them were fragments of uniforms and tin helmets, tommy guns, Spandaus, Schmeissers and hand-grenades.

Of the Monastery itself there remained only an enormous heap of ruins and rubble, with here and there some broken columns. Only the western wall, over which the two flags flew, was still standing. (Two, since Anders, characteristically, had ordered the Union Jack to be hoisted as well.) A cracked church bell lay on the ground next to an unexploded shell of the heaviest calibre, and on shattered walls and ceilings fragments of paintings and frescos could be seen. Priceless works of art, sculpture, pictures and books lay in the dust and broken plaster.

However, nothing encourages soldiers more than success, and the Poles, far from being incapable of further effort, threw themselves into their new tasks. Cairo was cleared by two reconnaissance regiments acting as infantry, the Carpathian and the 15th Poznan Lancers. Piedimonte fell on May 25 after much hard fighting by a battle-group composed of the 6th Armoured Regiment, the 18th Lwow and the 5th Carpathian Rifle Battalions and the 12th Lancers supported by intense artillery fire. The total Polish casualties between the 12th and 25th were 281 officers and 3,503 NCOs and rank and file, of which 72 and 788 respectively were killed. Bearing in mind that Anders' divisions had only two regular brigades of infantry each, and that the heaviest casualties are always in the rifle companies, a total at full strength of say 3,600 men, these are awe-inspiring figures.

We must now return to events in the valley below, where the two corps had been regrouped with a view to rushing the Hitler Line before resistance had hardened. Keightley had to surrender the 26th Armoured Brigade to conform with Kirkman's original plans to have the 6th Armoured Division re-formed and intact ready to follow through after any success. Instead he was given two of Murphy's armoured regiments, leaving Vokes The Three Rivers, the place of the Ontario and Calgary Regiments being taken by the British 25th Tank Brigade, equipped with Churchills. (An "armoured" brigade contained a motorised rifle battalion and often a self-propelled artillery regiment, a "tank" brigade, three "battalions" of tanks, usually manned by the Royal Tank Regiment and specialising in tank–infantry co-operation.) Each corps had room to operate with only one reinforced division forward, the 1st Canadian Infantry Division followed hope-fully by the 5th Canadian Armoured Division on the left, and the 78th followed by the 6th Armoured, joined later by part of the 8th Indian Infantry Division, put in to bring the talents of the Indian infantry in hill-fighting on to the shoulders of the heights.

The problem that faced both Keightley and Vokes was that the Liri valley, so promising a line of advance on the map, looked very different on the ground when examined with the eye of an infantryman trying to spot a sniper or a Spandau, or the commander of a tank scanning the nearby bushes or trees for a lurking infantryman waiting to set his tank on fire with a *Faustpatronen* or an *Ofenrohr*. (Hand-held and deadly to the tanks of those days. One was a grenade-thrower, the other resembled a US "bazooka".) The country was close with thickets of oak and tall crops, and the going difficult as the neighbourhood of irrigation ditches was muddy enough to bog a tank, and the Spalla Bassa and the Formio d'Aquino, tributaries of the Liri, had steep sides and required to be bridged by engineers before tanks could cross. The only first-class road running the length of the valley was the Via Casilina. Elsewhere there were only farm tracks until the engineers had bull-dozed roads, and in places in the Canadian sector not even battalion tactical vehicles could move forward without engineer assistance, and the infantry had to carry forward their heavy weapons and the ponder-ous rear-link radios and their batteries.

Feuerstein had also reorganised his dispositions on the Liri front after the 16th, a difficult process as his forward troops were under continual pressure; part of the 361st Panzer Grenadier Regiment, for instance, was at one stage encircled by the 78th Division and had to fight its way out. The 44th Division's HQ was relieved and the Liri sector divided between the 1st Parachute Division and the 90th Panzer Grenadier Division. The intended line-up once back in the Hitler Line was as follows. KG Schultz occupied Piedimonte. Next came KG Heilmann, basically the 3rd Parachute Regiment, whose junction point with the 90th Division was about 1,000 yards south of Aquino. The left of Baade's Division was held by KG Fabian, and the detail of the hotch-potch of units should be noted as it is evidence of the straits to which the 51st Corps, like the 14th Corps, was being reduced by constant attrition. The commander was Captain Fabian, the 2nd/361st Panzer Grenadier Regiment, the troops such remnants of that unit as had escaped from the trap, a variety of engineers acting as infantry, part of the 44th Ersatz Battalion, two anti-tank gun companies detached from mountain units up in the hills, and a company of tanks from the 26th Panzer Division. Between KG Fabian's left to the ruins of Pontecorvo on the left bank of the Liri the front was manned by SG Bode, by then composed of the remnants of the 576th Regiment, the rest of the 44th Ersatz Battalion, an equivalent battalion of engineers and a company of anti-tank guns, together with KG Strafner, three and a half companies of mountain troops with some engineers and assault guns, which was under the command of Colonel Bode.

It is difficult to assess the strength in infantry of the garrison of the Hitler Line, because it varied. Units were wasted by operations so that ordinary designations bore no relation to strength, and driblets of reinforcements scratched up from everywhere arrived from the rear or from quiet fronts. In the German records a "regiment" of only 300 is spoken of as being in relatively good condition, and others are below 100 all ranks. The Canadians estimated that they were faced by no more than 800 when Vokes made his final attack. Perhaps an estimate over the whole Eighth Army front of 1,500–2,000 is on the high side, but many of these were low-grade troops, not "regular" infantry, or artillerymen in the indirect fire role, and all had suffered severe wastage at the level of junior leader.

It was not this that counted, however, as long as morale held up. The strength of the defence lay in its fortifications, which multiplied the value of its man-power. (Fortifications had become very unfashionable after the First World War and the fate of the Maginot Line in the Second, but the Germans knew better. It is obviously better to fight a defensive battle protected from enemy fire than not.) Furthermore modern defensive tactics demand a very high ratio of fire-power to man-power; an example, theorists might argue, of the old principle of "economy of force". What made the northern sector of the Hitler Line a tough nut to crack was the as yet undetected Panther turrets, backed by an arrowhead formation of ordinary wheeled anti-tank guns and assault guns, and covered in front by a web of enfilading machine-gun fire. Fire-power had to be met with fire-power.

On the 18th Kirkman, encouraged by intelligence that the opposition in front of him was dwindling, urged Keightley on, but that officer refused to be hustled. That may be the case, he argued, but the country was close and infested with snipers, his infantry very tired and he had to proceed methodically from one firm foothold to another for, as had been seen so far, the enemy was still prone to counter-attack. Kirkman could only acquiesce, but later, in the evening, Keightley came on the telephone ". . . a very different Charles . . ." Keightley had for the time retained under his command the Derbyshire Yeomanry, the reconnaissance regiment of the 6th Armoured Division, and a motor rifle battalion, which he had sent ahead to probe, and at last light its commander had reported that he had found an unguarded stretch of the Hitler fortifications and his tanks were shooting into the outskirts of Aquino. This was great news, but it was too late to exploit it, so Keightley intended to attack at first light the next morning, with "a brigade and 100 tanks". This proved a fiasco. The Derbyshire Yeomanry was an efficient regiment, but on this occasion its commander had made a gross error in map-reading or was not clear of the exact location of the Hitler Line, which in fact still lay ahead. He had also failed to reconnoitre the ground, for a steep ravine, sufficiently deep to stop a tank, looped round the front and flanks of Aquino. In the morning the attackers were first helped and then betrayed by the treacherous early-morning fog. The infantry came up against uncut wire and machine-gun fire. The commanding officers of both leading battalions were hit, one killed, and the mist then lifted to reveal to the German anti-tank gunners the Ontario tanks spread out in the open. The whole area was subjected to a torrent of artillery fire. Nine tanks were lost, but fortunately the rest of the forward troops, covered by the British and Canadian artillery firing a smoke screen which used up every smoke-shell in the limbers and wagons, were able to extricate themselves from a most unpleasant situation. Keightley ordered a pause and prepared to resume the attack after dark.

The 1st Canadian Infantry Division greatly distinguished itself on the 17th and 18th in what their official historian said "included nearly the heaviest fighting of any day of the Liri valley campaign". Vokes may have been rather nettled by a message from Leese that reached him via Burns saying that the army commander was dissatisfied with the rate of progress so far, for he sent his infantry off at a cracking pace. "It was a thrill to see the battle-wise Van Doos [the Royal 22nd] march straight forward half crouching," said an admiring observer in a tank of The Three Rivers Regiment. The 3rd Brigade reached the Formio d'Aquino three miles further on by nightfall, and the brigade commander pushed the 22nd over during the night to establish a good bridgehead. The 1st Brigade was opposed by bits of the 576th Regiment and the fresh 190th Reconnaissance Battalion of the 90th Division. The Hastings and Prince Edwards forced their way across the Spalla Bassa after a day-long fight, and by nightfall the division was up to the Formio d'Aquino all along its front. The tanks came along as best they could but had to wait for the engineers before they could cross the Spalla Bassa and most of the day's fighting was by infantry using their own weapons to get forward.

Two outstanding feats were the capture of a battery of field guns by Lieutenant N. A. Ballard, leading his platoon who, his supply of grenades being exhausted, forced the surrender of the gun-position officer by clouting him with his fists, and the repulse of a counter-attack made by night on the 48th Highlanders of Canada by infantry and assault guns of the 190th Battalion. Sergeant R. J. Shaw, commanding the anti-tank platoon, destroyed two assault guns, asking for the battalion mortars to fire illuminating shell and laying and firing a 6-pounder gun himself. After this the courageous but much-battered German battle-groups were allowed to fall back directly to their Hitler positions, while Vokes prepared to see whether it was possible to "bounce" it – to go through before the defences could be coordinated.

It was not until 6.30 a.m. on the 19th that the 3rd Infantry Brigade supported by the 51st Battalion, Royal Tank Regiment, attacked KG Fabian, but the infantry were stopped by a hot machine-gun fire and an 88-mm gun (possibly a "hornet" assault gun) which knocked out several tanks. It was hoped to resume the attack with full artillery support, but for the moment all the army artillery was concentrated on targets on the 13th Corps front and Vokes called off the attack. At this stage Leese intervened. He cancelled the night attack planned by the 78th Division and decided that the Hitler Line had to be breached by deliberate attack, and that this had to be made in the Pontecorvo sector by the Canadians with the full weight of the Eighth Army's fire-power on May 23. This was to be a crucial date, for the indications across the whole front were that the turning point of DIADEM had arrived. On Alexander's orders the break-out from Anzio was to be synchronised on that date with operation CHESTERFIELD, the breakthrough attack by the 1st Canadian Corps.

This was preceded, somewhat to Leese's anxiety, by yet another opportunistic attack by the Canadians. Vokes had detected a weakness in the manning if not the weapon strength of the Hitler positions, and he also felt that the progress of the French 1st Division across the river could be exploited when he learnt that General Brosset's troops had entered the part of Pontecorvo south of Liri. He wondered whether it would be possible to turn the Hitler Line by an assault crossing from the French-held bank, but this on inspection proved too dangerous as the 90th Division had refused its right flank and the steep opposite bank of the river was lined with machine-gun posts. Nevertheless, Vokes obtained permission to attack Pontecorvo with one brigade. This rather rash adventure failed, though not because of any lack of determination. It advanced 400 yards and captured 60 prisoners, but to have pressed it would have incurred severe casualties so it was called off after a warning to Burns from Leese that it might interfere with and delay the arrangements for CHESTERFIELD.

The staff of the 51st Corps was fully aware of the storm that was about to break on its right flank. Intense air activity prevented an orderly transfer of units to the threatened front, masses of tanks could be seen moving up the Via Casilina and there was constant patrolling. The only misapprehension was that the probing attacks of the 19th were seen as the main assault, and Kesselring and von Vietinghoff were premature in congratulating Baade and Heidrich on successfully repelling it. The situation on the 14th Corps front, where the French had defeated the 26th Panzer Division's attempts to stabilise the situation, worried them far more. No directions were given to Feuerstein to make provisional orders for a withdrawal. The next warning

293

was the preliminary counter-battery programme, followed at three minutes before 6 a.m. on the 23rd by a barrage by 682 guns on an opening line 3,200 yards wide behind which the assaulting infantry lined up to cross the start line precisely at 6 o'clock, H-hour.

The course of one "set-piece" battle does not differ essentially from another. There are the same successes, the same reverses, desperate moments when, as happened on the 23rd, the significance of the uninterpreted dark dots on the air photographs of the Hitler Line defences was revealed as the Panther tank turrets unmasked and the front was lit up by scores of burning British and Canadian tanks. Later the infantry were separated by accident from their own anti-tank guns and overrun, and yet again, numbers of prisoners were captured by the Panzer Grenadiers who, marching them off to a rear area, found it in Canadian hands and captors and captives exchanged roles. Baade's division fought with all the tenacity of which the German soldier was famous but the chief of staff of the 51st Corps realised the game was up. He rang up the operations officer at HQ Tenth Army in the morning and again in the afternoon, urgently requesting "directives for a withdrawal so that the Corps could make preparations that would prevent the loss of arms and equipment". The second call was recorded in those words under the heading "Official note of Fact", a staff procedure only used when there was likely to be a subsequent search for a scapegoat. (Responsibility for failure was always deemed to be shared by the General Staff officer whose duty it was to give correct advice to his commander.) It was repeated when at 11.30 p.m. the chief of staff rang up General Wentzell himself, informing him that "KG Strafner must be considered as destroyed" and that "the Corps commander therefore orders the withdrawal from Pontecorvo . . ."
Vokes had broken through the Hitler Line in a single day's fighting. It had cost the Canadians 47 officers and 832 NCOs and rank and file, and 7 officers and 70 men of the attached Royal Tank Regiment units. Subsequently the Canadian staff made a thorough and self-critical analysis of the whole operation, but the historian patiently following the course of events in the Liri valley between May 16 and May 23 need say no more than that it established the 1st Canadian Division as the equal of any of the formations in the armies of Italy.

VII

France Wins the Diadem

GENERAL JUIN'S PLAN

Le rythme de manoeuvre sera adapté aux circonstances, ce qui nécessitera de tous ardeur, compréhension et souplesse.

Le Maréchal de France Alphonse Juin

We left the French relieving the British 10th Corps in the Garigliano bridgehead. By the middle of April the whole CEF was assembled there under General Juin, a total of four regular infantry divisions, one of which was held back east of the river, and a large force of irregular Moroccan levies. The CEF had been equipped by the United States and was organised along US Army lines, and in view of this and of the historic bond between the two nations the CEF was appropriately placed under Clark's command. With one specialised mountain division and the whole corps being adapted to mountain warfare it was correctly placed in the mountain region where McCreery's over-mechanised troops had been decisively checked. Nevertheless, for the moment Clark planned to allot Juin only a modest role in his part of the DIADEM operation. The fact was that neither he nor his staff, nor the staff of AAI had at that time any idea of the spirit and fighting-power of the French, nor an inkling of Juin's ability as a commander.

Their underlying feeling was that though the French were more than welcome as reinforcements after the departure of so many seasoned US and British troops in preparation for OVERLORD, the reason for their presence was political as well as military; they had to be seen playing a part. Neither the British, in the person of Alexander, nor Clark rated them very highly. In England the French Army had been somewhat oversold by some senior British officers, and also by Liddell Hart. Inevitably, after the terrible catastrophe of 1940 the British had written off the French Army as useless and reverted to their habitual if

297

mild Francophobia. (This was ungrateful, for a sacrificial defence by some French troops had helped to make the "miracle" of Dunkirk possible.) By the end of 1943 this attitude had softened a little, by virtue of French cooperation with the Eighth Army, especially the courageous stand of a French brigade at Bir Hacheim in 1942, and the performance of their ill-equipped divisions in Tunisia. The French, they felt, after all, had proved themselves sportsmen, still game for a fight after a bad beating.* The American attitude was rather different. Cultural and historic ties apart, Americans only valued success and had no time for losers. In any case, US officers as a class hardly shared the cultural interests of their Francophile countrymen: they were as insular as their British opposite numbers. Like them they tended to look down on coloured troops, or any that were not white Americans, very much as British service officers looked down on the Indians. The strongest bond between American and Frenchman was a common dislike of the "limeys" and "les Anglo-Saxes". (The French had neither forgotten nor forgiven the British attacks at Mers-el-Kebir, on their forces in Syria and the invasion of Madagascar, dictated though they may have been by the harsh necessities of war.) All this was an added incentive for the French to prove themselves, and as it turned out, their performance in Italy was to astonish Americans and British alike.

The French divisions in Italy were the surviving hard core of what in 1918 had been one of the finest armies of Europe, the softer tissues it had acquired in the inter-war years having been worn away by the harsh acid of defeat, capitulation and the occupation of the sacred soil of France. The men of the 1st Free French Division had either escaped from France, been caught by the war in North Africa, or had rallied to the flag from the most distant quarters of the French empire, including many women. The colonial units contained a high proportion of French, roughly in the proportion of one to every two indigenous soldiers, as it was the French practice to have French officers and under-officers commanding right down to platoon level, alongside

---

* There were, all the same, some British senior officers who should never have been allowed near foreign troops. One such, commanding an artillery group sent to reinforce General Monsabert's division in Tunisia, avoided the formal midday meal the French HQ staff sat down to whenever possible in operations – a very sensible custom – as he considered it effete. This was discourteous and impolitic, whatever his private feelings. When later, in Italy, two US artillery battalions were attached to his group and his staff drew up a useful English–US artillery glossary he tore it up. Foreigners, in his view, should conform to British ideas, and learn to speak English. Such is the grit in the gearbox of coalition war.

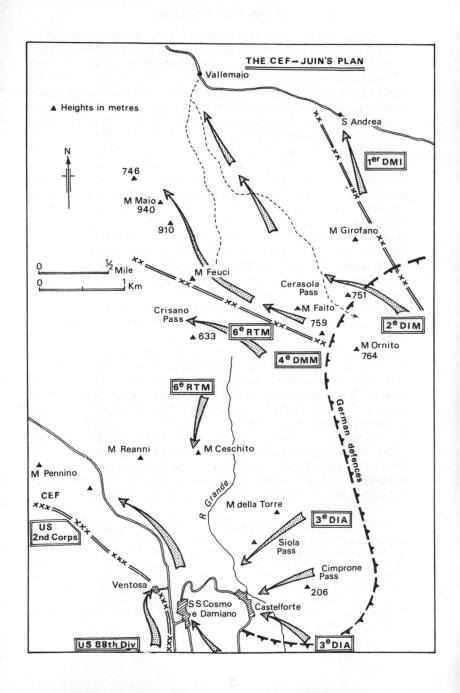

THE CEF—JUIN'S PLAN

▲ Heights in metres

Vallemaio

N

S Andrea

1er DMI

746 ▲

M Maio ▲
940

910 ▲

M Girofano ▲

0   ½ Mile
0   1 Km

M Feuci

Cerasola
Pass

▲751

2e DIM

Crisano
Pass

M Faito ▲
759

633 ▲

6e RTM

M Ornito
764 ▲

4e DMM

6e RTM

M Reanni ▲

▲ M Ceschito

M Pennino ▲

▲

M della Torre ▲

3e DIA

CEF
xxx

Siola
Pass

US
2nd Corps

xxx

▲

Cimprone
Pass

Ventosa ▲

206 ▲

S S Cosmo
e Damiano

Castelforte

German defences

US 88th Div

3e DIA

relatively few Moroccan or Algerians of equivalent rank. The CEF, therefore, in spite of its predominantly colonial composition, was essentially French; in its heart, its leadership and notably its mental processes.

In 1906 when the British Secretary of State for War, Haldane, took up his office and embarked on his period of reform, he was asked by an anxious general what kind of British Army he had in mind. "An Hegelian army" was his gnomic reply. A French general answered in such terms would not have been puzzled or surprised, although his own thought processes might, possibly, have been influenced more by the Frenchman Descartes rather than the German. General Juin would probably have responded to the accusation of being a Cartesian with some earthy barrack-room phrase, but he himself was a compelling example of the French belief in the application of pure reason to the solution of the problems of life, military or otherwise. His own "appreciations of the situation" and directives are models of logic and lucidity. It must not be thought, however, that the French system of command was based solely on arid, intellectual analysis. The French have given the word "martinet" to the universal military vocabulary, but their post-Revolutionary armies were remarkable for their individuality, dash and flexibility. They understood, as all good soldiers do, that discipline and obedience are essential, but also that they must be balanced by allowing free play to initiative, which means the freedom of subordinates to act on the spur of the moment but strictly in light of their mission. With this went a belief in the ardent spirit, the blazing courage French soldiers were expected to display on the field of battle; not suicidal, like the Japanese, but directed with intelligence. There is no exact translation for this quality in English. Montgomery, delving into his schoolboy slang, used to call it "binge". Juin expressed it perfectly in a sub-paragraph dealing with the phase of exploitation in his directive setting out for his staff his outline plan for the forthcoming operation to break through the Gustav Line: "Le rythme de la manoeuvre sera adapté aux circonstances, ce qui nécessitera de tous ardeur, compréhension et souplesse."[1]

General Juin was of relatively humble origin, the son of a police officer from the Vendée and a Corsican mother, whose family had settled in Constantine, a small town in Algeria. He was an active lad, given to long rambles in wild country in search of game; once rashly taking on a wild boar with a charge of small-shot. Encouraged by his parents, he worked hard at school, winning a scholarship to the Lycée, thus ensuring his secondary education and then, the French Army being a career open to talent, to the great military academy of Saint-

Cyr. There he passed out top of his term and so was allowed the privilege of selecting the regiment he wished to join. He chose the native regiment of his natal country, the Algerian Light Infantry or, to give it its proper title, the 1er Tirailleurs Algériens. Later he served with Moroccan troops, for whom he had the greatest admiration. The North African regiments, the Spahis, and the Moroccan, Tunisian and Algerian Tirailleurs resembled in many ways those of the British Indian Army. Their officers remained with them permanently, or for long periods, were expected to have a thorough understanding of the manners, customs and religion of their indigenous soldiers, and regarded themselves as an elite. Like the Indian Army, part of the colonial forces were almost always in action, sometimes against the very tribes from which they recruited their soldiers. Africa was an excellent school of tactics. Juin, had he ever met him, would have found much in common with the ex-Gurkha Rifleman, Francis Tuker, whose division was committed to what he later called the "idiocy" of Cassino. Like General Tuker, Juin had a profound aversion from bull-headed frontal attacks against strength – *"bille en tête"* – unless absolutely necessary, and a preference for surprise, the attack on the unexpected line and rapid manoeuvre.

Juin joined his regiment in 1911 and saw his first action in Morocco in 1912. The war took him to France with the Tirailleurs Marocains. There he was badly wounded in the right arm while leading an attack and afterwards served as brilliantly on the staff as in the field; famous for his left-handed salute, forthright manner and his perpetual cigarette. By 1940 he had been noted as an officer fit to hold the highest appointments and was in command of a French motorised division on which fell the full force of the *Blitzkrieg*. Juin kept his outnumbered force in being during a long withdrawal, from Gembloux to Lille, beating off repeated attacks and inflicting heavy losses, to surrender only when his exhausted troops finally ran out of ammunition. For this feat he was raised to the rank of Commander of the Legion of Honour. In the unhappy months that followed Juin was released from captivity and sent to organise the skeletal French forces in North Africa, ostensibly for defence against aggression from any quarter, in reality as far as Juin was concerned to prepare for the moment of liberation. He threaded his way deftly but without any loss of honour through the unhappy maze of post-war French politics, and when the Allies arrived in Algeria in the autumn of 1942 he was able to place a number of French units at the disposal of General Eisenhower, ill-equipped and with a strangely old-fashioned look, but full of enthusiasm and able to play a useful part in battle. Subsequent events brought him, in

November 1943, to Italy at the head of the CEF, with the full backing of the emergent French leader, Charles de Gaulle.

General Juin had not found much to admire in the Allied conduct of the war in Tunisia and still less in Clark's efforts between Cassino and the sea, or the *bille en tête* efforts to force the Gustav Line at the strongest defensive position in Italy: Cassino. He represented, at that moment, France, and was in no way disposed to defer politely to the views of Clark and Alexander. Now that he was in position with his full force assembled he was determined on two things: he was going to fight the battle in his own way, and that the only active army of France should play a part worthy of the French soldier. This was made abundantly clear when, on April 12, Clark sent his trusted aide, Brigadier-General D. W. Brann, his head of G3 (Operations), to brief Juin's chief of staff, General Carpentier, on his plans for the employment of the CEF. (And not his chief of staff, Gruenther, as would have been proper when dealing with a commander of Juin's status, or indeed himself as army commander.) Brann's message, in brief, was that the main thrust was to be made at Cassino, with a view to breaking through the Gustav Line to Rome. The role of the CEF was to open a route through the mountains and seize the important pass at Esperia. The US 2nd Corps would then go through, operating on the left flank of the Eighth Army, and the CEF would revert to army reserve.

Brann, accustomed to US Army practice which barred any discussion or criticism of plans emanating from higher HQs and required subordinate commanders merely to obey orders, was surprised by General Carpentier's hostile reception of his instructions. After vehemently expressed objections to the general plan which, as he understood it, was simply the repetition of an attack on an axis on which there had been already a complete failure and, moreover, was against the strongest part of the Gustav Line, Carpentier explained to him his own commander's views on a suitable mission for the CEF, as Juin had already set out in an aide-memoire for the guidance of his staff. Brann was "stunned" and "shaken" by the audacity of the proposed scheme of manoeuvre. He was then taken in to see Juin himself, who snubbed him. It was his plan, he said, in his blunt way, and he would discuss it with no one but General Clark.[2]

Juin's "appreciation of the situation", to use the British term, was very thorough, and developed his proposed operation to its logical limit. He began with a thorough study of the unpromising terrain fencing in his bridgehead. From the window of his office in his headquarters he had a magnificent view of a wall of snow-capped peaks, hiding the vast, tangled massif of the Auruncan Mountains some twelve miles square, varying in height between 3,000 and 4,500 feet, roadless, traversed by only two rough tracks barely fit for mules. The valleys were narrow and boxed in by cliffs, offering only narrow and difficult and easily blocked avenues of advance. Nevertheless, for a commander who understood warfare in mountains (which is not exactly the same as "mountain warfare", apt to be elevated into a mystery by specialists) and had a suitably equipped and trained force, as a battlefield it had some promising features. It was crossed by two good lateral roads. The first ran from Pontecorvo on the Liri river to S. Oliva, through the Esperia pass and then south through Ausonia and the Ausente valley which lay immediately behind the Gustav Line, connected to Highway No. 7, the Via Appia, and one of the classic roads to Rome. The second, twelve miles to the west, connected Highway No. 6, the Via Casilina, the other highway to Rome, to Highway No. 7 from Arce via Pico and Itri. Intelligence reports indicated that the Germans were relying on the difficulties of the ground to economise in troops for the defence of the sector. The German positions, running more or less north and south-east of M. Maio, though as strong as engineers could make them, were linear in pattern and without any depth, and apparently with no supports or reserves close behind. On the far side of the Ausente valley south of the Esperia pass, where the way was barred by the massif Ms. Revole –Fammera–Chiavica–Petrella, there was not so much as an automatic weapon or a piece of artillery, let alone a complete unit. Moreover, the boxed-in nature of the terrain was as much a hindrance as a help to the defence, because if the attackers could penetrate the first mountainous stretch behind the Gustav Line and cut the Ausonia–Ausente lateral, it would be they who had the advantage of the ground and the defenders who would find it difficult, even impossible to move reserves to the area so unexpectedly threatened.

Juin's plan in outline was to break through, capture the pass at Esperia on the run and advancing on as wide a front as possible seize control of the second lateral, Highway No. 82; but it must be understood that though that was his *objective*, possession of a piece of useful ground was not his *object*: that was the vulnerable right–rear of the German Tenth Army. He intended to lever apart the Gustav Line and so free the 2nd Corps, the CEF and the Eighth Army to form a mass of manoeuvre for the break-out and the march on Rome. This was a bold operational concept, but it is perhaps understandable that both Alexander and Clark and their respective staffs looked at it rather doubtfully. Neither man possessed the strategical insight that distinguished Juin from "*les bons chefs ordinaires*", but they could at least see that it did not detract anything from the DIADEM plan, and that it made sense to make full use of the four French divisions. As for the new role Juin recommended for the US 2nd Corps, to force a passage up the narrow strip between the sea and the mountains, it would be no more difficult than to try to fight along the narrow and winding road from the Esperia pass into the heart of the mountains. If Juin failed it could not do any harm, and if he succeeded, so much the better. The obstinate Frenchman was allowed to have his way.

Juin's plan as finally developed was as follows. The whole rested on the fact that through his foresight the CEF was an instrument well adapted for operations either on the plain or in the mountains. Its divisions were, with certain significant variations, organised and equipped on the US model. Each had nine battalions of infantry in three regiments, with a battery (or "cannon company") of light artillery included in each. The divisional troops consisted of an armoured reconnaissance unit equipped with light tanks, an artillery regiment of three groups (battalions) of 105-mm and one of 155-mm howitzers, engineers, signals and supporting services.

The order of battle was:

1ère Division de Marche d'Infanterie, (1ère DMI) Commander, Général de Division (equivalent US or British Major-General) Brosset. Formed as the 1st Free French Division in February 1943 and retitled as a normal French "marching" division in April 1944. Its infantry consisted of various independent battalions, including a "demi-brigade" of two battalions of the Foreign Legion, a North African battalion and battalions of marines grouped in three "brigades". (Not "regiments". The French are exact in their use of military terms. A regiment is a unit, of three battalions, with a single identity.) The armoured regiment had been formed by converting the 1st Regiment of "Fusilier-Marins", commanded by a naval *capitaine de frégate*. (Equivalent to a commander RN or USN.) Effective strength was 15,500 all ranks, of which 9,000 were Europeans or ethnic Frenchman.

2e Division d'Infanterie Marocaine (2e DIM) Commander, Général de Division Dody. Raised May 1943. Basically Moroccan; its infantry three regiments of Tirailleurs Marocains, the reconnaissance unit a regiment of Moroccan Spahis; the guns manned by the African Artillery Regiment. Effective strength, 14,000 all ranks.*

---

* "Tirailleurs", literally "skirmishers", in fact normal infantry. "Spahis", similarly were originally light cavalry, converted to armoured reconnaissance units.

3e Division d'Infanterie Algérienne (3e DIA) Commander, Général de Division Monsabert. Raised May 1943. Infantry, Tirailleurs Algériens and Tunisiens, 3e Régiment Spahis Algériens de Reconnaissance, artillery as above. Effective strength, 13,000 all ranks.

4e Division Marocaine de Montagne (4e DMM) Commander, Général de Brigade Sevez (equivalent US Brigadier-General, British Brigadier). Raised June 1943. Effective strength, 19,000. Unusually for a mountain division, it also had an armoured regiment, 4e Spahis Marocains. The artillery consisted of three battalions US type M116 75-mm light mountain howitzers with a useful range of 8,000 metres carried in mule pack; and its first and second echelons of transport were also pack mules. Effective strength, 19,000 all ranks.

"Corps" troops included medium and heavy artillery and the logistic services were adapted to work in mountainous country off the roads using pack animals as well as motor transport. US tank battalions were attached and anti-tank defence by a regiment of the famous Chasseurs d'Afrique equipped with M 10s. A large number of devoted French-women served in the hospital and ambulance units. When General Lucas met General Dody in January he expressed his anxiety about their employment in the forward areas, to which Dody retorted that they were as ready to die for their country as the men. Lucas wrote in his diary: "Surely France still lives!"

When the French were establishing their colonial empire in North Africa their most intractable opponents were found among the mountaineers of northern Morocco, and on the principle of converting poachers to gamekeepers the French Army formed irregular levies recruited from the hill villages to act as local internal security troops. Accustomed from early youth to fight not only the French but each other in their private vendettas, they required little drill or training. The basic unit was a "goum", based on a village or group of villages and families, led by specially selected French officers able to speak Arabic and well-versed in every nuance of clan and custom. A "goumier" was allowed to wear his own costume of *djellaba*, a striped woollen cloak, and trousers confined by *tighiwines* or woollen gaiters; the only concession to modernity being a steel helmet in action instead of the *rezza*, a small turban. The colour of undyed homespun plus the dirt collected in campaigning provided better camouflage than khaki battledress blouse and trousers. They were encouraged to fight in their own way as practised in their native mountains, as they were masters of the art of patrolling and reconnaissance, infiltration, ambuscade and minor tactics of every kind.

When the CEF was committed to operations in Italy Juin immediately saw that there was an essential role for these resourceful quasi-guerrilla troops, and asked for a large contingent to act not as "auxiliaries", their official rating, but front-line troops to work in close conjunction with the regular divisions, especially in the mountains. The units sent to Italy retained their basic irregular characteristics and their riding ponies and mule transport, but were modernised by the addition of heavy weapons including mortars, Jeeps and radios for tactical control.

A goum, equivalent to a company of infantry, had an establishment of 209 French and Moroccans, three goums plus an HQ Goum containing heavy weapons, signals and a troop of mounted scouts made a "tabor", and three tabors a "Groupement de Tabors Marocains" (GTM), commanded by a French full colonel. The 1st, 2nd and 4th GTMs joined the CEF, their total strength being 7,883 all ranks (170 French officers, 422 French under-officers and 53 French privates) under the command of an officer with great experience of these unique soldiers, Général de Brigade Guillaume. Such were Juin's resources.

As shown, the right-hand boundary of the CEF with the British Eighth Army was the north (left) bank of the Liri. The left with the US 2nd Corps ran westwards through the mountains from Castelforte, skirting the southern slopes of the peaks of Castella, Petrella and Revole to M. Calvo, after which it turned north-west. The 14th Panzer Corps held the right wing of the German line, and the garrison of the Gustav positions on the front of the CEF was approximately six and a half battalions of the 71st Infantry Division, lavishly equipped with machine guns and mortars, manning defences largely proof against anything but a direct hit with a 100-pound shell. This was the hard crust that had to be decisively broken by frontal attack if the whole daring manoeuvre was to develop.

The plan for all four divisions was to attack simultaneously by night and after a brief but intense preliminary bombardment by 400 guns. Then, from right to left, 1ère DMI would sweep forward on an axis following the right bank of the Liri; 2e DIM would strike north-west, clearing M. Maio, and make for the bend in the road between S. Giorgio and Ausonia; 4e DMM was to make a short hook into the valley of the River Grande; and 3e DIA, having broken through at Castelforte, would divide into two columns and advance on Esperia as fast as possible.

The key role was alloted to 4e DMM with all three groups of tabors under command, forming a mountain corps 27,000 strong. On the left a powerful Group commanded by General Guillaume would advance directly into the heart of the Auruncan massif, his axis skirting the inter-corps boundary and running north of the main peaks, Petrella and Revole, while another under Colonel Bondis performed a bizarre manoeuvre which no doubt caused the staff officers of Alexander's and Clark's respective headquarters when they read it to "suck their teeth", as the soldiers say. Owing to the constraints of the mountain terrain Bondis could not start clear of the columns of 3e DIA, moving up the road from Castelforte to Coreno, so the two axes had to cross over, a "*cisaillement*", the units passing through the intervals between each other; a movement usually left to horse artillery at displays of driving skill, and a solution unlikely to gain any marks in a staff college exercise. In the event it worked perfectly; a tribute to the intelligence and discipline of the troops concerned. These axes of advance were projected twenty miles, from the Gustav Line to the lateral Highway No. 82 and beyond.

The great merit of this plan, given the numerical weakness of the defence and the difficulties of moving reserves to a threatened sector, was that once the attackers had crossed the Ausente valley and cut the road through Ausonia, as each division advanced it uncovered the flanks of the enemy opposing its neighbour. In the south Juin intended that the progress of the mountain corps would assist the US 88th Division on its left, and that in its turn would allow supplies for General Guillame's mountaineers to come up by road from his flank instead of from behind up the mountain tracks. More ambitiously, his whole advance would arrive in the rear of the 14th Panzer Corps so that he could roll it up from an inner flank and open the road to Rome. Juin had no doubt that the aim of DIADEM was the liberation of the Eternal City for the simple reason that this had become the prevailing obsession of General Clark. In consequence, the subtle but real difference between Alexander's strategy and a direct drive on Rome had been filtered out of the original Fifth Army plan as described by Brann to Carpentier.

(General Juin would have been the first to have grasped its significance, but by his own account he seems to have believed firmly that it was the mission of the British Eighth Army to liberate Rome, although it was clear from the DIADEM plan that its main axis and its left boundary when projected lay north of Rome, which had always been in the Fifth Army's zone of action.) Juin had every reason to be satisfied. He had provided the commander and staff of the Fifth Army with a much better plan than their own. The French had a role worthy of them. General Keyes and his corps were now to be usefully employed in opening the Via Appia, the direct route to Rome. As for the goal, above all it was symbolic and would serve to focus the eyes of the French on a tangible object and intensify the *ardeur* with which they would throw themselves against the Gustav Line. This was to prove strong enough to survive the harrowing failures of the night of May 11, D-day for DIADEM.

20

BREAKING THE MOUNTAIN LINE

In one respect General Juin's plan was somewhat overoptimistic. It depended on the successful rupture of the Gustav Line in his sector where it was strongest – opposite the towering bulk of M. Maio, dominating the zone south of the Liri valley as M. Cairo and the heights above Cassino did the north. To reach it General Dody's 2e DIM would have to climb the sentry peaks to the south-east, Girofano, Feuci and Faito, their slopes honeycombed with fox-holes and weapon-pits. He hoped to do this between 11 p.m., his chosen H-hour, half an hour before moon-rise, and dawn. For such a task the British, by then very experienced in the bloody and difficult work of cracking open a well-organised German position, would have thought 800 guns barely adequate. Juin could only dispose of half that number, not counting the light howitzers in the infantry cannon companies, and this had to support the simultaneous attacks of all four of his divisions.

Nor was this the only difficulty facing his artillery commanders. There are certain technical problems to be solved when engaging targets many hundreds of feet above batteries deployed in the plain on steep reverse slopes and, as in parts of Dody's line, where the opposing sides are almost within grenade-throwing range of each other, so that the forward enemy posts can be engaged without endangering one's own troops. The solution of very careful registration by fire of all the difficult targets was not acceptable because it gave away the point and timing of the attack. (As it was discovered later, the German artillery, already alerted by some preliminary adjustment, had moved to fresh positions, and so was able to fire uninterruptedly on the night of the first French attack.) Juin's artillery commanders hoped to overcome these difficulties, at least in part, by preceding the assault with a long bombardment to soften up the defences, but this ran into objections from the British. The Eighth Army H-hour was half an hour later, at moon-rise, as this was essential for the engineers who had to put down the bridges for the assault crossing of the Garigliano, and in any case it was British policy to avoid any preliminary bombardment if possible, and they feared that the artillery preparation by the CEF would only serve to alert the German front from end to end. A compromise was reached by which Juin attacked at 11 p.m., but his guns only opened fire at that moment.

Within these technical and tactical constraints the French made the best plan they could. Covering fire for the attack on the enemy positions, counter-battery fire and harassing fire on tracks and areas designed to prevent the movement of reserves were fired on a timed programme. To deal with the unexpected, or positions already struck and coming to life, lists of prearranged targets and reference points were issued to the forward observers and attacking units so that fire could be called down by transmitting a simple code-word or number. Artillery liaison officers were exchanged with neighbouring formations, the British to the north and the Americans to the south so that mutual support could be quickly arranged. In spite of all these admirable arrangements, however, the artillery plan was a failure. Many targets were not hit at all, and others not hard enough to neutralise them. The moment Dody's assault troops left their trenches they came under an accurate and heavy fire from every German weapon, including flame-throwers, a horrid surprise.

Everything went badly across the whole front, and nowhere worse than in the centre. Two regiments of Moroccan infantry led the initial assault of the 2e DIM who, after the most sacrificial efforts, succeeded in penetrating the enemy defences, but were unable to reach their first objectives or even maintain their footholds. On the left only five men, the survivors of one whole battalion, succeeded in reaching their objective and stayed on it until they were ordered to withdraw. Another battalion lost 400 men, including many officers, until the regimental commander called off the attack. After four hours of bitter close-quarter fighting nothing had been gained and General Dody ordered the whole offensive to be abandoned and the troops back to their start line until he could reassess the situation by daylight.

Elsewhere there was little or no progress. The battalions of Marines from the 1ère DMI sent up into the mountains to cover Dody's right flank were halted by heavy fire causing many casualties and an armoured battle-group sent to work along the road leading to the left bank of the Liri made some progress in the elbow of the Garigliano until checked by anti-tank guns and mines. On Dody's left General Sevez's mountain troops from 4e DMM were halted by intense artillery fire. On the extreme left an armoured battle-group leading the advance of 3e DIA spent the morning of the 12th negotiating an immense minefield east of Castelforte and doing no more than cautiously examining its defences at close range. All in all the first-light situation reports contained nothing encouraging.

Nevertheless, grim as things looked on his front, at 7.30 a.m. Dody gave orders for the attack by 2e DIM to be renewed, but he was forestalled, very fortunately, although he possibly did not view it in that light at that awful moment. It is a cliché of infantry fighting that one way of winning a fight offensively is to turn it into a defensive action by seizing a piece of ground and forcing the defender to counter-attack it and so wear him down. It was also, as we saw at Salerno, German doctrine to defend by counter-attack, not merely to recover ground, but to hit the attacker when he has been badly shaken by defensive fire, or as he relaxes for a brief moment on the objective he has seized with so much anguish. As the commanders of the Moroccan regiments strove to reorganise and issue fresh orders a sharp artillery fire descended on them, and a counter-attack force scraped together from three separate units advanced on their assembly areas. The Moroccans, still licking their wounds, threw it back with severe loss, but when they in their turn moved up the slopes again, in mid-afternoon, the intensity of the artillery fire caused Dody to halt it. Clearly a new initiative was required. Juin came up to see the situation for himself, and after a thorough examination decided to suspend operations until the 13th. His new orders went out that night.

In the meantime General Monsabert was considering an initiative of his own. So far only part of his division was engaged, and that only in a position of readiness in front of Castelforte. His artillery was deployed ready for action, but the rest of his 3e DIA was still east of the Garigliano. He was faced with the defences of Castelforte, and these were so perfect an example of the German field fortifications that the Allies encountered everywhere in Italy that it is worth describing them in detail.

The road chosen as Monsabert's axis of advance leading from the Garigliano to Coreno, Ausonia and to the Esperia pass rose in three steps. On the first, 500 feet above the plain, stood Castelforte itself, well-named. On the next was the large village of S. Cosmo e Damiano, almost a suburb of the town, and 600 feet above that the equally aptly named Ventosa, perched on its own crag. All three were built in the style of the medieval hill-towns of Italy, the houses closely packed together and, except for where the main road ran through them, with the narrowest of streets. During the heavy fighting of the winter incessant bombardment by the British 10th Corps had reduced the buildings to ruins – treatment that only serves to make the task of the defenders easier – and the population had fled, bar a few who still crouched in their wrecked homes. Behind Castelforte a huge cirque of mountains provided a dramatic backdrop and buttress for the defence, M. Cianella on the left and M. Siola on the right. This natural rampart had been improved by the skill of the German engineers and the strong arms of German soldiers, who had learnt by bitter experience in Russia and now in Europe that if they wished to survive the hellish bombardments of the enemy artillery they had to burrow like moles. (The British and US soldiers, soft, lazy and urban as many of them were, never troubled to go to such lengths, or depths, though more use of their picks and shovels could have saved many lives.)

The German garrison amounted to about two battalions of infantry with a battalion of artillery in direct support, spread thin on the ground, some in the buildings and some on the key heights round about. The weapon-emplacements of those inside the town were carefully concealed in the rubble, supported by tanks and SP guns in the streets, ready to run out on to their firing platforms. Others occupied machine-gun posts hewn or blasted into the rocky outcrops on the commanding hills. The ravines behind the town bristled with mortar batteries, their crews when not in action sheltering in caves, and the field-guns, further back on the reverse slopes, were in deep gun-pits roofed over with layers of logs and stones so as to be proof against anything less than a 100-pound shell unless it entered through the narrow embrasure. The plain below Castelforte and the immediate approaches to the town – the "keep" – were sown with anti-tank mines, and belts of booby-traps and anti-personnel mines were interwoven with the defences in depth. (The German engineers were fiendishly inventive. It was unsafe to open a door or pick up a souvenir in any freshly captured building, and there were traps in innocent-looking slit trenches where an attacker might in his turn seek cover from enemy fire. "Schu-mines" the size of a cigar box could blow off a man's foot, and the equally horrible jumping-mine, if kicked or touched leapt into the air to explode and throw out a fan of steel shot waist-high with sufficient force to disembowel or castrate the victim.)

True to form, the French plan rejected the option of a frontal attack. Instead it was proposed to pick out the Castelforte defences by two converging attacks made from above and behind them. The boundary with the US 88th Division of the 2nd Corps was adjusted so that it could come in from the left, clear M. Cianella and take Ventosa in reverse, while on the right the 4e RTM from Sevez's mountain division (4e DMM) reinforced by one of Monsabert's Tunisia battalions (I/4e

RTT) would break through the Gustav Line in front of Furlito, work down the Rivo Grande and secure M. Siola. When this manoeuvre had been completed, and only then, an armoured battle-group based on the 4e RTT and commanded by its CO, Colonel Guillebaud, would tackle the Castelforte defences frontally. (The French, like the Germans, were adept at forming task forces or battle-groups very smoothly and rapidly from units required for a specific mission. They were termed *"groupements"*, and known by the name of their commanders.) Groupement Guillebaud consisted of the 4e RTT, less the battalion attached to the Moroccans, the 4th Moroccan Spahis (4e RSM), the 7th Chasseurs d'Afrique (7e RCA, equipped with US SP M10 3-inch anti-tank guns), an attached battalion of US medium tanks with Shermans and a company of the divisional engineer regiment, with the whole of 3e DIA's artillery in support. Guillebaud's mission was to send one of his infantry battalions to open a small pass on his left, to assist the thrust by the Moroccans, mop up in Castelforte and when the pincer attack had disrupted the defenders go through to act as spearhead for the division during the advance to Esperia.

Things went at first no better around Castelforte than anywhere else. The Moroccans on the right were stuck in the Grande valley, the I/4e RTT was held up in front of M. Siola and the company sent to occupy the Colle di Cemorone also failed. By the afternoon of the 12th the pre-conditions for launching Groupement Guillebaud had therefore not been reached, when the good news of the fall of Ventosa to the Americans arrived. General Monsabert felt that he could not allow his division, fresh and virtually intact, to stand idle at such a moment. He acted, in accordance with his commanding general's demand, with both "understanding" and "flexibility". He ordered Guillebaud to attack as soon as he could, and the rest of his division to be ready to move across the river at first light on the 13th.

Guillebaud's battle-group had been already formed into two task forces, an "East Column" and a "West Column" whose commanders had been examining the approaches to Castelforte all day, and they jumped off without delay at 4 p.m. The West Column lost three tanks and two SPs on mines outside S. Cosmo e Damiano, but the rest of the armour formed a fire-base and under its point-blank fire two companies of infantry disappeared into the ruins and began to ferret out the defenders. A tank of the East Column, whose commander was perhaps showing an extreme example of French *ardeur*, jammed itself in one of the entrances of Castelforte, and there too the infantry managed to infiltrate and begin half a dozen little duels with the defence. Tunisians were lowest in the North African pecking order. They, the saying went,

"were women, the Algerians men and the Moroccans heroes" –
coined, no doubt, by a Moroccan. At Castelforte the Tunisians showed
what skilled and daring infantry could do. By 7 p.m. Guillebaud's line
ran from Ventosa, which he had taken over from the Americans,
through the southern parts of S. Cosmo e Damiano and Castelforte
and out on to the high ground on his right, S. Sebastiano and M. della
Torre, and he had taken eighty-two prisoners.

During the evening Juin had cleared his mind and decided on his
next moves. He approved Monsabert's initiative and ordered him to
wait for no one and open up the road through the Castelforte defences
and press on to Coreno. To assist him Sevez was to make a fresh
attempt to clear his right by converging attacks from the north and east
to eliminate the Gustav positions in the Grande valley. At the same time
General Brosset was to get his armour moving again, for the British
were over the river in strength south of Cassino town and it was
important that he masked the enemy on the south bank of the Liri. At
the same time his left wing, the brigade of Marines, was to keep in
touch and in step with Dody's right. All now rested with Dody
regrouping for if he could not quickly clear the peaks in front of him
and reach Vallemaio Juin's whole plan would founder. There was no
time to reorganise or try a fresh line. Therefore, although to resume the
attack on the front of 2e DIM was to batter against strength, just what
Juin disliked most and where one attack had already failed, he ordered
Dody to try again, but with an important difference. This time there
would be a thorough preliminary bombardment and where necessary
the infantry would withdraw so as not to hamper the artillery when
engaging the forward enemy positions. For this Dody was allotted no
fewer than eighteen *groupes*, or battalions, of artillery; 176 pieces of
105-mm and 102 of 155-mm. Dody decided to take two bites at the
cherry this time. He would begin with a limited attack made at 4.0 a.m.
after a bombardment lasting three-quarters of an hour, mop up,
reorganise and mount a fresh attack to complete his breakthrough at
8.0 p.m.

Once again the German commander played into Dody's hands. His
meagre allotment of artillery had been reinforced and every German
gun opened up a violent counter-preparation, followed by a determined counter-attack. This was repelled by defensive fire from the
French artillery, and the opening attack delayed for over an hour. Later
another was launched by a reinforcing battalion of panzer grenadiers
but it too withered under the French fire, the battalion commander was
captured and the remnants drifted off to the rear in disorder, pounded
by mortar fire. There were now only a few scattered and discouraged

parties to resist the Moroccans, whose attack gathered momentum. By mid-morning Faito and Feuci were in French hands. On the right the fighting went on until 2.0 p.m. when M. Girofano fell, and an hour later the four kilometres from Dody's forward positions to M. Maio had been covered. If any of the embattled troops on the DIADEM front had eyes for anything but the enemy immediately in front of them they might have seen, at 3.0 p.m. on May 13, an enormous *Tricolore* being hoisted on the summit of M. Maio, visible from the Tyrrhenian Sea to the Monastery of Montecassino.

The whole CEF was by then on the move. Brosset's tanks were well on the way to S. Apollinare. Sevez's regiments had broken a gap two and a half miles wide in the Gustav Line between M. Feuci and M. Siola and he was preparing his lunge into the Aurunci massif. Guillebaud, leaving some infantry behind to mop up in Castelforte, had broken through its defences and was well on his way up the road, the rest of Monsabert's division filing over the Garigliano bridges and preparing to follow up. The French had now ruptured the Gustav Line in four places, its defenders were either recoiling in disorder – having lost between 30 and 40 per cent of their fighting strength and leaving 900 prisoners in French hands. It had not been a cheap victory. The French had lost 2,150 killed and wounded, the Moroccan divisions suffering particularly heavily and Guillebaud's battle-group 335, balanced by 377 prisoners of war it had captured, of whom 11 were officers.

The situation as seen from Kesselring's headquarters was by now extremely alarming, even for a commander of such strong nerves and optimistic disposition. He had been disagreeably surprised by the whole unfolding of the Allied offensive. Like a boxer, he had been watching his opponents right and left, the Liri and Anzio fronts, only to be butted suddenly in the face. The centre of the Tenth Army front had collapsed, the one sector he believed was impregnable. Kesselring could see what Clark obsessed with his private goals could not, that it was the combination of the Allied thrusts – their "articulation", to borrow the useful French term – that posed the threat. He had three panzer divisions in reserve, but was reluctant to commit them until he could judge the progress of the various Allied formations, including the as yet unleashed attack from the Anzio bridgehead. It should be possible to hold the British in the Liri valley where the defences were immensely strong and the front narrow, but the defence was like a cork in a bottle. If he allowed it to be loosened it might blow out, with fatal results for his whole defensive plan. If he had no reserves with which to buttress the Fourteenth Army his worst case might occur, the Tenth

Army being encircled by a thrust from the Anzio bridgehead. He was reluctant at this early stage to commit even part of his precious general reserve and so play into his opponent's hand, but the Gustav Line was breached and he had no other course open but to reinforce the 71st Division and man the forward defences of the Hitler Line. Accordingly on the 13th he ordered the 90th Panzer Grenadier Division to move from its position in observation near the mouth of the Tiber, and by the morning of the 14th its 200th Panzer Grenadier Regiment had covered seventy-five miles by night, to avoid the attention of the Allied air forces, and was taking up positions west of Esperia. At the same time von Vietinghoff began the parsimonious but effective method of creating a reserve at which the Germans excelled. He ordered his corps commanders to thin out where they could, withdrawing a company here or a platoon there. Artillery, engineers and reconnaissance troops were to be used as infantry, including those instruments of last resort, the ZBV* companies scraped up from any spare man-power in the rear areas, and formed into battle-groups. This sort of hotch-potch could only work in the German Army, where every man was indoctrinated to fight without hesitation in company with others and under the nearest officer or NCO, whether he knew them or not.

Allied Intelligence was, of course, well aware of the existence of the Hitler "switch line", which ran near Piedimonte, four miles west of Cassino on the north side of the Liri valley, to Pontecorvo, thence westwards to curve slightly south through Fondi until it reached the coast at Terracina. (The French referred to a fortified line, or line of fortified posts between Esperia and Highway No. 82 as the "Hitler Line", but this is easily explained. These German "lines" were in great depth [in German not "lines" but *Stellungen*, or positions] and in this sense the fortifications already prepared on the Esperia front could be regarded as the outposts of the Hitler Line proper.) During the battle the intelligence staff of the CEF gathered from German prisoners captured in the M. Maio sector that their units had been ordered to hold the ground to the bitter end – undoubtedly the reason for their officers' persistence in their suicidal counter-attacks, but those captured by Guillebaud further south spoke of an "Orange Tree Line" on which they hoped to fall back, running south-west from Coreno across the Ausente valley. French Intelligence also became aware of a "Dora Line" extending from the right bank of the Liri and barring the approaches to Esperia, after which it followed the heights west of the road as far as Ausonia. All the prisoners confirmed the opinion of

* *Zur Besonderen Verwendung*, troops for special employment or emergencies.

the forward French troops that German resistance had collapsed and the remnants of the Gustav Line garrison were making their way back across the mountains in small parties. They had left behind, as well as their dead, 1,200 prisoners of whom some 20 were officers including 6 battalion commanders, and all their guns except two. At the same time French Intelligence obtained clues pointing to the arrival of the 200th Panzer Grenadiers. Now was the moment for the CEF, exhausted as it was, to push on with all possible speed before the Hitler Line could be manned.

21

JUIN TRIUMPHANT

The CEF began its exploitation on May 14/15 and by the 21st its leading units stood on the heights commanding the Pico–Itri lateral. On the 23rd the Hitler Line was overrun. Juin's operation was one of the most remarkable feats of a war more remarkable for bloody attrition than skill, and deserves to be better known; instead of being a briefly noted incident of the secondary Italian campaign, or ignored altogether. It was orchestrated with extraordinary skill. The thrust lines of divisions split into two or three as the ground or the situation demanded, to reconverge and divide again, and battle-groups were formed, dissolved and reconstituted in a bewildering manner, but if they are patiently unravelled a pattern becomes visible as Juin and his skilled divisional commanders maintain the rhythm of their advance. This great success was not cheaply won. There were ten days of hard fighting, marked by many a fierce little battle and from time to time a dramatic coup. The German soldier might give way, but he never gave in without a bitter struggle. A whole volume could be devoted to the subject of the French in the mountains, but all that can be done here is to convey some notion of the flavour and style of their operations. Inseparable from these was the contribution of Major-General Geoffrey Keyes' US 2nd Corps, for just as the operation of the Allied armies was "articulated" – parts of a well-designed machine – so were the two corps of Mark Clark's army.

General Keyes, as we have seen, so far had not had a particularly happy time in Italy, and once more he was faced with a difficult task. Operationally it was extremely unpromising. He had to bash his way up a narrow corridor with the sea on one side and the mountains on the other, rising sharply from the coastal strip along which ran the Via Appia, over terrain ideally suited for a long spoiling German defence. The only option was to move up to the shoulders of the hills and unblock the road by a series of turning movements. The staff at corps

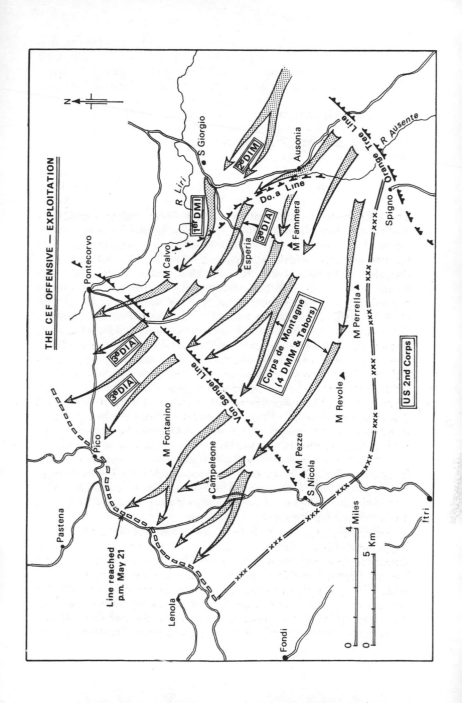

THE CEF OFFENSIVE — EXPLOITATION

and in the divisions worked hard at the problem. Models of the ground were constructed so that the attacking regiments could study their plans in detail, all the available intelligence was collated, and patrols were sent out to fix the enemy posts and familiarise the troops with the front.

Unfortunately General Keyes' two divisions, the 85th and the 88th, had neither the experience nor the training to carry out a sophisticated scheme of manoeuvre. American mass production systems of training, the use of standardised tactical procedures and rigid direction from above, though essential for the creation of a huge citizen army, did nothing to inculcate the initiative and cunning required when fighting in mountainous terrain; a lonely business, demanding independent action by companies and platoons – even squads. The art of moving by night, patrolling, stalking enemy posts and infiltration can only be acquired by constant practice. Physical fitness is equally essential. To carry all the gear and supplies required by an infantryman in action – radios, ammunition, water, machine guns, mortars – comes as an unpleasant shock to soldiers trained on flat ground and accustomed to moving all their heavy equipment in Jeeps or trucks. The US official historian records that patrols sent out by 2nd Corps units to pinpoint the enemy forward localities duly did so, but produced little information which the intelligence staff could use to identify enemy formations.[1] This is a symptom of inadequate mental preparation as distinct from skill at arms, resulting in a reluctance natural enough in conscript soldiers of urban origin to engage the enemy closely and secure a prisoner, or at least a body. (The British made a fetish of patrolling, a legacy of the trench warfare of the First World War, when the policy was to "dominate" no-man's-land, vigorously pursued by, e.g., General Hawkesworth of the British 46th Division. An officer from that formation, now a distinguished military historian, when on patrol one dark night near Cassino was puzzled to see what appeared to be a fiery glow-worm approaching him. When it was closer it proved to be a large US infantry patrol off-course, in file at close intervals, every man smoking a cigarette.)[2] Such shortcomings were not confined to the US Army, but can occur in all hastily trained armies of citizen soldiers regardless of nationality.

Bearing all this in mind it is remarkable how well Keyes' men did once they had found their feet, but during the opening days of DIADEM it illustrated this stark process. Units lost their way in the dark, ran into opposition they should have discovered existed long before D-day, men threw away their combat packs[3] (just as the idle 46th Division and the green US 36th Division had discarded vital extra loads such as reserve ammunition and radios at Salerno), or they went to ground or fell back on meeting strong opposition. One company including its commander fell into a state of collective panic and refused all orders to advance, and only recovered when the battalion S3 (Operations Officer) came forward and led a few men forward by his personal example. He was an example of those natural leaders who emerge when the chips are down and, often unexpectedly, assert themselves. One such was Sergeant Shea of the 350th Infantry who went forward alone and killed or captured the crews of three machine guns who were holding up the advance (to be awarded the Congressional Medal of Honour, the highest US decoration for courage in the field) and was promoted lieutenant. Lieutenant-Colonel R. E. Kendall, commanding a battalion of the 351st Infantry, got his shaken men on the move by walking about bolt upright under a heavy fire prodding them with his cane and genially inviting them to advance: "Come on, you bastards, you'll never get to Rome this way!" Later when held up by a strongpoint he fell mortally wounded after leading an attack on it, "firing every weapon he could lay his hands on" and personally grenading a machine-gun pit and killing its occupants. A candid history of any regiment in any army would reveal similar stories of young troops entering combat for the first time.[4]

In spite of these gallant efforts, however, Keyes shared the mortification of every other commander, bar one (Russell of 8th Indian Infantry Division), in that his initial attack was almost everywhere a complete failure. Only on Cianella had the right of the 88th Division, as related, completed its mission of clearing Cianella and capturing Ventosa against light opposition and with very few casualties. When Keyes renewed his attack on the 12th his troops again failed to make any real progress. The fact that his opponent, Generalmajor Bernhard Steinmetz, commanding the 94th Infantry Division, was a worried man, having lost men he could ill spare in the combats of the past two days and more to the constant, intense fire of the US Artillery, was not at that moment known to him, and would not have been of any great encouragement if it had. American generals had to work in a bleaker command environment than their British or French counterparts. They were given the mission and the means to accomplish it, and they were expected to succeed. Keyes knew that Clark was breathing down his neck, so he had to breathe down the neck of his two divisional commanders. He sent for them on the 13th, convinced, accurately, that his opponent was rapidly reaching the end of his resources, and ordered them both to continue the attack that afternoon, a move endorsed and amplified by Clark, who told Keyes that the attack was to be sustained all through the night into the next day, with the village of Spigno as objective, a suitable jump-off point for the parallel attack he intended the 2nd Corps to launch through the mountains in step with Juin's "Corps de Montagne", shortly to get under way as soon as the French had mopped up in the Ausente valley.

The result was more brutal losses, and little progress. The S3 of one of the battalions of the 351st Infantry reported to its regimental commander: "Two years of training have gone up in smoke . . . my men . . . about half of them – almost all my leaders."[5] This did not perturb the American commanders, at least not at that stage in the war. Keyes, unusually, had attached to his corps a large force of replacements, what the British termed "first reinforcements", trained and assigned to regiments, instead of having them fed up the lines of communication on a demand basis. Casualties did not move or deter him, any more than they did any other American general. To put it crudely, their philosophy was that to make omelettes it was necessary to break eggs, and in any case to attack *à outrance* all the time in the long run was cheaper and more humane than pussyfooting around looking for a soft option. As far as they could applaud any limey general they felt that Picton's cry of "Go on you dogs, do you expect to live for ever?" revealed that he had grasped the root of the matter. Of course soldiers did not want to be killed, and naturally officers like the S3 of the 3rd/351st Infantry mourned when the rookies they had so carefully turned into trained soldiers were cut down, but soldiers were expendable and had to be driven. It is important to emphasise this, for it is the reason why the Americans despised the paternalism permeating the British "regimental system", and why Mark Clark dismissed Richard McCreery contemptuously as a "feather duster", for not pushing his subordinates hard enough.

Clark certainly felt by the 14th that his determination had paid a dividend when the 2nd Corps reported after resuming its attacks that the German defenders of their first objectives had slipped away. What in fact had happened was that the French had overrun the right of the 71st Division, uncovering the left of the 94th, so Steinmetz was only too relieved when he received orders to withdraw. His units disengaged with their customary skill and fell back to their next position. Urged on by Keyes, the Americans now began to roll, or to "go", as the British infantry used to say.

The French were "going" already, and with a brief pause to regroup, which never seemed to take them any time, and to mop up in the newly opened Ausente valley, Juin's next phase began to unfold. Somewhat simplified, it was for the DMI to secure S. Giorgio a Liri and the higher ground of its neighbourhood south of the river; an area doubly important because its possession offered a protective flank to the operations against Esperia and the Dora Line beyond, which also provided observation over the Eighth Army's axis in the Liri valley. (Dora was the name given by the Germans to the stretch of the Hitler–Senger Line extending southwards from S. Oliva.) Beyond S. Giorgio the right bank of the Liri became low and marshy, so General Brosset dissolved his armoured battle-groups and reverted to his normal brigade organisation so as to give his infantry free play, and forced his way through the mountains past the Dora Line, much vexed by fire from north of the Liri, as the Canadians were now lagging nearly four miles behind him having been held up by the Formio d'Aquino stream. Dody went up through the mountains, positioned his division on the high ground commanding the junction of the roads leading to S. Giorgio, Ausonia and Esperia and deployed his artillery so as to support Monsabert coming up on his left. Then, pinched out by Brosset on one side and Monsabert on the other, the 2e DIM went into reserve and a well-deserved rest. In five days it had lost 1,120 killed, wounded and missing, but captured 20 officers, 500 under-officers and NCOs and 2,300 rank and file, a mass of equipment and 12 guns. Its supporting artillery had fired 68,000 rounds.

Monsabert was now "carrying the ball" for the CEF, for spectacular as the success of the newly forming Corps de Montagne was to be, the exploitation of Juin's success depended on forcing the Esperia bottle-neck with the utmost rapidity. Monsabert was to have the hardest battle, while Sevez had to grapple with the most difficult manoeuvre. His 4e DMM had suffered almost as severely as the 2e DIM, and he decided that he had to regroup so as to make the best and maximum use of his goums. Accordingly he formed three battle-groups:

Groupement Guillaume, under Général de Brigade Guillaume, overall Goum commander, with RTM (less a battalion), and 4e GTM (groups of tabors) and a battalion of the divisional artillery; two regular battalions, and six tabors or eighteen goums, plus engineers.
Groupement Bondis, Colonel Bondis, with under command a battalion of the 1er and a battalion of the 2e RTM, and the 3e GTM, a battalion of the divisional artillery, engineers.
Groupement Louchet, Colonel Louchet, the 2e RTM (less the battalion with Bondis) and a heavy regiment from the corps artillery: to serve as reserve.

General Monsabert, in true cavalry style, wasted no time after the fall of Castelforte. He had been freed from the responsibility of mopping up the remnants of the 71st Division behind, this having been handed over to the reserve group of 4e DMM. By the 15th Ausonia was in his hands, and he decided to turn the southern end of the Dora position. A steep winding road led from just south of Ausonia up to the mountain village of Selvacava, and one of his armoured battle-groups pushed boldly up it, forced the Dora Line and captured it. From there it sent on a battalion of Algerian Tirailleurs to seize La Basta, a height 1,000 yards north overlooking Dora from the rear. At the same time, Groupement Bondis (which had successfully performed the famous "scissors movement" and crossed the 3e DIA's column of route into the mountains) escaladed the southern slopes of M. Fammera and occupied its 3,800-foot summit. So far, so good. However, another armoured group pushing north along the road ran into a hot fire from assault and anti-tank guns a mile and a half out of Ausonia. This was a battalion of the 200th Panzer Grenadier Regiment, ordered to establish a strong front barring the way to Esperia. It was learnt later from prisoners that they had been told they had been ordered to hold their positions at all costs, for the outcome of the battle for the Hitler Line depended on it. That evening HQ CEF issued orders to Monsabert to accelerate his efforts to seize the Esperia defile and push on to M. Oro, and to Brosset to cover Monsabert's right flank by vigorous offensive action to penetrate the Dora Line and capture M. Calvo. Similarly, the Bondis battle-group was to support Monsabert's left by continuing its successful operation westwards from M. Fammera.

Monsabert regrouped again that night. Colonel Chapuis with two battalions and a battalion of artillery was to keep closely in touch with Groupement Bondis and turn the Esperia position from the south. The rest of his division was to force its way through to Esperia along the road, with Colonel Linares with four battalions of infantry supported by two battalions of heavy mortars and two battalions of artillery working his way along the crests on the left of the road, while Lieutenant-Colonel Lambilly with an all-armoured force of tanks and anti-tank guns (the Spahis, the American medium-tank battalion and the Chasseurs d'Afrique) tried the approach along the road. Groupement Lambilly was stopped dead two miles outside Esperia by a number of cunningly sited anti-tank guns, while Groupement Linares' infantry made assault after assault against a web of strongpoints in the hills. As this promised to take all day a battalion was left to continue the fight and mop up while the rest slipped by and moved on towards the objective but met further strong opposition. Monsabert decided that he had now to mount a formal attack, which duly took off. One more great heave, and Groupement Linares arrived in Esperia to find it deserted and a scene of devastation, bodies everywhere, victims of the artillery bombardment, masses of abandoned equipment, and some fifty shocked German soldiers who readily surrendered, the remnants of the 2nd/104th Ersatz Panzer Grenadier Regiment, which was thus annihilated. Groupement Lambilly pushed on west of Esperia to run once more into the stiffest opposition, this time from elements of Kesselring's general reserve rushed in to bottle up the apparently irresistible flood of French troops into the Aurunci, but with no better success. The whole CEF was now on the move, in spite of fatigue and severe casualties, so much so that the 1ère DMI was now about five miles ahead of the Canadians, and much vexed by fire from the left bank of the Liri – see p. 319. Success generates its own momentum, and the sole result of committing these good German units piecemeal was that they were destroyed in detail. "Detail" is perhaps the key word in describing these little-known operations, whether in the sense of attention to detail, victory in detail, or that the many small but fierce combats that were a mosaic of the whole were in the greater context of DIADEM mere details. They provide perfect models of what are sometimes dismissed as "minor tactics", minor perhaps by definition, but on which the eye-catching structures of "grand tactics" or the "operational art" and "strategy" rest.

Meanwhile, the goumiers with Corps de Montagne demonstrated their peculiar skills. Two examples are enough. General Guillaume's columns, marching and fighting, covered the nine-odd horizontal map miles to M. Revole in forty-eight hours to find it unoccupied, so Guillaume, whose men were exhausted by sheer physical effort and lack of any refreshment except what was in their water-bottles and haversacks, halted, took up defensive positions and waited for his mule trains to catch up. (It will be obvious to anyone who has experience of climbing or hill-walking that distances measured off a map mean nothing in mountains when horizontal progress of two or three miles may require an ascent and descent of 1,000 feet.) On the 17th the look-outs detected an approaching enemy column, marching in column of route without so much as a point or a vanguard. It was the 400th Reconnaissance Battalion and a battalion of the 104th Panzer Grenadier Regiment, on their way to extend the emergency stop line to the south by putting M. Revole in a state of defence. Guillaume himself arranged their reception. The main defensive positions were carefully camouflaged and there was enough cover in front of them for the goumiers to make themselves perfectly invisible in ambush positions on the flanks of their approach. Unsuspecting, and confident that the French could not reach a point so deep in the mountains for three or four days, the hapless Germans actually marched up to and inside the French main positions before they were cut down by close-range fire. Then, as they recoiled or tried to deploy, the goumiers in ambush opened up and massacred them. The commander of the force, a colonel, and a few of his men were captured and the rest annihilated. Guillaume's columns, refreshed by a supply drop from the air, went on to seize their final objective, M. Pezze, overlooking S. Nicola and Highway No. 82. There they were subjected to a more formal counter-attack by another battalion of the 104th and a detachment of German mountain troops, beaten off after some fighting at close quarters assisted by the fire of the French mountain batteries. The attackers left ninety dead on the battlefield and lost thirty-six men, prisoners of war.[6]

This action was supported by a brilliant little patrol made by Second-Lieutenant de Kerautem and two sections of No. 4 Goum, sent to establish an artillery observation post inside the enemy lines. De Kerautem succeeded in crossing the main road without being spotted by the force preparing to assault M. Pezze. At dawn he arrived on his objective, M. Vele, 1,000 yards to the west of the road, having silently eliminated a defence post. His little patrol was now behind the German front line. All that day his artillery observer directed a telling fire on to the rear of the enemy attacking the French on M. Pezze, throwing it into disarray. During the day the enemy discovered the intruders, and parties of German soldiers scrambled up the hill to eliminate them but were successfully held off. By nightfall, however, the goumiers were beset from all sides, and as his artillery observer could no longer see to shoot de Kerautem decided to slip through the German cordon and rejoin his tabor. This he did, only to stumble on what turned out to be the command post of the battalion directing the operation against him. His goumiers took this out in their own inimitable manner, and de Kerautem reported to his tabor bringing with him the command-ing officer, three of his staff and fourteen soldiers as prisoners of war.

By the 23rd the CEF having crossed Highway No. 82 was able to brush away the largely unmanned section of the Hitler Line (or the Senger extension), and possession of the lateral prevented any further attempts to move troops against the 2nd Corps, unless they came head-on down the Via Appia. Those that did were rudely disposed of by the 85th Division; both it and the 88th had now found their form in spite of their initial repulse and severe casualties, and the whole of the Fifth Army was free to advance. None of the Allied corps had stinted their efforts, but the organiser of victory was Juin and the laurels belonged to the French Army. The next and urgent question was what use was to be made of it by Clark, and his chief, Alexander.

THE GLITTERING PRIZE

Who shall polish this plated vessel,
This treasured cup? The company is elsewhere . . .
Terrible slaughter has carried into darkness
Many hundreds of mankind.

Beowulf
(Michael Alexander's verse translation)

In the third week in May the hopes and fears of the high commanders on both sides focused on the southern front. The crisis of DIADEM had arrived. Von Mackensen was aware of the build-up in the Anzio beach-head and awaited the American offensive with increasing pessimism as he saw the Army Group "C" reserves being sucked into the battle on the Tenth Army front only to be destroyed piecemeal. Von Vietinghoff watched his 51st Corps still holding on east of the Melfa but being ground to powder in the process, while the 14th Corps, though reinforced, seemed unable to check the momentum of the French and the Americans. Kesselring was too clever a soldier not to perceive the terrible predicament in which he would find himself if he did not order a timely withdrawal but, torn between sense and the irrational orders from the Fuehrer and the remote OKW, he delayed, maintaining the expression of ineffable optimism which so infuriated his army commanders. Von Senger, who had returned from his unwanted and untimely leave in Germany on May 17 to find his whole corps in disarray, perceived at once the danger to it posed by an attack out of the beach-head. Alexander was poised to unleash the 6th Corps from the beach-head as soon as Burns was ready to launch CHESTERFIELD which, as we know, was on May 23. General Clark was also agonising over a question of timing. So far, whatever he may have hinted to Truscott, he had not outwardly defied Alexander's clear wishes and instructions that Truscott's offensive would be in.accordance with plan BUFFALO; objective Valmontone. Privately he had other ideas. He was prepared to allow BUFFALO to go ahead as an opening move, not so much with the intention of deceiving the enemy but the Commander-in-Chief of the Allied Armies in Italy.

Finally there was the protagonist in the concluding act of the drama of DIADEM, Major-General Lucian K. Truscott, Jr. He was faced with two tasks, both essential to his mission. The first was the purely operational one. The Fourteenth Army position though not fortified like the Gustav and Hitler Lines was very naturally strong, especially on the western flank, and during the lull since the German counter-offensive had been thoroughly entrenched, minefields laid in depth, the front protected with wire and the ruins of the small town of Cisterna converted into a redoubt. Truscott's attack had to go through in a single continuous rush, for if there were any delay or BUFFALO were to take the form of a battle of attrition, as had HONKER, it would ruin the whole plan. In addition he had to raise the morale of his corps, which although so far victorious was worn out and suffering from the acutely unpleasant conditions in the beach-head.

Military historians since Xenophon have always been fascinated by the topic of a dynamic new commander reanimating a tired or dejected army. Here Truscott offers little literary scope. He seems to have been as unflamboyant a leader as has appeared in the history of the US Army since Ulysses S. Grant. He gave no pep-talks, he issued no stirring orders of the day, he was never seen to wear bizarre uniform or headgear or carry pearl-handled pistols, he generated no anecdotes and was guilty of no witticisms. The photographs of other generals tell us something about the man – the smirk of "Smiling Albert" Kesselring, the craggy features of "Iron Man" O'Daniel, the comical-cheerful expression of Leese and the determination radiating from Juin. Truscott's gives away nothing. We might conjecture that if he played poker it would be rather well, and we know he could be mildly convivial off-duty and enjoyed relaxing with his staff. We can only be sure of one thing: he was a first-class professional soldier. He had commanded the US 3rd Division (in the opinion of a discerning British observer the best in the Allied armies in Italy) which had emerged unshaken from sixty-five continuous days of combat in the bridgehead.[1] Truscott used the lull after FISCHFANG to set his corps hard at work preparing and rehearsing every detail of the forthcoming offensive. An energising current flowed from him down through the command hierarchy to the rank and file. To work soldiers hard for objectives that they clearly see are purposeful is as good a tonic for morale as any.

The operational problem facing Truscott and his staff was straight-forward but tough. The Fourteenth Army order of battle reflected von Mackensen's own belief that the Allies would strike north-west, directly at Rome. Therefore his three best divisions, the 4th Parachute, the 63rd Infantry and the 3rd Panzer Grenadiers under HQ 1st Parachute Corps were ranged in that order from the sea. The line was continued to the Mussolini Canal by Traugott Herr's 76th Panzer Corps with the 362nd and the 715th Infantry Divisions. (Divisions with three digits were recently raised and deemed second-rate, but only by German standards.) Von Mackensen had no reserve. All that Kessel-ring had left was the half-formed and half-trained 92nd Division, not counting the troops in northern Italy which included the useful Hermann Goering Panzer Grenadier Division. The Allied left in the beach-head was held by the under-strength British 5th and 1st Infantry Divisions, no longer under the 6th Corps but receiving their orders directly from the Fifth Army advanced command post near Anzio. Clark had a low opinion of them and recorded his contempt for their commanding generals. They had few tanks and no artillery other than their own 25-pounders and were allotted only a subsidiary role. (In any case Clark's secret plans for Rome excluded any but US Army units.) The 6th Corps line-up left to right from the boundary with the British 1st Division was the 45th and 34th Divisions to the little Astura river, with the 1st Special Force, a combined US–Canadian ranger-type unit extending the right as far as the Mussolini Canal.

Between there and the rear areas of the 14th Panzer Corps was a void, subject to desultory patrolling, since the 29th Panzer Grenadier Division was by then locked in combat with the US 2nd Corps. In reserve and preparing to act as the spearhead of BUFFALO were the US 1st Armored Division, Major-General Ernest Harmon, and the 3rd Infantry Division, Major-General John O'Daniel, last seen striding about the Salerno beach-head converting chaos into order. The 36th Infantry Division, still under General Walker, was brought into the beach-head shortly before D-day for BUFFALO. (It will be noted that the 34th, the 36th and the 3rd Divisions had all been engaged in strenuous and costly operations in the past six months, which shows the impact of Truscott, for they were shortly to prove the masters of the best soldiers in Europe.) For artillery Truscott could assemble some 180 guns augmented by three battalions of 90-mm anti-aircraft guns used against ground targets; few compared with British practice – Leese used over 600 in support of CHESTERFIELD – but type for type the US

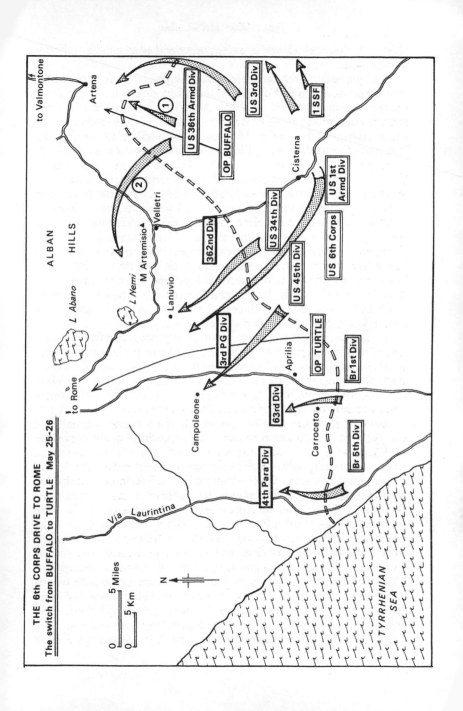

THE 6th CORPS DRIVE TO ROME
The switch from BUFFALO to TURTLE May 25-26

ALBAN HILLS

to Valmontone

Artena

US 36th Armd Div

OP BUFFALO

US 3rd Div

1 SSF

①

②

L Abano

L Nemi

M Artemisio

Velletri

Lanuvio

Cisterna

US 34th Div

US 1st Armd Div

US 6th Corps

362nd Div

US 45th Div

3rd PG Div

to Rome

Campoleone

Aprilia

OP TURTLE

Br 1st Div

63rd Div

Carroceto

Br 5th Div

4th Para Div

Via Laurintina

N

0   5 Miles

0   5 Km

TYRRHENIAN SEA

Artillery had the advantage in weight of metal and especially in heavy guns. (The US Artillery was also technically very skilled and in the 6th Corps its tactical employment was equally skilful. In British opinion its only faults were a habit of taking command decisions in the rear, treating the junior officers used as forward observers as mere rapporteurs and not fire-controllers, which occasionally led to tactical errors or omissions, and the accidental engagement of friendly troops, and to over-reliance on telephone cables, all too easily cut by tanks or enemy fire.)

In outline the plan for BUFFALO was for the 3rd Division to attack on the right, with its thrust line passing through Cisterna and then Cori, and the 1st Armored on the left directed on Velletri, the corps objective being, as said, the Via Casilina in the area of Valmontone. As the avenue of advance was dominated on the left by observers in the Alban Hills behind the enemy line and would be later from the north-western spurs of the Lepini range, two subsidiary attacks were to be mounted: one by the 45th on the left with limited objectives, the other on the right by the Special Force, with its final objective a dominating summit of the Lepinis, M. Arrestino. The whole of the left flank of the corps was to be extensively screened by artillery smoke.

The fire-plan compared with ordinary American practice was unusually elaborate. (The preferred method was the simple one of "artillery preparation", i.e., giving the enemy positions a good bashing and following up with infantry. They considered the British mistaken in their addiction to "covering fire" in the shape of moving barrages and timed programmes. There is a lot to be said on either side. The US methods were designed to be simple and standardised, suitable for operators in hastily trained, mass-produced units.) The artillery support was to be in two phases, the first preparatory and counter-battery fires against all HQs, strongpoints and hostile batteries whose locations had been fixed by every intelligence means, followed by a barrage to cover the approach and initial assault. Elaborate arrangements were made to provide additional support from the tactical air forces. The logistic planning included the accumulation of combat supplies, chiefly artillery and tank ammunition for no fewer than forty days at "intense" rates. Truscott, like the British general Horrocks the following year in the break-in phase of the Reichswald, saw little room for manoeuvre until he had reached Valmontone, and that like Horrocks he would have "to blow his way through". A number of Quartermaster Corps truck companies were brought into the beach-head and pre-loaded with ammunition, ready to make good expenditure without delay.

The assault echelons would pass through the positions of the 34th

Division, whose commander was made responsible for thoroughly patrolling his front, locating all strongpoints and positions, gapping minefields where possible and removing his own, clearing the obstacles and generally arranging for the smooth passage of two divisions through his own, never the easiest of manoeuvres.

General Harmon was alarmed by the unorthodox proposal to use a tank or armoured division for a breakthrough, instead of reserving it for the exploitation phase. He feared that he might lose 100 tanks in a matter of hours, but Truscott was adamant. The 1st Armored Division was exceptionally strong in tanks, 232 as compared with approximately 180 in other, slimmed-down divisions, and it included an armoured infantry regiment, four armoured artillery battalions and a tank-destroyer battalion. Truscott's resources were not so large that he could keep this powerful force in reserve for exploitation. To assist it in its breakthrough operation he reinforced it with another infantry regiment, the 135th from the 34th Division, additional fire-power in the form of 4.2-inch mortar companies and engineers, including a specialist mine-lifting company.

The result of this decision was that the staffs of Corps HQ and Harmon's division had to get to work to solve the problem of breaking in without undue loss. Analysing previous operations they concluded that the greatest single cause of tank losses was mines. Accordingly the US Engineers designed a modern version of the "bangalore torpedo" called a "Snake". This was rigid steel pipe filled with explosive with a shoe, or nose, on the far end, pushed by a tank into a minefield where it was fired, clearing by sympathetic detonation the mines along a path wide enough to accommodate a Sherman. It proved highly successful. An even more ingenious device was used to clear a path through anti-personnel mines which a squad of infantry could negotiate in single file. It consisted of a mortar-bomb towing a line which in turn pulled a string of small explosive charges.

Anti-tank guns were an even greater menace than mines, for a mined tank was usually recoverable, but one hit fair and square by a 75-mm or 88-mm gun was often a total loss, together with its crew. If engaged, the normal method was for the whole squadron or company to pause while the tank commanders searched the landscape for some tell-tale sign of the offender, a cloud of dust or smoke, or slight movement. It took time, and if it proved negative the tanks advanced again to provoke the hidden gun into revealing action, which was expensive. Something better had to be devised, for this would not do if a rapid breakthrough was the aim. Harmon practised his division in advancing with the leading tanks in echelon or arrowhead formation. As soon as the lead tank came under fire or was hit the cover in which the offending weapon might be hiding was drenched with cannon and machine-gun fire by all the others, indeed some units adopted prophylactic fire tactics, shooting up any suspicious-looking cover that might conceal a weapon whether fired on or not, while the supporting field artillery followed suit, confident that expensive though such a policy was, the tanks and guns could soon replenish from the ammunition trains following close behind the assault echelons. A second line of tanks followed some 300–400 yards behind, each carrying three specially selected infantrymen perched on top who, if the threat came from infantry hand-held weapons lying in ambush, dismounted to flush them out. An alternative weapon for moving infantry in close co-operation with armour was the brain-child of General O'Daniel: a sledge towed by a tank on which two semi-cylindrical hulls were mounted side by side in which the infantry lay prone. This was an interesting piece of "lateral thinking", but the infantry took a dislike to these springless steel coffins. They were glad when they proved unable to negotiate the numerous dry or wet irrigation ditches characteristic of the terrain and they were once more allowed to proceed in the manner more appropriate to foot soldiers.

Truscott perceived that he could not conceal from his opponent that an offensive was to take place but attempted with some success to surprise him on its direction and timing. The British were ordered to make a feint attack on their sector, which in fact did help to confirm von Mackensen's belief that Rome was the objective. As regards timing, the 6th Corps artillery and armour mounted a number of what the British Army used to call "Chinese" attacks. The planned H-hour was in the early morning, as soon as the tank crews could see to shoot, and at that time a violent bombardment would begin on odd or irregular days giving the impression that it presaged the long-awaited attack. At the same time masses of tanks were seen advancing, when the firing would suddenly cease, and the tanks withdraw. This, it was hoped, would lead the defenders to treat the real attack as yet another such apparently pointless waste of ammunition, and to delay responding with their defensive fires until the attackers were through the defensive zones and at close quarters. This policy paid off in other respects. The defending batteries were forced to open fire and so provide indications for the instruments of the counter-battery organisation and to reveal the location of standing defensive barrages. More subtle was the ploy adopted by the tanks. Not all withdrew. After each sortie some went into hides near their jump-off positions close to the front, so by the real D-day they could pounce on the forward enemy defences without giving the enemy warning. The noise of tracks and engines was audible for miles, and if the weather was dry clouds of dust would have revealed their approach from normal positions far in the rear. Nothing, in fact, that thought, professional skill, imagination and attention to detail might contribute to success was overlooked. (A British author might be forgiven for observing that it was just such attention to detail and careful planning when used by the British which led to American accusations of over-caution, even timidity.)

By these means Truscott obtained a well-deserved success. D-day was fixed for May 23, and in two days of bitter and costly fighting Harmon and O'Daniel broke the enemy line and captured Cisterna. By the evening of the 25th, the 715th Division was defeated and virtually ceased to exist as a fighting force. Valmontone was within arms' length of the triumphant Americans. Allied Intelligence had discovered that the Hermann Goering Division was on its way south, under heavy attack by air, which made it all the more urgent for Truscott to maintain the momentum of his attack and reach his objective before it arrived. He was therefore somewhat surprised when Brigadier-General Brann arrived at his command post with new orders from the army commander. BUFFALO was to continue with a token force, and the full weight of the 6th Corps was to be thrown forthwith into TURTLE, that is to say, it was to face left and advance directly on Rome over the Alban Hills. Truscott asked to see Clark, but Brann replied that this was a positive order to be carried out immediately, and in any case Clark had left the beach-head and was out of radio and telephone touch. (He had gone to Borgo Grappa, in the Pontine Marshes, where an engineer patrol from the 6th Corps had met a detachment of a reconnaissance battalion from the 2nd, and Clark had arranged to be photographed at a re-enactment of this event, symbolising the end of the long siege of Anzio.) Alexander was not consulted about the change in his plan and departure from his orders. The staff HQ AAI learnt of it only when the routine distribution copy of the "field order", confirming the verbal order passed by Brann, reached his HQ at Caserta. Alexander immediately visited Clark's main HQ but there found only Gruenther, whom he asked anxiously whether the advance on Valmontone was still in train. Gruenther, loyal to his commander, dissembled, but in fact BUFFALO was stone dead.

There is no point in waxing indignant or defensive over that extraordinary transaction. After all, an American might riposte to criticism of Clark by an Englishman by reminding him that England's hero, Nelson, won his laurels by twice disobeying the orders of his superior officer. He could argue, as Clark did, that possession of Valmontone was no guarantee that the withdrawal route of the Tenth

Army could be cut, and that von Senger did in fact manage to extricate his corps, and that it was the slowness of the Eighth Army that allowed him to escape, not Clark's change of plan. All that is special pleading, based in any case on a misconception of how the exploitation phase of DIADEM should go.

Clark himself was perfectly candid about his motives. He revealed them to all three of the distinguished historians employed in the Office of the Chief of Military History to cover aspects of the war in Italy. S. T. Matthews wrote in *Command Decisions*: "He considered Rome a gem belonging rightly in the crown of the Fifth Army."[2] Ernest F. Fisher, *Cassino to Salerno*, dispassionately recorded Clark's suspicion that the British were secretly planning to steal a march on him and enter Rome first, and his determination to win the prize before public attention was distracted from his feat by the momentous news of the landings in Normandy.[3] Were this not evidence enough he opened his diary and his mind to Martin Blumenson, author of *Salerno to Cassino*, his official biographer.[4] In short, the logic of his assessment of the situation did not rest on military factors but his overriding requirement to keep the British away from Rome. The switch from BUFFALO to TURTLE was not therefore a rapidly conceived strategic coup but entirely consistent with his conduct of the earlier battle on the Garigliano front and the First and Second Battles of Cassino. He had already decided to give no direct assistance to the Eighth Army on May 20, but before dealing with that incident it is necessary to describe how the situation appeared to von Senger, the thoughtful and able tactician who had defeated Clark's every move on the Cassino–Garigliano front in earlier battles.

Von Senger had been able to do this, he argued, because a corps was the right formation to control the vital Cassino–Garigliano sector. It was tactically indivisible, and a corps had sufficient resources to provide immediate reserves and the authority to handle the whole divisions in the deliberate counter-attack. Now, he was fully aware of the potential danger to his rear of a break-out from Anzio, and had identified the importance of Valmontone, for the same reasons as Harding. He had a provisional plan ready in case the forthcoming offensive breached the Gustav Line. It was to pivot on Cassino and withdraw into the Hitler Line without committing his Gustav Line garrisons to an intermediate series of battles, but retiring in good order so as to present the enemy with a well-organised defence when they arrived. He would then withdraw to the "C" Line* *north of Valmontone*,

---

* The "C", or Caesar Line was a projected but undeveloped defence position behind the Hitler Line. The title derived from the signals phonetic for "C". It was not a classical allusion.

in the same way, breaking clear to one phase line after another. When von Senger returned on the 17th to find his depleted corps reeling back from Juin's onslaught he urged Kesselring to allow him to put his withdrawal plan into action at once, but Kesselring refused him as he had refused Feuerstein earlier.

On May 18, seeing that Juin's advance had broken through the Hitler Line south of the Liri, out-paced the Eighth Army and outflanked the 51st Corps, Alexander sent Clark a warning order to be prepared to swing the whole weight of the 2nd Corps and the CEF round to the north. It was an obvious move. Clark had other ideas. On the 20th a reconnaissance squadron of the 2nd Corps found that Fondi was only weakly held, and he decided that it would be far better not to change direction and so lose momentum, but to order Keyes to press as hard as he could and join hands with Truscott in the bridgehead. This was a perfectly good decision, for Keyes and Truscott united doubled the potential of BUFFALO. Furthermore, if the Tenth Army could be pinned in the Liri valley until the combination of the 2nd and 6th Corps and the CEF had seized the Valmontone area its fate would be sealed. However, Clark seems to have thought that Juin's advance along his current north-westerly axis parallel to the south of the Sacco river and the Via Casilina would have the indirect effect of loosening the German defence opposing the Eighth Army. Ostensibly, therefore, he had good reasons for not ordering Juin to change direction as Alexander desired.[5] In fact, he had no intention of taking any action that might accelerate the dogged but slow advance of the Canadians and the 13th Corps, whose lack of progress he continually decried. So Clark simply ignored Alexander's "suggestions" and Alexander tamely accepted his disobedience. On the 19th the Eighth Army's attempts to bounce the Hitler Line were repulsed and Burns was committed to a deliberate attack.

One opportunity, to trap the right wing of the 51st Mountain Corps, created by Juin, had been lost. There still remained the original option. As Wentzell exclaimed on May 26 when the Hitler Line in the Liri valley had given way, "We have to get out of here as fast as we can or we shall lose the whole 14th Panzer Corps!" Indeed, by then it was being squeezed between the 6th Corps and the rest of the Eighth Army and was in danger of being cut off from the 51st Corps. The Allied situation on the 25th which had so alarmed him was as follows. In the Eighth Army sector the heads of its columns had emerged from the narrow gut of the Liri valley but were held up by the systematic German demolitions, mines, traffic congestion and the misfortune of a long Bailey bridge which was to carry the Canadian armour across the Liri river collapsing in the course of erection.[6] The only progress had been on foot, by the Canadians who had entered Ceprano, and the Indians in the hills flanking the 13th Corps axis on the right. The Eighth Army's operations should be measured as much by its successful attrition as by its limited territorial gains. The 51st Corps had suffered terribly. For instance, on the 25th Baade reported that he had lost seven battalions completely destroyed, five regular infantry, one engineer and one replacement battalion. He complained bitterly of being subjected to massed air and artillery bombardment, and that the enemy guns, unopposed by counter-battery fire, were able to deploy "in the open fields and mow down his infantry".

On the Eighth Army's left the CEF was fighting for every mile but still advancing with undiminished elan. The 1ère DMI had been squeezed out for lack of space and was in reserve and the 3e DIA having turned due north and cleared S. Giovanni, on the south bank of the Liri and the high ground immediately to its west, had halted. The two Moroccan divisions and the Goums pressed on into the mountains until Juin's front stuck out in a great bulge south of the river six miles deep to a point short of Castello de Volsci. By the 25th the French Intelligence staff had identified no fewer than nineteen battalions of infantry from various regiments, two or three non-infantry units fighting in the line and two newly arrived infantry regiments belonging to the 334th Infantry Division on the Adriatic sector. Many of these may have been only at 20 or even 10 per cent of establishment strength, but the total is evidence of Juin's success, and of the number of fish in the trawl – and not waiting to be caught, either. On the 26th only two fresh units were identified but there was ample evidence of a general movement from south to north, which was correct.[7] Von Senger had at last been given orders to break away. According to his plan he held on with his left, counter-attacking as necessary, and wheeled back his right.

Such terminology is, of course, archaic and only a figure of speech. In reality little groups of men, guns, tanks and horse-drawn artillery found their way along roads and track leading north through the night of the 25th/26th, the stragglers coming in by daylight, all hoping to meet a staff officer somewhere to show them their positions. Only the best troops and the best staff officers could execute the most difficult manoeuvre in war with such a hodge-podge of fragmented units, ZBVs and *Kampfgruppen*. On the 26th von Senger was firm on the line of the Sacco facing south. On the 27th he was able to disengage again to his next phase line, Guiliana di Romano–Cecano–Anaro, which he held all day on the 28th before moving back again and then the 14th Panzer Corps was in the clear.[8]

To return to the Allied side, on the 24th on Juin's left, Keyes' 2nd Corps had finally smashed the 29th Panzer Grenadier Division and on the 25th patrols from the 6th and 2nd Corps met at the village of Borgo Grappo. There was now a void between the left of the Fourteenth Army, unprotected by the shattered 715th Division and von Senger's units which began to trudge north at nightfall on the 26th. But only the French were pressing von Senger, so on the 27th a small *Kampfgruppe* of one battalion and five tanks re-crossed the Sacco and struck the right of the 2e DIM moving parallel to the south bank and was only beaten back after it had inflicted severe casualties. On the 28th, well to the south of the river in the French centre, a similar group acting even at that late date as rearguard supported by intense artillery fire threw back Groupement Louchet of the 4e DMM (*"ils sont bousculés . . ."*).

Returning to the 25th, there had been the promising development on the left of the 2nd Corps where a great horn was thrust out by the 6th Corps towards Valmontone threatening to cut the "C" Line and Army Group "C" in two. But on the 26th that threat was removed. The 6th Corps with admirable speed and flexibility turned through a right angle and began a fresh attack, leaving only a token force to continue the advance on Valmontone to preserve the appearance of complying with Alexander's plan, but really to protect Truscott's right flank from the threat of counter-attack by the Hermann Goering Division, whose move to that area had been detected by Allied Intelligence.

The question is, what were the correct moves that should have been made? In attempting to answer it we are conscious of the pitfalls of the "staff college syndicate room syndrome", wisdom after the event and freedom from the battlefield imperatives of luck, fatigue, the reaction of the enemy and Clausewitz's "friction" of warfare. It has also to be borne in mind it is not always profitable or easy to check a force in hot pursuit and order it to change direction without a loss of momentum and a pause that gives an alert and skilled enemy a chance to recover his balance. In fact, TURTLE succeeded more by luck than good judgment after it suffered a check that proved nearly fatal to Clark's ambitions.

What was needed was a fresh initiative on a fresh line, but one that left the troops already engaged to continue their advance without interruption. For the wedge and trap at Valmontone was only one possible vein for exploitation. What seems to have escaped the attentions of historians so far was the folly of not seizing the golden opportunity so unexpectedly offered by Juin's success. By the time the Eighth Army had broken through the Hitler Line and was stalled beyond it Juin had laid open the flank of the 51st Mountain Corps for some miles and he had two divisions in reserve, the 1ère DMI and the 3e DIA.

The first option was to shift the inter-army boundary north so that Juin could cross the Sacco behind the 51st Mountain Corps and use the Via Casilina. The two divisions available could have been re-inforced with British or Canadian tanks which, as they were US models, like their supporting armoured artillery, would have presented no logistic difficulties. He would also have required additional bridging, but in fact both the Germans and later Juin himself were able to cross the Sacco at will. If it had been done in time von Senger might have been trapped south of the Sacco, and von Vietinghoff forced into the difficult choice of either leaving Baade and Heidrich opposing Leese, with the risk of being cut off, or sending them against Juin's new right flank, which would take the cork out of the Liri bottle and let the Eighth Army loose.

From Valmontone there were the possibilities outlined, had Clark followed Alexander's order (or "suggestion") of the 18th, of squeezing von Senger from both ends along the Via Casilina or, depending on the degree of disarray of Army Group "C", making an armoured dash for the bridges over the Tiber behind him. A Patton or a Guderian might have dared to do it. It would be wrong to argue that any or all of these were certain to succeed, but it can be stated positively that to do nothing, to risk nothing, was absolutely wrong. That nothing was done was the consequence of the fatal conjunction of two such men as Clark and Alexander; the one with an iron determination to pursue a false aim, the other with the worthiest of intentions but lacking in backbone. Its malign influence was to be felt again in another botched operation before the year was out.

Another question is unanswerable or, at least, can only be the subject of conjecture: what might have followed had Army group "C" not escaped in good order? Hitler might conceivably have ordered a withdrawal as far as the foothills of the Alps to give him time to establish a new defence line in front of the southern approaches to the Greater Reich. ANVIL might have been modified. There might even have been the possibility of Alexander and Clark realising their dream of forcing the Julian Alps and the Lubljana "gap" and advancing into Austria before winter set in. The Allied armies might have reached the Apennines earlier, found the Gothic Line less well prepared and weakly manned and so been spared much hard and costly fighting that autumn and winter.

The rest of the story of DIADEM is soon told. Harmon and O'Daniel protested violently against the change of plan, with good reason, but

Truscott told them firmly that these were their orders and had to be obeyed. The corps and divisional staffs activated TURTLE with speed and efficiency, and the first troop movements were under way on the night of the 25th/26th and the switch completed by the 26th. The 3rd Infantry Division Armored Task Force Howze and the 1st Special Service Force were to continue the movement against Valmontone, but only to form a defensive flank against the threat of counter-attack by the 715th Division, which in fact was completely shattered, and the Hermann Goering Division, of which only the reconnaissance battalion had arrived. TURTLE was to be carried out by the 45th Division, already in position, the 34th and 36th Divisions, which had to face left and the 1st Armored Division, which had to retrace its steps and then face to its right. The first attack failed. German troops, unshaken and in strong positions, could only be shifted by a carefully prepared attack; they could not be rushed, even when outnumbered and out-gunned. By the 30th the operation had still to be set moving again by the initiative of the commander of the much-battered and hitherto unlucky 36th Division, still General Walker. Owing to a misunderstanding compounded by a shortage of troops M. Artemisio, a large wooded feature with steep slopes overlooking Velletri, had not been properly secured by the 1st Parachute Corps and some enterprising patrols from the 36th Division found it almost free of enemy troops. Walker, seizing the opportunity, sent two regiments to steal undetected up its slopes, assisted by engineers, and followed by tanks. This broke the front of the 1st Parachute Corps, but Kesselring had other bad news. He, too, had had his eye on Valmontone and the gap between the Lepini and the Alban Hills for some time, and by the 31st the US 88th Division of the 2nd Corps had swung up to that area from the coast, the French Corps de Montagne was pushing through the Lepinis and the 1ère DMI was moving rapidly along the north bank of the Sacco. It was time to get out and he ordered a general withdrawal, and so saved Army Group "C" to fight another day.

The US troops advancing in great spirits resumed their attack on the 31st and on June 4 Clark achieved his heart's desire and drove into Rome, which had been declared an open city. There he hoisted the Stars and Stripes and the Union Jack and, never a man to miss a trick, sent the first to the President of the United States and the second to the Prime Minister of England. Harold Macmillan, Old Etonian, signalled Harold Alexander to congratulate him on the liberation of Rome on so auspicious a date. Alexander, Old Harrovian, replied, "What is the Fourth of June?"

The two British divisions in the Anzio bridgehead played an undistinguished part in the final victory. They were hardly expected to do anything else, having been given the simple role of following up the retreating right wing of the 1st Parachute Corps. This they were glad to do, especially the infantry of the 5th Division who had been engaged in the murderous close-range fighting in their supposedly quiet sector, in the "wadis"; in particular between the 1st Inniskilling Fusiliers and the infantry of the 4th Parachute Division, neither belonging to the live and let live school of soldiering. They continued to clash in small-scale but bitter fights until the enemy disappeared. The British divisions were ordered by Fifth Army to halt and bivouac on the banks of the Tiber downstream of Rome. David Cole, the signals officer of the Inniskillings, was surprised to see that many of the formidable parachutists were no more than youths, in death still pink-faced and looking rather surprised. On June 5, having no duties to perform, Cole went into Rome for the civilised pleasures of a haircut and a cocktail in the Hotel Excelsior, in surroundings untouched and undisturbed by war. The Romans were very friendly, but they asked, "Why were you so long in coming?"

So ended DIADEM, marred in execution, but none the less a great victory. Alexander and his generals could justly claim that they had severely defeated the most powerful German army the Western Allies had yet encountered. Not the least benefit, bearing in mind the ultimate aim of the war, was the liberation of some three-quarters of Italy.

Kesselring with equal justice claimed that though defeated he had successfully carried out the Fuehrer's orders against heavy odds, extricated his armies from a trap, and was ready to fight again. He could also congratulate himself with the thought that it was the optimism of "Smiling Albert" and not the croaking of the *Hochwohlgeboren* army generals which had proved the better guide.

All the same, he was faced with immediate and grave difficulties. He had had severe losses. Army Group "C" had suffered 38,024 casualties, of which 2,127 were killed. (The last a surprisingly low figure, even allowing for its being a defensive battle, and that at this stage of the war the Germans had, like the British, been forced to adopt a policy of parsimony in man-power and prodigality in fire-power.) The true measure of his defeat was the loss of 9,484 prisoners (counting only Germans), 2,100 machine guns, 306 pieces of artillery and 250–300 tanks and other armoured fighting vehicles.

Kesselring soon patched up and rallied his divisions and was able to resume his fighting withdrawal. He intended to make his next stand on the Gothic Line, running from Pisa to Rimini along the forward slopes of the great north-west south-east diagonal of the Apennines. To give his engineers time to prepare it he fought two delaying battles, one astride Lake Trasimene, and behind that, on the line of the River Arno. The two German armies broke away cleanly, and the Allied soldiery, indifferent to the news of the fall of Rome and the landings in Normandy two days later, trudged or motored northwards, according to arm, resuming the familiar routine of replacing blown bridges, lifting minefields, scouting for an elusive enemy, coping with the self-propelled anti-tank gun round the next corner and occasionally being shot or blown up for their pains.

Clark was by no means mellowed by his personal victory and continued to be obstructive in a petty way. Ordered by HQ AAI to allow Leese running rights inside the Fifth Army sector to enable him to have a chance of cutting off the enemy in Orvieto, he refused until he had the order in writing, the delay frustrating the operation entirely. This hardened Leese's resolve never to fight adjacent to the Fifth Army if he could avoid it. What was now gnawing Clark was the certainty of soon losing seven divisions to ANVIL, together with HQ 6th Corps, which would make him numerically the junior partner in AAI. It exacerbated his by then obsessive dislike of the British.

Leese also had his troubles. He had formed a poor opinion of Burns during the Liri battle, and wanted him to be replaced if necessary by a British officer, which would have had unpleasant political results, and the staffs of Corps HQ and the 5th Canadian Armoured Division had not functioned well. Wisely the Canadian High Command was consulted and Burns on their advice was retained, but two senior officers were relieved: in retrospect unfairly, but that was a question for the Canadians. The 1st Canadian Corps was to show its prowess a second time in the Gothic Line battle.

Far more serious than these painful and difficult matters, after all part of the day-to-day work of generals, was the question of manpower. The British and Commonwealth commanders were already alive to this. The Americans so far were not. The US Army losses in DIADEM had been 17,931 (3,145 killed), the largest share of the total AAI casualties (some 40,000), but by June 4 the lavish and efficient replacement service had made them good. Casualty figures are notoriously difficult to interpret because of different methods of accounting and differing circumstances; besides cost–benefit equations are insoluble: what would have been a fair price for Cassino? The only thing that is certain is that battle is expensive; the French General Mangin said in 1918: "Quoi qu'on fasse, on perd beaucoup de monde." To take a single example: the two British divisions in Anzio were employed in a static defensive role from April 1 to May 22. On the 23rd they mounted a feint attack and from the 29th to June 3 they followed up the retreating enemy. Their total casualties for the period were 520 killed, 2,385 wounded and 450 missing.

An admittedly unsophisticated way of assessing casualties for a given operation, but one that does not lead to any great distortion is to obtain a comparative coefficient by dividing the total casualties by the number of infantry battalions engaged. This gives us: Poles, 307; US Army, 271; French, 259; Canadians, 196; British, 188. This result is very much what might be expected. The French, for instance, were fighting for the longest without a break and had attracted the bulk of the German reserves. American commanders drove their units on remorselessly, attacking again and again if the first failed. It is fallacious, however, to try to deduce from this a sort of league table of self-sacrifice on the one side or good tactics on the other. The point is that even the lowest loss of the order above is not one that can be sustained for one battle after another without an ample reservoir of replacements. Clark was to his chagrin to discover that even the American reserves were dwindling by the end of the year. The Allied commanders were to be faced with very difficult operations in the autumn and winter with these grim statistics hanging over them like a dark cloud.

VIII

The Gothic Line

23

OPERATION OLIVE

> I am told that the 5th Canadian Armoured Division was excellent . . . though
> not strong in numbers, the Canadians are right good soldiers.
>
> *Von Vietinghoff to Kesselring, September 7, 1944*[1]

The pursuit after DIADEM came to a halt in July, with Kesselring's
forces, battered but still intact and full of fight, ranged across Italy from
the Metauro river on the Adriatic coast along the Arno to the
Mediterranean, covering the Pisa–Rimini line according to plan. The
long debate over ANVIL (renamed DRAGOON) had gone against Alexander, and he was forced to halt and redeploy to fill the huge gap left in the
Fifth Army by the loss of seven divisions. The enforced pause enabled
Leghorn to be opened as a forward base and supply port and the
infantry were given a much-needed rest, for the pursuit had been a
hard-fought affair costing Clark 18,000 and Leese 16,000 casualties.[2]
All hope, however, of bursting through the Gothic Line and reaching
the plain of Emilia before the summer ended had evaporated and
Alexander prepared for an autumn offensive.

His mission, to contain Kesselring, remained the same and Harding
once again decided that the best course was an all-out offensive, with
the full weight of both armies concentrated and an elaborate deception
plan to conceal the point of attack. In the area of Ancona the Apennines
turn north-west in a great mountain rampart, rising from the rolling
foothills in the east to snowy peaks in Liguria, offering only two avenues
of advance. Harding discarded the Adriatic, with its alternation of ridge
and river valleys that had so troubled the Eighth Army in the winter of
1943. The most promising, he thought, was the main highway over the
passes from Florence to Bologna. This plan, which suited Clark, was
short lived.[3]

Kirkman's powerful 13th Corps was halted in line south of the Arno astride Florence and in his view the natural defences of the mountains facing him were strong enough to delay a mechanised army indefinitely. He decided that of two difficult options the eastern end of the Gothic Line was preferable, for only there could the great assets of the Eighth Army, a mass of tanks and thousands of guns, be realised. On August 3 when Leese visited him he pressed for the plan to be changed and found the army commander receptive. Leese, for emotional and personal reasons, had resolved never to fight shoulder to shoulder with Clark again if he could avoid it, and Kirkman now supplied him with a persuasive tactical argument. On the 4th Leese met Alexander and Harding, and Alexander, as compliant as ever, agreed with it.[4]

On the 10th Alexander summoned Clark to discuss the sudden change of plan. Clark agreed in principle with it, but was not prepared to see his Fifth Army reduced to a secondary role. Like Alexander, he was convinced that the correct strategy was to burst into the Po valley and thence into Austria and the Danube basin, and determined that he was going to play the leading part in this great enterprise. The "British", for whom by this time he felt nothing but profound contempt, could not "carry the ball" without his aid. (In DIADEM they had been "nothing but grief".)[5] There was also the danger that if Marshall and Devers thought the Fifth Army was not fully employed they might transfer it to France, a thought Clark could not endure. Keeping all this to himself Clark proceeded to negotiate in calm and masterly style. He brought the argument down to the tactical question of his right flank and who was to control the British division adjacent to it. His price for acquiescence was Kirkman's corps, complete.* British troops were better than none, and they would enable him to concentrate his trusted US divisions as his spearhead. Alexander, as ever, concurred. It made sense to put the left-hand corps under Clark so as to allow him to coordinate its operations with his own, and free Leese to conduct the battle on the coast, but Alexander's judgment of Solomon deprived Leese of a reserve, ignored the unsuitability of the central sector for tanks and divided his forces instead of concentrating them in one place or the other.

The staff, and the Canadians in particular, performed wonders transferring the Canadian Corps from its position south of Florence to the coast and in reversing the deception plan that had pointed to an offensive being launched on the Adriatic. That proved superfluous, for

---

* 6th British and 6th South African Armoured Divisions; 1st British and 8th Indian Infantry Divisions.

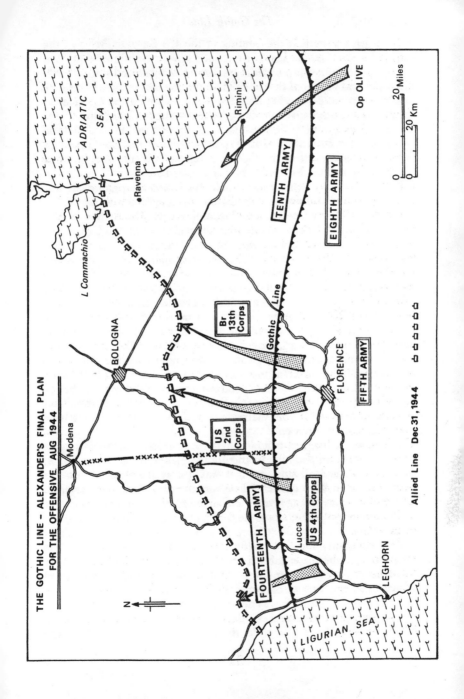

THE GOTHIC LINE – ALEXANDER'S FINAL PLAN
FOR THE OFFENSIVE AUG 1944

Op OLIVE

ADRIATIC SEA

Rimini

Ravenna

L Commachio

TENTH ARMY

EIGHTH ARMY

20 Miles
20 Km

BOLOGNA

Br 13th Corps

Gothic Line

FLORENCE

FIFTH ARMY

Modena

US 2nd Corps

FOURTEENTH ARMY

Lucca

US 4th Corps

LEGHORN

LIGURIAN SEA

N

Allied Line   Dec 31, 1944

in Kesselring's opinion the landing of the US Seventh Army in the south of France on August 15 precluded any major offensive in Italy. What worried him was his weakness, for he had suffered some 63,000 casualties and he feared that he might have to transfer some of his elite troops, his trouble-shooting 26th Panzer and 29th Panzer Grenadiers to France, and other divisions as well. Meanwhile the 2nd Polish Corps was pressing uncomfortably hard on the Adriatic flank. He ordered von Vietinghoff to withdraw the 76th Panzer Corps into the "Red Line", or forward defence zone of the Gothic defences in that sector, between the Metauro and the Foglia rivers, and awaited events.

Leese's Operation OLIVE was simple, bold and enterprising. He was faced by three divisions in the Red Line, the 1st Parachute on the Via Adriatica (Highway No. 16), the 71st and the 5th Mountain inland in the hills. He disposed of ten divisions altogether, and intended to open his attack with three corps in line abreast. Anders was to continue on the coast until he had masked Pesaro, and halt. Burns then would extend to the right and Keightley's powerful corps of five divisions, on his left, would press forward. Leese's intention was to overrun the Red Line, the outpost zone of the Gothic defences, in a surprise attack without artillery preparation, bounce both parts of the Green Line, the main battle zone, before it could be properly manned and then use his mass of armour to break through the rear defences, the Rimini Line, into the Romagna, the flat alluvial plain beyond. Following Montgomery's example, he visited as many units as possible, talking to the men and filling them with enthusiasm and confidence that this was to be the final victory in Italy. ("We'll meet in Venice!" was the cry.) Surprise was to be complete, with von Vietinghoff and Heidrich, the parachute commander, both on leave.

There was, however, trouble ahead. Leese had put his strongest corps, the 5th, on the hilly inland route, changing his original plan, since Anders had already found it was less well defended and the strongpoints on the coast could be turned from the higher ground. However, Leese, having given the Canadians what the Poles told him was the toughest route, along the coast, neither reinforced them, nor made arrangements to do so were they to break through on the direct route to Rimini. He had no flexible plan for his mid-battle, the "dog-fight", when inevitably a melee with the panzers and panzer grenadiers rushing up to counter-attack would develop, and it was vital to reach the ground with his own armour first.

Leese's third handicap was not of his own making. Deprived of the services of the experienced South African and British 6th Armoured Divisions, he had given Keightley the British 1st Armoured. Now in the course of the war in Italy the armoured divisions, following the German example, had learnt to fight in mixed teams of tanks and infantry, and like the New Zealand Division had added an extra infantry brigade. The 1st Armoured had not been in action since April 1943 in Africa, it was unaware of and untrained in the new tactics, its reorganisation on the new model had been only just completed, the armour and infantry were strangers to each other, and Major-General Richard Hull had only recently assumed command. In short, it was not yet battle-worthy. The consequences of all this lay ahead.

The men of the Eighth Army went into battle cheered by the presence of Winston Churchill, and in the best of spirits.

It was a clear night on August 25/26 when the 1st Canadian Division with the British 46th Division on its left passed through a screen of Polish troops and established bridgeheads over the Metauro. In daylight the 1st Canadian Division advanced, the 21st Tank Brigade in support. There was resistance, so they quickly learned that the enemy had not withdrawn. The advance was hindered by cratering and mining which delayed the tanks, radio communication failed here and there and some units lost their way in the confusing country. By the evening of the 26th the division had advanced about five miles.

Next morning the vanguards arrived at the hill-towns of Monteciccardo, S. Angelo and Ginestreto. In the afternoon Monteciccardo was bombed, unfortunately too early for the Edmontons to attack it at once, but in the small hours of the 28th their A Company entered the town and found it empty. Ten minutes later its forward platoon, having placed Bren guns to command the main street, was amazed to see a company of German infantry in threes marching down it towards them. Opening fire with two machine guns they inflicted about sixty or seventy casualties in less than a minute. Shortly afterwards, a tank appeared behind the Germans and the platoon was soon attacked by the rest of a German battalion; the company prudently withdrew to a ridge outside the town.[6] The Germans were, indeed, in some disarray and still unaware of the weight of the Eighth Army attack. They were playing for time to occupy the Green Line but also unwilling to weaken themselves so that they could not hold it. The Canadians had not attacked in great strength anywhere, and their tanks, delayed by demolitions, had not always been up with their infantry. Fortunately, this served to conceal their real strength from the Germans who did not positively identify their presence and took them for a force that was closing up to the Green Line, not one intent on pushing through it in strength.

By the evening of the 27th Burns felt less confident that he could bounce the Green Line. The 71st Division was giving ground and yielding prisoners, but though the Parachute Division had recently absorbed 2,000 half-trained replacements the Canadians found Heidrich's men their usual aggressive selves. When Burns asked Vokes whether he would reach the Foglia on the 28th he replied: "Seems unlikely."

Opinion in Army Group "C" was divided. Kesselring, supported by the staff of HQ Fourteenth Army, considered that the Eighth Army's *Schwerpunkt* would be in the centre, on the Arno front. The Germans had come to regard the Canadians and the New Zealanders as elite assault troops, whose presence on any part of the front was significant. Their intelligence staff was misled by identifications of both on the central front, and reports that the area behind it was buzzing with activity. This was correct, but the Canadians were from the independent 1st Canadian Armoured Brigade, attached to the British 13th Corps, and the New Zealanders were resting. Consequently, when Kesselring heard that Canadian prisoners had been taken on the coastal sector he told Wentzell that he believed that it was a diversion. This impression was strengthened by the fact that as the 76th Corps was already in the process of falling back from its outpost positions to the Green Line it had not felt the full weight of the Eighth Army's opening blow. The Canadians, in the opinion of the German staff, never took risks. Kesselring felt that his only immediate problem was to ensure that the Green Line was fully manned in good time, so he decided to wait for the battle to develop before altering his plans.

Wentzell disagreed. He told Kesselring that if the Canadian attack now under way was in fact the main Eighth Army effort, it was (in his view) on the correct axis. He recalled von Vietinghoff, who was on leave. "Then," in the words of the Canadian official history, "came one of those dramatic finds that sometimes fall to a groping Intelligence." The Germans got hold of a copy of the message sent by Leese to the troops on the eve of the battle. It spoke of "the last lap", secret concentrations of great strength to break the Gothic Line, and bringing the campaign to an end. On the night of the 28th, with von Vietinghoff back from leave, the Germans were at last convinced that the objective of OLIVE was, indeed, the Romagna. "Such was the cost of a single sheet of very inferior paper," wrote Lieutenant-Colonel Nicholson, the Canadian official historian.[7] In fact, Kesselring had already started the 26th Panzer on its way on the 27th and the 29th Panzer Grenadiers were warned to follow it as soon as they could be relieved. The Tenth Army ordered the 98th Infantry to relieve the 71st. On the 29th, the retreating divisions crossed the Foglia, with orders to hurry their occupation of the First Green Line. But despite that, Wentzell thought that the 30th would be a day of crisis, for neither the 98th nor the 26th Panzer Divisions could reach the front until that day at the earliest.

On the 29th Leese, Keightley and Burns considered whether to pause and mount a set-piece battle, for which fire-plans had been prepared in advance, or to try to bounce the Green Line. The 46th Division had kept almost abreast of the Canadians and patrols from both corps which had penetrated the two-mile-wide flat valley of the Foglia in the evening reported that the Green Line was lightly held. While the wire obstacles were formidable and the minefields well sited, the latter had been bombed and considerably disarranged by the Desert Air Force and so some patrols had passed through them without difficulty. On the morning of the 30th, when more aggressive patrols reached the road connecting the villages of Montecchio on the left, Osteria Nuova in the centre and Borgo S. Maria on the right, battalion commanders recommended that an immediate attack be attempted. By this time Burns had brought his armoured division into the line on the left of the 1st Division which was concentrated on a narrower front. He intended to attack with the two divisions in line, each with one brigade up, whatever form the attack took. After receiving the latest patrol information he recommended to Leese that his corps should attack immediately, pushing forward with companies, followed by battalions to make a lodgement while the Green Line was still only partially occupied.

From this time the "gate-crash battle", as Burns called it, was the responsibility of the "lieutenant-colonels who rose to the occasion and gave notable examples of leadership". This was well said, for the breaking of the Green Line was an occasion when Canadian units were faster to the punch than the Germans, exhibiting excellent minor tactics, out-fighting the parachutists and the 26th Panzer Division and opening the door for the Eighth Army to roll forward into the plain. Major-General Bert Hoffmeister sent his 11th Brigade infantry forward in the late afternoon of the 30th without a preliminary bombardment. Vokes' 3rd Brigade advanced at about the same time. The Cape Breton Highlanders on the left of them were to take Montecchio and Point 120, on the right the Perth Regiment went for Point 111 and then Point 147. Vokes' Princess Patricia's Canadian Light Infantry were to take Osteria Nuova and the West Nova Scotias Point 133. Behind the 11th Brigade, tanks of the 5th Armoured Brigade would cross the river and the anti-tank ditch, pass through the minefields as best they could and support the infantry as soon as possible. They could offer some fire-support even from the midst of the minefields but their direct presence would be required when the infantry fought their way through the German defences.

At first things did not go well because the Germans came to life and reacted strongly. (They had either been lying low or had arrived just in time to meet the advancing Canadians.) The Cape Breton Highlanders were thrown back from Point 120, where the 71st Division had been relieved by the 67th Panzer Grenadier Regiment of the 26th Panzer Division. However, the Perths took Point 111 and the Irish Regiment of Canada were brought across from the left flank and passed through between them and the battling Highlanders to attack Point 120 from the rear. The move took time in the darkness but when their attack with the tanks of the New Brunswick Hussars did go in at midday on the 31st it was entirely successful and freed the left for a further advance. In the meantime the West Novas had a dreadful time in the minefields, especially from the "schu-mines". The "Princess Pat's" persevered, cleared the village of Osteria Nuova of enemy, went on to take Point 115, pushed a company down the road to contact the 11th Brigade, and collected a good haul of prisoners from the Parachute Division.

During the night the tanks of the British Columbia Dragoons worked their way through the minefield with much shouting and cursing and not a little chaos to catch up with the Perths during the morning. The Perths had outflanked and taken Point 147 from the rear and sent a company up the spur beyond leading to the heights behind the Green Line, only for it to be pinned down by fire. The Dragoons were ordered forward to pick up the Perths and make a joint attack on their objective, Point 204 and Tomba di Pesaro, but the Perths were immobilised by "the severest shelling and mortaring that we had ever experienced", and the Dragoons went on alone. So difficult was the climb that the tank commanders dismounted to pick out a route for each tank, to be sniped and ambushed by the parachutists, until they were down to eighteen tanks, but they reached the goal, Point 204 in the very heart of the enemy position. Now the Dragoons could shoot into the rear of the enemy holding up the 3rd Brigade at Pozzo Alto, and had cut the road from the top of the hill to Borgo S. Maria.

It was now vital to get infantry on to Point 204 before dark, when the parachutists would certainly counter-attack. Fortunately the tanks of Lieutenant-Colonel McAvity's Lord Strathcona's Horse by then had passed through the minefields and they picked up the Perths' infantry late in the day. Fighting a model action, troop covering troop as they climbed the ridge with the battalion, they relieved the British Columbia Dragoons at nightfall. The BCD had lost their commanding officer,

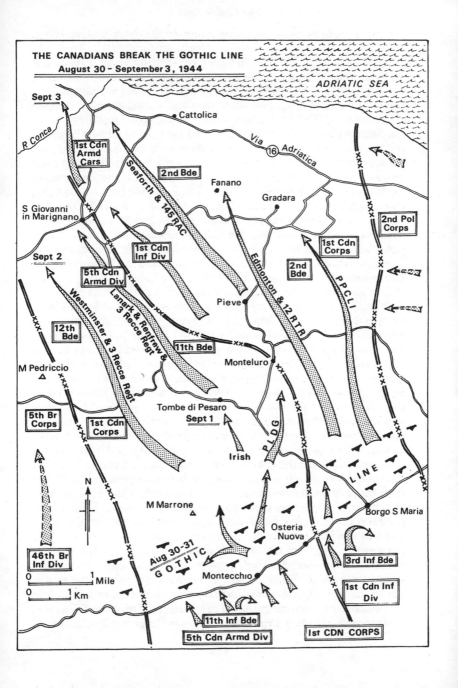

THE CANADIANS BREAK THE GOTHIC LINE
August 30 – September 3, 1944

ADRIATIC SEA

Sept 3

R Conca

Cattolica

Via Adriatica 16

1st Cdn Armd Cars

Seaforth & 145 RAC

2nd Bde

Fanano

Gradara

2nd Pol Corps

S Giovanni in Marignano

1st Cdn Inf Div

1st Cdn Corps

2nd Bde

Edmonton & 12 RTR

Sept 2

5th Cdn Armd Div

Lanark & Renfrew & 3 Recce Regt

Pieve

PPCLI

Westminster & 3 Recce Regt

12th Bde

11th Bde

Monteluro

M Pedriccio

5th Br Corps

1st Cdn Corps

Tombe di Pesaro
Sept 1

Irish

PLDG

L I N E

M Marrone

Borgo S Maria

46th Br Inf Div

Osteria Nuova

0   1 Mile
0   1 Km

N

Aug 30-31
G O T H I C

Montecchio

3rd Inf Bde

1st Cdn Inf Div

11th Inf Bde

5th Cdn Armd Div

1st CDN CORPS

Fred Vokes, brother of the commander of the 1st Division, killed, together with twenty-one others, and forty-nine wounded.

There was no sleep that night for the men on Point 204. Attack followed attack by parachutists and sniping assault guns. A farm cart was driven into the position and set on fire, brilliantly illuminating the tanks. Solid shot flew in all directions and mortar bombs crumped persistently, but the Perths gave as good as they got, chased away their assailants and at sunrise still held the position. Their friends on either side benefited immediately as the Strathcona's tanks were able to shoot at Pozzo Alto and help the 1st Division forward. Had Hoffmeister been able to listen to the agitated telephone calls between the 76th Panzer Corps, Tenth Army and Kesselring's HQ he would have been greatly encouraged. What the Germans most feared – a thrust from Point 204 to the summit of the ridge at Tomba di Pesaro and M. Peloso – was to be his next step. It would split the German defences and enable the 1st Canadian Division to take M. Luro and drive from there to the sea. The 1st Parachute Division would be cornered in Pesaro and the Green Line rolled up from the east.

The plan was for the Straths and the Perths to take both objectives early in the morning of September 1. However, the Perths had been fighting hard for two days and were too weak to go on. (Their commander Lieutenant-Colonel Reid, twice wounded, was awarded the DSO for outstanding leadership.) Their place was taken by the 4th Princess Louise Dragoon Guards – the "Plugs" – fighting for the first time as infantry, with the Strathcona's tanks. They were not deterred by a sharp artillery bombardment that greeted them as they arrived on Point 204, costing them several men, and at 1 p.m. jumped off together with the tanks supported by an artillery fire-plan. The newly converted infantry scored a great success, recorded blow by blow in the Strathcona's radio log. Working closely together tanks and foot soldiers remorselessly drove the enemy from one fire position to another; from behind corn stooks, hedgerows and inside houses until, when all was over, his dead lay in rows and a bulldozer had to be summoned to dig a trench for a mass grave. (Lieutenant-Colonel W. W. G. Darling, the commanding officer of the "Plugs", who controlled the battle, was also awarded the DSO for "sheer gallantry and personal example".) The victors from the grassy slopes of M. Peloso now had a panorama of the Second Green Line: M. Gemmano on the left, Coriano beyond the Conca river and to Riccione on the Via Adriatica, where the routed enemy was flying in the hope of occupying it during the night.[8]

A wonderful opportunity waited to be seized. If M. Luro fell as well as Tomba di Pesaro, a swift thrust by the 1st Infantry Division would seal the fate of the whole 1st Parachute Division, which had already lost its 4th Regiment; with it eliminated the Second Green Line could not be held. In the 5th Armoured Division the 11th Infantry Brigade was exhausted and needed time to reorganise, and the armoured troops, equally tired, required time to recover and repair damaged vehicles and to replenish. General Hoffmeister still had in reserve his second infantry brigade, the 12th. Reinforcing it with his 3rd Armoured Reconnaissance Regiment (tanks and armoured infantry), he sent it forward that night.* The 11th Brigade followed up in their troop carriers. Hoffmeister's objective was S. Fortunato in the third or reserve German line south-west of Rimini – the Rimini Line – and he had the satisfaction of driving through the Second Green Line before it could be occupied by the enemy. On his right the 1st Division had taken rather longer to get off the mark. It did not capture M. Luro until five hours after M. Peloso had fallen, and then Vokes had to organise a pursuit group with the tanks of the British 21st Tank Brigade, just too late to catch the remnants of the Parachute Division. The Canadians were now in full cry.

Earlier that afternoon General Burns had reported to Alexander and Leese at Eighth Army tactical HQ that the Green Lines had been crossed and his pursuit had begun. Leese and Alexander expressed their delight but seemed startled by the news that the advance had actually started and the speed of Burns' coup. Burns formed the impression that both men were completely at a loss. When he made to leave, Leese called him back. Alexander told him that he would recommend him for the DSO. In the book he wrote later Burns recorded that he took this to mean that at last Leese and Alexander had decided he was fit to handle his command and that "confidence had replaced the doubts that had formerly existed".[9] This was all very well, but Burns' immediate need was not a DSO but another armoured division. Leese's first error, his failure to provide Burns with a reserve division before OLIVE started, was one of judgment. Now, condoned by a passive Alexander, he was guilty of criminal inertia. The door to the enemy position, if not open, was at least ajar. Leese could not have been in any doubt that given the shortest breathing space Herr, like any German commander, would leap to slam the opening door in Hoff-

---

* One lesson of DIADEM had been that armoured divisions in Italy required extra infantry. Canada could spare none for its 5th Armoured Division, so the requirement was met by converting the 4th Princess Louise Dragoon Guards (an armoured reconnaissance regiment) and the Lanark and Renfrew Infantry (anti-aircraft artillery, reverting to its original role) to form the 12th Canadian Infantry Brigade.

meister's face, nor could he have been in any doubt that according to his own plan the 1st Armoured Division could not reach even the line of the Metauro for twenty-four hours. It was not impossible to improvise a mobile group to exploit Burns' success. A German or an American general would have galvanised his staff into immediate action. Any action would have been better than none. Leese did nothing.

On the 3rd, having crossed the Conca river, Hoffmeister's division pushed on and took Misano but on the 4th, as they were fighting their way down the ridge which terminated in the village of Besanigo, beyond the Second Green Line, the New Brunswick Hussars were heavily fired on and attacked by troops from their left flank. It transpired that the ridge from Coriano in the north to the villages of Passano and S. Savino in the south was held by the enemy. The corps boundary ran down the Besanigo stream, the Coriano ridge was in the 5th Corps sector. What had happened was that the 98th Infantry Division had arrived on the 3rd, and that night the 29th Panzer Grenadiers' 71st Regiment. It is questionable whether closer action between the 46th Division, held up at S. Clemente, and the Canadians would have been able to dislodge the 98th Division which was now supported by the 26th Panzer Division. However, the Irish and the Cape Breton Highlanders pushed on and took the hamlet of Besanigo on the 5th. Meanwhile on the 4th the 1st Division was echeloned back on the right of the 5th, held up in the Second Green Line by parachutists in S. Maria di Scacciano. That night it threw them out by turning their seaward flank and moved forward to the Melo stream crossing it on the 5th, but was held up there. The 1st Brigade lost 300 men in these few hours of fighting. Neither it nor the armoured division could go any further as long as the Germans were firmly entrenched in their left rear. Where was 1st Armoured Division, which was supposed to dislodge the enemy from the Coriano ridge?

It was not until the late afternoon of the 2nd that the 4th Hussars, the armoured reconnaissance regiment of the division, was ordered forward in advance of the main body of the division, which had not yet reached the Metauro, over twenty miles behind the Conca. The 4th Hussars drove all night over treacherous tracks under the impression that they were to find crossings over the Conca and then lead an advance through and beyond Coriano. Next morning they were bogged behind Clemente where they found the infantry of the 46th Division dug in.[10] On the night of the 3rd/4th the Hampshires of the 46th Division attacked but were halted by fire from S. Savino. In the morning they were shelled from the hills on their left flank and rear where Croce and Gemmano were firmly held by the Germans. During the 4th General Hawkesworth was still assuring General Hull that he

358

was holding "the gate" open for him and one of Leese's liaison officers reported that Hawkesworth had the enemy on the run. All this, the 4th Hussars discovered, was fantasy, but could not pass the truth back to HQ 1st Armoured Division. (Presumably because the radio distance was too great.)

For the state of affairs in front of Clemente the 46th Division was not altogether to blame. The 5th Corps terrain was difficult and Leese had underestimated the effect of the high ground on the left of the funnel into which he had committed it. When the 46th Division had been drawn along in the slip-stream of the 5th Armoured, a gap occurred on their left. Keightley filled it with the 56th Division and urged it to cross the Conca quickly. Its commander, Major-General John Whitfield, understood that he was not to be distracted by high ground on his flanks and ordered his leading brigade to push on, leaving a battalion following behind to occupy M. Gemmano. By the time the battalion arrived and climbed the steep hill to the fortified village of that name on top, it found the 100th Mountain Regiment already in occupation and could not dislodge it. Gemmano was the hinge of the Second Green Line and as long as it was in their hands the Germans could hinder an advance on Croce and narrow the corps front to virtually that on which the 46th Division was halted. The general form that the battle on the left had taken could have been anticipated from Leese's plan, given the terrain, even if it could not have been avoided. What was incomprehensible was the failure to bring the 1st Armoured Division to a point close behind the front from which it could exploit the opportunity on September 1 for which Leese had been hoping.

A number of circumstances contributed to the situation. In the first place Leese had been surprised by the speed of the Canadian penetration. Second, he had deliberately kept the 1st Armoured well back to avoid blocking the roads forward. Had he been prepared to commit it to the Canadian Corps that would not have been a problem, for there was plenty of room immediately behind them. Third, Leese's mind worked at infantry pace. At Alamein he had commanded the 30th Corps which had done most of the infantry work to crack the line, for the armour had at first refused to fight its way through the German positions, insisting that its task was to go through "the gap" and "pursue" the enemy. The 1st Armoured Division still held that outdated notion – shared, apparently, by Leese. It was looking for a gap.

Hull could reasonably complain about the way his division had been prepared for battle, particularly of the lack of time to weld the brigades together, but a more alert commander might at least have insisted that his division was positioned closer to the front. How had the 1st Division been briefed for its mission? What did it expect? Keightley emphasised a pursuit. Driving off from one visit with a flourish he called out, "Meet you on the Po," and left the expectation of a "sure-thing gallop". Richard Goodbody, who commanded the armoured brigade, had run a training programme in June to practise the tactics used by the Canadians in the Green Line but for OLIVE he had been briefed for a task which called for the armoured brigade to work alone except for its motor battalion. He and Hull told the officers they would "pass through the Rimini gap after the infantry had broken through the Gothic Line defences and then to go on, and on and on, day and night, until we are too exhausted to see the target".

The plan was to concentrate the division on the Foglia only on the morning of the 3rd. At dawn on the 2nd it was still at Senigallia about forty miles away. The leading elements reached the Metauro in the evening. Driving through the night the wheeled vehicle column reached the Foglia by appallingly difficult tracks on the morning of the 3rd; the drivers exhausted, the columns having been on the move for fifty hours. The tanks had an even worse journey. After a scant two-hour halt at the Metauro they moved on:

> The dust flung up by the sliding, churning tank tracks of the Shermans was so thick that drivers in the rear of the column could not see at all, but drove by listening above the roar of their engines to the bellowing of the tanks in front. Sometimes a tank would slew to the side of the road, one of its tracks ripped from the bogies by some too-exacting strain. Here and there a tank attempted an impossible gradient to try to get round some obstacle while its bruised and shaken crew clung hard to the ammunition racks inside the turret.

By the time that the fighting echelons of the division reached the Foglia on the 3rd men were stupid with exhaustion, and tanks were scattered down the line of march being recovered and repaired. Brigadier Richard Goodbody's own armoured command vehicle overturned with him in it. He was unhurt but far from fresh when he gave out his orders at about midnight on the 3rd. His 2nd Armoured Brigade would concentrate north of the Conca at S. Savino by first light on the 4th, after yet another night march. They would pass through the 46th Division and advance to the Marano and beyond. They were to start at 2.30 a.m. There was a delay to allow stragglers to catch up and to net radio sets. When the column started the regimental net of the Queen's Bays was superimposed on a BBC channel. Throughout the night the voice of Alvar Liddell reading the news was heard every half hour. Brass bands playing stirring marches cut into every message passed over the net. It was another one of those unsettling and ominous signs that the regiment was engaged in what was called "a nonsense". By 8 a.m. little more than six miles had been covered because of a late start and negotiating diversions around broken bridges and culverts.

At about noon on the 4th the main body of the 2nd Armoured Brigade was across the Conca and Goodbody was still being told that Coriano was "expected to fall soon". He was to attack through the 46th Division even though the infantry brigades in the lorries were far behind. But his leading regiment, the 10th Hussars, with a company of the 1st King's Royal Rifle Corps (the motor battalion) had gone over the S. Clemente ridge and met the Canadians on the Besanigo ridge, where they were told the real situation. The Germans held Coriano and the ridge in front in strength, Croce on their flank, and the hill-fortress Gemmano which overlooked their right rear. Keightley was misinformed and so were they as a result. The 46th Division's attack on the night of the 3rd/4th failed. The battle had slipped out of Keightley's hands, and the front was stalled.

There followed a classical situation in which a commander of a lower formation could not tell his superiors that they were talking through their hats. Goodbody had to change his plan and make what was to have been his jump-off line his objective. The artillery fire-plan was dislocated and the attack delayed. What ensued was the inevitable conclusion to three days and nights of marches and committing semi-trained units to an improvised plan without a proper reconnaissance. The history of the British Army, like others, is marred by such lapses. It was sad, though, that a débâcle like this should have occurred so late in the war.

The 2nd Armoured Brigade – without infantry, which was still south of the Conca – attacked with great courage into a setting sun against an enemy whose location had not been determined across an unsecured start line. It smacked of the Western Desert and what most soldiers then hoped were the bad old days. The attack failed, of course, and at great cost. The Queen's Bays had only nineteen out of fifty-two tanks running at the end of the battle, the 10th Hussars thirty and the 9th Lancers thirty-two. Many of the casualties were recovered, it is true, but the brigade had been thoroughly discomfited. As Kesselring had once caustically observed, "The first battles of green formations are nothing great." (Of the 5th Canadian Armoured Division on the Arielli at the end of 1943.)

The Germans' friend, the rain, fell that evening and continued in torrents on the 5th and 6th. The dust, cursed by everyone, became mud, which was worse. Streams, so easily crossed on the 4th, were impassable on the 5th. The 1st Armoured's infantry did not cross the Conca into action until the 6th, but one factor must be added. The battle was undoubtedly lost because of lack of forethought, bad management, inertia and the passage of no or faulty information and the failure of what throughout the Italian campaign had proved a second-rate infantry division. It was won by rapid reaction and sound judgment of the German commanders who unerringly sent their reserves to the correct places. The 98th Division, partially trained and untried, rushed its 117th Regiment to help the 1st Parachute Division on the evening of the 2nd, and the rest took over from the battered 71st on the 46th Division's front on the 3rd. A mixed group from the 162nd (Turkoman) Division was thrust into the line opposite the 1st Canadians. The 278th Division appeared in front of the 56th Division to relieve the 5th Mountain, of which the 100th Regiment remained at Gemmano. What remained of the 71st Division, about three weak battalions, took over a narrow front between the 278th and 98th Divisions. The crisis had been on the 3rd when the 98th Infantry Division, with the assistance of the 26th Panzer, stopped the 46th Division and ensured that the left flank of the Canadians would be exposed. When the 29th Panzer Grenadiers were available on the 4th, they used their flank position to strike at the Besanigo ridge. On the coast the 1st Canadians were held for most of September 4 in the Second Green Line by the parachutists, even though the 5th Division had turned the inland flank. Had the line not held the two Canadian divisions might have been able to by-pass the Coriano ridge on the 4th. On the night of the 3rd Kesselring had returned from a visit to the Fourteenth Army to find Herr and von Vietinghoff considering a further withdrawal. "Prolonged plain speaking crackled over the wires till past midnight, when the more even-tempered von Vietinghoff managed to calm his superior by alluding (among other things) to the German casualties, and declaring that he knew of no man who could better the performance of Herr." No retirement was ordered.

On the morning of the 6th Leese, recognising that a set-piece assault was necessary against the Coriano position, ordered the 5th Corps to carry it out while Burns crossed the Marano and exploited to the Marecchia. For this Burns was to be given the British 4th Infantry Division and a Greek brigade. The New Zealand Division, under him from the 4th for liaison purposes, was to be fully under his command on the 13th. The attack was timed for the night of the 12th/13th. After discussion with Keightley, Burns suggested that his 5th Armoured Division should be responsible for taking Coriano itself, leaving the 1st Armoured Division to attack from San Clemente.

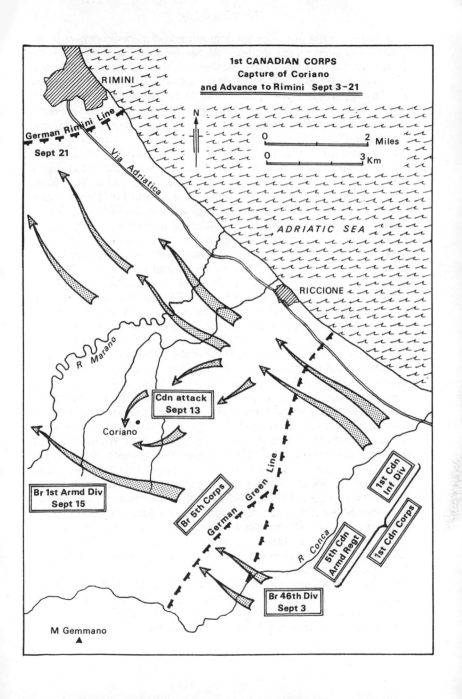

1st CANADIAN CORPS
Capture of Coriano
and Advance to Rimini Sept 3–21

N

0 .... 2 Miles
0 .... 3 Km

RIMINI

German Rimini Line
Sept 21

Via Adriatica

ADRIATIC SEA

RICCIONE

R Marano

Cdn attack
Sept 13

Coriano

Br 1st Armd Div
Sept 15

Br 5th Corps

German Green Line

R Conca

1st Cdn
Inf Div

5th Cdn
Armd Regt

1st Cdn Corps

Br 46th Div
Sept 3

M Gemmano
▲

Judging that the pause in operations marked the maximum shift of German divisions to the Adriatic, Alexander gave Clark the order to attack and directed the Desert Air Force to transfer its main effort to his front. As it happened the 1st Parachute Corps was already slowly withdrawing to the main defence zone in its sector, so the Fifth and Eighth Armies' attack coincided, marking "the beginning of a week of perhaps the heaviest fighting on both fronts that either Army had yet experienced".

The action against Coriano was highly successful. While the infantry of the 1st Armoured Division drove off the enemy from Passano and San Savino, the 5th Armoured Division took Coriano. The New Brunswick Hussars supported each battalion of the 11th Brigade, the Perths on the ridge south of the town, the Cape Breton Highlanders to the north and the Irish who cleared the houses one by one. Exploitation was done by the Westminster Regiment (Motor Infantry) and Strathcona's Horse. The preliminary bombardment was devastating and smoke screens blinded German observers and their anti-tank guns. The air operations of the Desert Air Force were particularly effective and virtually prevented the movement of German reserves, stifling local counter-attacks. In the twenty-four hours ending at sunset on September 13 more than 500 tons of bombs were dropped in 700 sorties against battlefield targets. The town was not finally cleared until the morning of the 14th by which time the 29th Panzer Grenadiers reported "considerable losses" and 14 officers and 775 other ranks were taken by the 1st Armoured Division, which bagged part of the garrison which fled from the Canadians. The 26th Panzer, 98th Infantry and 71st Infantry lost heavily too. It remained only to exploit the victory.

How shaken the Germans were is evident from a conversation between von Vietinghoff and Kesselring on the evening of the 13th:

Kesselring:	I have just returned and heard the terrible news. Will you please inform me of the situation.
Von Vietinghoff:	The depth of the penetration cannot be ascertained with accuracy as yet . . . The front has been greatly weakened.
Kesselring:	We must realise that tomorrow will be a day of great crisis.
Von Vietinghoff:	We are certain of that; all day we have been racking our brains about how to help, but we have nothing left . . .

All that Kesselring had to offer were three divisions, none of them immediately available, partly due to their having been held up by air force interdiction, but luck was with him. The 1st Armoured Division found the Fornacci stream swollen by rain and their tanks could not cross. The 4th Infantry Division was held up by shelling while passing through the 5th Armoured Division and then by Germans on the Ripabianca Ridge. The Canadians were briefly relieved and did not resume the advance until the 14th. The Germans needed no more time than that to recover. There followed a week of hard fighting first for the Ripabianca Ridge and then for S. Martino and finally S. Fortunato by the 1st Canadians with the 4th Division on their left. The Greek Brigade with the New Zealand Motor Battalion fought its way along the coast. Rimini fell to it on the 21st, and on the same day the 1st Canadian Division crossed the Marecchia into the Romagna.

In the week the Eighth Army suffered a daily average of 145 killed and 600 wounded. From the beginning of OLIVE the total figure was 14,000 with the Canadians' share being 4,511, their highest casualties for any period of equal length either before or after the Italian campaign.[11] Tanks were replaceable, the men were not. The 1st Armoured Division was disbanded, every UK infantry battalion was cut to only three rifle companies. The Germans were in worse condition. For the period August 26 to September 15 the 76th Panzer Corps reported 14,604 casualties, including 7,000 missing. By the 25th, of the Tenth Army's 92 infantry battalions only 10 had a strength of over 400 men, 16 were over 300, 26 were over 200 and 38 had less than 200.[12]

When the Canadians crossed the Marecchia on the 21st Leese signalled to Burns: "You have won a great victory. By the bitterest fighting since Alamein and Cassino you have beaten eleven German divisions and broken through into the Po Valley. The greater part of the German armies in Italy were massed against us and they have been terribly mauled. I congratulate and thank you all. We must now hit hard day and night and force them back over the Po." To Burns' units he signalled: "Well done Canada!"

It had, indeed, been a great and hard-fought victory. Mauled the enemy might have been, but not destroyed, for prolonged rain on September 20/21 helped the 76th Panzer Corps to withdraw in good order. The song sung by the 1st Canadian Division to the tune of "Lilli Marlene" – "We will debouch into the Valley of the Po" – seemed inappropriate on the 21st, not only because it was to be the New Zealand Division who would "debouch", but because the "plain" had proved a soggy disappointment. "Half seen through the fine drizzle of

September 21st it offered a dreary prospect of flat, watery and characterless land receding monotonously towards a grey horizon" to the platoons of the Princess Patricia's Light Infantry and the 48th Highlanders as they crossed the Marecchia, walked cautiously over a road on the other side and began to dig in. That was as far as they were to go and they were not at all sorry. Not many of them may have considered it, but their crossing "marked the end of an era . . . Behind lay the memorials of Eighth Army's past, San Fortunato and the Gothic Line, Florence and the Paula Line, Cassino and the Gustav and Hitler Lines, Orsogna and Ortona, and farther back still, beyond the many rivers and hills, the toe of Calabria where the army had first touched Italy one year and 18 days before."

Of all the divisions fighting in OLIVE, only the 1st Canadians and their old adversaries, the 26th Panzer and 29th Panzer Grenadiers, had been in action from the beginning, although the 46th and 56th Divisions, veterans of Salerno, could claim almost as long a service.

24

CLARK AGONISTES

In many a mountain pass,
Or meadow green and fresh,
Mass shall encounter mass
Of shuddering human flesh;
Opposing ordnance roar
Across the swathes of slain,
And blood in torrents pour
In vain – always in vain.

War Song, *by John Davidson, 1857–99*

Clark flew back to his HQ on August 10 not satisfied, for he was never to recover from the trauma of being robbed of the better part of his army, but at least in better heart. He had acquired four "British" divisions, a poor exchange for Americans he thought, but better than nothing. He could now continue to play an active and honourable role, and with good fortune debouch into the Emilian plain and take Bologna before the worst of the winter set in. Though he had convinced himself that the "British" were poor fighters and British commanders had no drive, if the 13th Corps exerted itself it could at least take some of the weight off the US divisions he intended to use as his spearhead.

In August the Fifth Army was drawn up in line along the Arno, with Lieutenant-General Willis D. Crittenberger's 4th Corps from its mouth to west of Florence. His corps itself was to be shortly transformed into a small coalitionary army. His US units were reinforced by British artillery and engineers, the 6th South African Armoured Division detached from the 13th Corps, later by the Brazilian Expeditionary Force and, briefly in December by the 8th Indian Division.

After Clark had redeployed, Keyes' 2nd Corps was concentrated behind Florence, and Kirkman's three remaining divisions extended his front to the boundary with the Eighth Army east of Highway No. 67; order from west to east the British 1st (Major-General Charles Loewen),* 8th Indian Infantry Divisions (still Major-General "Pasha" Russell), the British 6th Armoured Division (reorganised with two infantry brigades, the 1st Guards and 61st),[1] and the 1st Canadian Armoured Brigade as corps troops in support of the infantry divisions.

Clark's left and centre faced General der Panzertruppen Joachim Lemelsen's Fourteenth Army, with von Senger's depleted 14th Panzer Corps, the 16th Waffen SS Panzergrenadier Division and the 65th Infantry Division, opposite the 4th Corps; and in the vital centre covering the approach routes to Bologna, Generalleutnant Ernst Schlemm's 1st Parachute Corps with the 362nd, 4th Parachute and 356th Infantry Divisions. The 13th Corps faced, from west to east, the 715th, the 334th and 305th Infantry Divisions, part of the right wing of the Tenth Army under the 51st Mountain Corps. All these were occupying the forward or outpost zone of the Gothic Line, whose main defences ran eastwards from a point on the coast south of La Spezia, along the forward slopes of the Apennines to cover the Futa and Il Giogo passes and so into the 51st Corps sector.

As Harding had perceived, the most promising axis of advance was in the centre where there were three possible routes: Highway No. 64 connecting Pistoia and Bologna, the direct Highway No. 65 from Florence running through the Futa and Radicosa passes, and a secondary route joining it via the Giogo Pass and the town of Firenzuola. Further east there were secondary routes leading to Imola, Faenza and Forli, all in the 13th Corps sector.

None of these routes was at all easy, and Clark, without any trained mountain troops to infiltrate the high ground, had a very tough nut to crack, but he did not flinch. He had absolute confidence in his US troops and the ability of his commanders to drive them on through every obstacle. According to conventional tactics, when crossing a river or a range pierced by a number of passes, the best plan is to attack on as many routes as possible, and exploit a breakthrough with the reserve, but Alexander's division of the armies had left the Fifth Army too weak for this. Accordingly, Clark decided to hold with his left, ordering Crittenberger to maintain sufficient pressure to contain the 14th Panzer Corps with his 4th Corps, preventing any transfer of its

---

* Loewen was a Canadian officer, late Royal Artillery, in the British service, who was to have a distinguished career. He was refreshingly direct, outspoken and humorous.

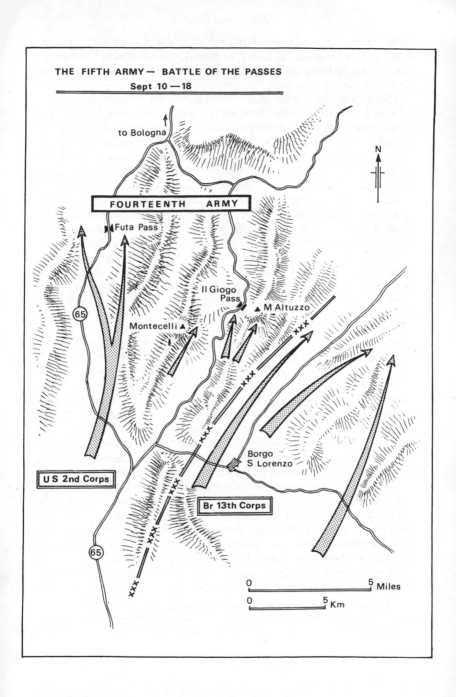

THE FIFTH ARMY — BATTLE OF THE PASSES
Sept 10 — 18

to Bologna

N

FOURTEENTH ARMY

Futa Pass

Il Giogo Pass

M Altuzzo

65

Montecelli

Borgo
S Lorenzo

U S 2nd Corps

Br 13th Corps

65

0   5 Miles

0   5 Km

divisions to the centre, and launch Keyes' 2nd Corps in the centre against the Futa pass. Kirkman, he hoped, would exert enough pressure on his right to keep up with and broaden the front of his main attack.

There was one factor that compensated for Clark's lack of an adequate reserve. If Operation OLIVE prospered it would draw off Kesselring's army group reserves, especially the 26th Panzer and the 29th Panzer Grenadier Divisions and hold the 1st Parachute Division on the Eighth Army front. When these elite troops were detected on the Eighth Army front Alexander would "pull the lanyard", and the Fifth Army would explode into action. Before this major attack could be developed the German outpost positions had to be driven in, a formidable enough task in itself, but while preparations were being made for this Kesselring, who by this date had seen the advantages of an orderly occupation of the main defences, ordered a phased withdrawal, closely followed up but not unduly hustled by the Fifth Army. The main attack was not to be launched until September 12/13.

As, in Clark's opinion, Kirkman was to prove as great a disappointment as had McCreery and Freyberg earlier in the year, and their mutual incompatibility was to prove a stumbling block in the operations that followed, it is necessary to explain and, we emphasise, understand their opposing points of view. As said, Clark's military philosophy was to go all out with every man he had as long as there was an infantryman on his feet until the objective was secured. We have already described the limitations in his tactical knowledge. Kirkman was no pussyfooter, far from it – he too could drive his divisional commanders – but no British officer could afford to purchase ground with a lavish effusion of blood. Even Clark, as we shall see, was to run out of that precious currency. Patience and skills were necessary ingredients of British tactics, because the 13th Corps, with the merest trickle of replacements available, could only afford one battle fought *à outrance* on Clark's lines.

There was, however more in their relationship than military differences. Neither was an outgoing personality. Clark could be formally cordial, but he lacked geniality. On August 12 Kirkman when he reported to HQ Fifth Army after coming officially under Clark's command was greeted with a band and a guard of honour. What Clark could not do was to sit down with a bottle of whisky and two glasses and in the course of an intimate discussion on the forthcoming battle see what made this reserved English general tick, though whether that would have worked is doubtful. Kirkman had excellent manners but he was not convivial. In his diary is an amusing but slightly disapproving account of a luncheon given at HQ Fifth Army for the British Prime

Minister, where there was (in his opinion) too much to eat and far too much to drink, and "everyone sweated a lot". (Winston Churchill appeared greatly to enjoy himself.) In any case Clark, on his side, had a low opinion of British generals, if not of British soldiers, and deeply distrusted the British hegemony in the Mediterranean theatre and this had struck too deep a root to allow any relationship with a British officer to prosper. Clark, except for one occasion we shall describe shortly, disliked confrontations, as we have already seen. Unlike Eisenhower, who once squashed Montgomery with "Hey, you can't talk to me like that! I'm your boss," Clark preferred to dissemble, or to send the egregious Brann with difficult questions or unwelcome orders. On his side Kirkman was a high-minded, dignified officer, impossible to ruffle, but stiff in bearing and opinion. For him behaviour was either good or bad, military solutions either right or wrong. He was not the far too common bigoted Englishman who looked down on Americans, but he would not give an inch when he considered some proposed action tactical "nonsense". He was amused rather than gratified when, on being asked by Brann to surrender his only good road to the 2nd Corps, he agreed at once and Brann, probably greatly relieved, described his attitude as "most public spirited". Kirkman wrote in his diary, "A peculiar attitude, and typically American. The operation is not a competition between the 2nd and 13th Corps!" (But he was mistaken, it was.)

While Clark developed his plans for the offensive Kirkman wrestled with the problems of working with the Fifth Army. Many of these could have been obviated by consultation, good staff duties and a strong chief of staff, but there is no record of Gruenther ever visiting Kirkman (in the way Harding did, even after the transfer, to keep Kirkman *au fait* with Alexander's future plans): it was always Brann. His first disappointment was with Clark's plan. Unreasonably, Kirkman could not see how impossible it was for Clark to accept the subsidiary role implicit, as he thought, in the revised plan for two separate offensives. He was dismayed when Clark told him that far from limiting his aim to deceiving Kesselring about the location of the Allied *Schwerpunkt*, followed by a push when the Fourteenth Army had thinned out, he planned to mount a full-scale offensive in which Kirkman's jaded and under-strength divisions were to play a leading part: "And so again I am involved in planning a thrust for Bologna, under Fifth Army who are not easy to work with, and with very doubtful resources. Clearly we must do all we can when the time comes, but if our attack is put in prematurely the very thing will happen which I wanted to avoid, heavy casualties and slow progress and in fact not a profitable operation." Not

371

surprisingly HQ Eighth Army were "unhelpful and unsympathetic" when Kirkman complained; the harder Clark pushed, the more it would help OLIVE.

When weighing the evidence of private diaries it should be borne in mind that they serve the useful purpose of allowing the diarist to let off harmlessly the steam of resentment, frustration or temporary annoyance, and this is as true of Kirkman's as it is of Clark's. The rigid loyalty Kirkman gave to whoever was ordained to be his commander, and demanded himself, was being severely tried by disappointment, fatigue and irritation with the Fifth Army's (to him) untidy methods and unsound tactics. He was "grousing", to use his own phrase. Keyes was being obstructive about the use of roads and the inter-corps boundary. (Keyes was not an easy man. Kirkman made a point of calling on his neighbour before the transfer, but Keyes' response was that he was not empowered to discuss any operational questions with him, an unnecessary snub, and a foolish one.) The next thing that annoyed him was an order that Keyes with two divisions would attack the German positions north of the Arno through his own right-hand sector, right across his communications, which Kirkman considered "nonsense". Then the reconnaissance parties of nine US artillery battalions arrived without warning inside the 13th Corps boundary to prepare their positions. These differences were resolved on the 29th by the German withdrawal, but they could have been prevented by a little foresight, the essence of staff work. Kirkman did not allow his own subordinates the luxury of grousing. He spoke sharply to Major-General Charles Loewen when he did, telling him that if the Fifth Army wanted things done in a certain way its orders had to be obeyed.[2]

By September 6 the Fifth Army had advanced without much opposition to a depth of five to six miles all along its front. During this period Clark received, via the British, information from the Ultra source that led him to review his plans. Hitler had intervened to instruct Kesselring to hold the Futa pass as strongly as possible, as that is where he believed the enemy was likely to make his main effort. It was also revealed that the inter-army boundary between the Tenth and the Fourteenth lay a short distance east of the Il Giogo pass. Though the natural defences of the Giogo were far stronger than the Futa, Clark correctly decided that to shift his main attack to the right would surprise the enemy, and it was conventionally good tactics to strike at the seam joining two armies. This required a readjustment of the boundary between the 2nd Corps and the 13th. The road over the Giogo was the secondary Road No. 6524, which branched off Highway No. 65 south of S. Pietro, looped its way up the steep slopes to the

Giogo and ended at Firenzuola where it joined Road No. 6528, leading back to Highway No. 65 on the left, and on the right swung north over the mountain range to Imola. It was obvious that this important road net should be under one command and used by troops with the same logistic requirements, and so was willingly ceded by Kirkman to Keyes when (as said) he was approached by Brann.

The new plan was a typical American broad-front approach. On the right of the 4th Corps the South African Armoured Division was to put in a limited attack, and Major-General Charles W. Ryder's veteran 34th Division was directed on the Futa pass, with the mission of convincing the enemy that this was still the American objective. The initial assault on the Giogo was to be made by the 91st Division (Major-General William G. Livesay) which had joined the Fifth Army in July, with the 85th (Major-General John B. Coulter) in reserve, each reinforced by an artillery group. On the right again Kirkman was ordered to extend the front of the attack with his two infantry divisions from Borgo S. Lorenzo up Road No. 6521 across his front to Highway No. 67. This was a perfectly good plan, but at first it was botched in execution. The Giogo pass was guarded to left and right by two great summits, Montecelli and M. Altuzzo, it was strongly fortified with the usual concrete casemates, earth and log firing positions and caves in which the infantry could shelter, all well concealed. The slopes were steep, broken by low, rocky cliffs and outcrops, and corrugated by spurs, the whole covered with dense brushwood. It was not country that demanded the skill of a mountaineer, but it required very fit and active men, and was impossible for the manoeuvre of formed bodies.

For some reason the attack was spread too wide and the 85th Division's delayed, possibly because of erroneous intelligence that the pass was only lightly held. In fact its defenders were the 12th Regiment of the 4th Parachute Division, under strength and full of replacements, but with ample fire-power. (Its other two regiments were in the area of the Futa pass.) Two of Livesay's regiments were directed against the heights west of Montecelli as far as Highway No. 65, and only one regiment on Montecelli itself whose commander believed that he could also capture M. Altuzzo. The unwisdom of such dispersal of effort and of underestimating such an enemy as the German parachute infantry was soon to be painfully demonstrated.

Alexander duly gave the order to "pull the lanyard" and the Fifth Army offensive began on September 12. The 34th Division, whose role was simply diversion, pressed so hard and unremittingly towards the Futa pass that, combined with the feebleness of the attack by the 363rd Infantry on Montecelli, made with two battalions, Lemelsen was completely deceived, and unable even when he saw the danger to move any reserves to the Giogo. The 363rd, toiling up the slopes, lost in the brushwood and afflicted by the radio blackouts, went to ground under intense fire from artillery, mortars and machine guns.* Their forward positions being unknown they could not be given artillery support and so the attack in the key sector failed.

The American system then was effectively applied. Clark applied the spur to Keyes, who passed it on with redoubled emphasis to Livesay, who in turn gingered up the regimental commander, ordering him to recommence his attack. Once more it faltered, but the last reserve, the third battalion, was thrown in and a slow advance was sustained towards the long crest of Montecelli. The US Army official historian has well described the tremendous and successful fight of the 363rd: ". . . those who bore the brunt of the fighting at critical points sometimes constituted no more than a platoon or less, seldom more than a company. Little clusters of men struggled doggedly up rocky ravines and draws separated by narrow fingers of forested ridges, climbing laboriously squad by squad, fighting their way forward yard by yard, often not knowing the location of the closest friendly unit . . ." – a description any soldier who has had the doubtful pleasure of fighting in mountainous terrain will recognise as vivid and accurate.[3] There is another frustrating aspect of such fighting. It is impossible for inexperienced staff officers and commanders, looking at their maps far below, to understand why the situation reports, such as they are, are so vague and concerned companies and platoons and not the generous chinagraph "goose-eggs" representing battalions and regiments, and also why there is so little progress. The reason is that if movement is largely vertical, half a mile forward may mean a climb of 400–500 feet.

On the 15th it was an officer and ten men of Company B who opened the way for it to set foot on the crest of Montecelli, and paved the way for the fall of the position, with severe loss. Attacks were followed by counter and re-attack, and many deeds of heroism and self-sacrifice went unnoticed, but one which was recognised and rewarded by the Congressional Medal of Honour was the defence of his company perimeter by Private (First Class) Oscar G. Johnson. He, the last man in his squad left on his feet, collected his comrades' weapons and ammunition and during part of the 16th and all the following night kept up so steady and well-directed a fire that every attack on his front failed.

* The reader should bear in mind that in all these mountain battles the crude radios of those days were liable to interruption by "shadow", due to the lie of the land, loud static and interference; to say nothing of being dropped over cliffs, the operators being hit or running out of batteries until the next convoy of porters scaled the mountainside.

Later forty of the dead around the company position were in front of his post. On the 18th Montecelli fell to the 363rd Infantry, and Altuzzo to the 338th of Coulter's division after an equally hard fight. The US infantry, assisted by excellent gunnery by the artillery, had broken through the Gothic Line, at the cost of 2,713 casualties in six days' fighting. It was a magnificent feat of arms, and a victory that must rank high even in the annals of the US Army. Lemelsen conceded defeat. Denied reinforcement, as every unit that could be spared had gone to the aid of the Tenth Army, now under continuous heavy pressure, he ordered a general withdrawal. The mountains behind the Gothic Line, he thought rightly, offered suitable fall-back positions where he could delay the Fifth Army almost indefinitely as winter set in.

While the battle of the passes was being fought the 13th Corps successfully breached the Gothic Line in its sector. Kirkman's plan was also to attack with all his divisions at once. The 1st Division supported by a squadron of the Ontario Regiment's tanks was to advance up the road Borgo S. Lorenzo–Faenza, the 8th Indian with a squadron of the Calgaries over the roadless watershed that lay between the Faenza road and Highway No. 67, and the 6th Armoured Division up Highway No. 67 to Forli, as Harding had told Kirkman it would be needed later as a supply route for the Eighth Army. On September 11 Clark warned Kirkman to be ready to attack on the 13th, but both the infantry division commanders immediately protested in a manner that would never have been tolerated in the US Army. (Nor indeed in the Eighth under Montgomery.) Loewen argued that it was wrong to attack in his sector at all, and "Pasha" Russell complained of being rushed and demanded more time for preparation. Kirkman promptly sat on both of them, pointing out that only the 715th Division opposed them, and ordered them in for a coordinating conference, where no further difficulties were voiced. The real difficulty was poor communications made impassable in many places by demolitions.

Nevertheless, the difficulties were overcome. On the 13th and 14th the corps battled away with very little progress, but on the 15th both the infantry divisions reported that they were through the main Gothic defences, collecting prisoners and deserters from the luckless 715th Division. (The one already shattered once by Truscott in May and since rebuilt.) On that day Kirkman was summoned to meet the Army Commander, General Keyes and General Coulter at HQ 1st Division for the purpose of arranging the move of one of Coulter's RCTs through Loewen's sector so as to loosen up the enemy on the extreme right of the 2nd Corps. The American officers were understandably downcast by their lack of progress after three days of intense fighting:

"They are bitterly disappointed and do not know what to do," he recorded, adding some scathing criticisms of American tactics. Clark was, however, cheered by the 13th Corps' success. He generously complimented Kirkman, and General Gruenther telephoned him from HQ Fifth Army to add his congratulations. Sadly, this marked the end of the honeymoon, such as it was, between the Americans and the British, though eventually the operation ended with the 13th Corps on its objectives. The 1st Division secured the Cascaglia pass on the 20th, and reached Marradi and Palzuola on the 24th, the Mahrattas captured M. Veruca, on the 17th the Gurkhas stood triumphant on the peak of the strangely named Femmina Morte and the 6th Armoured captured S. Benedetto in Alpe on Highway No. 67.

On September 24 as soon as mopping up at the Il Giogo pass was complete Clark wasted no time in setting Keyes going again, with three divisions aligned on the direct route to Bologna and the 88th Division trying a fresh line on Road No. 6528, the road to Imola. Brigadier-General Paul W. Kendall, a great thruster, formerly the deputy-commander during DIADEM, who was shortly to earn his second star in the field, captured the village of Castel del Rio on the 25th. Assisted by a new factor in the war, Italian partisans, he occupied the important height of M. Battaglia ("Battle Mountain" to the Americans) and held it against a number of desperate counter-attacks. However, it was soon found that the road was too small and too badly damaged to carry more than a division. It followed the winding course of the Santerno river along a valley with precipitous sides, long stretches of its corniche sections blown and the bridge at Castel del Rio destroyed. Clark ordered Kirkman to relieve the garrison of "Battle Mountain" and take over the route.

Progress everywhere now became slow. The laconic entry "rain" recurs in Kirkman's diary, with descriptions of the horrific demolitions: "The sappers under continual shell and mortar fire." Engineers were once more as important as infantry, their efforts were assisted by Italian labour and any troops who could be spared, such as the now unemployed anti-aircraft artillery. They, under Royal Engineer instruction, soon learnt how to erect Bailey bridging. It was a very difficult period for the 13th Corps, between infantry wastage, lack of replacements and sheer physical exhaustion. When General Clark complained that British officers did not drive their men like his he was perfectly correct. They had no alternative course to keeping the pressure up by small, skilled attacks and tactics designed to economise in life and limb. There was an unofficial phrase in vogue in those days, "leaning on the enemy". In essence it was based on vigorous patrolling with the aim of locating the forward enemy posts, obtaining prisoners and generally harrying the enemy. Most battalions formed a special patrol unit of selected men, but this cut two ways, as though it made for efficiency it increased the wastage of the best. The artillery observers kept the enemy under close scrutiny and made their lives as uncomfortable as possible. When opportunity offered, exposed positions were taken out, often with the help of tanks. It was a not uncommon sight to see a troop commander and his crews hacking away at rocks and boulders with pick, shovel and crowbar to get a single tank up to a firing platform.

It was a form of warfare unpopular with British soldiers who, if given a choice, would have preferred either a policy of live and let live, or to "have a good bash at the buggers". The artillery brigadier of the 6th Armoured Division was addicted to strolling about in the front line. On one occasion when a minor operation was taking place, he found the artillery observing officer trying to land a shell on a knife-edge crest, the assault force resting peaceably in some well-chosen ground dead to enemy observation while he alternated his "plus" and "minus" rounds, and the supporting infantry mortar platoon silent. He asked the NCO in charge why he was not engaging the enemy, to receive the reply, "Well, sir, if we shoot at them they'll only shoot back at us." It is not suggested that this extreme attitude was typical or widespread, but it was certainly symptomatic.[4] There was a certain amount of the inevitable "skiving" in the front line, as in all armies, born of excessive fatigue as much as anything else. Great pains were taken to rest men, especially the junior leaders, rotate units out of the line and if possible send parties to rest camps. The result was that the soldiers, confident that they were not being treated as expendable cannon-fodder, were able to keep going in the line for about twice as long as the hard-driven GIs. When an all-out effort was required they responded, as the 78th Infantry Division was shortly to demonstrate.

Clark's third drive on Bologna began on October 1, on the same pattern as before, a broad-front offensive with the South Africans on the left and the 34th, 91st, 85th and 88th Divisions astride Highway No. 65, with the objective of forcing the line of the Livergnano escarpment, marked by the peaks M. Adone, M. Belmonte and M. Grande, which continued eastward through another tangle of summits, M. Pieve, M. Spaduro and M. Acqua Salata, ending in an extraordinary feature, the Vena del Gesso, like a black sea-cliff, ending at the Santerno valley opposite Tossignano. Clark had asked for a reinforcement for the 13th Corps and Alexander had sent him the veteran 78th Division, newly returned to the Eighth Army from Egypt, where it had been resting and re-training. It was down to three instead of four rifle companies per battalion, but still full of fight, and Kirkman hoped to strike some heavy blows with it.* Clark ordered Kirkman to relieve Kendall's 88th Division, which had been slowly forcing its way towards M. la Pieve, and move his left boundary once more to the west. Accordingly he introduced the 78th Division, and gave Arbuthnott the mission of capturing the tangle of summits north-east of M. la Pieve.

Ten days of bitter fighting had seen little progress. By the 15th the US 2nd Corps had secured only one of its three objectives, M. Grande, and the 78th Division was not to clear the Pieve–Spaduro–Acqua Salata triangle until the 24th. In the opinion of its veterans that three weeks' fighting was the most severe of all its battles from the autumn of 1942 to the end of the war. Its 38th all-Irish Brigade arrived on the 5th/6th and attacked an enemy outpost position on Point 382 the following night, and secured it after three attempts. The 11th Brigade made five consecutive attacks on M. la Pieve and occupied it after the sixth, the enemy having abandoned it. The 36th Brigade took M. Acqua Salata at its second attempt. The Irish returned to the attack with two unsuccessful attempts against M. Spaduro, then secured a lodgment half-way up it with the third and took it at the fourth. None of these successes was cheaply bought. The 2nd Lancashire Fusiliers lost 93 men in one attack, leaving it with only 165 in its rifle companies.[5]

Clark persisted in his offensive with a determination that might have earned the admiration of Earl Haig in the earlier war, but he was defeated by a combination of appalling weather, bitter German resistance and some chilling arithmetic which became apparent by the end of the first fortnight. His casualty rate rose to a level which the US replacement system in Italy could not match, and the supplies of artillery ammunition on which he depended for the intense bombardments now necessary to prepare every advance began to fall short because of the demands of the US armies in France. Deeply chagrined, Clark was forced to halt his offensive on the 27th. He blamed Kirkman, whose divisions, extended over a long front with atrocious communications, were now echeloned well behind the 2nd Corps. His temper became frayed and not only his, Kirkman noted:

> Everyone is getting slightly quarrelsome these days. Mark Clark rang me up in a bad temper before I went out and said that it was never his intention that his 88 Div should attack high ground to get

---

* General Keightley had left to command the 5th Corps in Eighth Army, and his successor had fallen ill. It was commanded from October 10 by the most experienced and able officer who for the past year had commanded its 11th Brigade, Major-General R. K. Arbuthnott.

78 Div on and that it should stop at once.(!) I pointed out that 88 Div were attacking within their own boundary as laid down by his own staff and that 78 Div had taken over within their boundary to help them. To this he had no reply. Charles Loewen groused that . . . 8th Indian had done nothing for days and did not protect his right flank, Russell groused about 1 Div . . . when he wanted to use their roads they made endless difficulties . . . Arbuthnott rang up saying that 1 Div were not planning to get along quickly enough to protect his right flank . . . Everyone sees only their difficulties and never anybody else's . . . the fact is every one is getting a bit tired.

Two days later, on the 14th, when Kirkman was making his usual round of his front and clambering up to view-points on mountain tops, he was peremptorily summoned to a meeting with Clark. There he found Gruenther, Keyes, Brann and various staff officers ready to present the latest casualty figures for the Fifth Army, and was virtually arraigned in public for his lack of drive. The significant figures were: US troops, 13,082 casualties, prisoners taken, 2,451; British (Indian and Canadian), 7,087 and 506. Kirkman does not make it clear how he defended himself, if at all. He recorded that "it was all most unpleasant" and concluded characteristically: "Arrived here [back at his HQ] exhausted and ill-tempered at 17.30 having been on the road, climbing mountains and listening to Clark for 11 hours." This was extraordinary behaviour on the part of Clark, even allowing for his deep disappointment, his highly strung nature and his conviction that the British lacked all fighting spirit. He was politically extremely acute and knew perfectly well how a senior Allied officer should be handled, and that it would have been unwise to administer so calculated and public a rebuke to even a senior US Army officer. He had a perfect right to demand greater exertions from a subordinate, but the proper course was to speak to him privately, and if that had no effect, to ask Alexander to relieve him. The fact was he had never failed to cover himself after a failure. Now he smelt complete failure in the autumn air, and he needed a scapegoat, the last in the line of Dawley, Lucas, McCreery and Freyberg.[6]

Only two miles of the high country separated him from the watershed after which it was downhill for fifteen miles to Bologna. One more heave, 5,000 replacements more might enable his army to make it. He railed at the Eighth Army for keeping five divisions in reserve, and that Alexander had some 50,000 uniformed men in his vast command and logistic organisation. There were 5,000 infantry replacements in the theatre, earmarked for Devers' army group in France, but he, on the brink of success, was stalled for want of men. His mood was not improved by a letter from Devers telling him that he was driving his troops too hard. It was all the fault of the British, who wished the Eighth Army to get the credit for a victory in Italy. "We are caught in the British Empire machine." He was sent 3,000 infantry replacements at the end of October, but it was not enough. His divisions were burnt out, and had to be left in peace to recover until the final offensive opened on April 14. The official figure for the Fifth Army's casualties from September 20 to October 26 was 15,716. The hard-fighting 88th Division alone lost 5,026, and after receiving replacements was short of 1,243 all ranks; the majority combat soldiers. These are terrible statistics.[7]

Clark did not have long to repine. On November 24 a salve was provided for his bruised spirit. A signal, apparently quite unexpected, arrived from the British Prime Minister, with the glad news that he was to be promoted to command of the Allied Armies in Italy. General Dill, the British representative to the Combined Chiefs of Staff in Washington had died, Maitland Wilson was to replace him and Alexander was to command the Mediterranean theatre. Many changes took place. Leese had left at the end of September for Burma and, to Clark's disgust, the "feather duster" McCreery had been given command of the Eighth Army.[8] Truscott returned from France to command the Fifth. Kirkman was attacked by arthritis and returned to a home command in England. The 13th Corps was returned to the Eighth Army and Harding left HQ AAI to command it in its last battles. Clark assumed command of the Allied armies in mid-December, re-named HQ 15th Army Group once more, taking Gruenther and Brann with him. There were also changes on the other side. On February 15 von Vietinghoff was relieved by Traugott Herr, and on March 9 Hitler appointed Kesselring Commander-in-Chief, West, and so the firm hand that had directed the German defence for so long was removed. His place was taken by von Vietinghoff. Kesselring showed a last flash of his old spirit when von Vietinghoff asked for terms in April. He suspended him at once, and also General Wentzell his chief of staff, but on learning of Hitler's death, relented.

The Canadian Corps complete was withdrawn by the Canadian Government from Italy and united with the Canadian Army in 21st Army Group in time for the final battles on the frontier of Germany.

Under McCreery's careful handling that tired old steeple-chaser, the Eighth Army – "good for one more race" – battled on until the end of December.[9] On October 24 it crossed the Savio, on the 31st the Ronco, on November 9 it captured Forli and on the 16th Highway No. 64 was cleared through the length of the Apennines. On the 26th it crossed the Lamone, Ravenna fell on December 4, Faenza on the 16th, and all operations ceased on the 29th. The Eighth Army may not have been able to carry the ball alone, but it certainly made a number of touchdowns or, as McCreery might have preferred, could still take a number of stiff fences until it required a rest before the next meeting.

BREAKTHROUGH

It brings to a conclusion the work of as gallant an army as ever marched, and brings to a pitch of fame the military reputation of a commander who has always enjoyed the confidence of the House of Commons.

Winston Churchill, in the Commons, May 2, 1945

No one who has followed our account of the Allied operations in Italy is likely to conclude that they were a model of the military art, yet Churchill's tribute was fairly earned. Alexander, Clark and their generals consistently displayed two qualities – "leadership" and the "maintenance of the aim" – without which all other military virtues are of no value. Their leadership ensured that their much-tried troops were willing to make yet one more effort; in 1945 after an autumn and winter of hard fighting. Condemned to what they perceived as a subsidiary mission, and weakened by further detachments – three Commonwealth divisions to cope with internal strife in Greece, the Canadians and a British infantry division to north-west Europe – their determination to continue to attack the enemy never faltered.

The question of morale was certainly a matter for concern. The winter of 1944–5 was exceptionally cold. Some of the 11th (Ontario) Armoured Regiment, no strangers to arctic conditions, who maintained a vedette on the slopes of M. Grande in the 13th Corps sector with no shelter other than their tanks, asserted that it was by far the most unpleasant period of their service in Italy. The front-line troops dug in more for warmth than protection from fire – burrows they were reluctant to leave – while in the rear the more self-reliant built themselves a wonderful collection of shacks, shanties, hoochies, wigwams and bustees from looted material. Patrols on being sent out to reconnoitre or secure prisoners went to ground once out of sight of their own front line, to return after a plausible interval and report that they had made no contact with the enemy. On the banks of the Senio, where the Tenth and Eighth Armies were separated in places only by the width of the great dykes twenty-five feet high, things were different. When Kesselring had decreed that the German static defence was to be aggressive, and the policy of live and let live was forbidden, the Eighth Army responded in kind.

The morale of the Polish Corps and the US 92nd (Negro) Infantry caused great anxiety. The Polish problem was by far the most serious, as it could have deprived Clark of the services of the whole of the 2nd Polish Corps. The Poles were highly politicised down to the youngest private soldier, and when they heard that Allied leaders had agreed at the Yalta Conference to cede part of eastern Poland to Soviet Russia there was a very real possibility that they would refuse to fight for an alliance that had betrayed them. This was averted by the tactful handling of McCreery and Clark, by the loyalty of Anders and the influence of the Polish Government in exile in London.

The trouble with the 92nd Division arose from the fact that it was, in effect, the American equivalent of a "colonial" division, with black NCOs and rank and file, some black officers, but the command and staff mainly white. Such a unit can only be effective if pride of race is actually encouraged and only the best of white officers employed, and it was precisely these two essentials that were ignored. The weakness of its infantry was aggravated by the general practice of filling the ranks with what was left after the demands of the technical arms and services had been met. Some 13 per cent of the black riflemen were illiterate.

The division held a perhaps over-wide sector of the long US 4th Corps front and, like the rest of General Crittenberger's units, its defensive localities were widely dispersed and expected to cover the gaps and the front by active patrolling, which it failed to do. The German 51st Mountain Corps had identified the positions of the 92nd Division and after careful observation decided that it was a ripe target for a raid designed to wreck it as an effective fighting unit. On Boxing Day, December 26, 1944 a *Kampfgruppe* of two line and two mountain infantry battalions with ample artillery support achieved complete surprise, and though some of the infantry fought with great courage the great majority fled the battlefield leaving a wide gap in the 4th Corps front. For a brief period Operation WINTERGEWITTE ("Winter thunder-storm") caused a considerable "flap" as it was thought that it prefaced a larger offensive. Ironically, the gap was plugged and the raiders chased back by two brigades of the 8th Indian Division lent by the Eighth Army to the Fifth to provide General Crittenberger with a corps reserve. Later, in February, the division was entrusted with a local offensive with the object of improving the corps line, but failed again dismally. It was then reconstituted as a mixed division with one black regiment composed of the best of its infantry, one "Nisei" (US-born Japanese) regiment and a regiment of anti-aircraft artillerymen re-trained as infantry. It fought rather better in the April offensive, when its role was to mount a diversionary attack up the Ligurian coast.[1]

Apart from the obvious measures of regular rest, recreation and close attention to health and general well-being, the most effective way to maintain morale is purposeful activity. Though the great offensive was not to be launched until the first week in April both the Allied armies were kept busy. The last service of the gallant and ever aggressive Canadians in Italy was to eliminate two troublesome bridgeheads on the right bank of the Senio. McCreery kept his divisions out of the line hard at work in strenuous river-crossing exercises. Truscott was more fortunate in the matter of replacements, as he was allotted 7,000 surplus to divisional establishments. These he attached for training to the regiments they would join to make good casualties. Better still, a new specialist unit, the US 10th Mountain Division, joined the Fifth Army. Elitism ran counter to US Army traditions (although the superiority of the US Airborne divisions had already breached that principle) but inevitably when the 10th Division was formed it attracted fit, adventurous young men with college educations, including expert rock-climbers and skiers.

Truscott put this welcome reinforcement to good use. Soon after he had assumed command he concluded that it would be bad tactics to renew the attack on Bologna along the direct axis (Highway No. 65) where the autumn offensive had already failed. Although the US 2nd Corps was tantalisingly close to the city it still had to traverse some very difficult mountain country and the German defences on this obvious approach were well developed and proof against even the heaviest bombardment. Far better, thought Truscott, to choose the longer and more difficult route west of the River Reno and Highway No. 64. There the right flank of the 4th Corps, held by the Brazilian Expeditionary Force, angled back from the left of the 2nd Corps as General Crittenberger's role in that sector was to guard General Keyes' left flank. The mission given to the 10th Mountain Division, supported by the Brazilians, was to clear the heights west of the Reno and secure a good jump-off line some six miles ahead. This was accomplished between February 18 and March 5, the division greatly distinguishing itself in this its first action. The opening move was the escalade of a 1,500-foot precipice flanking the axis of advance of the 86th Mountain

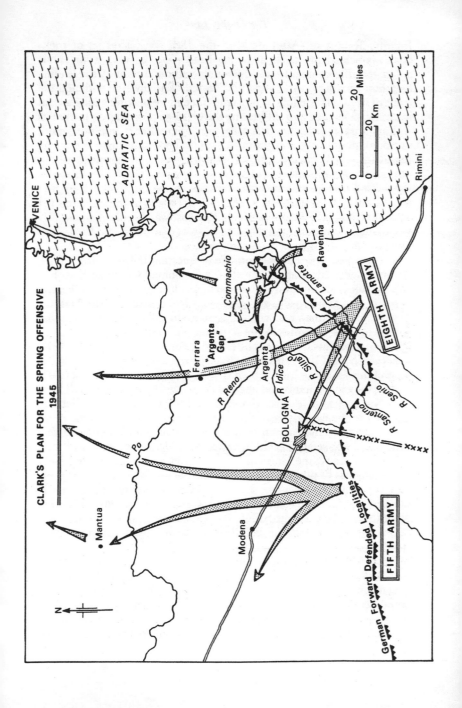

CLARK'S PLAN FOR THE SPRING OFFENSIVE 1945

Infantry Regiment. After dark on the 18th special teams of rock-climbers scaled the cliffs attaching fixed ropes as they went. Thus aided, the rifle companies clambered up without difficulty, the leading battalion arriving on the crest undetected. The division widened the front of its attack the following night, once more making a long ascent in complete silence and infiltrating the German positions on the crests without attracting hostile defensive fire. Thereafter it employed more orthodox tactics with maximum air support and, well supported by the Brazilians, established a nine-mile-wide new front commanding the northern descending slopes of the range. It was an admirable display of specialised battle-craft and strict discipline for a division in its first action, but not cheap, bearing in mind that many of the rank and file were potential NCOs and officers. The cost was 1,140, of whom 309 were killed. Truscott then closed the operation down and turned his attention to planning his main offensive.

In retrospect it seems reasonable to question the need for a final, all-out offensive in Italy. After all, the Combined Chiefs of Staff had already ruled out any far-reaching strategic development in the theatre, it was bound to be costly, not least in civilian casualties. Surely it was obvious that German resistance was about to collapse? In the west the victory of the US armies in the Ardennes had virtually eliminated the German capability for further offensive action. In February the American, British and Canadian armies had cleared the "Siegfried" positions west of the Rhine. In March both British and Americans were across it and fighting in the industrial heart of Germany. By April 1 the US First and Ninth Armies encircled the Ruhr, trapping 325,000 German troops. On the eastern front the vast Soviet armies were on the move from Danzig to the eastern frontier of Austria. Nevertheless, at that time it did not seem that the war was likely to end as early as it did. Hitler was urging the German armies to fight to the bitter end, there were rumours of plans for a fanatical last stand in the Bavarian Alps, and the solid evidence of the extraordinary courage and tenacity displayed by German soldiers on every front. The only possible option open to the Allies once they had decided on the goal of unconditional surrender was to continue at full pressure in Italy, as on every other front.

Alexander's mission remained clear – to pin as many German divisions in Italy as possible. He considered, quite correctly, that the best means to that end was the liquidation of Army Group "C". To this could be added the personal and perfectly legitimate ambitions of his three newly appointed commanders. Neither Truscott nor McCreery would have been fit to hold their high appointments had they lacked basic aggressiveness, the urge to engage the enemy. Clark was rather different. He ardently desired renown and at last he was in an operational position to win it, preferably with a spearhead of United States Army divisions. Rightly, he insisted that the 15th Army Group offensive should not be delayed until May, when the weather and going would be perfect, but launched in the first week in April.

While HQ 15th Army Group improved its positions and discussed the plans put forward by its army commanders, Army Group "C" braced itself to meet the expected Allied offensive. Its new commander, von Vietinghoff, considered his position, and found it dire. Admittedly his main front was naturally very strong. The stretch of mountains from the Ligurian coast to Highway No. 64 was easily defended. The centre, in front of Bologna, was naturally strong and well fortified. If the Allies chose to make their main effort on the Adriatic flank they would be faced in succession with assault crossings of the Senio, the Santerno, the Sillaro, the Idice (all prepared for defence) and finally the Reno. But those and the fighting-power of his soldiers were von Vietinghoff's only assets. He had no strategic reserve. Kesselring, still his superior commander, had removed four divisions from Italy, but there remained eight divisions in each of the two armies, two veteran divisions, the 90th and 29th Panzer Grenadiers as his only mobile operational reserve, two German divisions for the security of the rear areas against the swarming Italian partisans, and five useless Axis-oriented Italian divisions constituting the "Army of Liguria". Von Vietinghoff's sole hope of keeping his armies in being, endorsed by Kesselring, was a fighting withdrawal from his winter position first to the line of the Po, then the Adige and finally to the "*Voralpenstellung*" guarding the passes through the Alps. This plan, the one most feared by Alexander and Clark, because it could rob them of a quick success, was vetoed by Hitler, who thus ensured that Army Group "C" would be hammered to pieces on the anvil of its winter line.

Von Vietinghoff's difficulties did not end there. The Allied air forces in Italy had systematically wrecked the communication system on which his logistic arrangements depended. Road and rail traffic was disrupted, and the supplies of motor-fuel reduced to a trickle. The German marching divisions were frugal in their requirements and rubbed along with animal draught and even hand-carts, but without petrol the rapid reinforcement of a threatened point in the front by panzer units or transfer of the forward troops to a rear line was impossible. Air power had turned Army Group "C" into a 1918-type force, moving at the infantryman's pace of two and a half miles an hour.

Meanwhile the first hair-line crack in German resolve to fight to the bitter end became visible in Italy in, of all things, Hitler's praetorian guard. Obergruppenfuehrer Karl Wolff, head of the SS in Italy (the security, not the fighting, or Waffen SS) was in a position to know the full facts of the situation, and also the least likely to be suspected of treachery. It is evidence of how completely the high officials of the Third Reich were cut off from world opinion that Wolff believed that the United States and Britain could be persuaded to sign a separate peace, leaving Germany to defend her eastern frontier against the "Bolsheviks". Wolff employed an Italian business man as a go-between to make contact with Mr Allen Dulles, representative of the United States Office of Strategic Services, based in the United States embassy in Zurich. These negotiations began in February, but made little progress until the Allied breakthrough in April convinced the German commanders that unconditional surrender was their only option.[2]

For the Allied commanders in Italy, the question was how best to bring this about. When Clark succeeded Alexander at HQ 15th Army Group he believed, as we now know, that at last he could fight the war in the way he wanted, free from the trammels of British direction. His promotion, made at the suggestion of the British Prime Minister, to command a force in which British and Commonwealth units predominated, did nothing to mollify his distrust of the "British" or weaken his conviction that they – with whom he included the natives of the United Kingdom, the Canadians, the New Zealanders, the Indians and the South Africans – were no good, that they could not "carry the ball". Only real Americans (he believed) could do that. What a man holding great responsibility writes in his private diary or to his wife to relieve his feelings should always be read with tolerance, but to despise the majority of his command is hardly the best qualification for a general.

When General George Marshall visited Clark in his new HQ on the way back from the Yalta conference Clark paraded for him detachments from every national army and ethnic group in the 15th Army Group. Marshall in response declared that the Italian campaign was "the most perfect example of team work among many nations united in a common cause". This was not Clark's view. What he had intended to show the Chief of Staff was that his was a "hodge-podge outfit", lacking in flexibility – its units "can't be switched around". "I cannot put a British division or an Indian division on a snow-capped mountain like I can the Americans . . ."[3] Fortunately Clark had the ability to dissemble, essential for a man in high office. Except to Kirkman his Anglophobia was never revealed until his diaries became available to historians. As a result, his original intention for the April offensive was

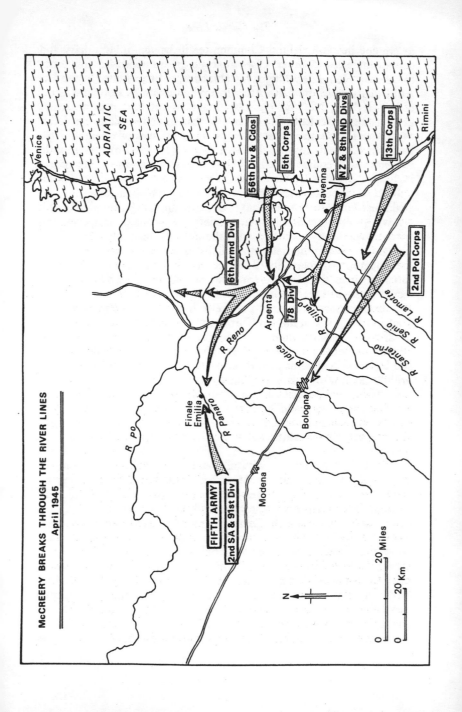

MᶜCREERY BREAKS THROUGH THE RIVER LINES
April 1945

ADRIATIC SEA

Venice

56th Div & Cdos

5th Corps

NZ & 8th IND Divs

13th Corps

Rimini

Ravenna

6th Armd Div

2nd Pol Corps

Argenta

78 Div

R Silaro

R Idice

R Reno

R Santerno

R Senio

R Lamone

Finale Emilia

R Panaro

Bologna

R Po

Modena

FIFTH ARMY
2nd SA & 91st Div

N

0   20 Miles

0   20 Km

to employ the British and Commonwealth troops in subsidiary and supporting roles. As ever, Clark attached great importance to a territorial goal. He made Bologna his objective, to be captured by the US Army divisions in the Fifth Army in a renewed attack along the direct route, Highway No. 65. He soon found, however, that as an army-group commander he had to defer, as he had forced Alexander to defer, to the views of his army commanders. Truscott insisted on fighting his battle in his own way, as did McCreery. The final plan was not a compromise, a course invariably fatal, but contained the inputs of two highly professional army commanders.

It seems to be a characteristic of wars waged by democracies – and coalitions – that every lesson has to be learnt afresh. The final offensive – it was given no comprehensive code-name – was, at last, after five botched ventures – planned with the aim of the destruction of the German armies in the field; the first principle of warfare. Because of the topography of the winter line there it was not a single concentrated thrust. Instead, the plan was for a double encirclement, what German tacticians termed the "*Keil und Kessel*" or "wedge and trap".

Truscott's intention was to strike into the plain of Emilia west of Highway No. 64 with the 4th Corps, and then side-step the 2nd Corps on to an axis clear of Bologna. One wing of his army was to make for Verona, while the other swung north and then east behind Bologna and south of the Po. To this plan he stuck like glue, remembering Clark's predilection for prestige goals, like Rome.[4]

McCreery proposed a similar strategy. He wanted to strike northwards as hard as he could, his first objective being to cross the River Po. As part of his plan he organised a river-crossing task force under HQ 10th Corps. If this went well he would order part of his right wing north-west to meet the right of the Fifth Army behind Bologna. Here he had a tussle with Clark, who still hankered for the rapid fall of the city. Lacking confidence in McCreery and the Eighth Army, he considered that a major breakthrough on the Adriatic flank was unlikely. The Eighth Army, he ordered, was to attack eastwards up Highway No. 9 towards Bologna. Privately, it seems, he thought the best that McCreery could do would be to draw the Army Group "C" reserves away from Truscott. McCreery was to start two days before the Fifth Army, on April 9, with the added advantage of the whole Allied air effort devoted exclusively to his support until the 12th. (As it turned out Truscott had to delay his D-day until the 14th because of bad flying weather on the 12th and 13th by which date the Eighth Army had broken the winter line.)

McCreery's operational plan for his northward thrust was imaginative and masterly. His left was in the mountains, his centre was barred by the eastward flowing rivers backed by the Reno, which swings in a great loop behind Bologna and then east and south into the Adriatic, receiving the waters of the others on its way. His right faced the twenty-mile-wide Lake Comacchio, a brackish lagoon separated from the Adriatic by a strip of land. Much of the low-lying ground to its west had been flooded by the breaching of flood-banks and the destruction of pumping stations by the German engineers, who had also prepared defensive positions along each river line. However, he perceived one weak spot. Between the Reno and the southern shore of the lake there was a corridor free of any major water-obstacle running north-west to Argenta on Highway No. 16. A number of amphibious, armoured, tracked assault vehicles ("landing vehicles, tracked" or LVTs) had arrived in Italy, and McCreery obtained sufficient to lift a brigade. Their use could convert L. Comacchio from an obstacle to a highway leading to the German left rear and to control of the "Argenta Gap".

The Eighth Army's main attack was entrusted to the 5th Corps (Lieutenant-General Charles Keightley). The 56th Division was to cross L. Comacchio, the New Zealand and the 8th Indian Division were to force the passage of the Senio and Santerno, followed by the reinforced 78th Division, virtually a large "panzer grenadier" division. Once a bridgehead over the Santerno had been secured the 78th was to cross, wheel right, make for the bridge over the Reno at Bastia, join hands with the 56th Division and clear the Argenta corridor. HQ 13th Corps (Lieutenant-General John Harding) was to be ready to take command of the left wing of the 5th Corps when it divided. The direct thrust to Bologna aligned on Highway No. 9 was to be undertaken by the 2nd Polish and British 13th Corps.[5]

As usual the 15th Army Group plan included deceptive measures designed to play on the abiding German fear of a landing behind one or other of their sea flanks. Von Vietinghoff was sufficiently convinced to move the 29th Panzer Division to cover the Adriatic coast north of Venice, and when the US 4th Corps mounted a diversionary attack on the Ligurian coast directed on Massa and La Spezia he shifted a regiment of the 90th Panzer Grenadier Division to that area. German intelligence was certain of only one thing – that as soon as the weather improved the Allies would attack in great strength. Traugott Herr, commanding the Tenth Army, torn between exact obedience to the Fuehrer's orders and his professional judgment, chose to be guided by the latter, but in doing so made a fatal error which was to ensure the success of McCreery's plan.

Defying the explicit instructions of OKW, Herr decided to establish his main line of resistance along the Santerno out of range of the formidable artillery of the Eighth Army, maintaining only an outpost line on the Senio. His reasoning was sound, but he was unlucky. McCreery had indeed assembled 1,020 guns supplied with 2,000,000 rounds of ammunition to support his opening assault, but he had also been allotted air support on a huge scale. (As the Russians had overrun the targets of the Allied strategic bomber force based in Italy it was free to join the US 22nd Tactical Air Command* and the RAF Desert Air Force in the land battle.) Clark's decision to attack with his armies in succession from left to right had the great advantage of concentrating this mass of fire-power first on McCreery's front and then on Truscott's. On April 9, as Herr had foreseen, a tremendous artillery bombardment struck his attenuated defences behind the Senio, but at the same time repeated attacks by the US heavy bomber force laying "carpets" of twenty-pound fragmentation bombs reduced his main line of resistance along the Santerno. On the 12th the New Zealanders and the Indians had established bridgeheads over it, and on the 13th Major-General R. K. Arbuthnott, commanding 78th Infantry Division, began his flank march along the north bank to Bastia.

There is an often-quoted saying that no operational plan ever survives contact with the enemy. That is certainly true if both sides are equally matched or, at least, equally determined. The fact that the plans of both Truscott and McCreery were brilliantly realised does not mean that the spring offensive was a walk-over; that the Allied armies rolled over the emaciated German divisions behind a vast curtain of artillery and air-power. All the records are of intense fighting against a ferocious, last-ditch defence lasting for sixteen days. After that only small isolated groups continued the struggle. Some of the 14th Panzer Corps, hotly engaged with a task force of the 10th Mountain Division, finally laid down their arms at Riva on the north shore of Lake Garda on May 3, one day after the official cease-fire. It took the Poles until the 21st to break through the 1st Parachute Division and enter Bologna. "*Une très jolie petite bataille*," said Anders to Harold Macmillan with grim joviality, "*Nous avons tué plus que deux mille Boches . . .*"[6]

Four private soldiers received awards for valour, two posthumously, all four for personal attacks on groups of machine-gun posts. On April 5 a Japanese of the 442nd (Nisei) Infantry, Private (First Class) Sadao S. Munemori took over a rifle squad when the NCO in command was wounded and captured the objective, personally silencing two machine guns with hand grenades. Almost immediately an enemy grenade, its

---

* So named when the 12th TAC joined the 6th Army Group in France.

fuse burning, fell among his comrades. He threw himself on to it, saving their lives, but losing his own. On the 14th Private (First Class) J. D. Magrath of the 85th Mountain Infantry fell mortally wounded to a stray shot, having attacked and silenced four posts, using captured weapons when he had expended his rifle ammunition. He and Munemori were awarded the Congressional Medal of Honour.

On the 9th two sepoys (privates) of the 4th Indian Division won the Victoria Cross during the assault crossing of the Senio. It involved climbing the twenty-five-foot-high dyke on the enemy bank, beyond which lay concealed machine guns whose crews had survived the artillery bombardment. Haidar Ali of the 13th Frontier Force Rifles accounted for two, though wounded in leg and arm, charging out alone ahead of his company which was pinned by their fire. Namdeo Jadhao, 5th Mahratta Light Infantry, was the "runner" (messenger) of one of the attacking companies, whose HQ was moving close behind the leading platoon. Once over the bank it came under fire from three machine-gun posts, leaving Namdeo the only man not killed or wounded. He first carried back two wounded and then equipped with machine pistol and grenades attacked single-handed, returning once for more grenades. The guns silenced, he returned a third time to cheer the rest of his company on, standing on top of the flood-bank shouting the Mahratta war-cry. That the awards for heroism were distributed among a Japanese, a white American, a Muslim and a Hindu was, perhaps, symbolic, and certainly appropriate to the multinational character of the Allied armies.

The Eighth Army at last achieved the breakthrough it had been denied four times. The crossing of Lake Comacchio achieved complete surprise, and Arbuthnott, who kept up a rolling attack by day and night, passing one brigade through another, reached Argenta on the 17th. There the 78th and the 56th Divisions met stiff resistance, as by then von Vietinghoff perceived that he had been the victim of the Allied deception plan, and committed the 29th Panzer Division to the Argenta corridor. It was too late. On the 16th McCreery placed the 6th Armoured Division under Keightley, who ordered Major-General "Nat" Murray to pass through the Argenta Gap and make for the Po without slackening his attack by day or by night. Refreshed and encouraged by its return to the mobile role after its dismal slogging match in the Apennines, the division (four cavalry regiments in tanks, motorised Guards and Greenjackets) set off in a burst of the true cavalry spirit. On the 23rd, patrols of the Derbyshire Yeomanry stood on the south bank of the river, and the Scots Guards and engineers prepared to cross.[7] By then the hard-pressed von Vietinghoff had received a harsh and, indeed, insulting reply from OKW to his last appeal to be allowed to disengage to the Po defence line. It accused him of a "defeatist attitude", reaffirming that his mission was to defend "every inch of Italian soil", concluding ominously by reminding him of the "serious consequences" of not carrying out the "Fuehrer's orders to the last word". That was the death warrant of Army Group "C". Kesselring was no help. He, from his distant HQ, was now simply reaffirming Hitler's manic decrees.

On the 14th the Fifth Army opened its attack, two days late, having been delayed by bad flying weather. The mountainous terrain left Truscott with little room for manoeuvre, but by attacking in succession first with the 4th Corps and then with the 2nd, he too achieved a complete breakthrough, using the full weight of the Allied air forces to support each corps in turn. The US Army staff reaffirmed its aptitude for organising large and complex troop movements in mid-battle by side-stepping the 2nd Corps on to Highway No. 64, along which it advanced, not without hard fighting, west and north-westwards into the plain of Emilia, by-passing Bologna. At the same time the 6th Armoured Division reached the Po, and the leading regiment of its left-hand group was preparing to clear the village of Finale Emilia. There the 16th/5th Lancers met the tanks of the 11th South African Armoured Brigade attacking the same objective from the west, while a liaison officer from the 17th/21st Lancers fortunately arrived at HQ US 91st Infantry Division just in time to dissuade it from advancing to the attack supported by a full-scale artillery bombardment -- on to the rear of the 16th/5th.*[8] Joining hands, the right of the US 2nd Corps and the left of the British 5th Corps trapped the bulk of the 76th Panzer Corps south of the Po. On the 25th, when the 27th Lancers of the 78th Division captured Generalleutnant Graf Gerhard von Schwering, he was asked to reveal the locations of his corps. He replied laconically that "it could be found somewhere south of the Po". Everywhere the fields were covered with abandoned vehicles and heavy weapons, some defiantly set alight, among them roaming hundreds of draught horses turned loose to graze. The orders given to the German soldiers had been to make their own way to the Po, but many of the bridges and ferries organised to take them across had been destroyed by air attack. Over 100,000 men stood around waiting to be rounded up and, they hoped, fed and protected from the anti-Fascist and anti-German partisans. (These, lavishly armed by the Allies, and capable of little

---

* Illustrating the difficulty of control when two friendly armies meet head-on in a double envelopment. One of the tank commanders of the 16th/5th loosed off at a South African tank, but fortunately missed.

more than murder and noisy fire-fights with their fellow Italians of a different political hue, had been summoned into action to support the final offensive.)[9]

The confusion in the battle area extended back from the units of Army Group "C" to its high command and beyond. Kesselring, though privately a realist, for the moment came down on the side of the diehards who wished to fight on to the bitter end. Those who, like von Vietinghoff, saw no alternative to surrender, still felt bound by the oath of loyalty they had so foolishly sworn. Only SS General Wolff, whose task it was to punish traitors, felt strong enough to cut through the bickering and hesitation and persuade Alexander to accept emissaries empowered to arrange a surrender.

At last in the presence of Alexander's chief of staff, Lieutenant-General Sir William Morgan, an agreement for the unconditional surrender of all the German and pro-Axis forces in Italy was signed at Caserta, on April 29. The cease-fire became effective on May 2.[10]

The Allied victory evoked no euphoria, no sense of triumph, no victory parades. The fighting troops after a good sleep were fully occupied in collecting, disarming and making arrangements to administer 145,000 prisoners of war, demobilising the partisans and restoring the public utilities of towns wrecked by bombing. The older men could remember the first air-raid sirens of 1939, the victory and defeat in France and the beaches of Dunkirk. The younger men, most of them veterans of twenty-four or twenty-five, had known nothing but a state of world war during their adult lives. It was, at first, hard to grasp that it was all over.

REFLECTIONS

It is better to be wise before the event than after; but it is still better to be wise after the event than not to be wise at all.

Enoch Powell*

The end of the war in Italy was overshadowed by the death of Hitler, the collapse of the Third Reich and the explosion of the atom bombs at Hiroshima and Nagasaki. All that remained in popular memory was an impression of bungled operations; the landing at Anzio and the destruction of the Abbey of Montecassino. The British, nostalgically obsessed with defeats, heroic or otherwise, dwelt on Dunkirk, Singapore and the earlier battles in the Western Desert. American attention was divided between the war in the Pacific and, understandably, OVERLORD, as it was the task of liberating north-west Europe and the defeat of Germany that brought the US Army across the Atlantic. Italy was a diversion.

Yet the Italian war is of abiding interest. It demonstrated the self-generating momentum of military operations once begun, it is full of examples of the pitfalls of coalitionary war, and offers an insight into Anglo-American relations at a period fraught with mutual dislike and suspicion. The debate centred about the aim of the campaign and the question, never satisfactorily answered, of how far the military resources poured into what was manifestly a subsidiary theatre of war paid a dividend. We suggest that this is too simple a way of assessing so complex an activity as warfare – perhaps the question is not a valid one at all. Nevertheless, it has to be answered; first, though, it is necessary

* One-time professor of classical studies, brigadier and now MP for County Down, *The Times*, September 22, 1984.

to draw attention to an ironic circumstance. The military ideology, or "doctrine" of the British and United States Armies was fundamentally the same. Theoretically there was no need for the bitter differences between the British and American chiefs of staff. Both adhered to a set of maxims for the conduct of large-scale operations, which the British somewhat misleadingly termed the "principles of war". Both Marshall and Brooke would have unhesitatingly agreed that the *Object* should first be carefully and exactly defined, and thereafter every resource be devoted to its attainment according to the principles of *Concentration* and *Offensive Action*. Forces diverted to necessary subsidiary operations, such as the protection of an open flank, or to mask the direction of the main thrust should, according to the principle of *Economy of Force*, be no larger than required for the task. The invasion of mainland Italy was launched in the hope that a brief and limited effort could bring about large gains. As so often seen in history of warfare, this had proved a delusion.

A further irony was that the early studies leading to a British war doctrine had been based on the lessons of the Civil War in the United States. The definitive work, and the operational bible of the British Army, was the *Field Service Regulations* (Volume II, *Operations*) as written and later revised after the First World War.*

The authors of the *Field Service Regulations* attached great importance to economy of force, which had been at the heart of the great debate between the "westerners" and the "easterners" during the First World War. The "westerners" (like Roosevelt and Marshall in 1943) believed that the best, indeed the only way to defeat the Central Powers was a direct assault on the German positions in France and Belgium and the defeat of the German armies in the field, leading to the occupation of Germany itself. The "easterners" argued for a more imaginative, wider strategy, attacking the eastern and southern perimeter of the Central Powers wherever they could – in Iraq, Egypt, the Dardanelles, Salonika and Italy. "*FSR* Vol. II" was, in effect, a post-war endorsement of the policy of the "westerners". The Staff College students and instructors of the inter-war years who were to

---

* The author was Aspinall Oglander, a soldier and the author of the volume of the official history dealing with Gallipoli. Archibald Wavell revised it later and added a further volume on grand strategy. The principles of war were drafted by J. F. C. Fuller, pioneer of armoured, mobile warfare. In 1929 Major-General Sir Frederick Maurice, Professor of Military History in King's College, University of London, published *British Strategy*, the classic exposition of the "principles of war" as understood by the General Staff. For "economy of force" see his Chapter 6. In Chapter 2, especially p. 44, he explains the reason for exclusion of political considerations.

reach high positions during the Second World War were accordingly indoctrinated, but a further irony was that the supreme director of the British war effort was to be Churchill, a convinced, obstinate and, indeed, obsessive "easterner". This is not to say that Churchill was wrong and Marshall was right. Marshall was a military fundamentalist of a narrow and rigid kind. The British and American soldiers agreed on the exclusion of all political considerations. In their philosophy there was no question of gaining public opinion, or regarding war as a final and legitimate means of gaining political objectives. In democracies it was for governments to set political goals, and for soldiers to secure military objectives.

The principles of war were no more than maxims – some of them mutually exclusive and contradictory – intended to fix the minds of soldiers on operational essentials. It is not known whether Churchill ever opened a copy of *FSR* Vol. II, but if he did he would have approved of "the fifth principle", *Offensive Action*. As for the rest, he was not the man to allow doctrinaire considerations to deflect him from courses of action which his acute political sense told him were correct. Churchill may or may not have been whole-heartedly behind the OVERLORD enterprise, but that question lies outside this particular discussion. What he did understand was that the Allies were not mentally or physically prepared to invade north-west Europe in 1943. (A view reinforced by the experience of invading Sicily and the Salerno landing, both successful, but revealing serious errors in Allied planning, execution and the morale and training of the troops.) Churchill also perceived that inactivity in 1943 was politically and morally impossible. It was necessary to engage in offensive operation in mainland Europe as soon as possible to reassure the Russians and to convince the Western Europeans inside and outside the frontiers of Nazi-dominated Europe that their prison wall could be breached, and that the German Army could be defeated by the Western soldiers, in mainland Europe, and not only in distant Africa and off-shore islands in the Mediterranean. In 1943 Italy was the only place where the Allies could be certain of obtaining a foothold.

The success or failure of the Italian campaign has, therefore, to be assessed in the wider, political perspective of grand strategy. It cannot be satisfactorily judged by the crude method of striking a quantitative balance, for that would not be comparing like with like. On the one side there were the lean German divisions, all but the few elite panzers and panzer grenadiers marching on their feet, their few guns and scanty supplies relying on horse draught and, for most of the campaign, virtually without air support. On the other, there were the lavishly supplied Allied armies, counting their tanks and guns by the thousand and their artillery ammunition by the million rounds, supported by a powerful tactical air force. Nor was this all. They were backed by an elaborate logistic infrastructure stretching across the Mediterranean from Morocco in the west to Suez in the east. It could be said, therefore, that it was not Alexander who was drawing in forces that could otherwise be employed against Allies in north-west Europe, but Kesselring who was containing Alexander. That was the logic behind the diversion of six US and French divisions to the south of France in the summer of 1944.

An alternative, suggested oddly enough by Churchill himself (at the QUADRANT conference in 1943), was to close the theatre down. Once the Allies had reached a line sufficiently far north of the airfields in southern Italy required by the USAAF for the southern limb of the Combined Bomber Offensive, it would be fortified and garrisoned by no more troops than required to hold it. The impracticability of such a course is obvious. If too weak the garrison would invite a German offensive; if strong enough to hold it the object of freeing forces for use elsewhere would be defeated. If entirely passive the morale of the garrison would suffer, but a policy of raids and patrols, as obtained during lulls on the Western Front in the earlier war, would only serve to disgust the troops, always quick to resent pointless effort and unnecessary casualties. Divisions could be moved from theatre to theatre, but the logistic base in the Mediterranean with its string of ports and airfields could not easily be picked up and put down somewhere else. It was not only the accessibility of Italy that invited invasion: the essential machinery to mount and sustain it was already in existence.

There is more weight in the argument that once Alexander had been given his final directive and the DIADEM offensive was seen to have gathered momentum, he should have been given his head and all the resources available. This had the support of Mark Clark, at least from the moment when he realised that the only opportunity to distinguish himself would be in Italy in command of the Fifth Army. In his own memoirs he asserted that the removal of six of his divisions after DIADEM was "one of the outstanding mistakes of the war".[1] His biographer, quoting him, writes: "Had the Allies reached Bologna in 1944, moved into the Balkans and been in eastern Europe before the Russians . . . 'they might have changed the whole history of relations between the western world and Soviet Russia.' "[2] It is not clear exactly what Clark meant by "the Balkans"; conventionally Yugoslavia, Albania, Romania, Bulgaria and Greece. None of these was accessible to the 15th Army Group, and it is highly unlikely that the Russians would have tolerated such an incursion into territory they had marked out as their own, even if Clark could have reached them.[3] Clark was in fact to reach Austria in May 1945, and it made little difference to the course of events in central Europe in the long term.

The military side of this option, put up in outline by Alexander, to be immediately rejected by the Combined Chiefs of Staff, was to gain the head of the Adriatic by a combination of land and amphibious thrusts and then advance on Vienna via the so-called "Lubljana Gap". The plan ignored the fact that the Allies had taken over a year to battle their way up the length of Italy where the natural defensive lines, though strong, at least were long enough to offer some room for manoeuvre and surprise. Yet it envisaged an advance in winter along a narrow mountain route 250 miles long, first over the Julian Alps, then through the high pass or "gap" near Lubljana, no more than thirty miles wide and offering many good defensive positions, along the valley of the Save and then over a great Alpine massif. Central Europe as a goal was political and military moonshine.

A better option might have been to turn north-westwards after breaking the Gothic Line and invade France by the classic route along the coast and over the Alpes Maritimes. (Provided that the advance of the Allied armies had not perforce been halted after the ANVIL-DRAGOON contingent had been removed.) Not only would the CEF have been ideally employed in the mountains, but the fact that it was advancing into France would have fired it with enthusiasm. This was never given serious consideration, except by Churchill. The rigid, unimaginative decision to launch ANVIL-DRAGOON had been taken unilaterally by the Americans, as the dominant partners in the alliance and, moreover, redeploying forces that were theirs or under their control. All Churchill's protests were therefore in vain.

It may seem that in recapitulating these arguments we have put up targets made of straw for the purpose of knocking them down, but they were options seriously considered by at least some of the great personages involved, and deserve a mention before discussing the more practical aspects of the campaign.

The overriding direction given to Alexander was to contain as many German troops as possible in Italy. First, therefore, the doubtful aid of statistics must be invoked to see how far he was successful in fulfilling the specific demands made on his gradually depleted armies. The Allied armies marched some 800 miles from Calabria to the Brenner Pass in almost exactly twenty months, fighting most of the way, and mounting five deliberate offensives, or six if Anzio is regarded as a separate operation. Throughout they had a numerical advantage on the battlefield, although it is not immediately apparent. The strength of Army Group "C" was 195,000 in July 1943, 411,000 in July 1944 and 439,000 when Kesselring's command was briefly expanded in 1945 to include *OB West*, excluding the Italian troops in Liguria. Applying Martin van Creveld's ratio of combat to supply in German Army theatres of war, 84.5 per cent of total strength may have been 339,480 in the final battle.[4] US statistics give the Fifth Army strength including its British element in the last twelve months of the war as 359,565, and the Eighth Army in round numbers as 190,000 total forces. If 60 per cent of the Fifth and 70 per cent of the Eighth were combat troops, 216,000 and 133,000 respectively, the grand total is 349,000. The total strength of the Allied forces was the figure of 1,677,000, including the headquarters and line of communication staffs, the air forces and the logistical infrastructure required to support a force overseas. In terms of the divisional slice, that is, the total numerical strength available divided by the number of divisions, the US Army was more lavish than the British, and both were luxurious compared with the German Army.* These figures suggest that the forces actually engaged on both sides were roughly equal in numbers. The Allied commanders did not try (or at least not very hard) "to comb out their tail" to obtain more men on the battlefield.

A second measure of relative strength is to compare the number of divisions in the battle zone and in the theatre as a whole, bearing in mind the warning already given of the wide variation of establishment strength, ration strength, weapon availability and fighting-power of German divisions. Those available in the battle zone is the significant figure, as Kesselring, though he had a larger reserve than Alexander, had to retain a number of divisions to secure his communications from partisans, overawe the anti-German population in the industrial north and guard against amphibious operations in his rear. The figures are:[5]

	Allied battle zone	*German battle zone*	*Total German*
1943–4	18	15	23
Diadem	25	18	24
Gothic Line	20	22	26
1945	17	19	21

* This figure also is only an imperfect indicator, as it does not take into account non-divisional troops such as independent tank brigades and corps and army artillery, unless specially adjusted, but it is a useful coefficient of efficiency. However, a modern army requires a large and effective logistic back-up, repair workshops, hospitals, reinforcement holding units, rest camps, etc., if it is to remain efficient for long periods. A large "slice" is as much an indication of efficiency as waste of man-power.

Some of Kesselring's reserve divisions were second-rate, but they enabled him to react swiftly and effectively in an emergency, as he did at Anzio. This, however was by no means the whole picture. The Allied presence in Italy and the Mediterranean roused, and kept alive, Hitler's fears of Allied armed intervention in the Balkans, especially in Greece or Yugoslavia. It was also important to cut off logistic support to the active Yugoslav partisans. General von Westphal stated that "about one fifth of the German ground forces", possibly about forty "divisions" of sorts, were stationed in the area to ensure its security. It can, of course, be argued that such units, with few heavy weapons, no tanks, low-grade personnel and rudimentary logistics, would have been of little value in the critical fighting in the West and that the demands of internal security would have required them to be stationed in the region anyway, but that ignores the fact that good German officers and men could not be used where they were most needed elsewhere. In terms of divisions pinned down, the Italian theatre seems undoubtedly to have been a profitable investment for the Allies.

A third measure is the balance of killed, wounded and missing. This, however, has to be treated with the same reserve as the first two. Different armies used different systems of accounting. "Killed" may not include "died of wounds", and wounded permanently incapacitated may not be distinguished from wounded returned to unit. The Germans, as they were always retreating, were unable to tell how many of their "missing" had been killed or made prisoners of war. The sick, whose numbers grew in the severe winter of 1944–5 in the Apennines, are not included, nor the cases of neurosis arising from battle exhaustion which were battle casualties as much as those caused by the bullet. Robert H. Ahrenfeldt, in *Psychiatry in the British Army in the Second World War*, refers to the work of two US Army investigators on the psychiatric "life" of infantrymen in the Fifth Army. It is not easily compressed, but they concluded that "just as an average truck wears out after a number of miles", so did a soldier in combat, the figure being 200–240 combat days (ten "combat days" being equivalent to seventeen calendar days). The casualties were not necessarily young or poorly motivated soldiers, but more often junior leaders and decorated veterans. Some were irretrievably damaged though they could carry out useful non-front-line jobs. Many patients were "ineffective" after 140–180 days. The comparative British figure was of the order of 400 days, attributed to their policy of "left out of battle", and frequent rest and relief. In the Fifth Army the American soldier might be in the front line without relief for twenty to thirty days, frequently for thirty to forty and occasionally for eighty.

The reliable official historian of the US Army states that the round number of Allied killed, wounded and missing in Italy from September 9, 1943 to the end was 312,000, of which the Fifth Army share was 188,746, the Eighth Army therefore approximately 123,254. Of the national contingents to take two examples, the Canadian figure from the landings in Sicily to their departure on March 25, was 26,254, the French 22,171 in DIADEM and the subsequent pursuit. In his final despatch Alexander reported that the total German loss was 536,000, which presumably included the mass of prisoners taken in the final débâcle. The US Army historian, relying on official German sources (which excluded the small number of Waffen SS, Luftwaffe and Kriegsmarine casualties and may have been incomplete for the last days of April 1945) gives the smaller figure of 434,646, which included 48,067 killed, 172,531 wounded and 214,048 missing. It would seem therefore, that the balance of attrition favoured the Allied armies, contradicting the accepted theory that the defence is more economical. The explanation possibly lies in the fanatical German belief in defence by local counter-attack, and certainly in the overwhelming Allied fire-power: in the opinion of many Germans far more severe than anything they experienced on the Eastern Front, where the Red Army generals calculated their fire-plans in terms of hundreds of artillery barrels per kilometre. The Allied losses in the far shorter campaign in north-west Europe were 766,294, and in the Battle of Normandy the ground forces lost only 209,672, of which 39,976 were killed, compared with the German loss of 240,000 and 210,000 made prisoner. It is clear therefore that in simply the grim figures of attrition the Allied effort in Italy was profitable and not unduly severe.*

The next question, having reviewed the slippery evidence of military statistics, is the conduct of operations on the highest level. It has been claimed that the aim the Allied high command gave Alexander was consistent throughout. This is an over-simplification. We have seen that the aim changed repeatedly, from a cheap victory over Italy, to prove to the Russians that the Western Allies were really fighting in Europe, to support the strategic bombing policy, and finally to contain Army Group "C". From the German point of view there were two threats. Operationally Kesselring feared amphibious end-runs round his flanks all through the campaign. In terms of grand strategy Hitler saw his whole rickety empire in the Balkans threatened. It was only by exploiting these threats that the vast military assets poured into Italy

---

* By way of contrast, on the Western Front, in the First World War when the BEF was made up to approximately fifty-five divisions, the average loss per month during "quiet" periods was 15,000, rising to 100,000 during intense fighting.

could have been made to pay a strategic dividend. It was not a question of waltzing off on some hair-brained strategy through the Lubljana gap into the Danube basin. Given the landing craft used for DRAGOON Alexander could have avoided the battles of attrition on the pattern of the Western Front, fought in muddy river valleys and up precipitous mountain slopes. Instead he could have upset all Kesselring's careful strategy and nice calculations. With the forces diverted to ANVIL-DRAGOON he would have had a fair chance of overrunning the Gothic Line in the summer of 1944. It is ironical that the final, definite order to remove them issued on July 5 was preceded four days before by an emergency conference Kesselring held with his generals to discuss their heavy losses, and the need for more elastic and early withdrawals. DRAGOON succeeded only in removing a whole army from effective action in both Italy and France for a vital four weeks. No hindsight is needed to imagine the consternation in OKW if the collapse in Normandy had coincided with an equal débâcle in Italy. The failure of Allied grand strategy, as determined by the Americans, was due to treating the two theatres as rivals when they should have been seen as a single, strategic whole. The American insistence on the elementary principle of concentration was in reality a rationalisation, to conceal misunderstandings, jealousies and rival aims.

These are political and strategic questions, open to debate and disagreement, but susceptible to rational analysis. There were other, deeper, more opaque forces at work. The mere existence of two opposed armies within striking distance of each other seems to generate "offensive action". We have seen how the generals, manifestly for the best reasons, all became identified with their armies and missions, feeling that what coincided with their ambitions was militarily correct. They were, after all, human.

We argue that a great war in Italy was inevitable from the moment that the Anglo-American forces were built up in French North Africa. It was then found, as ever, that it is easier to start a war than stop one.

Dominick Graham, Fredericton, N.B.
Shelford Bidwell, Wickham Market, Suffolk

Appendices

CHRONOLOGY OF PRINCIPAL EVENTS

August 1943
Axis forces withdraw from Sicily. Allied high command approves BAYTOWN and AVALANCHE plans for invasion of mainland. Badoglio opens secret surrender negotiations.

September
3rd. Italian surrender signed. BAYTOWN launched.
8th. Allied HQ orders broadcast news of Italian surrender. GIANT II (airborne descent on Rome) cancelled.
9th. Germans disarm Italian armed forces. AVALANCHE (Salerno) and SLAPSTICK (Taranto) successfully launched.
16th. Eighth Army and Fifth Army in contact.
17th. Germans disengage at Salerno and begin phased withdrawal to winter (Gustav) Line.
22nd. Eighth Army captures Bari.
23rd. Fifth Army begins advance on Naples.
27th. Eighth Army reaches Foggia airfields.

October
1st. Fall of Naples.
3rd–6th. Eighth Army action at Termoli.
12th–15th. Fifth Army forces passage of Volturno.

November
5th–15th. Fifth Army (British 10th Corps) fails to take M. Camino.
8th–28th. Eighth Army crosses Sangro river but autumn rain and floods halt operations.

December
2nd–17th. Fifth Army resumes offensive. 10th Corps clears M. Camino and US 2nd Corps S. Pietro and M. Sammucro. Fifth Army faces Gustav Line from Cassino to mouth of Garigliano river.
4th–28th. Eighth Army front: 2nd NZ Division fails to take key position at Orsogna, but 1st Canadian Division captures Ortona. All operations on Adriatic Front halted by bad weather. Leese succeeds Montgomery in command of Eighth Army. Harding appointed chief of staff to Alexander.

January 1944

8th.   Maitland Wilson succeeds Eisenhower in Mediterranean theatre, with Jacob L. Devers, US Army, as his deputy.

17th.   Fifth Army offensive opens; 10th Corps establishes bridgehead across Garigliano.

19th.   46th Division fails at S. Ambrogio.

20th.   36th Division fails at S. Angelo ("Bloody River").

22nd.   SHINGLE launched: US 6th Corps lands at Anzio.

23rd.   German counter-moves against Anzio landing begun: HQ Fourteenth Army and 76th Panzer Corps fence in bridgehead.

24th.   Fifth Army (US 2nd Corps and CEF) begin First Battle of Cassino.

February

Fourteenth Army fully operational. US 6th Corps at Anzio on defensive. Alexander reinforces Fifth Army in Cassino sector with *ad hoc* corps under General Freyberg composed of 2nd NZ and 4th Indian Divisions.

15th–18th.   Second Battle of Cassino. Abbey ("Monastery") on Montecassino bombed, NZ Corps attack fails.

16th–21st.   German counter-offensive against US 6th Corps (FISCHFANG) at Anzio fails.

Combined CoS agree that proposed removal from Italy of troops and landing craft required for invasion of southern France (ANVIL) should be postponed pending spring offensive by AAI.

March

15th.   Third Battle of Cassino unsuccessful. Allied offensive operations halted. British 13th Corps relieves NZ Corps, which is disbanded.

April

Preparations for spring offensive (DIADEM), planned by Harding. Garigliano front reorganised, CEF and US 2nd Corps take over from British 10th Corps, inter-army boundary moved south to Liri river, Eighth Army concentrates 13th, 2nd Polish and 1st Canadian Corps in Rapido–Cassino–Montecassino sector.

May

11th.   D-Day, DIADEM. After initial setbacks Allies break through on all fronts. Spectacular success of French.

26th.   Clark orders Truscott to change the axis of his attack and make for Rome. Tenth and Fourteenth Armies extract themselves from potential trap.

June

4th.   Fall of Rome.

Kesselring relieves von Mackensen of command of Fourteenth Army. Army Group "C" withdraws in good order.

July
HQ US 6th Corps with three US divisions and the whole CEF, plus supporting troops, withdrawn from Italy to prepare for ANVIL, now called DRAGOON.
18th.   Ancona falls to 2nd Polish Corps.
19th.   Leghorn falls to Fifth Army.
Pursuit by AAI halted. Pause to rest and reorganise.

August
Army Group "C" completes its fighting withdrawal to outposts of Gothic Line north of R. Arno.
10th.   Alexander sets aside provisional plan for concentrated attack by both armies in centre directed on Bologna in favour of two separate attacks, by Fifth Army in centre and Eighth Army on Adriatic coast. British 13th Corps transferred to Fifth Army.
25th.   Eighth Army opens offensive (OLIVE). Canadian Corps drives in German outposts.

September
2nd.   Canadian Corps breaks through Gothic Line, but 5th Corps fails in attack on Coriano. OLIVE temporarily checked.
10th.   Fifth Army opens offensive.
13th–21st.   Fifth Army forces Il Giogo and Futa passes and drives towards Bologna.
12th–21st.   Canadian Corps breaks through main Gothic defences at Coriano. Rimini falls. Eighth Army continues methodical advance.

October
1st.   McCreery succeeds Leese in command of Eighth Army. Fifth Army, accepting heavy losses, fights through central Apennines to within nine miles of Bologna.
27th.   Fifth Army halted for lack of infantry replacements. End of its autumn/winter offensive.
Eighth Army advances across Fiumincino, Savio and Ronco rivers.

November
9th.   Eighth Army reaches Forli.
16th.   13th Corps, having reverted to Eighth Army, clears the trans-Apennine Highway No. 67 to the Emilian plain. Eighth Army reaches Lamone river.
24th.   Alexander relieves Maitland Wilson in command of the Mediterranean theatre, Clark relieves Alexander in command of Allied armies in Italy, renamed 15th Army Group, Truscott appointed to command Fifth Army; all effective in December.

December
4th.   Eighth Army advancing up Highway No. 9 (Via Emilia) captures Ravenna.
16th.   Eighth Army captures Faenza.
26th–28th.   German spoiling attack in Serchio valley against US 4th Corps.
29th.   Eighth Army winter offensive closed down.

January–March 1945
Fifth Army carries out local operations to improve its position preparatory to the spring offensive. The 1st Canadian Corps leaves the theatre for N.W. Europe. SS General Wolff begins clandestine negotiations for an armistice in Italy. Kesselring departs to become C-in-C West, succeeded by von Vietinghoff. (Von Vietinghoff had already stood in for Kesselring when he had been gravely injured in a motor accident. Traugott Herr who went to HQ Tenth Army in von Vietinghoff's place, retained that appointment when von Vietinghoff was posted to the Russian front, from which he was recalled.)

April
9th/14th.   Eighth Army and Fifth Army open spring offensive in succession.
23rd–25th.   Eighth and Fifth Armies join hands at Finale, trapping Tenth Army. Fifth Army captures Bologna and breaks out into plain of Emilia. Destruction of Army Group "C".

May
2nd.   German delegates formally surrender to Alexander at his HQ in Caserta near Naples.

SOURCES

Official Histories

1.   For basic information we gratefully relied on the labours of the official historians listed in our select bibliography, and in the absence of the volumes that should follow the late Brigadier C. J. C. Molony's *The History of the Second World War: The Mediterranean and the Middle East* (Vol. V), turned to General Sir William Jackson's *The Battle for Italy*, which as a campaign narrative is equally serviceable. Where the text requires support by a detailed reference it is identified in the Chapter Notes by the author's name and page number.

Unpublished Papers

2.   In the US National Archives, Suitland and Washington: The War Diaries of all units of the US Fifth Army and of the 16th Panzer Division.

3.   At the Military History Institute, Carlisle Barracks, Pennsylvania: The Institute's collection of German studies written for the US Historical Division *c.* December 1947. In particular the following. "The Campaign in Italy" with chapters written by General Westphal, von Vietinghoff, General Schmalz (Hermann Goering Division at Salerno), Albert Kesselring, The Diaries of Frido von Senger. The Institute also holds copies of the interviews by US Army historians of many of the officers who took part in the campaign, both American and others, and an extensive collection of their private papers, including those of John P. Lucas.

4.   At the Centre for Air Force History, Bolling AFB, Washington, the records of the US Army Air Forces in the Mediterranean and interviews with air force officers.

5.   At the Directorate of History and the National Archives of Canada, Ottawa, the unit war diaries, the papers of the official historian, and at the Directorate of History a collection of translated German documents compiled by J. Steiger of the Directorate in the 1940s.

6.   At the National Archives of New Zealand, Wellington are the records of the New Zealand Expeditionary Force, private papers of campaign participants and the papers of the official historians.

411

Sources

7. Various papers written in support of the battlefield tour undertaken by Nicholas Straker and Dominick Graham in 1970 and in the year following were compiled from Cabinet Office papers, particularly those written for C. J. C. Molony by his "Enemy Documents Section", and from unit war diaries. Douglas Graf von Bernstorff, chief of staff 26th Panzer Division, provided narratives for German operations. Straker was a participant in the 56th Division from Salerno to Anzio, where he was wounded.

8. Two army battlefield studies were used: British Troops Malta Command Study of Cassino and the British 3rd Infantry Division Study of Salerno, Exercise Gipsy Moth, September 1969.

Private Diaries

9. General Sir Sidney Kirkman, in the Liddell Hart centre for Military Archives, King's College, London, covering his service as commander, 13th Corps.

10. Colonel J. S. Mennell, kindly lent to author, covering the participation of the British 6th Armoured Division in the 1945 offensive, when he was GSO2 (Operations) of that formation.

Authors' Experiences

11. Bidwell served with the 2nd Army Group RA as Brigade Major at Salerno and as Brigade Major, RA 6th Armoured Division during the pursuit after DIADEM and part of the autumn fighting in the Gothic Line. Graham walked the length of Italy as an escaping prisoner of war in 1943 and undertook battlefield tours of Salerno, Cassino, Anzio and the Gothic Line in 1970 and 1985.

Naval

12. By Admiral H. Kent Hewitt USN, commander Western Naval Task Force: "The Allied Navies at Salerno, Operation AVALANCHE, Sept. 1943": *USN Institute Proceedings* (Sept. 1953): *The Naval Review* (British) vol. XLII, No. 1 (Feb. 1954).

Imperial War Museum

13. Letters and diaries concerning the Italian campaign in the Department of Documents.

SELECT BIBLIOGRAPHY

Ahrenfeldt, R. H., *Psychiatry in the British Army in the Second World War* (Routledge and Kegan Paul, London, 1958).

Ambrose, Stephen E., *The Supreme Commander: The War Years of General Dwight D. Eisenhower* (Doubleday, New York, 1969).

Anders, Wladyslaw, *An Army in Exile* (Macmillan, London, 1949).

Ball, Edmund, *Staff Officer with Fifth Army; Sicily, Salerno and Anzio* (Exposition Press, New York, 1958).

Beddington, W. R., *A History of the Queen's Bays 2nd Dragoon Guards* (Waren, Winchester, 1954).

Bidwell, Shelford and Graham, Dominick, *Fire-Power: British Army Weapons and Theories of War, 1904–45* (Allen and Unwin, London, 1982).

Blaxland, Gregory, *Alexander's Generals: the Italian Campaign 1944–45* (Kimber, London, 1979).

Blumenson, Martin, *Salerno to Cassino* (Office of the Chief of Military History, Washington, 1969).

— *Bloody River: the Real Tragedy of the Rapido* (Houghton Mifflin, Boston, 1970).

— *The Patton Papers* (Houghton Mifflin, Boston, 1974).

— *Mark Clark* (Congdon and Weed, New York, 1984).

Boehmler, Rudolf, *Monte Cassino* (Cassell, London, 1964).

Boulle, Georges, Volumes under series heading of *Le Corps Expéditionnaire en Italy (1943–1944)* (Etat-Major de L'Armée de Terre, Service Historique, Imprimerie Nationale, Paris).

— *La Campagne d'Hiver* (1971).

— *Les Campagnes de Printemps et d'Eté* (1973).

Bowlby, Alex, *The Recollections of Rifleman Bowlby* (Leo Cooper, London, 1969).

Burns, E. L. M., *General Mud* (Clark and Irwin, Toronto, 1970).

Carver, Michael, *Harding of Petherton: Field-Marshal* (Weidenfeld and Nicolson, London, 1978).

Cederberg, Fred, *The Long Road Home* (General Publishing, Toronto, 1984).

Chamb, René, *Le Maréchal Juin: Duc de Garigliano* (Presses de la Cité, Paris, 1968).

Churchill, Winston, S., *Closing the Ring* and *Triumph and Tragedy*, Vols V and VI, *The Second World War* (Cassell, London, 1954, 1956).

Clark, Mark W., *Calculated Risk* (Harper, New York, 1950).

Cole, David, *Rough Road to Rome, A Foot-soldier in Sicily and Italy 1943–44* (William Kimber, London, 1983).

Copp, de Witt S., *Forged in Fire: Strategy and Decisions in the Air War over Europe, 1940–45* (Doubleday, New York, 1982).

Creveld, Martin van, *Fighting Power: German and US Army Performance, 1939–45* (Greenwood Press, Westport, 1982).

Ehrman, John, *Grand Strategy*, Vol. V, *The History of the Second World War* (HMSO, London, 1956).

Ellis, John, *Cassino. The Hollow Victory: The Battle for Rome January–June 1944* (André Deutsch, London, 1984).

Ferrell, Robert H., *The Eisenhower Diaries* (Norton, New York, 1981).

Fisher, Ernest F., *Cassino to the Alps* (Centre for Military History, Washington, 1977).

Fraser, David, *Alanbrooke* (Collins, London, 1982).

Gavin, James M., *On to Berlin* (Bantam, New York, 1981).

Graham, Dominick, *Cassino* (Ballantine, New York, 1971).

Greenfield, Kent Roberts (ed.) *Command Decisions* (Office of the Chief of Military History, Department of the Army, Washington DC, 1960).

Hamilton, Nigel, *Monty: The Making of a General, 1887–1942*, and *Monty: Master of the Battlefield, 1942–1944* (Hamish Hamilton, London, 1981 and 1983).

Hapgood, David and Richardson, David, *Monte Cassino* (Congdon and Weed, New York, 1984).

Hastings, Max, *Overlord: D-Day and the Battle for Normandy* (Michael Joseph, London, 1984).

Hinsley, F. H., *British Intelligence in the Second World War*, Vol. III (HMSO, London, 1984).

Howard, Michael, *Grand Strategy*, Vol. IV, Book 5, *The History of the Second World War* (HMSO, London, 1972).

— *The Mediterranean Strategy in World War II* (Weidenfeld and Nicolson, London, 1968).

Hunt, David, *A Don at War* (Kimber, London, 1966).

Jackson, W. G. F., *The Battle for Italy* (Harper and Row, New York, 1967).

— *Alexander of Tunis as Military Commander* (Batsford, London, 1971).

— *The Battle for Rome* (Batsford, London, 1969).

Kay, Robin, *From Cassino to Trieste*, Vol. II, *Italy: History of New Zealand in the Second World War* (Department of Internal Affairs, Wellington, 1967).

Kesselring, Albert, *A Soldier's Record* (Morrow, New York, 1954).

Kippenberger, Howard, *Infantry Brigadier* (Oxford University Press, 1949).

Kohn, Richard and Harahan, Pat (eds), *Condensed Analysis of the Ninth Air Force in the European Theater of Operations* and *Air Superiority in World War II and Korea* (Office of Air Force History, Washington, 1982 and 1984).

Lamb, Richard, *Montgomery in Europe, 1943–45* (Hamish Hamilton, London, 1983).

Le Goyet, Pierre, As under Boulle. *La Participation Française de la Campagne d'Italie 1943–1944.*

Lytton, Henry D. "Bombing Policy in the Rome and Normandy Invasion Campaigns of World War II", *Military Affairs*, vol. xlvii, no. 2 (April 1983).

Macmillan, Harold, *War Diaries: Politics and War in the Mediterranean January 1943–May 1945* (Macmillan, London, 1984).

Majdalany, Fred, *Cassino, Portrait of a Battle* (Houghton Mifflin, Boston, 1957).

Martineau, G. D., *A History of the Royal Sussex Regiment* (Moore and Tillyer, Chichester, 1955).

McAvity, J. M., *Lord Strathcona's Horse (Royal Canadians): a Record of Achievement* (privately published, Toronto, 1947).

Molony, C. J. C., *The Mediterranean and Middle East*, Vol. V, *The Campaign in Italy 3rd September to 31st March 1944* (HMSO, London, 1973).

Momyer, William W., *Airpower in Three Wars* (Office of Air Force History, Washington, 1983).

Nicholson, G. W. L., *The Canadians in Italy*, Vol. II, *Official History of The Canadian Army in the Second World War* (Queen's Printer, Ottawa, 1956).

Nicolson, Nigel, *Alex: The Life of Field-Marshal Earl Alexander of Tunis* (Weidenfeld and Nicolson, London, 1973).

Orgill, Douglas, *The Gothic Line: The Autumn Campaign in Italy, 1944* (Heinemann, London, 1967).

Pal, Dharm, *The Campaign in Italy* (Oriental Longmans, 1960). *Official History of the Indian Armed Forces (India and Pakistan) in the Second World War.*

Phillips, N. C., *The Sangro to Cassino*, Vol. I, *Italy: the History of New Zealand in the Second World War* (Department of Internal Affairs, Wellington, 1957).

Pogue, Forrest, C., *The Supreme Command. The European Theater of Operations* (Office of the Chief of Military History, Washington, 1954).

Pond, Hugh, *Salerno* (Kimber, London, 1961).

Ray, Cyril, *Algiers to Austria: A History of the 78th Division in the Second World War* (Eyre and Spottiswoode, London, 1952).

Richards, Denis and Saunders, Hilary St George, *The Royal Air Force*, Vol. II, *The Fight Avails* (HMSO, London, 1954).

Roskill, Stephen, *The War at Sea*, Vol. III, Pt I (HMSO, London, 1960).

Roy, Reginald, *Sinews of Steel: the History of the B.C. Dragoons* (British Columbia Dragoons, Kelowna, 1965).

— *The Seaforth Highlanders of Canada, 1919–65* (Evergreen Press, Vancouver, 1969).

Sallagar, F. W. *Operation Strangle: a Case Study of Tactical Air Interdiction* (Rand, Santa Monica, 1972).

Senger und Etterlin, Frido von, *Neither Fear nor Hope* (Macmillan, New York, 1964).

Slessor, Sir John, *The Central Blue* (Cassell, London, 1956).

415

Starr, Chester G., *From Salerno to the Alps: a History of the Fifth Army, 1943–45* (Infantry Journal Press, Washington, 1948).

Stevens, G. R., *Fourth Indian Division* (McLaren, Toronto, 1948).

Sunderland, Riley, *Evolution of Command and Control Doctrine for Close Air Support* (Office of Air Force History, Washington, 1975).

Tedder, Arthur William, baron, *With Prejudice: the War Memoirs of Marshal of the Air Force Lord Tedder* (Little, Brown, Boston, 1967).

Trevelyan, Raleigh, *Rome '44: the Battle for the Eternal City* (Viking, New York, 1982).

— *The Fortress: a Diary of Anzio and Afterwards* (Collins, London, 1972).

Truscott, Lucian K., *Command Mission* (Dutton, New York, 1954).

Tuker, Sir Francis, *The Pattern of War* (Cassell, London, 1948).

Verney, Peter, *Anzio 1944: an Unexpected Fury* (Batsford, London, 1978).

Vokes, C., *My Story* (Gallery Books, Ottawa, 1985).

CHAPTER NOTES

Chapter 1. Two Armies in Search of a Battlefield, pp. 15–26.

1. Hamilton, *Monty: Master of the Battlefield*, pp. 393–4.

2. Molony, pp. 13–27, Hamilton, op. cit., pp. 245–72.

3. Carlo D'Este and Eduard Mark kindly communicated their conclusions, based on their respective researches. Briefly, of the total Allied air effort over the period, amounting to some 7,000 sorties, the proportion directed against the Axis crossing places in the Messina Straits (according to D'Este no more than 8.95 per cent) lacked concentration, was sent against the wrong targets and was too easily deterred by the concentrated German flak. The Royal Navy's contribution was virtually zero, owing to an overestimate of the strength of the Axis coastal artillery commanding the straits. The figures for German – as opposed to Italian – forces evacuated to the mainland was troops, 38,846; vehicles and war-like equipment, 10,356 items; stores, 14,949 items. The German commanders believed that without this powerful reinforcement to their troops already in position it would not have been possible to hold the Allied armies south of Rome for so long.

4. For this vexed question see primarily Michael Howard, *The Mediterranean Strategy in the Second World War*, p. 35,

and *The History of the Second World War: Grand Strategy*, Vol. IV, Book 5, Chapter 26, pp. 497 et. seq., 499, 502. For the contrasting views of Brooke and Marshall: Fraser, *Alanbrooke*, pp. 358–65, and Forrest C. Pogue, *General George C. Marshall: Organiser of Victory 1943–1945*, pp. 293–4.

Chapter 2. General Eisenhower's Problems, pp. 27–42.

1. For a good account of Eisenhower's problems see Stephen E. Ambrose, *The Supreme Commander: The War Years of General Dwight D. Eisenhower*, and for interesting perceptions, H. Macmillan, *War Diaries: The Mediterranean 1943–1945, passim*, under "Eisenhower", also p. 118.

2. Nigel Nicolson, *Alex, The Life of F.-M. the Earl Alexander of Tunis*, pp. 193–4, and Macmillan, op. cit. pp. 137–8. It will be understood that both greatly *admired* these characteristics.

3. Mark Clark's own explanation in *Calculated Risk*, but it is clear from Blumenson, *Mark Clark*, pp. 137–8, that he did not understand the factors involved.

Chapter 3. The Board and the Pieces, pp. 43–57.

1. Extract from J. Steiger's AHQ Report Number 18 in D. Hist (Ottawa)

417

981.011 (D3) on German documents for the period of September–December 1943 with his commentaries:

German units were indeed handled as interchangeable pieces of machinery and quite often found themselves under commanders of varying personality. The great flexibility of the battle groups offered tempting advantages of a tactical nature but the German records show that it made it also more difficult for higher commanders to keep fully posted, tended to loosen the bands between the regular commanders and their troops and sometimes tended to a situation where nothing seemed to be more important than a pause for the sorting out of the troops and the untangling of the administrative confusion. The German proclivity for regrouping the natural parts of the Army structure did complicate the task of Allied tactical intelligence. It remained simple to ascertain the division to which an identified unit belonged, but the fact that elements of a division had been recognized in a certain area by no means proved that the other parts of the division were to be found in the same area. (The ad hoc manner in which German units at Salerno were rushed on their arrival into battle groups that were sent straight into action and their continuous aggressive action led Allied intelligence and operational commanders to overestimate the strength of the German 10th Army. In turn that has been one root of the current interpretation of the battle as a near-run thing.)

2. The fate of all but two is unknown. They probably succumbed to naval bombardment or assault. MOLTKE and LILIENTHAL were actually sited on beaches selected for the 10th Corps landings.

3. Molony, p. 268. Note that the locations are hide or harbour areas. Once battle was joined the KGs and their sub-

sidiary task forces conducted a mobile, aggressive defence.

Chapter 4. Avalanche and Hurricane, pp. 58–76.

1. Rocholl diary, fragment, IWM/AL/144.

2. See oral testimony of soldiers in Pond, *Salerno*. Even allowing for the tendency of interviewees to exaggerate, men under fire tend to magnify its effect many times: it appears that it is all directed at them personally, as veterans will testify.

3. G. F. Worsop, 2nd/5th Foresters, 46th Division, IWM/T357, p. 85 et seq., a graphic account of the fighting at Salerno as seen by a frightened and bemused young soldier in his first action. For another excellent account from a private soldier see G. Allnut, 8th Royal Fusiliers, IWM/80/46.

4. War Diary, HQ 16th Pz. Div. (National Archives, Washington). The garrison commander returned to KG Stempel during the night of September 9–10.

5. A/Brigadier, later Major-General L. O. Lyne, Letter of November 13, 1943, IWM/71/2/1–7.

6. Strawson, McCreery, IWM.

7. Molony, pp. 284–5. Herr Meierkord gave his own account of this action during the British 3rd Division's battlefield tour of Salerno.

8. Douglas Graf von Bernstorff on February 28, 1971 wrote: "Actually [the Americans] did not seem to have noticed that on the evening of the 9th the 16th Pz. Div. had been broken into two pieces, and that a quick advance on Persano via the railway station could have decided the battle on the first day."

9. Blumenson, *Salerno to Cassino*, pp. 108–9.

Chapter Notes

Chapter 5. Von Vietinghoff Shoots his Bolt, pp. 77–90.

1. War Diary, HQ 16th Pz: "121208 [i.e., 12.08 p.m., September 12] We get the impression that the enemy is going to embark again."

2. Ibid. 131105.

3. Ibid. 131250.

4. Ibid. 140005:
1a [i.e. chief operations officer]: It [KG *Stempel*] goes on attacking?
Ruenkel: It goes on!
1a: Is that an order?
Ruenkel: You bet! That is the corps order!

5. Blumenson, *Salerno to Cassino*, pp. 130–2: f.n. p. 132.

Chapter 6. Salerno – The Postscript, pp. 91–102.

1. There are various accounts of the mutiny, e.g., Pond, *Salerno*, D. Hickey and G. Smith, *Operation Avalanche* (Heinemann, London, 1983), and a BBC television feature of dubious value. We incline to the view that the excuse offered by the ex-mutineers when interviewed is a rationalisation and the basic cause was the belief that all had been assured of following the 51st Highland Division home. For McCreery's reaction, see Strawson. Molony does not mention the mutiny, which remained a secret so well kept that all except a very few in the bridgehead ever heard of it.

2. US National Archives, Suitland, Maryland, 226/Infantry/143-04, 14 October 1943.

3. Compare Molony pp. 244–6 with Blumenson, *Salerno to Cassino*, pp. 141–3.

4. Lucas, Diary.

Chapter 7. Mines, Mud and Uncertain Trumpets, pp. 103–22.

1. Martin van Creveld's instructive *Fighting Power: German and US Army Performance 1939–1945*, pp. 69–71 and Table 7.2. He shows that in the US Army the ground combat arms, except the armoured corps, received a disproportionately low percentage of first-class recruits as classified on a scale of I to V. Curiously, the field artillery and engineers did worst of all, yet external observers of the US Army rated both arms highly for morale and efficiency.

2. James M. Gavin, *On to Berlin*, pp. 77–9.

3. C. Ray, *Algiers to Austria: A History of the 78th Division in the Second World War*, one of the better divisional/regimental histories, pp. 87–91.

Chapter 8. An Odour of Gallipoli, pp. 123–41.

1. Blumenson, *Salerno to Cassino*, p. 248. Lucas, Diary, November 23, 1943; Military History Institute, Carlisle Barracks, Pennsylvania.

2. Blumenson, ibid. But Blumenson interprets Eisenhower's predictions more charitably.

3. Ibid., p. 180. "Eisenhower's personal belief in the efficacy of waging a vigorous campaign during the fall and winter to capture the Po valley underwent a startling change about October 7."

4. Ibid., pp. 180, 183, 246.

5. Ibid., pp. 180–1.

6. Ibid., pp. 239–40.

7. Ibid., p. 177. Marshall's first estimate of the force levels required in the Mediterranean made about August 7 was Italy ten divisions, invasion of southern France, fourteen.

8. For one assessment of Wilson, see Macmillan, *War Diaries: the Mediterranean 1943–1945*, pp. 367, 371.

9. Report No. 24. Steiger papers, Directorate of History, Ottawa.

10. Correspondence, General H. Kippenberger, Editor-in-Chief NZ official histories, National Archives, Wellington, 1A: 181/32/12, 6 March 1956.

11. Ibid. Correspondence with N. C. Phillips, 27 January 1956.

12. Lucas, Diary.

13. Ibid. 2 January and also on 4th: "Unless we can get what we want the operation becomes such a desperate undertaking that it should not in my opinion be undertaken."

14. Ibid. 10 January. Bracketed passages added as afterthoughts to the previous day's entry.

15. Ibid.

16. Ibid.

Chapter 9. The Soldier's Art, pp. 142–58.

1. Blumenson, *Mark Clark*, p. 154.

2. Ibid. p. 160.

3. The definitive account is Blumenson; *Bloody River: The Real Tragedy of the Rapido*. See also *Salerno to Cassino*, pp. 328–47. Brigadier Howard Kippenberger's 5th New Zealand Brigade took over the front from the 36th Division later. His account of the battle from information given to him by the survivors is in the Kippenberger Papers, in particular Kippenberger to Fred Majdalany, n.d. (March 1956?).
For Clark's reactions, Blumenson, *Mark Clark*, pp. 167–9.

4. The Harmon Papers, Military History Institute, letter from Harmon to Lucas February 12.

5. Peter Verney, *Anzio 1944: an Unexpected Fury* (Batsford, London, 1978) p. 180. We have relied on Verney's excellent account for this narrative of the battle.

6. Blumenson, p. 424. Blumenson, *Salerno to Cassino*, pp. 360–65.

7. J. R. Wood Papers, MHI, Carlisle Barracks. Interviews with W. E. Narus 1973–4. "Clark never let allies see him upset even though he was 'biting his Goddamned lip!' " e.g. Clark made some general comments in his diary on Sir Andrew Cunningham's performance:

> Evidence accumulates that Admiral Cunningham and his navy are in no way cooperating with me. He does not come direct to me but insinuates to everyone that he has been hoaxed into the position which makes it necessary for him to maintain my forces in the Anzio bridgehead. He not only does not cooperate in the supply set-up but with his naval gun fire he imposes so many restrictions and makes it so difficult that it is easier, in most cases, to do without his naval gun fire support than to accept the restrictions he imposes. He continually screams about enemy gun fire in the harbour, knowing full well that there is nothing that can be done on this situation that is not already done.
>
> Cunningham has set an arbitrary limit of 2,500 tons per day which not only is insufficient to maintain my forces but thereby precludes the essential build-up for my counteroffensive. [Clark wanted 2,700 tons.]

Chapter 10. Fear, Hope and Failure, pp. 159–75.

1. Hapgood and Richardson, p. 20, "later . . ." a Roman princess would tell Clark that "he was only the second barbarian to conquer Rome from the south". In her eyes Belisarius was a barbarian.

2. Information about the German disposition is from the narratives prepared

420

by the Enemy Documents Section of the Cabinet Office in support of Molony.

3. Hapgood and Richardson, pp. 38–9.

4. The diary of von Senger und Etterlin was the source for his book, *Neither Fear nor Hope*. A copy of it is at the MHI, Carlisle Barracks, Pennsylvania.

5. F. Majdalany, *Cassino: Portrait of a Battle*, p. 89.

Chapter 11. The Torch is Thrown, pp. 176–90.

1. Blumenson, *Salerno to Cassino*, p. 383.

2. A note in Freyberg's log reads as follows: "11.30 a.m. 11 Feb. Gruenther asked Freyberg if GOC wanted Americans to go forward when he attacked. GOC said he did not think they could. Gruenther said they had started on their attack this morning and were fully hopeful but if it was a question of betting he would be forced to bet against them."

3. Clark, *Calculated Risk*, p. 298.

4. Majdalany, pp. 117–18. Both Majdalany and the New Zealander Phillips served in the British 78th Infantry Division.

5. Hapgood and Richardson, pp. 238, 240. HQ Fifth Army avoided admitting that this was so, even when they were asked to comment on reports that shells were falling on the place, saying that "erratic bursts" were responsible. In fact the zones of guns were too large to avoid hitting the place when targets close to the walls were engaged.

6. Hapgood and Richardson, *passim*.

7. Blumenson, *Mark Clark*, pp. 185–6.

8. And say to this day.

9. C. J. C. Molony, *History of the Second World War: The Mediterranean and Middle East*, Vol. V. (HMSO, London, 1973), p. 713. A total of 143 Fortresses, 70 Mitchells and 40 Marauders actually set out for the mission.

10. Neville C. Phillips, *Official History of New Zealand in the Second World War, 1939–1945: Italy*, Vol. 1. *The Sangro to Cassino* (Wellington, 1957), pp. 26–30.

Chapter 12. A Hateful Tapestry in the Sky, pp. 191–202.

Note on research:
Operation AVENGER *and the bombing of the Monastery.*
   Our study is based on N. C. Phillips' volume of the Official History of the 2nd New Zealand Corps (1957), and on Martin Blumenson's *Salerno to Cassino* (1967) in the series published by the Office of the Chief of Military History in Washington, examination of the Fifth Army, 2nd Corps, 34th and 36th Divisional records in Washington, the New Zealand Archives in Wellington and the narratives written by the British historians responsible for Enemy Documents working in the Cabinet Office, London.
   Phillips' files record his efforts to discover the truth. He was, unfortunately, doubly handicapped. Disgruntled as Freyberg may have been by *Calculated Risk*, which laid the blame for the destruction of the Monastery at his door, he was reluctant to provide Phillips with ammunition for controversy. Also, Phillips was unable to travel to the US to examine the American documents for himself. He wrote on June 22, 1954, and also to Harding for confirmation of Clark's story in *Calculated Risk*. The Americans replied on July 7 saying: "Our historian has failed to find any such Fifth Army transcripts. The information is based on Clark's diary which is still in his possession." On September 22 they wrote again saying that a memorandum on which Clark appeared to have based his information in *Calculated Risk* had been found written by Gruenther and dated

February 12. It was still classified. However they sent extracts from it which were to be included in Blumenson's account (1967) and were incorporated into Phillips', although in some important respects Gruenther's disagreed with the New Zealand evidence. In reply to a letter from Phillips F.-M. Lord Harding said that he did not disagree with Clark's account in *Calculated Risk*, but had no evidence to support his opinion. Phillips' account of the events of the 14th, when the final decision to bomb on the 15th was apparently made, relies on a "weather forecast" and is based on Freyberg's memory. Freyberg told him that Gruenther stated that the bombing had to be on the 15th because the weather was expected to deteriorate and FISCHFANG would require all aircraft to be used at Anzio on subsequent days. "It was then or never," and so Freyberg had no choice. This version of events served to explain the unreadiness of the 4th Indian Division to exploit the bombing and has entered into some, but not all, accounts. In fact, Blumenson does not mention it, nor does he suggest that the bombing was advanced a whole day or even a few hours from the afternoon to the morning. Blumenson is correct for the bombing was never intended to be on the 16th. Furthermore, the weather forecasts did not predict wet weather on subsequent days, and, in fact, the 16th was fine and the heavy bombers were not used at Anzio. However, the bombing was advanced from the afternoon to the morning which was a casual act by the air force and went unreported by Fifth Army staff until the last moment.

The American account relies heavily on Gruenther's memorandum, but it was a red herring. It was purportedly written on the 12th, yet Gruenther intimates that the first that he had heard of the bombing plan was when Freyberg phoned to ask for the mission on the evening of the 12th. This is wrong, because Freyberg discussed the matter with Clark on the 9th. Freyberg's requisition on the 11th for tactical support was turned down by Fifth Army on the morning of the 12th, which caused Freyberg to ask Harding to have the decision reversed on the afternoon of the 12th, and Gruenther had been engaged the rest of the afternoon and evening discussing the matter with Harding and Clark. Clark's account confirms this. Gruenther is also wrong about the Bomb Safety Line (BSL) and the initial postponement of the mission from the 13th to the 14th. He says that he warned Freyberg that the Americans would have to be withdrawn behind the BSL on the evening of the 12th, and that was when Freyberg phoned back later to say that the withdrawal could not be arranged and that the mission was postponed until the 14th. Clearly he has confused the events of the 12th and 13th. The mission was not cancelled until 10 a.m. on the 13th and then at the behest of the 2nd Corps. He makes no mention of the introduction of the heavy bombers, since his account concerns only the 12th. The purpose of his memorandum, though, is clear. It is to maintain a causal link between the original "softening" mission of fighter-bombers as requested by Freyberg, and the ultimate destructive attack in the interest of Clark. Freyberg is, thereby, set up as the originator of the attack by the heavy bombers and Gruenther omits all the events in the interim, including his own cancellation of the fighter-bomber mission.

Misled by Gruenther, Blumenson observes that there is no explanation for the introduction of heavy bombers when only fighter-bombers were requested, and suggests that the airmen were responsible. Ira Eaker may have flown over the Monastery in a light aircraft on the 13th and reported signs of German occupation. Yet that seems unlikely, since the 13th was a day of snow storms and there was no flying. Eaker says that he made the flight on the 15th, which would have been too late to influence the matter – a convenient alibi. Probably he flew on the 14th, but only after the decision had been made, with his reluctant agreement. No doubt he hoped to see some confirmation that the Monastery was occupied and he did. He agreed to the mission only because he was under pressure from Arnold to use his aircraft to blast a way into the Liri valley.

The American account reflects Gruenther's and Clark's impressions of the fighting. It does not explain that the 2nd Corps only relinquished command on the heights early on the 15th, and hence does not have to explain that was the reason for the confusion there. Far from mentioning the loss of ground by the 2nd Corps, it states that the Indians actually withdrew behind the BSL on the night of the 14th/15th and that the Germans followed them up; the rest of the fighting on the heights being devoted to recovering the lost ground (Blumenson, *Salerno to Cassino*, p. 416). This is completely erroneous and may reflect the confusion in the US HQs concerned. However, it also successfully avoids the need to explain the loss of the 2nd Corps' positions, to comment on Ryder's report on the morning of the 13th that he still held them, or to connect the loss with Clark's refusal to use the New Zealand Division as soon as it was available to him.

When was the ground lost? The Fifth Army documents make it clear that the 34th Division never claimed to have taken Point 593 or Albaneta. The 36th Division was brought up for both purposes in the fatal, final days of the battle, between February 10 and 13. It did not hold either for more than a few hours at most. The German account confirms this. On the night of the 11th/12th they were outflanked by Baade's Operation MICHAEL and gave up the whole front-line position that Ryder thought was still held on the 13th.

This leads us to Clark's critical error and the historians' treatment of it, of not reinforcing the exhausted 2nd Corps earlier. It partly ducks the issue and partly blames Alexander for the delay. The former was done by ignoring the results of it on the heights, as we have seen above, and omitting to explain how the plan had to be changed from a leapfrog operation to a relief and a deliberate attack, and placing blame for delays on the Indians. The suggestion that Alexander wanted to reserve the New Zealand Corps for the breakthrough transfers the blame for what actually happened to him. Yet on January 30 Clark, at Anzio, received a signal from Gruenther:

> NZ Corps will continue momentum of attacks now being carried out by French and 2nd Corps. Attack cannot take place before 8 February. [The first day of the 4th Indian Division's presence at Cassino.]

Clark's reply was:

> Your 915 not understood. How can Spadger Corps [*sic*] of two divisions carry on the impetus of four? Does Alexander understand the possible necessity of using some of this force if present attacks are unsuccessful? (Note 2 below.)

It was difficult for Alexander to deal with a man who did not understand that the best course was to maintain the momentum of an attack and not wait until it came to a halt through exhaustion before committing fresh troops. By the time Clark had indulged in his usual piecemeal tactics there was nothing that Alexander could do but restrict his aim to obtaining a limited bridgehead, and taking his time over it.

Behind the idea that the timing of the entry of the New Zealand Corps was never in question is the notion in the American account that it came over from Eighth Army just in time to relieve the 2nd Corps, according to plan. The options open to Clark are not then in question. Clark is represented as being in Alexander's hands; the reverse being the case.

The episode at Cassino demonstrates the problems that the official historians and their unofficial successors face in recounting a coalition campaign in a national history.

Our contribution, like those of Majdalany and Hapgood and Richardson in particular, has been to attempt to gather material from all the national archives of the armies concerned and to explain the contradictions between the official accounts. Clark's *Calculated Risk* is a valuable contribution, provided that it is borne in mind that it contains a general's apologia. Unfortunately for the historical record, Freyberg for the best of motives declined to counter by telling his own story. (A little inconsistently, he confided more to F. Majdalany in two interviews than the total of the information he gave to Phillips, but not enough to enable Majdalany to arrive at the correct answer.)

Hapgood and Richardson identify the key questions – Who ordered the bombing? Why were the heavy bombers brought in? Why was their attack made on the wrong day? – but cannot answer them satisfactorily. They rely on Gruenther's memorandum and have not compared the differing US and NZ accounts. However, they do point to the important clue of the BSL, without actually explaining its meaning, and they note the German use of the ground around the Monastery. Their *Monte Cassino* was not published in time to affect our research but did lead Graham to examine the notes he took in 1970 from the American archives when he was writing his *Cassino*. There he found the evidence that allowed the piece in the puzzle labelled "BSL" by Hapgood and Richardson to be inserted.

Ground is evidence as important as a typed letter, an operation plan or a message torn from a signal pad. In 1970, Nicholas Straker and Dominick Graham spent several days walking the ground of the Cassino battlefields with modern and contemporary maps in their hands. It appeared to them that some modern authors had misappreciated the ground and that even the participants in the battle, in particular officers at divisional and higher headquarters, were misinformed. That is not at all surprising, since few of them had seen the ground behind the Monastery, which is very broken and not easily read from maps. After seeing the ground Graham became sceptical about unit reports of their locations and achievements, which in some cases could be reconciled neither with the map nor the ground.

The battle sequences cannot be explained unless the reader understands that the whole German position consisted of pairs of interlocking sections. This was obviously not understood by the commanders at the beginning of the battle. These were the open, watery southern outskirts of the town linked to the main built-up area under the heights; the town linked to the hillside above it crowned by the Monastery; the front and back of the Monastery were linked together, and the back of the Monastery was joined to M. Castellone, a long, exposed flank. These five zones had to be attacked simultaneously to prevent mutual reinforcement. Piecemeal attacks therefore, were fore-doomed to failure.

That is the tactical dimension. Similarly, the operational dimension has also to be viewed as a whole, and as a (somewhat dislocated) continuation of the First Battle of Cassino.

Finally, we emphasise our debt to Martin Blumenson. Although our account of AVENGER differs from his in important respects, were it not for his labour, and that of his colleagues, revisionary studies such as ours would be immeasurably more difficult.

1. The National Archives of New Zealand, Wellington.
1A:1 181/32/12, Author's File, N. C. Phillips Part 1. This includes correspondence concerning *Calculated Risk*.
181/55/1 Kippenberger correspondence with Jerry Scoullar (narrator of an earlier volume) on the Monastery, and Dickens.
181/53/11 Reviews of Phillips' volume.
WA 2 Series 8/46 Freyberg Diaries. September 1943–October 1944.

Freyberg's "diary" in his papers; actually the log kept for him by his Military Assistant, now Justice Sir John White.

8/50 Historical, February 1944. (Tuker's Correspondence.)

8/51 Conference Notes (contemporary).

11/6 Kippenberger Papers.

3/26 Phillips. Investigation into the bombing.

21.1/1/50   G. Log, 2nd NZ Division.

21.1/1/50   G (operations) Log, 2nd NZ Division.

2. National Archives, Suitland, 105-3.2.

3. Kippenberger's diary, op. cit. n. 1 above.

4. Freyberg – White's log.

5. US National Archives, Suitland. Md. Fifth Army Papers, 105-3.2; AAT Operation Instruction No. 42, 11 February 1944.

6. Extract from the Diary of Jack Glennie in "British Troops Malta Command Study; The Battles of Cassino, January to May 1944". (HQ British Troops, Malta, 1968.)

2nd NZ Div/Corps G Log for 1400 Hours 12 February shows American locations: "1/141 reported 100 yards beyond crest of Point 593 towards Point 569. 2/142 on 'Hill 468'." (Hill 468 was Massa Albaneta. It was not a hill but a spot height in the valley below Point 593. The 142nd had never held it, but were halted at the pass on Cavendish Road above it.)

The US units were the 135th and 168th Infantry of the 34th Division and the 141st of the 36th Division.

7. Gruenther was clearly mistaken about the date and time of the *original* request for bomber support. By the evening of the 12th Freyberg, at last in possession of the facts of the situation on the heights behind the Monastery, had realised that a postponement was necessary.

He would not, therefore, have asked that same evening for air support on the 13th. Clark could not have been aware of the facts, or else he would not have asked for the mission to be delayed until 10 a.m. Disregarding the added misunderstanding about the bomb safety line, Gruenther did not cancel the mission *until* 10 a.m. on the 13th, and then only in response to the vehement objections of Keyes and Ryder. It should be noted that both Clark and Phillips give the date and time of the original request as p.m. 12th.

8. One inexplicable feature of a dreadfully muddled affair was that although the NZ Corps and the US 2nd Corps were under command of HQ Fifth Army, and the NZ Corps was about to carry out a major, independent operation, albeit in a sector believed to be controlled by the 2nd Corps, the channel of communication carrying the vital information about the timing of the bombing mission was *via* HQ 2nd Corps and thence to HQ 34th Division, both failing to pass it either to HQ NZ Corps or to HQ 4th Indian Division. Viz., "150158 [i.e., 1.58 a.m., February 15] As far as we know the first bombing will not take place until 1300 [1 p.m.]" "150730. Abbey will be bombed this morning between 0930 and 1015," 2 US National Archives, Suitland, pp. 334–3, 2. (Even if the mistaken belief that Keyes, Ryder *et al*, were in full operational control on the heights and therefore entitled to overrule the NZ Corps over matters affecting the safety of US troops still obtained in the American camp, the failure to pass such vital information directly to HQ NZ Corps can only be attributed to a disastrous failure in "staff duties".

Chapter 13. Scarcely any Goal, pp. 203–24.

1. Phillips, p. 239.

2. Phillips and others date this meeting the 18th: the Freyberg diary the 19th, which is the more likely.

3. Molony, pp. 833–7.

4. Ibid., pp. 838–46.

5. It was only after the war that Freyberg claimed to have laid down these conditions.

6. Alexander to Freyberg. NZ National Archives, Series 8/50.

7. NZ Archives, 447.28.5. Narrative of Private E. H. Groves, "D" Company, 25th Infantry Battalion, 2nd NZ Division.

Chapter 14. Look Out, Fighter Bombers!, pp. 225–40.

When this chapter was being researched Richard Kohn, the Chief of Air Force History, and his staff were undertaking a second-generation study on the component phases of FM 100-20 – "air superiority", "interdiction" and "close support". They allowed us to see proof sheets of their publication, *Air Superiority in World War II and Korea* – a volume in the USAF Warrior series, edited by Kohn and Joseph P. Harahan – in which interviews with senior airmen were recorded. Members of the staff were kind enough to read a couple of draft papers on the subject of army–air cooperation from which this chapter was distilled. Graham was also able to talk to Eduard Mark who was working on interdiction, and with Dan Mortensen on a number of subjects. The Air Force study provided a framework for the chapter.

Sources on microfilm at Bolling are extensive and the drafts and printed versions of numerous formation histories are on the shelves of the library. Historical studies used by the original official historians are available. We list here the more useful to us:

General
> The Ninth Air Force History chapter "The Genesis of an American Tactical Air Force in the United Kingdom".
> Historical Study Number 88, April 1954: "Employment of strategic bombers in a tactical role, 1941–51". Historical Study Number 35, 1948 (by Kent Roberts Greenfield of OCMH), "Army Ground Forces and the Air-Ground Battle Team, including organic light aviation".
> Narrative of close support by 12 TAC and its adaptation of FM 100-20 to conditions in Italy.

On Cassino
Reports on the bombing of the town on March 15 appeared in the two months that followed:
> H. R. Alexander, 4 May 1944, in 621.549 frame 662
> The New Zealand Corps, n.d., frame 664
> John K. Cannon (MATAC), frame 663
> Allied Forces Headquarters, 4 June, frame 672
> Ira Eaker, 12 April, frame 669
> HQ MAAF, April, frame 649

On STRANGLE
The subject merges with interdiction generally and has been viewed from the German side as well as the Allied.
> The Zuckerman Report, 28 December 1943. 519. 425-1 also 1211-16, 512,609c and 533.306-1.
> F. W. Sallagar, *Operation Strangle: a case study of tactical air intelligence* (Rand, Santa Monica, 1972).

Chapter Notes

Henry D. Lytton, "Bombing policy in the Rome and pre-Normandy invasion campaigns of World War II . . ." *Military Affairs*, vol. xlvii, No. 2, April 1983.

12th Air Force, "Op Strangle, 15 March–11 May", 650.454.4. Documents concerning German impressions and experience of Allied Air Operations in Italy from interviews and documents. K 113. 107–184.

Also: "The Supply Situation", by Colonel Ernst Faehndrich, "The Transport Situation", by Colonel Klaus Stange. K 512.621 VII/100. "Rail Transportation Problems in Italy", by Generalmajor Karl Koerner, April 1947, and "Advantages and Defects of European Transport Networks" (German Historical Branch Study), 512.621 VII/4.

AFHQ Assistant Chief of Staff (G2), "Appreciation of German intentions in Italy" from the point of view of their ability to control their communications. 512.621.

Recorded interviews with Ira C. Eaker are in K 239.0512-626, 627, 868.

With Carl Spaatz, 868 and Laurence Kuter, 810.

Letter and conversation with James Parton at Carlisle Barracks, in June 1983. (Parton was Eaker's military assistant and flew with him almost everywhere. He is Eaker's biographer.)

Printed sources in addition to those above:

Field Manual FM 100-20 drafted by Brigadier-General Laurence Kuter.

Staff Officer with Fifth Army, by Edmund F. Ball. K 146.01

Evolution of Command and Control Doctrine for Close Air Support, by Riley Sunderland (Office of Air Force History, March 1973).

1. The 12th Air Support Command became the 12th Tactical Air Force in 1944.

2. Captain Edmund Ball, author of *Staff Officer with Fifth Army*.

3. DeWitt S. Copp, *Forged in Steel: strategy and decisions in the airwar over Europe 1940–45* (Doubleday, 1982), pp. 426–8 and 440–2.

4. Bolling Air Force base. US Air Force Historical section. 168.7001-102; 20 April.

Chapter 15. A Man of Ruthless Logic, pp. 241–52.

1. Macmillan, *op. cit.*, pp. 47–8.

2. Carver, *Harding of Petherton: Field-Marshal*, Chapters 1, 6 and 8.

3. Macmillan, *op. cit.*, p. 374; Carver *op. cit.*, p. 125.

4. Carver, *op. cit.*, p. 126.

5. Diary and Papers of General Sir Sidney Kirkman, *passim*.

6. Macmillan, *op. cit.*, pp. 404–5 and n. 405.

7. Fisher, *Cassino to the Alps*, pp. 105–6 and n.

Chapter 16. The Battering Ram, pp. 253–64.

1. Based on the Proceedings of the Royal Artillery Historical Society, vol. xi, no. 3, "Cassino 1944" – papers read by Brigadier F. S. Siggers and General Sir Sidney Kirkman.

Chapters 17–18. Tiger Drive, and The Battle in the Liri Valley.

We have attempted to describe a great battle, in all respects except space on the same scale as El Alamein, October 1942, and our account is necessarily condensed. We have not concerned ourselves with the carping of Clark, who bequeathed to the US historians the notion that the Eighth Army was "drawn along" in the wake of the successes of the Fifth, nor with the fraught command relationships inside the Canadian Corps or between Leese and Burns, as neither affected the course of the battle. With regard to Leese, we are much indebted to Nigel Hamilton, who furnished us with much useful information, the fruit of his own research. Otherwise we have relied extensively on the accounts of Anders, Jackson, Nicholson's admirable volume of the Canadian official history, Ray's history of the 78th Division, the German sources as listed and Kirkman's diary.

Chapter 17. Tiger Drive, pp. 265–81.

1. Directorate of History, Ottawa, Report No. 20, p. 39.

2. The title is derived from that of the Grand Master of the Teutonic Knights, the ancient Prussian order of chivalry. It has been translated for us as: "The All-German Grenadier Division: The Grand Master of the Realm".

3. See note on Chapter 16 above.

4. A Polish officer suggested that HONKER referred to the cry of migrating wild geese, to whom he compared his fellow countrymen: migrants, but flying home. Alas, only a flight of fancy. J. Ellis, *Cassino: The Hollow Victory*, p. 324 and n. 28.

5. Verbal communication to the author (Bidwell) and article by Maynard Pockson, "Crossing the Garigliano" (actually the Rapido), RUSI Journal, vol. 4, no. 72, December 1972.

6. Jackson, *The Battle for Rome*, pp. 94–7. General Sir William Jackson speaks with the additional authority of a Royal Engineer and of one involved in the assault crossing.

7. Ibid.

Chapter 18. The Battle in the Liri Valley, pp. 282–96.

1. Directorate of History, Ottawa, Report No. 20.

Chapters 19–20. General Juin's Plan, and Breaking the Mountain Line

Based on the French official history, as given in Sources.
Also the *Revue Historique de l'Armée*, 23rd Year, no. 2, May 1967, *Hommage au Maréchal Juin*, containing biographical sketches by Juin's chief of staff, General M. Carpentier and others, and articles on the work of the Deuxième Bureau of the CEF and the services of the Moroccan Goums.
Ernest Fisher in Chapters I and II of his *Cassino to the Alps* provides an excellent and, for an official history, unusually candid account of the opening stages of the US 2nd Corps' drive along the Via Appia.

Chapter 19. General Juin's Plan, pp. 297–308.

1. In his staff memorandum of April 14, 1944: source *Hommage au Maréchal Juin*.

2. Op. cit., p. 29.

Chapter 20. Breaking the Mountain Line, pp. 309–17.

Nil.

Chapter Notes

Chapter 21. Juin Triumphant, pp. 318–27.

1. Fisher, p. 48.

2. Michael Glover, communication to author.

3. Fisher, p. 49.

4. Ibid.

5. Ibid., p. 68.

6. For an account of these actions see "Les Goums Marocain et leur emploi par le général Juin 1943–1944", Lieutenant-Colonel Y. Jouin, *Revue Historique de l'Armée*, May 1967, pp. 90–1.

Chapter 22. The Glittering Prize, pp. 328–46.

1. Major-General A. J. C. Block, late Royal Artillery, commanded the 24th Field Regiment, RA in support of the US 3rd Infantry Division in the Anzio bridgehead. He describes Truscott as "essentially a quiet, strong, and determined character. We all wished he'd been corps commander when we landed in January." Communication to Bidwell.

2. Mathews, in *Command Decisions*, p. 356 and n.

3. Fisher, p. 119 and n.

4. Blumenson, *Mark Clark*, pp. 208–15.

5. Fisher, pp. 89–90 and n.

6. Nicholson, p. 441.

7. Boulle, *Les Campagnes de printemps et d'été*, Table D, pp. 118–19.

8. Von Senger, diary, op. cit.

Chapter 23. Operation Olive, pp. 347–66.

Notes on Research

This chapter was originally researched in 1970 by Dominick Graham and Nicholas Straker as part of their battlefield tour in the summer of that year. The documentary support on the British side was sparse since the relevant volume of the Official History had not been commissioned. However, Straker wrote a narrative using what had been prepared by historians in the Cabinet Office, Jackson's *Battle for Italy*, Orgill's *The Gothic Line*, and British regimental histories. By then Nicholson's volume had been published and much of the documentation on which it was based, German as well as Allied, was available at the Directorate of History, Ottawa. Good regimental histories, such as those of Roy and How (BC Dragoons and New Brunswick Hussars), were also published. This ought to have served to balance the accounts of Jackson and Orgill which tend to concentrate unduly on the operations of the British 5th Corps, whereas it was the Canadian Corps that broke the German main defensive line, captured Coriano and finally broke through.

In 1983 Brereton Greenhous and William McAndrew of the Directorate of History conducted a battlefield tour to study the actions of the Canadian 5th Armoured Division. Many veterans, including the divisional commander, Major-General Hoffmeister, participated. We have used the papers written for the tour which reinforce our view that a great opportunity was lost. The inherent fault in Leese's plan was the lack of a reserve he could dispose of flexibly. As a result when the 5th Corps failed to loosen the strong German defence lines near the coast by a series of left hooks, the Canadians, whose role and strength were incompatible, were unable rapidly to exploit their success and help the 5th Corps forward, instead of *vice versa*.

Chapter Notes

Canadian Sources

"The 5th Canadian Armoured Division in the Gothic Line – 1944", by Brereton Greenhous.

"The 5th Canadian Division: the background 1943–4", by William McAndrew.

"Eighth Army at the Gothic Line", by William McAndrew.

"Interview with General Hoffmeister", Greenhous and McAndrew (1982).

"Correspondence of G. W. L. Nicholson with participants concerning drafts of the Official History. (948.013 D 21.) Folders 7 and 8.

(Mainly concerning General Burns and his relations with Leese and his own subordinates.) In Folder 7, 604–9, Burns comments:

> There did not exist any well-recognised authority with respect to the function of an armoured division when fighting in the Italian terrain. Conditions were completely different from those encountered by 7th Armoured Division in the Desert . . . General Leese, both at the Liri Valley battle and in the Gothic Line did not exercise the direction that might be expected of an Army Commander. In the former operation General Burns worked with the commander of 13th Corps [Kirkman], who appeared to have more concern with the running of the battle than General Leese. Similarly, in the Gothic Line matters seemed to be left in the hands of the 5th Corps commander.

"CMH Report No. 187. Canadian Operations: Olive to the Marecchia".

"AHQ Report No. 27. Captain Steiger's translations of German documents 11 August–31 October 1944. (981.011 D3)". In particular: "Material for the presentation of the Battle of Rimini within the framework of the treatment of the Italian Campaign from the standpoint of military history, August 1944–February 1945", written by Lieutenant-Colonel Pretzell, Operations Officer, 71st Division and later Colonel, Operations, Tenth Army. (His dates are twenty-four hours adrift and he denies that Tenth Army was surprised by Olive. The account was written during the period in which the American historians were collecting German recollections in 1947.)

"MS B-268 (Historical Division, HQ US Army, Europe), Italian Theatre, 23 August–2 September", by Adolf Haeckel and Dietrich Beelitz. (Another account written from memory and not documents.)

The war diaries of the units of the Canadian Corps were examined. Their value varies but some contained excellent after-action reports. One of these extra papers is the radio log of the Strathcona's in their attack on M. Pelosa with the Princess Louise's Dragoon Guards. Also Brigadier I. S. Johnston's appreciation for the attack of the 11th Brigade against the Green Line on August 30. There are also good accounts of the attacks of the Cape Breton Highlanders on Montecchio and Point 120 and the Perths and British Columbia Dragoons operations at Point 204.

1. Quoted by Nicholson, p. 564.

2. Fisher, p. 297.

3. Carver, *Harding of Petherton*, pp. 141–2.

4. The accepted version of how the change of plan came about – Carver, Blumenson (*Mark Clark*) and Fisher – is correct as far as it goes. The moving spirit, however, was in fact Kirkman, whose views were respected by all concerned (except Clark). It can be assumed that he had already weighed Harding's plan and found it wanting before August 3 when, according to his diary, he met

Leese and discussed "future fighting". In the days succeeding, this discussion was followed up by a telephone call to Leese and meetings with Harding and McCreery. On the 10th Kirkman was summoned to HQ Eighth Army, arriving after the conference between Clark, Leese and Alexander. "Alex took me aside ... the [new] plan is entirely according to my suggestion ... the only snag, and it is I am afraid entirely logical, is the 13th Corps will go under command of 5 Army."

5. Blumenson, *Mark Clark*, pp. 222–6; Fisher, pp. 306–7.

6. War Diary, Loyal Edmonton Regiment, quoted by Brereton Greenhous in a paper prepared for the Canadian Army battlefield tour of 1983.

7. Nicholson, pp. 511–12.

8. Ibid., p. 521.

9. Burns, *General Mud*, p. 189.

10. For a good account of the tribulations of the 1st Armoured Division see Orgill, *The Gothic Line*, Chapters 9–11.

11. Nicholson, p. 681 and n.

12. Ibid., p. 563.

Chapter 24. Clark Agonistes, pp. 367–81.

1. For as long as the gradually depleted infantry strength permitted British armoured divisions in Italy were organised on the basis of one armoured brigade and two infantry brigades. The 78th Infantry Division later absorbed the armoured brigade of the disbanded 1st Armoured Division plus extra armour, becoming in effect an "armoured" division.

2. The 6th SA Armoured Division was detached from the 13th Corps and placed directly under US command. Major-General Poole was equally dissatisfied with the standard of staff duties in Fifth

Army: "No consultation, impossible orders", Kirkman, diary.

3. Fisher, p. 328.

4. Bidwell, personal testimony. (He was occasionally invited by his chief, CRA Brigadier Clive Usher, to join him on these alarming perambulations.)

5. C. Ray, *Algiers to Austria* (History of the 78th Division), pp. 163–75.

6. Kirkman, diary. Blumenson, *Mark Clark*, p. 231.

7. Blumenson, op. cit., pp. 230, 232.

8. Ibid., p. 230. "They have relieved Leese and put in a washout like McCreery. He is a feather duster type." Quoted from Clark diary.

9. When McCreery assumed command of the Eighth Army he told a conference of his senior officers that it was "like an old steeple chaser, but if carefully handled was good for one more race". Strawson, op. cit. Also V. Ffrench Blake, History of 17th/21st Lancers, p. 153.

Chapter 25. Breakthrough, pp. 382–95.

1. Fisher, pp. 407–10.

2. Ibid., pp. 438, 485 et seq.

3. Forrest C. Pogue, *George C. Marshall: Organizer of Victory*, pp. 536–7; Blumenson, *Mark Clark*, p. 239.

4. Truscott, *Command Decisions*, pp. 478–9: "I had not forgotten the change of direction in the break-out from Anzio." Quoted by Fisher, p. 449.

5. The best account of the final battle and break-out is in Jackson, *The Battle for Italy*, Chapter 17, "Their Just Reward". McCreery's plan involved a somewhat complicated change of role of his corps HQs in mid-battle, depending on how it developed. The 10th Corps HQ was in reserve, with a special engineer task force under command to supervise the assault crossing of the Po, but at the crucial

moment its commander, Lieutenant-General Hawkesworth (commander of 46th Division since Salerno) succumbed to a fatal illness, and the 5th and 13th Corps each made their own arrangements for the crossing.

6. Macmillan, *War Diary*, p. 741.

7. Colonel Mennell, diary kept when GSO2 (Operations) 6th Armoured Division and kindly lent to Bidwell.

8. Ibid. Also Regimental History of the 17th/21st Lancers.
C. N. Barclay, *History of the 16/5 the Queen's Royal Lancers, 1925–1961*, p. 160.

9. For an amusingly sarcastic account of the partisans in action, Macmillan, *War Diary*, pp. 742–3.

10. On May 4 von Senger was escorted to HQ 15th Army Group to make the detailed arrangements – nominal rolls, collection of surrendered arms, rations, medical arrangements, accommodation, security, etc. – and inform HQ Army Group "C" accordingly. It was purely a matter for the staff. Characteristically this was blown up into a public relations exercise designed to give the impression that General Clark personally received the surrender of the German armed forces and armies in Italy. E.g., illustrations in Jackson *op. cit.*, facing p. 293, and Fisher, p. 530.

Chapter 26. Reflections, pp. 396–406.

1. Clark, *Calculated Risk*, p. 348.

2. Blumenson, *Mark Clark*, p. 233.

3. Not only the Russians. Tito, although prepared to accept Allied supplies and equipment and a strictly limited military presence, was determined to resist any attempt on the part of the Allies to invade Yugoslavia in strength or even to cross it en route to central Europe. See N. Beloff, *Tito's Flawed Legacy* (Gollancz, London, 1985), Chapters 2 and 3.

4. M. van Creveld, *Fighting Power*, pp. 55–8.

5. Jackson, *The Battle for Italy*, Appendix E, pp. 332–3.

INDEX OF MILITARY UNITS AND FORMATIONS

433

* Infantry units as opposed to Panzer Grenadiers were later called 'grenadiers'.

GENERAL INDEX

Index

443

comd. Fifth Army, 380, 384, 385, 386; plan for final offensive, 390; 392

Tuker, Maj.-Gen. Francis, 190, 192; demands air attack on Monastery, 194; 300

TURTLE, op., 335, 339

Twining, Maj.-Gen. Nathan F., 199, 227

Ultra, intelligence, 127, 153, 372

Uganda, H.M.S., 36

US Joint Chiefs of Staff, 230

Valmontone, significance of in DIADEM, 247–8, 251, 329, 335, 336, 337, 339, 340, 341

Vietinghoff *gennant* Scheel, Gen. Heinrich, 47, 49, 67, 75, 78, 81, 87, 149, 170, 202, 265, 268, 285, 293, 316, 328, 340, 350, 352, 362, 364; comd. Army Group 'C', 380; his problems, 387, 391, 393, 394

Vokes, Maj.-Gen. C., 263, 281, 284, 289, 292, 293, 294, 352

Vokes, Lt.-Col. F., 356

Volturno, R., passage of, 116–17

Walker, Maj.-Gen. Fred L., 53, 62, 75, 85, 87, 99, 118, 330; coup at M. Artemisio, 341

Ward, Maj.-Gen. D., 273, 280

Webb-Carter, Lt.-Col., 154

Wedderburn, Lt.-Col. David, 155

Wentzell, Col. W., 168; uncertainty of Allied dispositions, 212–13; *ibid.*, 265–6, 294, 337; reaction to op. OLIVE, 352–3; 380

White, Maj. John, 197

Whitfield, Maj.-Gen. J., 359

Wilkinson, Lt.-Col., 274

Wilson, Gen. Sir H. Maitland, 132, 182, 192, 199; proposals for use of air-power, 208; 228; and relief of Clark, 251

Winter Line, *see* Gustav Line

WINTERGEWITTE, op., 383

Wolff, *Obergruppenfuehrer* (SS), Karl, 388, 395

Zuckerman, Hon. Gp. Capt. S., 228 and f.n., 229, 233